Prelude to Quebec's Quiet Revolution:
Liberalism versus Neo-nationalism, 1945–1960

In this study of the intellectual origins of Quebec's Quiet Revolution of the 1960s, Michael Behiels has provided the most comprehensive account to date of the two competing ideological movements which emerged after World War II to challenge the tenets of traditional French-Canadian nationalism.

The neo-nationalists were a group of young intellectuals and journalists, centred upon *Le Devoir* and *L'Action nationale* in Montreal, who set out to reformulate Quebec nationalism in terms of a modern, secular, urban-industrial society which would be fully "master in its own house." An equally dedicated group of French Canadians of liberal or social democratic persuasion was based upon the periodical *Cité libre* – one of whose editors was Pierre Trudeau – and had links with organized labour. Citélibristes sought to remove what they considered to be the major obstacles to the creation of a modern francophone society: the all-pervasive influence of clericalism inherent in the Catholic church's control of education and the social services, and the persistence among Quebec's intelligentsia of an outmoded nationalism which advocated the preservation of a rural and elitist society and neglected the development of the individual and the pursuit of social equality.

Behiels delineates the divergent "societal models" proposed by the two movements by focusing upon such themes as the critique of traditional nationalism; the roles of church, state, and labour; the response to the "new federalism"; the reform of education; and the search for a third party. He shows how the rivals combined to help bring down an anachronistic Union Nationale government in June 1960. In one form or another, he concludes, *Cité libre* liberalism and neo-nationalism have remained at the heart of the political and ideological debate that has continued in Quebec since the Duplessis era.

Michael D. Behiels teaches history at Acadia University.

Prelude to Quebec's Quiet Revolution

Liberalism versus Neo-nationalism 1945–1960

MICHAEL D. BEHIELS

McGill-Queen's University Press
Kingston and Montreal

© McGill-Queen's University Press 1985
ISBN 0-7735-0423-0 (cloth)
ISBN 0-7735-0424-9 (paper)

Legal deposit second quarter 1985
Bibliothèque nationale du Québec

Printed in Canada

This book has been published with the help of a grant
from the Social Science Federation of Canada using
funds provided by the Social Sciences and Humanities
Research Council of Canada. Publication has also been
assisted by the Canada Council and Ontario Arts
Council under their block grant programs.

Canadian Cataloguing in Publication Data

Behiels, Michael D. (Michael Derek), 1946–

Bibliography: p.
Includes index.
ISBN 0-7735-0423-0 (bound). – ISBN 0-7735-0424-9 (pbk.)
1. Nationalism – Quebec (Province). 2. Quebec
(Province) – Politics and government – 1936–1960. *
3. Quebec (Province) – Economic conditions – 1945–
1965. * 4. Quebec (Province) – Social conditions –
1945–1965. * I. Title.
FC2924.9.N3B43 1985   971.4′04   C85-098028-3
F1053.B34 1985

In memory of my father
and for Linda, Marc, and Justin

It is not the concept of *nation* that is retrograde;
it is the idea that the nation must necessarily be
sovereign.

Pierre Elliott Trudeau *Federalism and the French
Canadians*

Quebec, the state of Quebec, is the axis of all
French-Canadian life ... *Any blow struck at
Quebec, the political framework of French Canada,
is a blow struck at our very heart and head.*

André Laurendeau *The Essential Laurendeau*

Contents

Preface

This study is essentially a descriptive analysis of the intellectual origins of Quebec's "Quiet Revolution" of the 1960s and 1970s. In the decade and a half following World War II two competing ideological movements, liberalism and neo-nationalism, emerged to challenge the prevalent ideology of traditional French-Canadian nationalism. A group of young, dedicated French-Canadian intellectuals and journalists, centred around *Le Devoir* and *L'Action nationale* in Montreal, set out to reformulate and redefine traditional French-Canadian nationalism so as to reflect their intense commitment to building a modern, secular, Québécois nation-state in the province of Quebec. In the words of the neo-nationalist historian Michel Brunet, Quebec City was to become the capital of a modern Québécois nation-state just as Ottawa had become the capital of the increasingly centralized, social welfare nation-state of English-speaking Canadians.

Neo-nationalists were challenged by a group of similarly young and dedicated French Canadians of liberal and social democratic persuasion centred in the periodical *Cité libre* and in organized labour movements. Inspired by the philosophy of Catholic social action originating in France and other parts of Western Europe in the 1930s and 1940s as well as by the Keynesian liberalism prevalent in North America, the Citélibristes attempted to undermine what they considered to be the two major stumbling blocks to the emergence of a modern francophone society in Quebec, one capable of integrating on its own terms with the mainstream of Canadian and North American life. Citélibristes questioned the all-pervasive influence of clericalism inherent in the Catholic church's control over education, health, and social welfare services in Quebec. A pluralistic, democratic, and innovative francophone society was only possible if there was a complete separation of church and state, thereby bringing an end to all forms of clericalism. In addition, the long-standing ideological unanimity represented by traditional French-Canadian nationalism had to be destroyed. The continued prevalence among Quebec's intelligentsia of a nationalism which preached the preservation of an outmoded rural and élitist society while neglecting the urgent necessity for socioeconomic and political reforms to secure equality of opportunity and improved living conditions for all citizens had to be buried along with the paternalistic and antidemocratic regime of Maurice Duplessis. Ending the tyranny of clericalism proved to be a lot easier than undermining the influence of nationalism, especially in the new form articulated by contemporary neo-nationalists. Indeed, *Cité libre*'s liberalism and neo-nationalism, in its various forms, set the stage for the social, economic, political, and constitutional struggles that engulfed Quebec and Ottawa in the 1960s and 1970s as proponents of both of these ideological currents strove to attain and retain control over the levers of power, provincial and federal, in order to put their respective ideas into action. The "quiet revolution" of the fifties was swept aside by the "not-so-quiet revolution" of the 1960s.

This study, which originated as a doctoral thesis for York University, could not have been completed without the support and encouragement of many people. Robert Hett and Stewart Mackinnon, both of the Department of History at the University of Alberta, sparked my interest in contemporary Quebec. I am grateful to Richard Jones, Jacques Rouillard, and Alan MacIntosh for reading drafts of the study at various stages of its development. The financial support of the Social Sciences and Humanities Research Council of Canada and Acadia University was most helpful, indeed indispensable. I am most thankful for the always-inspired guidance, advice, and moral support of Ramsay Cook. Joy Cavazzi, Carolyn Bowlby, and Eli Ives were responsible for typing the innumerable drafts. Finally, I owe a special debt of gratitude to my inordinately patient and supportive wife, Linda, who along with our two boys, Marc and Justin, often revived my flagging spirits, thereby keeping the project on the rails. This work is dedicated to them.

Translations of all French-language quotations have been provided, with the intention of making the material accessible to as wide a readership as possible.

Prelude to Quebec's Quiet Revolution

Introduction

The image most often associated with Quebec's French-Canadian people during the 1940s and 1950s was that of a church-ridden, agricultural society outside the mainstream of the urban-industrial North American way of life. Even when perceptive English-speaking Canadian journalists, politicians, and educators acknowledged that hundreds of thousands of French Canadians lived in cities and earned their living in industrial occupations, they usually concluded with the caveat that the role of French Canadians was, and would be for some time, one of subservience. A second, rarely articulated caveat was that as French Canadians joined the urban-industrial mainstream they automatically became less French-Canadian. It was, many English-speaking Canadians thought, only a matter of time before the Catholic church ceased to be a governing factor in the lives of urban French Canadians of all classes. In a generation or two, the only remaining distinctive feature of urban French-Canadian society, the French language, would become a quaint dialect spoken only in the intimacy of the family setting, at meetings of anachronistic national associations, and perhaps occasionally in public for nostalgic and commemorative purposes. Finally, the unattainable dream of assimilation, expressed so vividly by Lord Durham in 1840, would come to fruition as the majority of French Canadians became fully integrated with the mainstream of North American society.

Many English-speaking Canadians, operating on a level of simplistic wishful thinking, felt quite comfortable in this soon-to-be-outmoded conception of Quebec's French-Canadian society and its projected evolution. Parenthetically, this dated perception of Quebec and its French-speaking majority coloured and, in many cases, warped the prevalent interpretations of Maurice Duplessis' second regime, 1944–59. The vast majority of English-speaking Canadians, in and outside Quebec, welcomed and supported Duplessis' unwavering commitment to greater and more rapid development of the province's natural resources. Rapid industrialization and urbanization, most English-speaking Canadians hoped and believed, would speed up the demise of the conservative and outmoded French-Canadian society. French Canadians would be propelled into an urban-industrial way of life where individual economic progress and social welfare took clear precedence over cultural and linguistic survival. Nevertheless, many English-speaking Canadians continued to feel uncomfortable with the traditional nationalist and antiliberal overtones of Union Nationale policies and practices. Many rationalized away their fears and unease by claiming that Duplessis' recourse to nationalist rhetoric and antiliberal administrative and political practices was merely a necessary and astute political strategy intended to keep his party in office. After all, had not Wilfrid Laurier claimed that French Canadians had no opinions, only sentiments, and therefore required strong leaders? No doubt the shibboleths of traditional French-Canadian nationalism went a long way in perpetuating this outmoded perception of wishful thinking on the part of English-speaking Canadians. Had French-Canadian nationalists not repeated *ad nauseam* for two generations that French Canadians could not join the urban-industrial order and still remain genuine French Canadians?

The deaths of Maurice Duplessis in September 1959 and Paul Sauvé, his successor, in January 1960 were interpreted by many Canadians as the final nails in the coffin of French-Canadian nationalism. The victory of Jean Lesage's Liberal party was heralded as the end of the *ancien régime* and the beginning of the "Quiet Revolution," whereby Quebec's outmoded and archaic socioeconomic and political institutions would be fully modernized once and for all. Both French and English-speaking Canadians welcomed and supported the overthrow of the Union Nationale but generally for quite different reasons and motives. English-speaking Canadians were, on the whole, elated by the prospect that the dual process of industrialization and urbanization could proceed apace, unobstructed by the church, narrow and inward-looking nationalists, and an outmoded, scandal-ridden government that had become more a liability than an asset. English-speaking Canadians, sitting comfortably at the controls of the Quebec economy, would reap, they presumed, the lion's share from continued economic expansion while apprenticing bilingual and educated French Canadians to the processes of high finance and industrial capitalism, a world almost exclusively English in its linguistic operations and social ambiance.

The Quiet Revolution signified something quite different to French Canadians. Throughout the fifties and early sixties concerned French Canadians interpreted the Duplessis regime as the era of "la grande noirceur," an era characterized by social and political repression and increased foreign control over Quebec's economy. For Quebec's francophone intelligentsia the era was one during which little of significant and positive value had occurred, except perhaps for the famous asbestos strike in 1949, an event which symbolized the maturation of the Catholic labour movement. Knowledgeable and far-sighted French Canadians supported greater industrial expansion and political and social modernization while continually denouncing the state-of-siege mentality and regressive policies of successive Duplessis administrations. The persistence of archaic social and political institutions, the intelligentsia argued forcefully, almost guaranteed that French Canadians would not share equitably in the fruits of increased industrial and commercial productivity. The sweeping away of the Union Nationale in June 1960 was seen by a growing majority of French Canadians as providing the first and perhaps the last real opportunity to modernize fully their society while still guaranteeing the survival and *épanouissement* of the French-Canadian nationality. The challenge, it was correctly recognized by many French-Canadian opinion makers, involved enormous risks. But, on balance, those risks were not as dangerous as prolonging the status quo.

Beginning in 1960, the Quiet Revolution gathered momentum under the guidance of the Liberal team led by Jean Lesage, Georges-Emile Lapalme, René Lévesque, and Paul Gérin-Lajoie, to name only a few. The implementation of far-reaching reforms occurred in areas such as education, social welfare, and hospitalization, and essential services like hydro-electricity. Countless other reform projects – for regional development, greater francophone participation in the industrial sector, the renewal of governmental administration at all levels – flowed from the offices of senior bureaucrats, many of whom were recent recruits from Quebec's universities, the private sector, and Ottawa. That the Liberal regime was able to proceed so quickly in many areas was a clear indication that the true "quiet revolution" had already taken place in the hearts and minds of a small but dedicated minority of well-educated, middle-class French Canadians. To the astute observer it was clear that the seeds of change had been carefully and systematically sown and nurtured to fruition in the precarious environment of the postwar years. What conjuncture of character and circumstance allowed this ideological quiet revolution to take place? What was the main thrust and significance of this process of ideological renewal?

Essentially, two competing ideological currents emerged after the war to challenge the hold exercised by traditional French-Canadian nationalism over the established clerical and secular élites. Both ideological currents – neo-nationalism and *Cité libre* liberalism – were the products of the socio-economic and ideological developments experienced in Quebec since World War I. In the short run, both currents emerged from the inability of the traditional nationalist intelligentsia to cope adequately with the multiple crises created by the depression and an extensive national war effort.

Slow to be recognized but in many ways the first to take root in Quebec was the ideology of neo-nationalism. This significant metamorphosis of French-Canadian nationalism had its origins in the Bloc Populaire Canadien movement, 1942–8, which failed to reconcile the tensions between the older, established generation of socially conservative and federal-oriented nationalists and a younger generation of secular, liberal-minded Québécois nationalists. This latter group, led by André Laurendeau, Gérard Filion, Jean-Marc Léger, and others, became associated with *Le Devoir* and *L'Action nationale* after the war. Its members undertook the enormous task of reformulating the substance and thrust of the ideology of traditional French-Canadian nationalism so that it might correspond more closely to changing socioeconomic realities and the evolving aspirations of francophones in all walks of life and all social classes. Differentiating neo-nationalists from Citélibristes was the latter group's firm conviction that liberalism, in and of itself, was a universalizing and homogenizing ideological force. On the other hand, liberal and social democratic reforms in concert with nationalist preoccupations and aspirations could precipitate a regeneration and modernization of French-Canadian society, a national entity valuable in its own right but also because of the quality of uniqueness it gave to the Canadian nation-state.

More controversial, because it marked a distinct departure from the recent past, was the reemergence of the ideology of liberalism as articulated by Citélibristes, social scientists, and labour activists. The emergence of a liberal intelligentsia had its origins, not in the nineteenth-century *rougism* of T.D. Bouchard's Institut démocratique, but rather in the introduction and dissemination of the social sciences in Quebec's francophone universities as well as in the growth of organized labour. Proponents and practitioners of the former emphasized the need for increased secularization, freedom of inquiry and expression, and a renewal of liberal democratic traditions. Advocates and active supporters of organized labour contended that liberal democracy meant little for working-class people unless accompanied by a significant degree of social democracy. These views found a forum in the periodical founded in 1950 and co-edited by Gérard Pelletier and Pierre Elliott Trudeau, called quite appropriately *Cité libre*, at the annual sessions of the Institut canadien des affaires publiques after 1954, at countless symposia and labour congresses, and most importantly on the radio and television networks of Radio-Canada.

The present study begins with an overview of socioeconomic changes precipitated by a new round of economic expansion and goes on to assess the origins of the neo-nationalists and their comprehensive critique of traditional nationalism. The origins and central ideas of the *Cité libre* movement's "revolution of mentalities," as well as the Citélibristes' devastating critique of French-Canadian nationalism, are examined and a descriptive analysis is provided of the vigorous debate engendered by this flourishing ideological pluralism. Important themes discussed by protagonists of both ideologies include the changing role of the state and the economic inferiority of

French Canadians and the francophone society, the role of organized labour in the pursuit of liberal and social democracy, the urgency and potential direction of educational reform, Quebec's response to the new federalism, and, finally, the modernization of the political process.

This study culminates in an overview of the often bitter, mostly futile, but highly revealing search by both groups for an appropriate political vehicle to implement their respective societal models. Champions of *rougism* and ultramontane nationalism had in the mid-nineteenth century fought a vigorous battle for the allegiance of rural and Catholic French Canadians. It is now well recognized that moderated versions of both ideologies came to dominate Quebec's political and social institutions. Similarly, since World War II, protagonists of neo-liberalism and neo-nationalism have carried on a struggle to win the allegiance of secularized urban French Canadians. Two decades later it is becoming fairly clear that both ideological forces have influenced in very significant ways the evolution of modern Quebec and Canada. This study endeavours to elucidate why and how they did so by a careful scrutiny of the two groups that fostered and nurtured these competing ideologies.

CHAPTER ONE

Quebec in Transition

Quebec today can give the impression of a waking youthful giant. His facial features are familiar but his demeanour and his actions appear exaggerated. If, however, we looked more closely and especially if we recall the recent or even ancient past, we can recognize that these developments are all very natural. This awakening, unexpected as it may seem, was foreseen some time ago.[1]

World War II proved to be a turning point in the history of contemporary Quebec. The renewal of industrialization and urbanization on a massive scale guaranteed the decline of a fragile agricultural society and ensured the demise of a highly mythologized rural way of life. The industrial economy, with its smoke-belching factories, its centralizing and monopolistic tendencies, would henceforth have a predominant role in the development of the province and in the lives of its people. Quebec had experienced significant levels of industrialization and urbanization since the 1870s but these phenomena had never penetrated, to any significant degree, the collective identity of the French-Canadian people.

In particular, the socioeconomic changes had not altered the ethos or *mentalité* of French Canada's clerical élite or nationalist intelligentsia. The depression and World War II jarred French-Canadian society sufficiently to set in motion the process of ideological renewal.[2] This change in outlook was both heralded and symbolized by the work of two novelists. Roger Lemelin's *Au pied de la pente douce* (1944) and Gabrielle Roy's *Bonheur d'occasion* (1945) introduced French Canadians to the urban landscape, thereby making possible the imaginative assimilation of its best and worst features. Shattered beyond repair was the belief that Quebec was a society where nothing changed or would change. Indeed, much had changed in Quebec over the previous two centuries though never at the cost of continuity. The clichéd slogan "Notre Maître, le Passé," coined by the clerical nationalist Abbé Lionel Groulx, was a faithful reflection of that historical reality.

During the two decades following the outbreak of the war Quebec society underwent such deep, pervasive, and wrenching socioeconomic changes that, for the first time since the Conquest, the fragile thread of continuity with the living past was threatened with complete destruction. Quebec's citizens witnessed awe-inspiring changes in their physical surrounding and at the same time experienced a dramatic restructuring and reshaping of the pattern of their daily lives. "C'est le temps que ça change," the Liberal party slogan in the 1960 election, signified much more than a desire for a change of one set of political leaders for another. In fact, the slogan fell on receptive ears because so much had changed in "la belle province" in less than a generation and more change was perceived as necessary. Most of the direct pressure for change stemmed from the phenomenal growth of the Quebec population. With the birth rate still hovering around 30 per thousand in this period, coupled with the influx of thousands of immigrants, Quebec experienced a 22 per cent increase in its population in the 1940s and a whopping 30 per cent in the 1950s.[3]

THE PATTERN OF INDUSTRIAL EXPANSION

The long-held notion that Quebec was, economically speaking, a backward region has been laid to rest. Quebec, like Ontario, has experienced successive rounds of industrial growth since the last quarter of the nineteenth century.[4] The outbreak of World War II brought renewed economic growth, halted a decade earlier by the onset of the depression. This process was characterized by several significant developments, some new and others a reinforcement of trends established in the interwar years. An example of the latter was the rapid expansion of extractive and primary-processing industries, namely pulp and paper, ferrous and nonferrous metals, and the chemical industries.

The importance of the primary sector did not reside in its ability to absorb large numbers of workers or in its contribution to gross provincial production. In fact, between 1946 and 1966 the value of production in the primary sector dropped from 13.4 to 6.7 per cent of total provincial production while employment dropped from 26.8 to 8.4 per cent of the labour force, with most of the decrease attributable to the rapid decline of production and employment in the agricultural segment.[5] The extraction of Quebec's natural resources, while fostering a diversification of the economy and the creation of some highly skilled and highly remunerative positions, did involve negative features. The huge amounts of capital and complex technology required were, in the main, imported from outside the province and resulted in increasing foreign domination of Quebec's economy.[6] This was vividly apparent in the employment practices of the vast majority of non-francophone corporations which, even when French Canadians possessed the required technical and administrative training, continued to show a

TABLE 1

Indicators of Economic Growth in the Primary Sector, 1941–61

	Hydro-electric production (millions of KWH)	Mineral production (value in dollars) '000	Pulp and paper (value in tons) '000
1941	17,741	$ 99,700	5,343
1951	29,690	$255,932	7,706
1961	50,433	$455,523	8,544

Sources: Annuaire du Québec 1962, 619; Annuaire du Québec 1966–1967, 596, 628

marked preference for technical experts, managers, and administrators who shared their language and culture.[7] Finally, new urban conglomerations, often merely company towns like Baie Comeau and Schefferville, sprang up in remote regions of the province. Isolation, the high cost of living, and, often, oppressive company rule created new social problems not experienced in the more established urban centres like Montreal and Trois-Rivières.[8]

The secondary sector of the economy, including manufacturing and construction industries, expanded quite rapidly in the two decades following the war to provide employment for three-quarters of a million workers by 1966, an increase of over two hundred thousand jobs in twenty years. Value of production in the secondary sector rose by over 300 per cent between 1946 and 1966, from $1.2 to $5.1 million. This represented a respectable annual growth rate of 7.5 per cent for manufacturing and 8.0 per cent for construction and public utilities. Despite continued expansion the secondary sector lost ground in the overall economic situation, slipping from 41.2 to 38.8 per cent of the total value of provincial production and from 36.0 to 31.9 per cent of employment in the twenty years after the war.[9]

Quebecers have long compared their rate of economic growth to that of their neighbouring province, Ontario. It became increasingly apparent to concerned French-speaking Quebecers after the war that, compared to Ontario, Quebec's economy had serious handicaps because of its geographic location on the periphery of the North American economy and the severe climate, which resulted in higher rates of seasonal unemployment and placed restrictions on the agricultural sector.[10] More importantly, Quebec's manufacturing sector possessed deeply entrenched structural weaknesses. In broad comparative terms, Quebec possessed a relatively high concentration of resource and light consumer goods industries, many of the latter having been established after the implementation of the National Policy in 1879. While heavy industry (iron and steel products and transportation equipment) accounted for over 30 per cent of Ontario's manufacturing production in 1955, it accounted for only 13 per cent of Quebec's. In contrast, while textile and clothing output constituted 15 per cent of Quebec's industrial production they formed only 6 per cent of Ontario's. Nearly 60 per cent of Quebec's industrial employees worked for firms which produced nondurable goods compared with 40 per cent of Ontario's. These firms were generally less productive than durable goods producers, paid lower wages, and offered fewer fringe benefits. Further weakening the province's industrial sector was the fact that two of its nondurable goods industries, tobacco and leather, and one major heavy industry, transportation equipment, were all suffering steady decline after the war.[11]

Although both the resource and manufacturing components of the province's economy contributed greatly to the overall expansion in production, it was the service sector which provided increasing numbers of jobs for those leaving the farms and rural communities and for a large percentage of the urban young men and women entering the labour force. By 1960, 60 per cent of Quebec's labour force was employed in the service industries – commerce, communications, finance, public administration, education, health, entertainment – an increase of over 20 per cent since the war. The tertiary sector accounted for 55 per cent of total value of production in 1966 as compared with 41 per cent in 1946. Indeed, this was the fastest-growing sector of the economy with 3.6 and 8.9 per cent annual growth in employment and production.[12] As disposable income rose, enhanced in many cases by an ever-increasing number of women in the labour force, the demand for goods and services increased dramatically.

THE DECLINE OF AGRICULTURE AND RURAL LIFE

In the thirties, the rural way of life was still perceived as the ideal, symbolized by a vigorous "back to the land" movement supported by numerous voluntary associations and all political parties. By 1960, the vast majority of Quebec's inhabitants owed their livelihood to occupations related directly or indirectly to the industrial economy. The urban way of life, with its promise of better education, social anonymity, occupational mobility, and, for many, a higher standard of living, finally supplanted the "rural" ideal.[13]

In 1941, after the "back to the land" movement of the 1930s, 45 per cent of Quebec's French Canadians were classified as rural, 3 per cent more than a decade earlier. The pattern of the 1940s (see table 2) shows a 50 per cent decline of French Canadians on farms, but only 40 per cent of those abandoning farms moved directly to large urban centres. The remaining 60 per cent settled in villages or towns connected with resource industries such as mining and pulp and paper or migrated to the counties surrounding Mont-

TABLE 2

Urban-Rural Distribution of Population of French Origin, Quebec 1941–61

		Rural farm	Non-farm rural	Urban	Total
1941	'000	1,107	105	1,483	2,695
		41%	4%	55%	100%
1951	'000	714	522	2,091	3,327
		21%	16%	63%	100%
1961	'000	533	699	3,009	4,241
		13%	16%	71%	100%

Source: Census of Canada 1941 2, table 30; Census of Canada 1951 2, table 46; Census of Canada 1961 2.3, table 121.

real and Jesus islands and worked in the one-industry towns and villages or commuted to the islands, where they found employment in a wide range of skilled and unskilled occupations associated with a booming metropolitan economy.[14] Social life in these small rural/suburban communities was not all that different from life back on the farm. This fact undoubtedly softened the cultural shock inherent in the shift from farm life to the unrelenting demands of assembly-line production encountered in the factories.

The pattern of the 1950s was quite different. The active French-Canadian farm population declined to slightly over half a million or 13 per cent of the francophone population. The number of farms declined by nearly forty thousand from 134,366 to 95,777 between 1951 and 1961.[15] Not only was one out of every two sons leaving the ancestral home, as had been the well-established pattern of the past, but, by the mid-1950s, whole families were abandoning farming in pursuit of occupations that would ensure them a higher standard of living. Unlike in the 1940s, the flow was directly to Quebec's urban centres with Montreal and Quebec City getting the lion's share of those French Canadians leaving farming. This massive rural depopulation was prompted by a sharp decline in demand for agricultural commodities, attractive salaries and benefits in the industrial and service sectors, and the consumer lifestyle of urban society as portrayed in the urban-dominated electronic media of television and radio as well as in the large, advertising-oriented, urban dailies.[16]

The traditional mistrust and distaste for the urban way of life characterized by dependence, loose social controls, unhealthy environment, and a consumer economy – the antithesis of traditional rural living – had, by the 1950s, all but vanished in most parts of the province. While the traditional values continued to be preached, social behaviour reflected the new urban values as the younger generation of French-Canadian men and women prepared themselves for the move to the cities to find employment, get married, and raise their families.[17] Farming, in the process, ceased to be a way of life and became another occupation, a business. Like other occupations it was judged on its ability to provide a higher standard of living and was found wanting. Consequently, the status of farming along with that of its practitioners declined dramatically in the postwar years, leaving a residue of bitterness and social tension in rural Quebec, especially in areas where farming had always been marginal. The old and new urban-centred professional, business, and technical élites profited from the demise of the rural élites and eventually displaced them as the major force within the social and political institutions.

URBAN EXPANSION AND SOCIAL CHANGE

The counterpart of rural depopulation and industrialization is, of course, urban growth and development. All of the intellectuals referred to in this study were city educated. Most lived in Montreal or Quebec City and, despite their rural origins, reflected and advocated the aspirations and concerns of a burgeoning postwar urban society. Metropolitan Montreal, with 40 per cent of the provincial population by 1961, dominated the economic and cultural life of Quebec. The region was a powerful magnet for two-thirds of the internal migrants and virtually all the postwar immigrants. A combination of renewed prosperity and rapid population growth resulted in what one historian refers to as the "Great Transformation" of Montreal. Its nearly two and a quarter million inhabitants made Montreal the sixth largest city in North America, and second only to Paris among the francophone cities of the world. Adding a further enriching dimension was Montreal's cultural and linguistic pluralism, a mosaic of Central, Eastern and Southern European, British, and Asian peoples. This diversity added a complicating dimension to the long-standing French-English tensions of the city.[18]

While Montreal is the major urban centre for a majority of French Canadians it is also the hub of English-speaking Quebec, primarily the Anglo-Scottish commercial and financial élite that had built and still controls some of Canada's major economic institutions. Anglo-Canadian domination over Montreal's economic life predicated that English be the main language in the workplace. This reality prevailed despite the fact that only 18 per cent of Montreal Island's population in 1961 was of British origin, down from 24 per cent a decade earlier. As a result, the ambiance of Montreal remained, even in the 1950s, predominantly English. This was reflected in the fact that the vast majority of non-British immigrants chose English as a second language and cultural institutions like McGill University received international recognition.

This situation enraged the outspoken nationalists in the Société Saint-Jean-Baptiste de Montréal and their battle to have the Canadian National Railways change the name of its new hotel, the Queen Elizabeth, to a more appropriate francophone name symbolized the ongoing process of francization. French Canadians constituted over 60 per cent of the city's population, and a progressively larger proportion of this francophone majority spoke only French. Nationalists were determined that Montreal, like Quebec City, would become eventually a francophone metropolis, economically and socially speaking.

THE SOCIAL AND INSTITUTIONAL IMPACT OF ECONOMIC GROWTH

The visible signs of industrial expansion and social change – rural depopulation, urban sprawl, an improved transportation infrastructure – impinged on the individual and collective consciousness of most Quebecers. Less readily apparent but in many respects more important to the future evolution of their society were the social and institutional transformations necessitated by economic growth. At the heart of the demise of traditional French-Canadian society was a broadening and deepening of the class and occupational structures. The renewed expansion of the economy created a wide range of new occupations, closed out some others, enhanced upward mobility, and consequently altered the class structure considerably. A well-recognized pattern had emerged by the beginning of the twentieth century. Two distinct but related class structures had evolved in Quebec, one for the majority francophone community and one for the minority anglophone community. One Quebec sociologist describes this phenomenon succinctly.

To begin with anglophones played a dominant role in politics, commerce, professional services, and the development of natural resources. They trained francophones who would eventually succeed them. The progress of francophones allowed them to compete with and displace anglophones from certain areas of activity such as municipal and provincial politics and administration while creating a dual linguistic and religious structure such as exists in Montreal in education, hospital, and municipal services. It is clear that the evolution of the modalities of interdependence and competition had not occurred at the same pace in the various fields of activity. Industrialization, thanks to the growth of big business, experienced the same process as had taken place in other sectors, such as government administration, a century and a half earlier. Francophone cadres have succeeded anglophone cadres in various fields over the past two centuries. Certain areas, such as the cultural domain for example, were quickly abandoned by the anglophones and organized in distinct and autonomous regimes. Other fields, such as finance, were preserved as ancient fiefs while new areas of activity were continually emerging.[19]

The French-Canadian middle class was not entirely autonomous in relation to the English-Canadian middle class. In fact, the former was divided into two groups. The traditional francophone professional petty bourgeoisie fulfilled administrative and professional occupations inside institutions serving its own cultural community. This group's members enjoyed their virtual isolation and their opportunity for full upward mobility. But in the process they cut themselves off from the plight of the emerging French-Canadian working class, which was struggling against the demands of the factory system and its anglophone and American bosses. This professional petty bourgeoisie rationalized its economic inferiority by elaborating a myth of cultural superiority. Its members continuously supported political-religious élites who defended the values implicit in a highly symbolic and ostentatious Quebec-centred nationalism, isolationism, clericalism, and belief in free enterprise.[20]

Middle-class French Canadians belonging to the second group fulfilled administrative and professional functions in federal government and other national institutions and performed intermediary managerial functions in English-Canadian and American corporations. Invariably these middle-class French Canadians adjusted to the demands of the milieu in which they worked. They functioned in a predominantly anglophone environment and acted primarily in the private sector as "intermediaries between English-language management and a mixed customer group in large part French, and as intermediaries between management and a mixed labour force which was overwhelmingly French at the assistant foreman's level and below."[21] The vast majority of French Canadians working in these large corporations were concentrated in sales, public relations, and personnel work. High-powered French-Canadian commercial, financial, and industrial technocrats were rare indeed, even during the years of rapid economic expansion after the war. In 1961 French Canadians remained underrepresented in the categories of owners, directors, and administrators and overrepresented below the rank of foreman.[22] In short, the traditional French-Canadian "petite et moyenne" bourgeoisies were less modern and less dynamic than their English-Canadian counterparts. Furthermore, a French-Canadian "haute" bourgeoisie was conspicuous by its virtual absence, leaving the top levels of finance, commerce, and industry to English Canadians and Americans.

An increasing number of French Canadians, secular nationalists at the Université de Montréal, *Le Devoir*, and *L'Action nationale*, and the membership of the Chambre de Commerce du District de Montréal, were becoming acutely aware of the inferior position of the traditional francophone middle-class. Perceptive critics like Claude Ryan and Jean-Charles Falardeau could sense the tensions and frustrations which permeated the ranks of lower middle-class groups such as civil servants, journalists, and especially lay educators in the Montreal region. These groups were battling for improved salaries and some degree of social recognition of their worth and role in society. They noticed a considerable decline in the social status of the clergy and the traditional liberal professions, with a concomitant rise in the status of financial, commercial, and industrial occupations as well as those recently introduced technical professions of engineering, chemistry, and architecture.[23] The business sector of the francophone middle-class did not reap the rewards in this shift of status. For several reasons, including the persistence of weak and underfinanced family enterprises, the lack of investment capital and access to new technology, French-Canadian businessmen found their position in the Quebec economy, especially in the Montreal region, deteriorating rapidly.

By the 1950s, a small but increasingly vocal minority of French Canadians from all classes was receiving education in the physical, social, and administrative sciences as well as training at the business schools of Laval and the Ecole des hautes études commerciales in Montreal. Many of these well-educated French Canadians began their careers by working in the anglophone-dominated institutions where they acquired a taste for the rising social and economic status of the new middle-class professions only to discover that linguistic and ethnic factors seriously limited their chances of promotion. Eventually many would strike out on their own, as was the case with French-Canadian advertising executives in Montreal.[24] In doing so, they transferred their newly acquired secular conception of occupational mobility to the French-Canadian society at large. Young, aspiring, educated francophones were slowly acquiring new middle-class occupations in their own community on which they could model and build their own careers. The emergence of this new middle class marked the beginning, according to one sociologist, of Quebec's bureaucratic revolution.

The growth of bureaucratic urban institutions became the structural basis of a new social class called the new middle class . . . New middle class unrest dates back to the mid- and late fifties. The postwar period saw a massive migration of French Canadians to the cities, mostly the major ones. This massive urbanization altered the existing nature of urban institutions. Urban institutions of welfare, health, and education had rapidly to increase their size, their staffs, and their budgets to meet the new demographic needs.[25]

Well-educated French Canadians who sought and obtained employment in church-owned and administered schools, colleges, hospitals, and social service organizations discovered that, there also, upward mobility for laymen was strictly limited.

These ethnic and structural barriers to upward mobility for French Canadians become all the more real and important when one realizes that the modernization of the Quebec economy did not alter appreciably the proportion of administrative, professional, and semiprofessional occupations in the society. Between 1951 and 1961 the proportion grew only marginally from 15 to 18 per cent with most of the increase attributable to the 60 per cent growth in the category of intellectual workers, namely, teachers, specialists, technicians, and clerics.[26] Undoubtedly, the growing but still small minority of French-Canadian scientists, social scientists, administrators, and businessmen found the competition with anglophones in the private and public sectors to be particularly tough, while the opportunities in the francophone private and public sectors were limited severely for both historical and structural reasons.[27] As a result of this set of circumstances, a sociologist could, in 1960, make the claim that, despite the growth of the new francophone middle class, the traditional professional petty bourgeoisie remained the commanding group in French-Canadian society.

The decisive importance of the clergy and its ascendancy over the French-Canadian political and commercial spheres have not decreased in the transition from rural to the industrial society. Quite the contrary: the clergy's importance has been strengthened . . . The structurally significant group of the recently urbanized population is not the urban workers, but the new middle class, a rapidly increasing group of salaried white-collar workers with no definite political ideology. This new middle class staff the ever developing bureaucracies of government, business, and the church. The collective role of this new middle class is to be the improvised agent of an "administrative revolution," and this "administrative revolution" constitutes a new basis for the accrued power of the traditional élites. Their claim is being honoured without any dissent.[28]

The scenario did not evolve exactly as Hubert Guindon envisaged it in 1960 because the political and social climate shifted quickly and dramatically. No one, in fact, could foresee accurately the rapid evolution of events after the death of Maurice Duplessis' successor, Paul Sauvé. Undoubtedly the traditional élites were rejuvenated to some extent. The rejuvenation in the case of the clerical élite proved to be short-lived. The lay professions of the French-Canadian middle class had become wealthier and less traditional as a direct consequence of industrialization. French-Canadian businessmen, suffering from the powerful competition of the larger and more dynamic anglophone and American corporations, became increasingly supportive of the demands being made by this new professional middle class for an active, secular, francophone-oriented Quebec state. Consequently, the traditional professional élites and a certain segment within the church, fearing a loss of their control and power, also became sympathetic with the desires and aspirations of the new francophone middle class for a modern, secular and francophone-controlled society.[29]

Little did the traditional leaders realize that this new middle class, imbued with the ideologies of neo-nationalism and liberalism, and spurred on by the desire for recognition and power, would shortly challenge their control over the new urbanized and modernized French-Canadian society that had blossomed in Quebec during and after the war. As subsequent chapters will demonstrate, the struggle of this new middle class was as much against the status quo in the francophone milieu as it was for power and control over the anglophone-dominated sectors of the Quebec economy. In fact, the initial confrontation came within the former and not against the latter. "It is remarkable," wrote Jacques Brazeau,

that the expansion of the middle class had, to begin with, political causes. It was with a Quebec government, allied to a highly conservative and exploitive business community, that union leaders and militants, journalists, and university graduates crossed swords. These activists were an élite, a minority, who would arouse the urban middle and working classes. The cry of a few powerful voices would change our society by making the state undertake a number of responsibilities it has long neglected: the nationalization of public services, socioeconomic planning, the reform and control of education at all levels, and the administration of all social services. These new governmental and administrative responsibilities provided francophones with high-level career opportunities which they could not, at that point, obtain in the private sector.[30]

Clearly, then, Quebec in the forties and fifties was a province where much had changed. Furthermore, the seeds of even greater changes were being sown in a very comprehensive manner. Rural depopulation, on a scale unprecedented since the second half of the nineteenth century, virtually destroyed the last vestiges of the much-eulogized rural economy and way of life. While a great many of the rural migrants had been prepared, in varying degrees, psychologically to make the shift to their new urban environment, few, if any, had the necessary education to qualify for the better-paying occupations. Most filled the unskilled, dirty, low-paying, seasonal jobs left vacant by city dwellers moving on to greener pastures. The province's industrial economy continued to expand at a respectable rate while polarizing around Montreal and a few established and recently created resource-based hinterland communities. The historical structural weaknesses in the economy remained solidly entrenched and, to some degree, were aggravated further by an increasing reliance on the tertiary sector to provide employment for increasing numbers of young men and women entering the labour force. In the end, it was the social repercussions of industrialization and urbanization that set in motion, fed, and continually reinforced the demand of the new francophone middle-class intelligentsia for a rigorous examination and eventual reformulation of Quebec's socioeconomic and political institutions, and the ideologies, values, and norms of behaviour underpinning those institutions. It is to a descriptive analysis of this historical phenomenon that the substantive chapters of this study are devoted. Placed in the context of the comprehensive and far-reaching socioeconomic developments sweeping Quebec in the forties and fifties, the reemergence of liberalism and the rise of neo-nationalism take on a degree of significance that cannot be overestimated.

CHAPTER TWO

The Neo-nationalists: The Formative Years

In the decade and a half following World War II a handful of concerned and dedicated French-Canadian neo-nationalists undertook the long overdue task of redefining traditional French-Canadian nationalism. Rapid economic expansion and urbanization drove home the urgent necessity of adjusting nationalist doctrines to the prevalent class and occupational structures and the new aspirations reflected in the emergence of social welfare state liberalism. Neo-nationalists, to a greater and less extent, were all influenced by the tenor and thrust of the ideological debates and political experiences of the depression and war years. Like their nationalist mentors, especially Abbé Lionel Groulx and Dr Philippe Hamel, they were deeply disturbed by the Union Nationale's betrayal of the economic nationalist reforms of its political platform. The severe economic crisis of the 1930s had highlighted the economic inferiority of French-Canadian society and had accentuated the social and economic decline of the French-Canadian professional and commercial petty bourgeoisies.[1] The educated French-Canadian youth, products of the professional bourgeoisie but also of working-class and rural milieux, began the process of analysing and criticizing French Canada's educational, economic, and political institutions. This lively ideological debate, tentative and ill-defined at best, constituted, in the words of one Quebec sociologist, French Canada's first "quiet revolution."[2]

On the surface, the ideology of French-Canadian nationalism appeared to have altered very little since the Laurier years and the heyday of Henri Bourassa. L'Action nationale, the successor of L'Action canadienne-française of the 1920s, began publication in January 1933. Its contributors hammered away at the shop-worn and tattered themes of the past – the spiritual mission of the French-Canadian race, antisemitism, national education, 're-Frenchification' of Quebec, especially Montreal, and anticommunism, with back-to-the-land and Achat-chez-nous campaigns thrown in for good measure. Yet the economic stresses and strains of the 1930s produced undercurrents of criticism and reappraisal which would have far-reaching consequences. The question of the economic inferiority of French-Canadians, individually and as a collectivity, gained increased prominence with the appearance of Victor Barbeau's *Mesure de notre taille* in 1936 as well as the Action libérale nationale's valiant but unsuccessful full-scale public campaign against the hydro-electric trust companies in 1934–6. Second, a small but not insignificant number of young French Canadians began to question the nature of French-Canadian catholicism, thanks to the growing influence of the philosophy of personalism developed by French social Catholics, namely Jacques Maritain and Emmanuel Mounier. In seeking a Christian alternative to communism, fascism, and monopoly capitalism the young team of *La Relève*, founded in March 1934 by Robert Charbonneau and Paul Beaulieu, proposed a new social order based on the philosophy of personalism which focused on the universality of man rather than the glorification of the nation. Similarly, the Jeunesse étudiante catholique (JEC), a movement of militant Catholic action founded in 1935 by the Fathers of Sainte-Croix, deliberately ignored political and nationalist action in favour of concrete Christian social action undertaken to find solutions to the collective problems of the students' environment. Also, Rodolphe Dubé, writing under the pen name of François Hertel, attempted with some measure of success to popularize this philosophy of personalism by applying it to the realities of French-Canadian society. In essence, the philosophy of personalism sanctified and encouraged lay Catholics to undertake a reform of social institutions as the only effective means of achieving a humanitarian civilization in which all persons could develop to the full their material and spiritual potential.[3] This philosophy of personalism would free many young French Canadians from the constraints placed upon them by the "inward-looking" theology and practice of traditional French-Canadian Catholicism and nationalism.

The immediate postwar years would prove to be difficult and exasperating ones for many of the younger generation of French-Canadian nationalists. Their hopes and aspirations had been dashed by the rapid demise of the Bloc Populaire Canadien, a wartime movement of nationalist and socio-economic reform which foundered on the shoals of a bitter internal power struggle and the reemergence of a revitalized Union Nationale party led by *le Chef*, Maurice Duplessis.[4] The older, more tradition-bound nationalists of the Bourassa and Groulx schools reasserted their confidence in *le Chef* and actively supported the Union Nationale government's rearguard struggles to undermine the increasingly centralist social and economic policies and programs of the St Laurent federal government. The younger nationalists, led by Gérard Filion, director of Quebec's independent nationalist daily *Le Devoir*, and André Laurendeau, the paper's associate editor-in-chief, did not share the same confidence in Maurice Duplessis and his government. Filion and Laurendeau were exasperated by the premier's ineffectual defence of what was at most a very limited and passive conception of provincial autonomy as well as the Union Nationale's abysmal lack of a coherent program of socioeconomic reform policies aimed at modernizing Quebec's outmoded and beleaguered social-welfare and educational institutions. Finally, Duplessis and the Union Nationale, in the tradition of the Liberal regime of Louis-Alexandre Taschereau (1920–36), threatened democratic values and institutions through an all-pervasive system of patronage and political corruption.[5]

Gérard Filion had become director of *Le Devoir* in April 1947, replacing Georges Pelletier who had held the post since 1930 but had been in poor health for several years. This was a most fortuitous and auspicious development for the disenchanted young nationalists. *Le Devoir* had narrowly missed falling under Duplessis' influence. Several members of the board of directors who were Union Nationale sympathizers had attempted to appoint a director favourable to the Duplessis regime. The attempt was thwarted by a young nationalist lawyer, Jacques Perrault, who was made chairman of the board when Pelletier fell ill in 1944. Filion had refused at that time to be appointed assistant director so Perrault persuaded Pelletier to hand over his controlling shares in trust to Archbishop Charbonneau of Montreal. When Pelletier died in 1947 the socially conscious and liberal-minded archbishop, accepting the advice of the management board, named Filion director of *Le Devoir* and handed him all the controlling shares.[6]

Filion proved to be the perfect choice for a demanding and, at times, exasperating position. He would, with the full support of the board, guide *Le Devoir* through a very difficult decade, narrowly avoiding bankruptcy on a couple of occasions. He brought to the task solid credentials. Born in 1909, at Isle Verte near Rivière-du-Loup on the south shore of the St Lawrence, Filion had a tall, broad-shouldered physique and forthright manner that revealed his rural origins. He started his secondary education at the classical college in Rimouski but completed his bachelor of arts degree at Laval in 1931. He went on to acquire a "license en science commerciales" at the Ecole des hautes études commerciales in Montreal in 1934. During the depression Filion was only too eager to take a job with the Union catholique des cultivateurs. He soon made his mark as secretary of the organization and editor of its paper, *La Terre de Chez Nous*. He used his organizational skills to help increase the UCC's membership from ten to forty thousand and the circulation of the paper from thirteen thousand to eighty thousand.[7]

In less than a decade, *Le Devoir* under Filion's guidance became one of the most respected newspapers in all of Canada and the most influential daily in Quebec. This feat could not have been accomplished without a competent editorial staff. Heading *Le Devoir*'s highly effective editorial team was none other than the past provincial leader of the Bloc, André

Laurendeau. Having watched Laurendeau at first hand in the Ligue pour la défense du Canada and then in the Bloc, Filion was determined to appoint him as assistant managing editor to replace eventually an ailing Omer Heroux who had been with the paper since its inception in 1910. Laurendeau's ability to grasp quickly the essential aspects of any question from international politics to municipal affairs and his control of the French language made him in fact, if not in title, the managing editor of Le Devoir by 1950. Another leading member of the team was Paul Sauriol, on the staff since 1928. He dealt with social and economic aspects of provincial and federal affairs. The Ottawa correspondent, Pierre Vigeant, dealt extensively, until his premature death in 1960, with the thorny problem of French-Canadian participation in the federal government ministries and the civil service. Another key contributor was Pierre Laporte. He gained his fame and notoriety as the paper's Quebec City correspondent, a position which he interpreted very broadly, taking every opportunity available to denounce the policies and practices of the Duplessis regime, his favourite target.[8]

How did this team perceive the role of its small but influential daily? Its members were determined to publish a paper that followed the broad policies established by Henri Bourassa in 1910. Le Devoir had been created as an independent, Catholic, and nationalist daily. Filion, on numerous occasions, explained how his team interpreted these three characteristics. To those readers who criticized the paper for being so harsh on Duplessis and his regime, Filion quickly retorted that "Le Devoir was independent, that is, it was free from any external pressures, yet it was not neutral because it regularly took a position on problems of the day."[9] Le Devoir gave prior importance to ideas and interpretation rather than to the dissemination of so-called "objective" news information. The paper was never a corporate business enterprise. In the treatment of political, social, and economic problems the editorial staff's position always took clear precedence over the financial concerns of the administration. As a result, its circulation was very small compared with those of the other Montreal dailies, French and English. This policy kept Le Devoir independent of the ever-present pressures of the business community, both anglophone and francophone. The economic costs of maintaining this intransigent position of independence in relation to both the established political and economic élites were extremely high. By 1955 the paper was operating on an annual deficit of around $50,000 and the director almost declared bankruptcy. Le Devoir's financial position was stabilized when a group of concerned French-Canadian nationalists formed an association called Les Amis du Devoir, which managed throughout the 1950s to solicit sufficient funds annually to cover an ever-growing deficit.[10]

Le Devoir was not the organ of any political party or any particular social class. Its position on issues was based on very specific and explicit values and assumptions. The first of these assumptions was that the paper was a Catholic daily. This did not mean that *Le Devoir* was the property of the church or that the hierarchy inspired and censored its editorial content. It meant simply that the paper was published by Catholic laymen who supported Catholic causes, followed the church's direction on moral issues and questions of dogma but exercised complete freedom in all secular matters.[11] Filion's claim that the paper followed its own line of thought in secular matters is somewhat misleading. This was especially so during the early 1950s, when the paper continued to follow very closely the social thought of the church, much of which dealt with secular matters such as education, labour management, and social security. Nevertheless, by 1960 *Le Devoir* had come to interpret the role of a lay-dominated Catholic newspaper very broadly. To the delegates attending the paper's fiftieth anniversary celebrations Filion declared in part: "Freedom of expression is a law of progress both within and outside the church. Our refusal to conform to this law will enclose us in a sort of intellectual ghetto."[12] The imperatives of a modern secular society demanded public debate on all secular matters, even within the church.

While *Le Devoir*'s Catholic assumptions were still important in the 1950s it was clear that secular nationalist values and objectives were paramount in the minds of the director and his editorial staff. *Le Devoir* had, since its inception, become known as the official organ of the nationalist movement in Quebec. Filion reminded his readers that he had been a committed French-Canadian nationalist ever since his involvement in the Jeune-Canada movement of the 1930s and as a member of the Ligue pour la défense du Canada and the Bloc Populaire in the 1940s. He had attempted to give a clear nationalist orientation to the work of the UCC and therefore his move from that organization to *Le Devoir* was neither a change in direction nor a denial of his past. Rather, it was an attempt to pursue in a more systematic and positive manner the nationalist aspirations and objectives of the French-Canadian people. He was determined to demonstrate that the ideology of nationalism could inspire practical and realistic reforms and programs and it was his ambition that *Le Devoir* should become for French Canadians a guide to concrete action.[13] In short, *Le Devoir* was first and foremost an independent daily of nationalist thought and action.

Filion's deep commitment to the nationalist cause was demonstrated clearly by the fact that he chose André Laurendeau to head his editorial team. André Laurendeau's formative years had prepared him well for a career in journalism. He was born in Montreal on 21 March 1912, the son of educated middle-class parents. His father, Arthur Laurendeau, a musician by profession, was a staunch nationalist who played an active role in both *L'Action français* of the 1920s and *L'Action nationale* of the 1930s. Consequently, from an early age Laurendeau was immersed in endless discussions of French-Canadian politics, religion, and culture. This process continued during his five years, 1926–31, at the Jesuit-run Collège Sainte-Marie in Montreal, where Father Thomas Mignault infused the entire classical curriculum with a Quebec-centred French-Canadian nationalism.[14]

Laurendeau's penchant for French literature and creative writing prompted him to enrol in the Faculty of Letters at the Université de Montréal, where he pursued these interests as well as the Canadian history courses offered by Abbé Lionel Groulx. By the fall of 1932 Quebec was in the full grip of the depression with some 100,000 unemployed, most of them in Montreal. The incumbent Liberal government of Alexandre Taschereau lacked the will or the capacity to respond to the crisis while the federal Conservative government of R.B. Bennett displayed a callous disdain for French Canadians by refusing to hire or promote them within the federal civil service. [15] Where there is nationalism there is youth. Laurendeau, along with several Université de Montréal colleagues, including Gérard Filion, Pierre Dansereau, Pierre Dagenais, Jacques Vadeboncoeur, and several others, felt a need to act. Laurendeau prepared the *Manifeste de la jeune génération*, demanding that French Canadians be treated fairly by the federal government and the large corporations, and called upon French Canada's youth to become "master in their own house." The manifesto was made public on 19 December 1932 at the Salle Gésu in Montreal during a rally presided over by Armand Lavergne, speaker of the House of Commons and a veteran nationalist from the Laurier era.[16] The Jeune-Canada movement was born. Over the next three years the movement's leaders organized several noisy and well-attended public rallies throughout Quebec and distributed numerous tracts and pamphlets advocating a national reawakening, economic liberation from foreign trusts, and the reestablishment of a sound and stable social order. Jeune-Canada was marred by a mild strain of antisemitism and a virulent anticommunism, and pursued the search for the elusive *chef national* to lead the French-Canadian nation toward its highly "mythical" long-term ideal and objective, the full political independence of "la Laurentie." No active politician measured up to Jeune-Canada's stringent criteria. The movement's choice fell upon its mentor and nationalist historian, Abbé Lionel Groulx. Fortunately for Groulx, his cassock prevented him from having to be put to the test![17]

The Jeune-Canada experience was significant for Laurendeau in that it forced him to grapple seriously with the tenets of traditonal French-Canadian nationalism. His pamphlet, *Notre nationalisme*, was an attempt to undermine and refute Henri Bourassa's claim that French-Canadian nationalism had become imperialist, racist, and separatist.[18] For Laurendeau it was self-evident that French Canadians constituted culturally and sociologically a nation which they had every right and responsibility to conserve and develop. The most effective way of carrying out this responsibility was to identify this French-Canadian nation with a particular geographic region known as *la Patrie*, or to use Jeune-Canada's terminology, *la Laurentie*. "Sustained and nourished in this manner," claimed Laurendeau, "our nationalism will grow rich, harmonious, and mature."[19]

Yet Laurendeau clearly despised a "maple syrup" nationalism with its "apostrophes to the race."[20] A close reading of *Notre nationalisme* reveals a tentative break with the traditional nationalism of the period, especially in his attempt to reconcile the competing claims of personalism and nationalism: "We will give citizens of this corner of the earth a sense of collectivity as well as a sense of personalism ... Through this sense of personalism, of differentiation, of individuality, one's own sense of belonging to the collectivity is preserved. In this manner one learns to advance to a higher level, from the Nation to the Universe, to Creation and then its Primary Cause."[21] This new thrust had its origins in Laurendeau's growing interest in French Catholic personalist thought as expounded in the Paris reviews *Esprit*, under the director Emmanuel Mounier, and *Sept*, put out by Jacques Maritain and Etienne Gilson. Both Maritain and Gilson taught at the Université de Montréal as prominent visiting professors in the early 1930s and Laurendeau was able to absorb their ideas first hand. Laurendeau also joined a group of young French Canadians, led by Robert Charbonneau and Paul Beaulieu, who founded in March 1934 the review *La Relève* to explore and disseminate left-wing French Catholic personalist thought.[22] After considerable soul searching *La Relève* undertook a reassessment of nationalism which rejected the principle of political national self-determination and the total subordination of the individual to the collectivity. For *La Relève* the nation was essentially a centre of culture and "patriotism, which cannot be considered apart from the person, does not take on its true meaning and value unless subordinated to a Christian order, or more generally to a Christian conception of humanism."[23] *La Relève* managed to transcend the clerical and nationalist orthodoxy of its environment by drawing upon the liberal catholicism expressed by the authors and proponents of French Catholic personalist thought. Overall though, *La Relève*'s adherence to left-wing Catholicism was timid and only partial, its role limited to pursuing a "spiritual revolution" through the rehabilitation of universal man. *La Relève* refused to follow Maritain's and Mounier's plea to left-wing Catholics to engage in political action to bring about necessary socio-economic reforms.[24]

Laurendeau quickly transcended the nonactivist literary perspective of his colleagues in *La Relève*. He believed nationalist political action was imperative. This was due, no doubt, to his strong commitment to the development of a creative and autonomous French-Canadian culture, anchored fully in the future as well as the past.[25] Just as important was Laurendeau's personal encounter with the French leaders of left-wing Catholicism during his study sojourn in France at the Sorbonne, the Collège de France, and the Institut Catholique in 1935–6. Of this experience, Laurendeau later recalled that after searching in several directions he had finally come to accept the general position of the Catholic left and to regard Jacques Maritain, Nicholas Berdiaeff, and Emmanuel Mounier as "masters or guides," while remaining a French-Canadian nationalist.[26] From his encounters with Berdiaeff and Daniel Rops, Laurendeau learned that Christianity and modernity were not incompatible. In fact, a sincere and responsible Christian realized that the creation of the Kingdom of God on earth required a creative initiative on the part of all Christians to bring about the concrete transformation of society, even if this action meant the overthrow of the established social order and a clash with constituted regimes.[27]

From Mounier, Maritain, and Gilson, Laurendeau came to perceive what personalism entailed in the context of the European fascist and communist movements of the 1930s. He came to accept *Esprit*'s condemnation of the Franco insurrectionists in the Spanish Civil War and he agreed with Mounier's interpretation of the revolt as "capitalist, fascist, and feudo-clerical defensive reaction, directed by pitiless generals, some of whom are notorious Freemasons."[28] He also criticized the French-Canadian press for unthinkingly supporting the fascist cause and condemning the communists simply because Franco was ostensibly on the side of the Catholic church. He reminded his French-Canadian readers that "God is not some *bourgeois policeman* charged with defending the large property holdings of the aristocracy or certain religious communities, or supervising the shameless exploitation of the poor by wealthy capitalists."[29] Upon his return to Canada Laurendeau was struck forcefully by the rightist bias of French Canadians, and of French-Canadian nationalists in particular who more often than not thought that "God was on the Right." He reminded French Canadians that Catholics could and should reject communism not in the name of some fascist order but rather "in the name of the holy gospel and Christian philosophy."[30] Maritain and Gilson convinced him that it was suicidal for the Catholic church to continue to allow Christian doctrine to be identified with and used by right-wing regimes, especially the fascist regimes of Spain and Italy.

Yet Laurendeau shrewdly recognized that the political realities of Quebec differed considerably from those of France. Any successful strategy for political and social change had to take into account the fact that no highly distinguishable left, right, or centre constituencies existed in Quebec. There was only a strong but generalized tendency in favour of the Right. Consequently, Laurendeau proposed an approach to Quebec politics which entailed an amalgamation of French Catholic personalism with a socially oriented French-Canadian nationalism. "The formula of the future," he suggested, "appeared to be some kind of social-nationalism based on the philosophy of personalism, or a strong and dymanic *Centre* instead of the existing repugnant middle-of-the-road parties which serve as a balancing-pole in normal times but must be balanced during periods of crisis."[31] Little did Laurendeau realize at the time that he was setting himself a challenge that would literally encompass the next two decades of his life.

Laurendeau was well placed to state the case for this formula of social-nationalism and personalism and to gain converts from within nationalist circles. In the fall of 1937 he succeeded his father as director of *L'Action nationale*, a post he held for five years. Laurendeau immediately oriented the review toward concrete socioeconomic issues. He denounced the Duplessis government's antilabour policies and practices in the textile strikes of 1937 and he opened the review to François Hertel, who, like himself, had become firmly attached to personalism.[32] He denounced the spread of racist doctrines while reminding French Canadians that the papacy had condemned both Communism and Nazism.[33] He chided Duplessis for his anti-communist crusade, which was aimed primarily at the increasingly militant unions as well as at the Liberal leader Adélard Godbout's antifascist crusade against Duplessis' Padlock Law. Both crusades were merely rhetorical distractions which drew the public's attention away from the real villain, irresponsible and greedy monopoly capitalism.[34] Yet although these ideological movements may have served as distractions in Quebec, elsewhere they contributed to the outbreak of World War II. The dual threat of conscription for overseas service combined with the centralist ambitions of the federal government forced Laurendeau to set aside, momentarily, his task of redefining French-Canadian nationalism.

By 1942 Laurendeau and Filion along with several other colleagues of their generation found themselves at the centre of the nationalist vortex. Prior to September 1939 all Quebec nationalists had favoured a policy of complete neutrality. Once the Canadian government declared war, the French-Canadian nationalists proposed a policy of compromise. French Canadians would accept willingly limited voluntary participation in arms, money, and manpower, if Prime Minister King's Liberal government stood by its promise not to impose conscription for overseas service. If the Liberal government refused to abide by this reasonable compromise, the nationalists warned that they would undertake the task of organizing a massive systematic and nonpartisan public protest.[35] The nationalist challenge was put to the test when the King government, in the Throne speech of 22 January 1942, announced that a plebiscite would be held in April in which his government would ask the full Canadian electorate to free it from its promise of no conscription for overseas service. The nationalists were ready. The Ligue pour la défense du Canada was formed immediately with the support of all prominent and active French-Canadian nationalists and nationalist organizations including the Société Saint-Jean Baptiste, *Le Devoir*, L'Union des

cultivateurs catholiques, the Catholic union movement, and *L'Action nationale*.[36] Laurendeau and Filion were both members of the executive and
were instrumental in attracting to the organization the younger generation
of nationalists like Jean Drapeau and Michel Chartrand. The Ligue's objective was to get all Canadians, but especially French Canadians, to vote
overwhelmingly "no" to the Liberal government's request. The ideological
basis of the Ligue's anticonscriptionist campaign was the argument, eloquently stated by Laurendeau, that if democracy was to prevail in Canada
then the will of the English-Canadian majority could not be imposed by
force upon the clearly stated will of a significantly large and officially recognized ethnic minority, especially in a matter of life and death such as active
war service. In a pluralistic federal state the principle of majority democracy
had to be tempered by a sense of justice and fair play toward all components
if political strife and civil disobedience were to be avoided.[37]

The campaign conducted by the Ligue pour la défense du Canada
throughout Quebec was well funded, well organized, intensely passionate,
and highly successful. Despite the naïve urgings of Mackenzie King, and
those in his cabinet who would agree to participate, for a "yes" vote by
French Canadians, the result was a foregone conclusion. The plebiscite revealed a country clearly divided along ethnic lines. Quebec as a whole voted
72 per cent "no," while the other nine provinces voted 80 per cent "yes."[38]
The outcome, no doubt, was a powerful reminder to Prime Minister King
that French Canadians remained as bitterly opposed to conscription as in
World War I. Serious trouble could be expected in Quebec if his government
did not approach the issue with the utmost caution and political sensitivity.
The Liberal government pushed ahead with its Bill 80 to amend the National Resources Mobilization Act to allow conscription for overseas service.
To assuage French-Canadian fears Prime Minister King offered his immor-
tal phrase, "conscription if necessary, but not necessarily conscription."

While the Ligue continued a vigorous campaign of political education
against conscription and ran its "candidate of the conscripts," Jean Drapeau,
against General Laflèche in the Outremont by-election in November 1942,
others laid the groundwork for a nationalist third party. Marie-Louis
Beaulieu, René Chaloult, and Paul Gouin, with the help of Abbé Lionel
Groulx, Georges Pelletier, and Henri Bourassa, persuaded a vocal anti-
imperialist federal member of Parliament, Maxime Raymond, to accept the
leadership of this new party. In late September 1942 the party was named
the Bloc Populaire Canadien. "Canada for Canadians, Quebec for Quebecers!" became the Bloc's highly nationalist and emotional slogan.[39] In January
1943 Laurendeau was appointed secretary-general of the Bloc Populaire
and he undertook, along with numerous other colleagues from the Ligue,
the difficult task of developing the fledgling party's organizational structure,
program, and fund-raising efforts. These efforts were seriously hampered

by a power struggle which erupted at the outset between Dr Philippe Hamel, the Quebec city dentist who had come to symbolize the struggle against the hydro-electric trusts, and Edouard Lacroix, Quebec MP for La Beauce, a close colleague of Raymond's and a prosperous lumber and textile entrepreneur. Lacroix had made a private arrangement with Raymond according to which he would put $90,000 at the Bloc's disposal if he could control all the Quebec region ridings and if the party's program met his approval. When this arrangement became known, the dissident trio Hamel, Gouin, and Chaloult denounced Lacroix as a traitor to the nationalist cause and demanded that Raymond expel him from the party and put them in positions of responsibility. As long as Lacroix remained the trio would not participate. Raymond, unwilling to take action against Lacroix or appoint regional lieutenants, because of an agreement with Georges Pelletier, director of *Le Devoir*, to maintain full authority over the party, decided to delegate his authority over the provincial wing of the Bloc to André Laurendeau in February 1944. As a result, the imbroglio between the trio and the party evolved into a schism. The Bloc Populaire entered the 1944 provincial election deeply divided, lacking funds and effective organization, especially in the Quebec region. Moreover, without the crucial support and participation of the trio the Bloc had no chance whatsoever of challenging Union Nationale candidates or incumbent members in the rural constituencies.[40]

On the ideological level the federal wing of the Bloc centred its attack on British imperialism and the threat of conscription. These French-Canadian nationalists did not perceive that for the vast majority of English-speaking Canadians this was "Canada's War," rather than a knee-jerk, emotional colonial reaction in aid of a declining imperial power. The Bloc's leaders were more perceptive in their recognition of the Liberal government's use of the war crisis to implement piecemeal the highly centralist recommendations of the 1940 Rowell-Sirois *Report*, a form of internal imperialism dictated by an anglophone-dominated central government. The Bloc denounced Premier Godbout's decision to give Quebec's consent to a constitutional amendment providing Ottawa with full jurisdiction over a national unemployment insurance program. Godbout also came under harsh criticism for signing the tax-rental agreement in 1942, thereby relinquishing Quebec's rights in the field of direct taxation in return for paltry federal subsidies. The Bloc was successful in portraying the Quebec Liberal party as a mere puppet of the federal Liberal party, a fact which contributed considerably to its defeat in the 1944 provincial election. However, the Bloc was not able to convince the voters that Duplessis and the Union Nationale were proconscriptionist and soft on imperialists. Duplessis had, no doubt, modified his extremist position of 1939 but a great many farm families and urban working-class French Canadians still considered him to be their best defence against Ottawa and the Tory imperialists.[41]

On the provincial scene the Bloc adopted a program of social-economic reforms which was influenced heavily by the philosophy of social catholicism adapted to the Quebec environment by the lay and clerical members of the Jesuit organization, the Ecole sociale populaire. Laurendeau and his fellow nationalists denounced the foreign and Anglo-Canadian financial and industrial élites for the economic dictatorship they wielded over Quebec and its people. This system of monopoly capitalism enriched a few while exploiting the lives of working-class people, most of whom were poorly educated French Canadians of rural origins. Socialism, contended Bloc militants, was not the solution. The CCF program, as outlined in the Regina Manifesto, was unacceptable to French-Canadian Catholics because it destroyed private property through public ownership of all the major means of production, advocated class conflict, and avoided the moral and spiritual dimensions of society in its assumptions and reform proposals. Furthermore, the CCF program called for excessive centralization of power in the hands of the Canadian federal government and bureaucracy, replacing the dictatorship of an Anglo-Canadian financial élite with the dictatorship of an Anglo-Canadian dominated state.[42]

As an alternative, the Bloc Populaire advocated the building of a family-oriented society which would draw upon Catholic social doctrine to attenuate the worst features of monopoly forcign capitalism and bring about the economic liberation of the French-Canadian majority in Quebec. A regulatory, and if need be, interventionist Quebec state would help achieve this objective of economic liberation by encouraging the growth of small- and medium-sized francophone private corporations, the establishment of rural and urban, producer and consumer cooperatives, the regulation of large-scale private corporations, and finally the nationalization of some of Quebec's monopoly-controlled essential services such as hydro-electricity, the telephone system, and the importation of coal and petroleum. The Bloc also wanted to improve the standard of living of Quebec's farming families through rural electrification, rural credit, and improved roads, hospitals, and schools. The plight of the urban proletariat would be improved through the imposition of better working conditions, low-cost housing, urban-renewal, family allowances, and other social security measures, as well as the acceptance by employers and the state of strong unions capable of bargaining for "family" wages. The state's political leaders and senior bureaucrats would be advised and supervised by a social-corporatist inspired economic planning council which was made up of delegates from employer and professional associations, farm organizations, and the unions.[43] The Bloc's provincial program was both a reaffirmation of the essentially conservative nature of traditional French-Canadian nationalism and a harbinger of the liberal-oriented neo-nationalism that would emerge in the postwar years.

The Bloc Populaire, despite a Gallup poll taken in July 1944 giving it 27 per cent of the popular vote, did not do very well in the provincial election on 8 August. Conscription was not a concrete issue and the Bloc was hampered in the overrepresented rural constituencies by the Chaloult-Gouin-Hamel "imbroglio" as well as the party's incipient neo-nationalist socioeconomic reforms which inevitably would have led to the growth of the provincial bureaucracy and increased taxation. Bloc candidates garnered nearly 16 per cent of the popular vote but elected only four members to the provicial Assembly, including their leader André Laurendeau. Laurendeau, with the support and encouragement of René Chaloult who was elected as an independent nationalist, hammered away at the Duplessis government for its negative defence of provincial autonomy and its unwillingness to implement urgently required social and economic reforms. Laurendeau called upon the premier to undertake dynamic provincial programs on all fronts in order to counteract the centralist social-welfare and economic development programs of the postwar Keynesian-inspired federal government and bureaucracy. Unfortunately, the Bloc's resources were very limited and a nationalist consensus on how to respond to Ottawa had not as yet emerged. Many of the Bloc's activists, including Raymond, favoured leaving the provincial arena to Duplessis' Union Nationale. Laurendeau, Filion, and the younger nationalists could not accept this approach. Consequently, Laurendeau resigned the leadership of the Bloc Populaire in July 1947 and joined *Le Devoir* in September.[44] As a political endeavour the Bloc had failed miserably. As a training ground for the emerging generation of French-Canadian nationalists the experience proved, in hindsight, to be of immeasurable significance. It brought them face to face with the concrete realities of a rapidly changing Quebec society and made them realize the inadequacies and shortcomings of traditionalist nationalism. It also made them realize the folly and frustration of trying to create a nationalist third party without first building a widespread, grass-roots popular base for such an endeavour.

With the termination of his political career in the summer of 1948, Laurendeau was once again available. In September of that year the members of the Ligue d'Action nationale reappointed him for a second term as director of *L'Action nationale*. Laurendeau undertook, once again, the task of broadening the scope of the periodical by inviting younger, more socially and economically oriented French Canadians to contribute articles to the review and even join the Ligue d'Action nationale. Laurendeau's persistent efforts paid off. In 1948 the Ligue was dominated by traditional clerical and professional petty bourgeois nationalists like Anatole Vanier, Dominique Beaudin, Canon Lionel Groulx, Father J.-P. Archambault, and Antonio Perrault. But during Laurendeau's second term as director the Ligue and *L'Action nationale* came under the increased influence of the younger French-Canadian nationalists such as Jean Drapeau, Jean-Marc Léger, Jacques Perrault,

Jean-Paul Robillard, Paul-Emile Gingras, Gérard Filion, and Pierre Laporte who succeeded Laurendeau as director in 1954. *Le Devoir* concentrated on the application of nationalist doctrine to concrete problems and issues that arose in Quebec society. The major function of *L'Action nationale*, as Laurendeau conceived it, was the rethinking and reformulation of the basic tenets of French-Canadian nationalist thought. The roles of *Le Devoir* and *L'Action nationale* were therefore complementary, so that it is not surprising to find the leading personnel of these two journals largely composed of members of the younger generation that had participated in, and had been moulded by, the events of the depression and war decades.

One of the most innovative thinkers of the Ligue d'Action nationale and an active contributor to *L'Action nationale* was Jean-Marc Léger. Born in 1927, Léger attended Collège André-Grasset in Montreal and then proceeded to acquire degrees in law, social science, and history at the Université de Montréal, 1946–9, where he was taught by the neo-nationalist brother-in-law of André Laurendeau, Jacques Perrault. He edited, along with Camille Laurin, the student newspaper, *Le Quartier Latin*. As editors they focused their attention on the socioeconomic problems of the day and attempted to develop a dialogue between the self-centred bourgeois student milieu and the urban working-class milieu with its union and cooperative organizations. Léger and several of his colleagues, following a pattern established in France's postwar universities, spearheaded the setting up of the Equipe des recherches sociales in 1947 to inculcate a social conscience in their fellow students. At its peak in 1948, the Equipe comprised over one hundred and twenty students from the faculties of law, arts, and social sciences. The executive organized weekly seminars centred around talks given by invited guests from all political parties, the Catholic and international unions, the cooperative movement, the various Catholic action groups, and business organizations. The seminars were, in Léger's view, an excellent medium for making the students aware of Quebec's contemporary problems, especially the worker problem which had been neglected, by and large, by French Canada's lay and clerical leaders. In fact, in the spring of 1949 the Equipe organized a collection for the asbestos miners of the Eastern Townships who were on a lengthy strike and two hundred Université de Montréal students journeyed to Asbestos and Thetford Mines to present their donation and show their support for the strikers' cause. The influence of the Equipe experience encouraged many of its members, according to Léger, to pursue careers in organized labour, cooperative movements, social welfare and health organizations, and as journalists concerned with these fields. Léger himself pursued a career in journalism in the area of foreign affairs. In the fall of 1949 he headed for Paris, where he enrolled at the Institut d'études politiques. In 1951 he returned to Montreal with a "Certificat en relation internationale" and took a job at *La Presse* reporting on foreign affairs until he left in December 1956 to join the staff at *Le Devoir*.[45]

The transition was not difficult. In fact, Léger felt quite at home with the neo-nationalist team at *Le Devoir*. He and a couple of other colleagues from *Le Quartier Latin* and the Equipe had, at Laurendeau's invitation, joined the Ligue de l'Action nationale in 1948. They had come to the attention of the Ligue in the fall of 1947 when they submitted for publication in its review an article that was highly critical of the French-Canadian petty bourgeoisie's conception of nationalism, a conception which, they argued, totally ignored the socioeconomic, cultural, and linguistic problems of the francophone working class. Influenced by the personalist philosophy of *Esprit* and *Sept*, as well as by the *économie et humanisme* philosophy of the French Dominicans, Léger and his colleagues called for the reintegration of francophone workers with the nationalist movement by the development of closer contacts between the petty bourgeois leaders and the working class, the formulation and dissemination of a national doctrine reflecting the contemporary problems and aspirations of the francophone working-class majority, and the founding of a university for the workers and their children.[46] Reflecting the social Catholicism which had influenced Laurendeau in the 1930s and 1940s, Léger and his colleagues concluded that nationalism, "must it be repeated, was only a form of humanism adapted to particular circumstances and conditions, a unique humanism which remains in its most profound sense a contribution to the development of the individual."[47] Expanding on this desire to integrate individual and collective aspirations, Léger would become one of the leading neo-nationalists of the 1950s. After Laurendeau's premature and untimely death in 1968, Léger, who had been promoted to the post of editorialist in 1962, decided to write three articles supporting the concept of sovereignty-association for Quebec. *Le Devoir*'s director and editor-in-chief, Claude Ryan, published the articles on condition that Léger resign as editorialist. The following year Léger left the newspaper to become secretary-general of the Agence de co-opération culturelle et technique organized by several francophone countries.[48]

The Montreal neo-nationalists had, in the early 1950s, few active supporters in the Quebec City region apart from René Chaloult, who lost his seat in the Quebec legislature in the 1952 provincial election. Most of the first postwar generation of Quebec City intellectuals were graduates of Father Georges-Henri Lévesque's Faculty of Social Sciences at Laval. Like their dean they were highly critical of French-Canadian nationalism as exemplified by Maurice Duplessis and his Union Nationale administration. Duplessis responded accordingly and tried to have Father Lévesque ousted as dean but the move was unsuccessful.[49] Consequently, Jean-Charles Falardeau, Maurice Lamontagne, and Léon Dion gravitated toward *Cité libre* and L'Institut canadien des affaires publiques set up in 1954. One graduate who did not follow this pattern was Arthur Tremblay. Born in 1917 at

St-Bruno in the Lac Saint-Jean region, Arthur Tremblay completed his classical education at the Séminaire de Chicoutimi in 1937. He was encouraged by Father Georges-Henri Lévesque, whom he met in 1939, to complete a master's degree in social sciences at Laval, which he accomplished in 1942. He had helped finance his education by running a private career counselling service which was incorporated within the university in 1941 as the Institut Laval d'orientation professionnelle. In 1943, Tremblay was employed part-time in Laval's Ecole de pédagogie which was then under the directorship of Abbé Alphonse Parent. He spent 1944–5 obtaining a master's of education degree from Harvard and was subsequently appointed associate director of the Ecole de pédagogie. He became a full professor in 1949 and remained with the Ecole until 1960. In 1949–51 Tremblay studied the work of Jean Piaget at the Université de Paris and other western European institutions. Upon his return to Quebec he was appointed to the Comité de coordination de l'enseignement which was set up to establish some links between the truncated francophone secondary public system, called the Ecole primaire secondaire, and the universities, which were having great difficulty recruiting qualified students for their faculties of science. This experience was, Tremblay contends, a turning point for his career. Rather than concentrating on theoretical research, he focused his skills and energies on analysing the problems of Quebec's Catholic and French educational system and then proposing the necessary reforms. The Royal Commission of Inquiry on Constitutional Problems, known as the Tremblay Commission and set up in February 1953, provided an excellent opportunity to get all groups interested in education at all levels to express their views and was a marvellous vehicle to bring to the attention of the general public the serious shortcomings of Catholic and francophone education. Arthur Tremblay, because of his expertise in the area, was called upon to prepare the Fédération des commissions scolaires' and the Confédération des travailleurs catholiques du Canada's presentations on education to the Tremblay Commission. Impressed by his grasp of the issues, the commissioners then asked Tremblay to synthesize the 140 briefs presented to them on the question of education reform. In fact, the positions Tremblay adopted on education reform were closely aligned with those of the neo-nationalists. Tremblay's ideas were readily circulated in Le Devoir, and he was in great demand as a speaker throughout the province and on radio and television. In the late 1950s, as vice-president of the Association d'éducation du Québec and a member of the Association canadienne des éducateurs de langue française, Arthur Tremblay championed the need for progressive education reforms and supported the neo-nationalists' demand for a full-scale inquiry into education. In 1960 Tremblay became executive assistant to Paul Gérin-Lajoie, minister of youth in the Lesage Liberal cabinet and the person responsible for education in Quebec. The following year Tremblay, along with Gérard Filion of *Le Devoir*, was appointed to the Commission royale d'enquête sur l'enseignement, known as the Parent Commission, where he remained until he became deputy-minister of the newly created and long-overdue Ministry of Education in May 1964.[50] He was by then in an excellent position to influence the course of educational reform in Quebec!

Quebec's postwar neo-nationalists emerged from the francophone community's professional petty bourgeoisie. A few had their social origins in rural Quebec but had managed to join the ranks of the urban professional petty bourgeoisie via their education in the classical college system, the Ecoles des hautes études commerciales, or the traditional faculties of law and medicine. All were products of the depression and war experiences and all were influenced by the Quebec-centred nationalism of the Groulx school. This nationalism, expressed in the Action Libérale Nationale of the 1930s and the Bloc Populaire Canadien of the 1940s, was mixed with the social Catholicism of the Ecole sociale populaire of the Jesuits, the personalist philosophy of Mounier, Gilson, and Maritain, and, finally, the *économie et humanisme* philosophy of the Dominicans which had found favour with the Catholic labour movement after the war. All these ideological influences combined with the rapid demographic and socioeconomic changes in postwar Quebec to induce a young, dynamic, and deeply committed group of French Canadians to question seriously the basic tenets of their nationalism. They found the traditional version defective in several ways and then set out to formulate and disseminate a more progressive, secular, and humanist form of nationalism.

CHAPTER THREE

The Neo-nationalist Critique of Nationalism

At the centre of a universe in revolution our small world has changed profoundly. We are now fully aware of this situation and are starting to bring new solutions to new problems. *These proposed solutions are dividing us* – they divide nationalists because their love of the nation and their acute awareness of the dangers facing it do not necessarily imply a set of common options to deal with new questions.[1]

The profound changes referred to by André Laurendeau involved a conjuncture of four major developments. The first entailed the decline of British imperialism in Canada, especially noticeable in urban French Canada since the war. Second, the political equilibrium of Canada was being seriously undermined by the implementation of an Ottawa-inspired and controlled social welfare state. Third, the province of Quebec was experiencing an unprecedented era of industrial and commercial expansion which was creating dramatic social and demographic changes challenging the very roots of French Canadian society. Finally, the Catholic church in Quebec was in the process of changing its perception of nationalism and attempting to redefine its role within French-Canadian society.[2] One result of the growing awareness of the numerous crises within French Canada created by these developments was the realization by a small minority of nationalists of the need to examine critically the major assumptions and tenets of traditional French-Canadian nationalism.

THE EMERGING CRISIS

The thrust of their critique was conditioned, of course, by their understanding of the nature and import of the various crises confronting their society. The neo-nationalists of *Le Devoir* and *L'Action nationale* perceived correctly that the most significant development in contemporary Quebec was the renewal of industrial development, "because this created political, social and cultural upheavals which were disorienting."[3] Until the Great Depression, industrial and urban growth in Quebec was concentrated primarily in the Montreal region and had not seriously weakened the economic structures or the cultural and religious value system of rural society. In fact, the "communal" rural value system continued to retain considerable allegiance and resonance among the urban French-Canadian petty bourgeois intelligentsia and first generation working-class families. The first serious challenge to the economic and institutional structures of rural Quebec came with the closing of the three traditional outlets for its surplus young men and women – emigration to the United States, colonization of Quebec and northern and eastern Ontario, and employment in the province's expanding primary and secondary economic sectors – during the 1930s.[4]

The renewed prosperity and employment created by the war and postwar industrial expansion only attenuated and delayed the growing crisis in rural Quebec. But by the early 1950s French-Canadian nationalists realized the full extent and significance of the rural depopulation that had taken place since 1939. Not only were young men and women who were surplus to the needs of the rural society seeking and finding jobs in the cities and company resource towns but entire families were deserting the ancestral soil in search of better economic conditions and a higher standard of living. The most visible sign of this demographic and economic revolution was the rapid expansion of what Laurendeau termed "the fourth estate in the nation."[5] He estimated in 1947 that between 60 and 80 per cent of French Canadians, depending upon the region chosen, resided in urban centres. The working class was henceforth to be Quebec's largest social class and French-Canadian society would be "increasingly influenced, directed, saved or ruined by this class."[6] As soon as the political system had been readjusted to reflect this demographic revolution, the fourth estate would press upon the politicians the resolution of its major problems, problems substantially different from those of rural French Canadians.

Gérard Filion was convinced that no other people in the western world had undergone as rapid or as radical an economic and social revolution as the French-Canadian people. "A traditionally rural people," wrote Filion in 1954,"formed in the practice of the bourgeois virtues, accustomed to living on ancient traditions, has been transformed in a single generation into a proletarian people. Other countries have, like Quebec, become industrialized but none at such a rapid pace. Even England, the mother of the industrial revolution, took several generations to complete the transformation of its pre-industrial economy."[7] In contrasting the postwar crisis brought on by the new wave of industrial expansion with the one created by the Conquest of 1760, Laurendeau concluded that the more recent crisis, despite the fact that the French-Canadian nation was stronger and more mature, was much broader and deeper in scope than the upheaval created by the Conquest.

The industrial revolution had left and was leaving no institution – economic, political, or social – untouched. Everything in the society had to be re-thought, restructured, reconstructed, or, at least, reformulated in terms of the society's new socioeconomic structures and increasingly secular values.[8]

The massive demographic shift to urban centres created two distinct but interrelated problems. The first was the transformation of large numbers of habitants – semi-autonomous, land-owning producers – into unskilled, propertyless members of the urban working poor. But just as alarming for French-Canadian nationalists, young and old, was the destruction of the economic and social viability of the rural society. The belief that French-Canadian people had a "rural vocation" was an integral part of traditional French-Canadian nationalist thought. In the late 1940s even young nationalists like Laurendeau still believed, in part, that a strong rural society was important to the preservation of a sound balanced economy, as a guarantee of social stability and moral and physical health and as the only sector that the nationality could rely on "to replenish its élites and renew its population."[9] Considering the traditionally high birth rate in rural Quebec, there was a good deal of validity in Laurendeau's claim that habitant families had been primarily responsible for the phenomenal growth in the French-Canadian population since 1760 as well as being the main source of its leadership, lay and clerical.

Apart from the demise of the rural society, it was the nature and size of the new industrial proletariat that most alarmed young French-Canadian nationalists. The workers, no longer habitants, constituted the single largest social class in modern Quebec, and their problems and needs would increasingly dominate the political arena. How this class responded and adapted to its new urban-industrial environment would determine in large measure the future of French-Canadian society in Canada and North America. Would French-Canadian institutions and sociocultural values prevail among the working-class communities of the cities as well as they had for nearly two centuries in the rural parishes? In short, could French Canada modernize itself while still remaining a unique and valuable society? These were the questions that Laurendeau put to his nationalist colleagues in October 1947 in the leading article of an inspired symposium entitled "*l'humanisme ouvrier*." His own assessment of the situation was harsh and to the point. The working class, he declared, "constitutes, along with the big business community, *the group of men least influenced* by the national question, consequently the least prepared to accept sacrifices for the collective good."[10] The worker had a much weaker sense of tradition, of culture, than did the habitant or the petty bourgeois. In fact, the working class was almost totally indifferent and, on occasion, even hostile to the doctrines of French-Canadian nationalism and its spokesmen. The demise of the Bloc, in Laurendeau's estimation, had clearly shown that the workers placed economic and material gain far ahead of concerns such as provincial autonomy and French-Canadian control over the Quebec economy.

To a great extent, this process of redefinition was a natural outgrowth of the perception and understanding of the serious problems confronting French-Canadian urban industrial workers and their families. One broad explanation, offered by young and old nationalists alike, to account for the denationalization of the French-Canadian working class was that the very process of industrialization itself was a homogenizing, uniforming, and universalizing force that undermined all cultural and national particularisms. The industrial revolution had created a new class that was plagued by perpetual wage and job insecurity. Second, the industrial system depersonalized the individual worker because it demanded of him very little initiative and left him a minimum of responsibilities. The end result was a vicious cycle in which the worker, freed of his social responsibilities, lost the desire, even if he retained the means, to accumulate reserves. Meanwhile his position of permanent insecurity further encouraged an attitude of social irresponsibility. Industrial capitalist society induced the worker to regard the maximization of profits as of more importance than spiritual or cultural values.[11] Claude Ryan, an organizer of Catholic action movements, expressed the dilemma most eloquently when he wrote: "Perhaps the best explanation of the present dilemma facing French Canadians is that they have been drawn, somewhat unaware, into a vast universalizing movement. This process has taken them out of their traditional and historical environment and forced them to experience, on the cultural, social, and economic levels, the same great problems as the rest of mankind."[12] French-Canadian society was forced, therefore, to abandon its strategy of isolation because industrialization, which opened the society to outside influences, created problems that were common to all industrialized western nations.

The process of homogenization and denationalization as it affected the French-Canadian working class was readily visible. But in many ways it was also the most difficult phenomenon to control and remedy. As French-Canadian families abandoned their rural sociocultural values and ethos, these were being replaced by English-Canadian and American values and norms of behaviour. In short, the nationalists, to their dismay, could not discover a nascent French-Canadian culture developing in Quebec's urban centres. The movie houses, the theatres, the radio programs, consumer advertising, and magazines were all predominantly English and American. They reflected values and a lifestyle that were modern but, nevertheless, alien to the majority of French Canadians. What was just as alarming was that the working environment, especially in Montreal, for increasing numbers of French Canadians was primarily English-speaking and therefore an assimilationist experience. All the unions, except the Confédération des travailleurs catholiques du Canada (CTCC), were dominated by American bosses and American union ideology.[13] Consequently, as Jean-Marc Léger explained it, the worker

has to face a terrible disequilibrium which we feel constitutes the essence of the current crisis. He has to attempt an impossible adaptation of his French existence to an environment and structures which not only prevent his development but even worse attempt to destroy his culture. National interest, generally speaking, usually coincides with the immediate interests of the individual. Here the situation is quite the opposite for the worker. He is impressed by the quantitative values which inspire American movies and periodicals, thereby preventing him from appreciating the spiritual enrichment of the patrimony of French civilization.[14]

The problem was not limited to one of cultural imperialism. This was merely an extension of the foreign domination of the Canadian and Quebec economies. The development of Quebec's primary and secondary economic sectors had been and continued to be initiated, directed, and controlled by British, Anglo-Canadian, and American financiers and corporations.[15] While rapid economic expansion laid to rest once and for all the argument that the Quebec economy was backward, it also accentuated the long-standing problem of the economic inferiority of French-Canadian workers and the inability of society to create a powerful French-Canadian entrepreneurial and managerial bourgeoisie.[16] The major thrust for the expansion of the economy came from outside the province, while increasing numbers of French Canadians were called upon to provide the labour. The French-Canadian people, warned Filion, were undergoing, at an accelerated rate, the same social turmoil and economic oppression being experienced by the black peoples of Africa after Western European capitalists had invaded their native countries.[17]

The impact of the postwar economic expansion on two traditional French-Canadian institutions was devastating. The family and the parish no longer functioned as strong integrating social forces when transplanted into the urban environment. The economic role of the family as a semi autonomous, land-owning productive unit capable of placing all of its children in various occupations was terminated. Most, if not all, of the children of urban working-class families were forced, very early in life, to become independent wage-earners and make a place for themselves within a highly competitive and individualistic world. Compared to the small rural parishes, the urban parishes were large impersonal administrative units with four or five priests. Because these priests were generally much better educated than the rural immigrants, they often found it difficult to relate either to the traditional values or to the myriad of new problems created by the urban/industrial setting for this burgeoning working class. Moreover, the social and moral control exercised by the parish priest and by parents was not as pervasive or as effective in the cities and large towns as it had been on the farms and in the rural parishes. A society ordinarily dependent upon the external social controls provided by the family and the parish found it very difficult to adapt to the social freedom and pluralism prevalent in the large urban centres.[18] To some extent, however, neo-nationalists overemphasized the traumatic nature of the rural/urban transition, since many of the migrants had already absorbed in a variety of ways the secular values and norms of the urban and industrial environment.

The social tensions and instability resulting from massive rural depopulation led to the destruction of the traditional rural culture of the new arrivals. This culture, neo-nationalists contended somewhat erroneously, was not replaced by an indigenous French-Canadian working-class popular culture, but rather by the American and English-Canadian popular cultures that were readily available. In fact, neo-nationalists like their predecessors overlooked the existence of a genuine French-Canadian working-class culture, one which would be celebrated later by the contemporary Québécois playwright Michel Tremblay. This lack of insight led neo-nationalists to concentrate on the foreign aspects of French-Canadian working-class environment.

The relevant feature of these foreign popular cultures, according to Claude Ryan, was that they were as secular as the industrial revolution that had engendered them. This secularism resulted in a serious spiritual and moral crisis for a great many French Canadians and their families. The majority of urban French Canadians, he noted, continued to follow the external practices of their Catholic faith – weekly church attendance, baptism and marriage within the church, enrolment of children in confessional schools. Yet increasingly their daily life was becoming dominated by secular activities and values. A widening gap was developing between thought and action. French Canadians willingly signed petitions supporting temperance in alcohol use while the annual consumption rate continued to climb at an alarming rate. French Canadians supported religious and civic campaigns against indecent dress and pornographic literature. Yet French-Canadian women, young and old, were becoming increasingly daring in their dress habits, and parents of working-class families "are nourished weekly by tabloids that emphasize scandals and violence as well as by grotesque television wrestling matches, the outcomes of which are prearranged."[19] Once a major part of their daily lives was fully secularized, it would not be long before French-Canadian working-class families began to look down upon and eventually discontinue their remaining religious activities. For traditional nationalists who considered Catholicism to be an integral element of the French-Canadian identity this development posed a major threat to the future of the nation.

TRADITIONAL NATIONALISTS UNDER ATTACK

If the responsibility for the "denationalization" of the industrial working class did not rest in the hands of the workers themselves, who then was to blame? As we have just seen, much of the onus was placed on the industrial process itself. Yet this explanation was not completely satisfactory to the neo-nationalists. Their assessment of the inability of French-Canadian nationalism to penetrate the urban-industrial masses led them to question the relevance of that traditional nationalism and the astuteness of its major spokesmen. What were the major findings of this critical reexamination? The general thrust of the critique was that the intelligentsia had failed to live up to its responsibility of providing national leadership. Its members had cut themselves off from the people by failing to elaborate a realistic and meaningful nationalist doctrine and program of action.

According to a number of Université de Montréal students who formed part of the Equipe des recherches sociales, namely Jean-Marc Léger, d'Iberville Fortier, Pierre Lefebvre, and Camille Laurin, the nationalist élite no longer reflected the new social and economic structures of Quebec society. This élite continued to elaborate its nationalist doctrine for a predominantly rural community when in effect a new class, the urban industrial workers, had replaced the habitants as the largest social class.[20] "Ignorant of the working-class milieu," argued these students,

and barely aware of the extraordinary economic evolution taking place, the nationalist intelligentsia did not sense the terrible crisis facing the French-Canadian worker, especially his painful attempts to adjust to an environment in which he could find none of his origins. Therefore, ignorant of this drama, of the needs and the appeals of the people, the nationalist intelligentsia could no longer carry out its leadership role. It could not make the people hear its message because they no longer spoke the same language. The nationalists repeated antiquated slogans such as "faithfulness to tradition," "pride in one's origins," "preservation of the national collectivity." Meanwhile the workers demanded better salaries, housing, recreational facilities, social security measures, in short, a number of improvements which showed respect and dignity for them as men. Between the nationalist élite and the people no further dialogue was possible since all rapport had been broken.[21]

These Université de Montréal students were not alone in their scathing indictment of the traditional nationalists. A young cleric, Abbé Gérard Dion, who taught in the Department of Industrial Relations at Laval, and Joseph Pelchat both argued that the French-Canadian worker was convinced that he had often been misled, even betrayed, by white collar supervisors and managers. The workers believed that the political, intellectual, and professional élites that championed the cause of the French-Canadian nation did so primarily to advance their own vested interests under the guise of serving the general interests of the collectivity. Dion and Pelchat suggested that French-Canadian nationalism had never made a deep impact on the working class because the workers realized intuitively that it was inherently a bourgeois, conservative, and defensive ideology that offered them nothing concrete.[22] This interpretation was supported strongly by Claude Ryan and Jean-Paul Robillard, a former colleague of Laurendeau's in the Jeune-Canada and Bloc Populaire movements.[23]

Quebec's politicians and political parties came in for some of the strongest criticism for having smeared the reputation and undermined the credibility of nationalism among the urban masses. A wide gap had developed between the nationalist rhetoric of office-seeking politicians and political parties and their programs and policies once in power. Duplessis and the Union Nationale had championed the cause of provincial autonomy in the elections of 1944 and 1948 but, apart from granting the province a flag, the government had created few tangible and beneficial programs for industrial workers and their families. In the midst of a serious social crisis, the Duplessis regime continued to sell out the province's natural resources and to place the interests of the party ahead of those of the Quebec people, especially the working class.[24] In the scramble for patronage and electoral success, the political parties considered that the nation was merely a commodity that fell to the highest bidder. In normal times this auctioning process had consequences that could be overcome. But when the nation was in the throes of a serious social crisis, confronted by Ottawa's powerful push towards centralization and a growing wave of socialism, the eventual outcome could only be disastrous for the future of the national community.[25] It was painfully clear that the young nationalists could not count upon the existing political parties, Liberal or Union Nationale, to make nationalism more meaningful to the fourth estate.

A second major concern of the postwar nationalists was the evolution of the Quebec Catholic church's leadership away from its customary support of French-Canadian nationalist doctrine, programs, and institutions. The Catholic church's leaders in Quebec had in the late 1930s undermined the importance of the Association catholique de la jeunesse canadienne française, founded originally in 1904 to instil in French Canada's youth a deep love for their nation and their religion.[26] This highly nationalistic movement was replaced by a group of specialized Catholic action movements – Jeunesse étudiante catholique, Jeunesse agricole catholique, and Jeunesse ouvrière catholique – in which no special emphasis was placed on the elaboration of nationalist doctrines, objectives, or activities.[27]

André Laurendeau accepted the argument that the church's antinationalist reaction fulfilled an important historical function by destroying the strong link that certain nationalists had established between the French language and the Catholic faith. What he objected to most strongly was the fact that certain chaplains and lay leaders in the recently established Catholic Action movement denied, by their conduct, the national dimension of the milieu they wished to conquer. Many of these individuals had, in Laurendeau's view, confused the meaning of a universal humanism with "the will to uproot oneself, as if one had to cease belonging actively to a national community in order to be a Catholic, and in some cases even deny a prior solidarity with that community."[28] The tragedy of this confusion was that nationalist organizations, like the Societé Saint-Jean Baptiste, had lost their traditional supply of young militants from the ACJC. Furthermore, French Canada's universities were no longer militant centres for an active nationalist-oriented youth. The editors of *Quartier Latin*, the student paper at the Université de Montréal, had come to perceive nationalism as a barrier, "as a doctrine of denial, justifiable perhaps in another era but quite unacceptable in the modern age."[29]

There were a couple of other developments that prompted the young nationalists to view the church's attitude towards French-Canadian nationalism with some degree of scepticism. Church leaders had failed to object to, and in many ways had supported, the orientation of the Oblate-owned and administered University of Ottawa towards English unilingualism after 1950. Moreover, there was evidence that seemed to substantiate the frequent rumours that even the formerly nationalist sector of the clerical élite supported, in principle, federal grants to Quebec universities. Both of these developments marked a departure from the church's past behaviour. Laurendeau hypothesized that the church was giving warning that it no longer would serve as tutor to the French-Canadian nation and that French Canadians would henceforth have to take their temporal future into their own hands, even in church-controlled areas such as education. He nevertheless warned that an overtly antinationalist attitude on the part of church leaders could prompt the elaboration of a purely secular, even anticlerical nationalism. Such a development was indeed possible, especially if immediate national interests and institutions seemed compromised and their survival endangered.[30] One thing had become increasingly clear to neo-nationalists by the early 1950s. This was that the task of reformulating French-Canadian nationalism would have to be undertaken by lay nationalists. The long-standing predominance of clerical figures such as Father Papin Archambault and Abbé Lionel Groulx in the nationalist movement was a thing of the past.

TRADITIONAL NATIONALISM
UNDER ATTACK

The attack of the young nationalists was not restricted to a severe critique of the clerical and political nationalist élites. The attack was directed at the very heart of the ideology of traditional French-Canadian nationalism. The Achilles heel of that ideology resided in the fact that its spokesmen had not perceived the significance of the industrial revolution. For a long time traditional nationalists had continually applied old solutions to new problems. When traditional nationalists finally realized the full nature and import of the socioeconomic crises created by the industrial revolution, the majority of them interpreted these problems as passing phases caused by the malice of men. The main reason for this misinterpretation, suggested Laurendeau, was that these nationalists

failed to clearly understand the action of economic forces. For them the city remained, at least when they took time to ponder the issue, a bad environment which proved attractive because French Canadians were degenerating or because the politicians provided insufficient support to agriculture and colonization ... Even at the end of the Great War, when barely 10 per cent of Quebec's inhabitants worked on farms, a great many French Canadians continued to see themselves as an agrarian people. The following historical cliché could be found in most educational institutions: our future, like our past, is on the land; the cities are (morally and nationally) centres of perdition.[31]

In short, the traditional nationalists were guilty of perpetuating the myth of "agriculturalism."

Michel Brunet, a neo-nationalist historian at the Université de Montréal, offered the most comprehensive and least sympathetic criticism of the traditional nationalists' rejection of the new industrial order. Selectively marshalling his historical evidence, Brunet demonstrated to his satisfaction how French-Canadian nationalist thought had been dominated for over a century by the myths of agriculturalism, antistatism, and messianism.[32] The future of the French-Canadian nation, according to this inflexible triad of beliefs, was linked to the ability of the French-Canadian people to remain a nation of habitants dominated by moral values and spiritual objectives far from the tentacles of a secularizing, urban, interventionist welfare state. The continued predominance of these beliefs had effectively prevented French-Canadian nationalists from accepting the secular values, urban growth, and increased state participation inherent in the new industrial order.[33]

The most serious outcome of this prolonged rejection of the new industrial society was that French-Canadian nationalist thought had never been radically reformulated, so as to reflect and respond to the needs and the problems of a new socioeconomic class – the urban industrial workers and their families. The nationalists had defined their nationalism from a historical and juridical perspective, thereby limiting their preoccupations to questions of language and educational rights for French-Canadian minorities and the thorny issue of French-Canadian participation in the federal government. Certain gains had been made in the field of culture but traditional nationalists had failed dismally in the arena of politics. In the area of economic and social reforms they had concentrated the bulk of their efforts on the preservation and renewal of the rural economy and its sociocultural values and institutions. In brief, the social thought of the traditional nationalists was outmoded and incomplete because it did not reflect the complex realities created by rampant industrial and urban growth, phenomena which they had for the most part rejected or accepted only very grudgingly.[34]

André Laurendeau, while accepting the validity and implications of this rather severe judgment, felt obliged to make two qualifying points. Nationalism, he warned, was not an answer to all human problems. As a political ideology, he argued, nationalism was neither of the Left nor of the Right. Consequently, it did not imply a precise set of economic and social policies and programs for dealing with the industrial revolution and its problems. It was clear therefore that, in a given milieu, as Laurendeau explained,

nationalism will take on the demeanour of its authors: bourgeois with the bourgeoisie, intellectual with the intelligentsia. Neither the bourgeois nor the intellectual cease being themselves because they are nationalists; and a nationalist who does not respond as I do when confronted with the working-class question is no less a nationalist. I can argue that he is badly mistaken, that he is associating a living and dynamic idea with anachronistic forms and therefore doing it considerable harm. This alone does not justify my denying this person's nationalism.[35]

Second, Laurendeau reminded his young colleagues that traditional nationalists like Henri Bourassa, Édouard Montpetit, Abbé Lionel Groulx, Joseph-Papin Archambault sj, Esdras Minville, Paul Gouin, and Philippe Hamel had always been in the vanguard of the campaign for certain socioeconomic reforms. These nationalists had been partially responsible for whatever social progress Quebec had achieved since the turn of the century – two such examples were the Catholic labour movement and the cooperative movement. Quebec's postwar neo-nationalists, he warned, must not get caught up in a sterile attempt to use traditional French-Canadian nationalism as a convenient scapegoat. It was more important to channel their energies and insights into the creation of new concepts and practical policies and programs which would make modern French-Canadian nationalism a meaningful and viable ideology for all sectors of Quebec society, especially the emerging francophone urban working-class majority.[36]

DEFINING NEO-NATIONALISM

The fundamental difference between traditional French-Canadian nationalists and the neo-nationalists of *Le Devoir* and *L'Action nationale* was that
the latter accepted the reality of urban-industrial Quebec. Neo-nationalists
pointed to scientific surveys to substantiate their claim that Quebec's physical geography implied not an "agricultural vocation" for its people but
rather the challenge to adapt to and help create a modern urban-industrial
society using the province's vast natural and human resources.[37] "In 1950,"
Léger told the French readers of the review *Esprit*, "there is no longer a
rural and agricultural French Canada, but primarily an urban/industrial
French Canada."[38]

Gérard Filion went so far as to warn his compatriots that the industrialization of the province was as inevitable as the continuation of the planetary
system. The task confronting the French-Canadian people was whether
they could assimilate the modern industrial world and master modern technology for the defence and expansion of the French-Canadian culture.[39]
Laurendeau outlined the challenge in his usual eloquent style: "French-
Canadian culture must demonstrate that it is no longer strictly identified
with the rural society of yesterday. Rather, it must prove that it is capable of
immersing itself in an urban environment. This is an exciting question, one
that demands of all men today considerable imagination, courage, and intelligence. The present generation is one of transition. It must show what this
transition will entail, a slow advance towards nightfall or else a vital link
between two different lifestyles."[40] Quebec was no longer, in fact had not
been for a long time, the Quebec of Louis Hémon's *Maria Chapdelaine*,
where nothing changed or would change.[41]

In what way did this acceptance of the new industrial order allow neo-
nationalists to redefine the ideology of French-Canadian nationalism? What
alterations were recommended to make French-Canadian nationalism more
reflective of the new society and, it was hoped, more acceptable and meaningful to the urban masses? After much soul searching the neo-nationalists,
led by André Laurendeau and Jean-Marc Léger, arrived at the conclusion
that nationalists must quickly abandon their antisocial, conservative, reactionary, xenophobic, and petty bourgeois outlook and doctrines. Although it
was never made explicit in the early 1950s, it is clear that the neo-nationalists
wanted to break the long-standing link between Catholicism and French-
Canadian nationalism which had led to a definition of nationalism in which
moral values and spiritual objectives had predominated. French-Canadian
nationalism, in effect, would be secularized by the neo-nationalists, who
increasingly portrayed it as an ideology of socioeconomic change and of
individual and collective liberation for the French-Canadian people.

The first thing neo-nationalists attempted to do was to demonstrate that the ideology of nationalism was not inherently and irrevocably a preserve of the ruling petty bourgeoisie. The most effective way of accomplishing this was to point out that nationalism was born with the French Revolution and therefore was linked from its inception with liberal and democratic ideas and objectives. Nationalism, explained Jean-Marc Léger, "was, by its origins, not an ideology of the Right but clearly of the Left. It was with the slogan 'long live the nation' that the French revolutionaries opposed the monarchy and a dying aristocracy. The liberal aspirations of the eighteenth and nineteenth centuries took on the form of liberal nationalism in independent as well as colonial countries."[42] One sure way, contended the neo-nationalists, for returning the ideology to its proper origins was for French Canadians to strive for the abandonment of the monarchy and the establishment of a Canadian republic. It was this kind of thinking that prompted the 1948–50 campaign by Le Devoir and L'Action nationale for a Canadian republic.[43]

The neo-nationalists also thought it was important to illustrate that a nationalism of the masses had historical roots in Quebec, that in fact, it was the only authentic form of nationalism in that society. Bending the historical evidence to suit his interpretation, Léger contended that the most significant nationalist struggles of the French-Canadian nation were those in which the masses had played a strong and decisive role, such as the habitants' refusal to support the British in the American Revolution, the rebellions of 1837–8, the Riel affair, the anti-imperialist campaigns of 1899–1917, and the plebiscite of 1942. Furthermore, the nationalism of the French-Canadian masses, argued Léger, in contrast to that of the self-serving clerical and petty bourgeois élites, was liberal, democratic, and reformist in nature and objectives.[44] It was therefore imperative that neo-nationalists redefine their nationalism in terms of the needs and aspirations of the French-Canadian working class.

What was the nature of this new nationalism as it was thus reformulated? It was argued strongly that a rapprochement could be achieved between the French-Canadian nationalist movement and the working class by creating a synthesis between the concepts of "social" and "national." This indispensable synthesis, it was hoped, would produce "a doctrine which respected and safeguarded both the class and the nation, which created a situation whereby the worker felt that struggling for the national community no longer required the rejection of class solidarity. In short, a situation in which the worker did not feel obliged, in opting for his class, to abandon the nation."[45] The neo-nationalists were convinced that it was urgent to undermine the belief that there was a fundamental contradiction between the national rights of the French-Canadian collectivity and the social security and economic rights of French Canadians, especially the urban and rural working people.

Unlike right-wing nationalists, neo-nationalists accepted the fact that a certain degree of solidarity existed between French-Canadian workers and their fellow workers in other countries. However, contrary to socialist thinkers, neo-nationalists felt that a French-Canadian petty bourgeois had a great deal more in common with a French-Canadian worker or habitant than he did with an Anglo-Canadian petty bourgeois. This national solidarity, because it was primarily psychological rather than material in nature, could in times of crisis trigger "common reflexes and shared sentiments whereby a valuable and rich humanism was preserved and developed."[46] While neo-nationalists had come to accept class solidarity as significant and irrevocable, they nevertheless believed that the healthy development of a French-Canadian working-class consciousness need not imply a corresponding decline in national consciousness. The former could be achieved within the latter.

It was regarded as most important that nationalism become a militant force in the battle for socioeconomic reforms. If it failed to do so, socialism would be chosen by the masses as the only alternative capable of providing the workers with the security, stability, and greater equality of living conditions that both laissez-faire and monopoly capitalism had failed to produce. As Léger saw it, the industrial and technological revolutions had prompted the working man to abandon his attachment to doctrines of laissez-faire liberalism and increasingly to accept the concept of collective action and state intervention. The eighteenth-century concept of individual man, master of his own destiny, had in fact never become a reality for the working man. It was little wonder that if given the choice workers would opt for socialism, an ideology which promised individual security through collective action.[47] Neo-nationalists could not accept "pure" socialism as the alternative for the French-Canadian people. A redefined nationalism, Léger contended, was the only acceptable solution:

... between the ideology of conservative and individualistic liberalism, which develops within political democracy and economic capitalism, and the ideology of Marxism, a collectivism which leads via the political dictatorship of the proletariat and the socialization of the means of production to state capitalism, there exists another alternative. It is up to nationalism to inspire its discovery. Beyond liberal idealism and Marxist materialism, both misleading because they are incomplete, one must seek a conception of social organization which, based on an antideterministic dialectic, takes into account full recognition of all the elements which make up our history.[48]

A reform-oriented nationalism, unlike socialism, would in the view of the young nationalists reintegrate the French-Canadian working-class majority into the national community. As well, it would render the worker a greater degree of personal freedom and security than he was getting under the existing system of industrial capitalism. For the neo-nationalists there could be no "liberation" of the French-Canadian working classes without a simultaneous "liberation" of the French-Canadian nation. Increased provincial autonomy and improved social justice were two vital necessities that neo-nationalists had to pursue simultaneously. This stemmed from the fact that French Canadians, "a proletarian people," were the victims of a double oppression, a class oppression and a national oppression. There could be no real social justice without the liberation of the nation from the economic and political oppression of the American and Anglo-Saxon financial and industrial powers. A greater degree of political, social, and economic autonomy for the French-Canadian collectivity would allow for the emancipation of the working class without the risk of that working class becoming "denationalized."[49]

It is doubtful whether most of the neo-nationalists in the 1950s accepted the implications of this dual national and class struggle, as it was outlined by Jean-Marc Léger, the most radical member of this small group in 1951. What was clear, nevertheless, was that the majority of neo-nationalists had by the early 1950s adopted the view that substantial structural reform of Quebec's existing economic, cultural, political, and social institutions was urgently required.[50] Precisely what these reforms were and what sort of new society they would create was still unclear, but the long overdue debate had at last been initiated.

NEO-NATIONALISTS CONFRONT THEIR LIBERAL CRITICS

Ironically, the initial opposition to this attempt to redefine French-Canadian nationalism did not come from traditional nationalists. Rather, it came from another group of young French-Canadian intellectuals who were active in the Quebec labour movement and expressed their views in a small periodical entitled *Cité libre*. The co-editors of the review, Pierre Elliott Trudeau and Gérard Pelletier, along with Pierre Vadeboncoeur and Marcel Rioux, had produced by the mid-1950s their own highly critical assessment of traditional French-Canadian nationalism. These antinationalists, as they came to be called, vigorously rejected the attempt by the neo-nationalists to reorient French-Canadian nationalism toward democratic values and socioeconomic reforms, on the grounds that the ideology of nationalism was inherently a conservative, isolationist, and xenophobic force which had and would continue to retard the modernization of Quebec society.[51]

The first reaction of the neo-nationalists was one of disbelief, but this was soon followed by an attempt to find a compromise. Laurendeau and Léger urged the Citélibristes not to equate their neo-nationalism with traditional French-Canadian nationalism, thereby creating an artificial conflict between two groups of young socially minded French Canadians. Léger, writing in the French periodical *Esprit* in 1952, expressed the view that "the great hope of French Canada resides currently in the creation of an understanding between the two ideological tendencies represented by the young intellectuals associated with *Le Devoir* and *L'Action nationale* and those belonging to *Cité libre*."[52] Searching for common ground, Laurendeau offered two explanations for the Citélibristes' tendency to see "in one's attachment to the French-Canadian nation, in one's vigilant action in the service of French Canada," a serious obstacle to international cooperation and the persistence of a narrowness of outlook. To begin with, Citélibristes erroneously equated French-Canadian nationalism with certain xenophobic, isolationist, and racist movements in Europe which had grown up under the disguise of authentic nationalism. They also had a misguided belief that French-Canadian nationalism was indifferent and perhaps even opposed to contemporary appeals for social development and international coopera-tion.[53] These views were serious obstacles to cooperation. Neo-nationalists applied themselves assiduously to undermining them as effectively and as quickly as possible.

Laurendeau made it very clear that he and his nationalist colleagues abhorred all forms of racism as strongly as the Citélibristes. He and Léger denounced the common practice of evoking the names of Maurras, Barrès, and Gobineau by those wishing to denigrate French-Canadian nationalism.[54] Furthermore, even a cursory reading of neo-nationalist writing would reveal that they too rejected any form of nationalism that was reactionary, conser-vative, xenophobic, and isolationist. Citélibristes were reminded that *Le Devoir* and *L'Action nationale* had taken the lead in urging a more liberal and positive approach to questions such as immigration, communism, for-eign aid, recognition of Communist China, and the role of the Soviet Union in world affairs.[55] Indeed, the pages of *Le Devoir* were more open to a liberal and sympathetic discussion of international problems than they ever had been in the past.[56]

Neo-nationalists, in fact, perceived their nationalism as a form of human-ism. A creative, reformist, and pluralistic nationalism was, for them, the most lucid and potentially rewarding route to an authentic internationalism. Earlier, Laurendeau had drawn upon French Catholic personalist thought to reconcile the tensions between individual and collective rights and aspira-tions. In effect, the same approach could be used to reconcile the very real but not insurmountable tensions between genuine national rights and aspi-rations and the growing desire for international cooperation and the percep-tion of a universal humanism. Only by becoming a dynamic, creative force could the French-Canadian nation contribute to the latter processes.

Yes, it is certainly not by denying the very reasons for our existence or by satisfying ourselves with a dull and monotonous survival that we French Canadians can serve the cause of humanity. We have the lofty duty to devote ourselves, at every level, to the expansion of the French-Canadian culture and presence for which Providence deemed us to be the witnesses, the artisans and the proselytizers in North America. Clearly this is not an easy task! It will not be accomplished without struggle. Yet to reject this role would constitute not only a disservice to the nation but even more a breach of faith in humanity which has the right to expect of each and every one of its component parts, the nations, that they contribute to the growth and development of the common heritage.[57]

Nationalism was the perception of the human wealth of a distinctive cultural entity and the consequent will to provide that particular collectivity with the social, political, and economic tools necessary for its survival and development. All national groups – with either a shared or separate political existence – that achieved a high degree of socioeconomic and cultural development constituted a significant enrichment of humanity and could better contribute to a greater degree of international cooperation and development. The latter would never be achieved by denying cultural differences but rather by accepting them as necessary and valid and then working to transcend them.[58]

Rather than diminishing, the ideological dispute between neo-nationalists and Citélibristes had by the mid-1950s escalated into a polemic of major significance. Jean-Marc Léger was denouncing the Citélibristes as a bunch of crypto-centralizers and arm-chair socialists who preached, in the name of technocratic efficiency, democratic values, and socioeconomic progress, the "lucide integration" of Quebec society into the rest of Canada.[59] Pierre de Grandpré, *Le Devoir*'s literary editor and a committed neo-nationalist, took a more objective approach and continued to search for common ground. Grandpré none the less formulated two basic criticisms of the Citélibristes. First, he took them to task for what he termed their North American frontier mentality: "this tragic vital instinct, originating also within ourselves, which consists in rejecting what we sense is the very seductive superiority of Europe, while attempting to create everything from scratch. We care little for what might be lost in the process."[60] In the second place, while he was impressed with the brilliant, varied, and tightly woven criticisms of some of *Cité libre*'s contributors, he remained disappointed at their inability to offer creative and constructive proposals for the future of the French-Canadian collectivity. Perhaps this was due to the pessimistic and defeatist attitude of some Citélibristes. For example, Pierre Vadeboncoeur and Marcel Rioux had expressed the belief that the French-Canadian society was doomed to die because it had entered an era in which French Canadians would have to seek solutions to all their problems on a level indifferent to their ethnic survival. Grandpré felt that the resignation and indifference of

some French-Canadian intellectuals towards the future of their own community was the most frightening and tragic development of the 1950s. He
nevertheless concluded, with a great sense of relief, that neither Gérard
Pelletier nor Maurice Blain nor Pierre E. Trudeau was willing to stand by
and watch the collective suicide of the French-Canadian people.[61]

Neo-nationalists like André Laurendeau and Pierre de Grandpré were
determined to maintain an open mind toward the Citélibristes. They felt
that many of their ideas were valid and necessary if French-Canadian
society was to be modernized and regain control over its future. In trying to
bridge the gap between the neo-nationalists and the liberal and social democrats of *Cité libre*, Grandpré made a very astute and sympathetic assessment
of their motivations and intentions.

I see only men of my generation who refuse to repeat ancient and inoperative
anthems, who direct their attention to the social question and the industrial problem
because they possess an urgent desire to apply their skills to the real field of action
and combat, who are attempting to replace, in all fields, the ubiquity, the imperialism,
and the inanity of merely good intentions with authentic human realities and problems. The values linked to our collective destiny, the very foundations of our society
(to be precise, our spiritual faith and the French culture), I think it is the intention
of most of them, at least, to ensure that these can overcome without too much
difficulty the real obstacles! They have learned to use their critical faculties to
discover the most secret and most powerful impediments which exist within us.
These impediments reside in all the self-satisfying illusions against which these
critics struggle tenaciously, we believe, because they prevent us from maturing and
reaching our potential.[62]

The Citélibristes, concluded Grandpré, had forced the French-Canadian
nationalist movement to rediscover its real nature and true objectives.
French-Canadian neo-nationalism, because it expressed a deep faith in the
powers of man and the belief that it was important to oppose rigidity and
determinism with creative thought, courage, and "faithfulness to oneself,"
had a great deal more in common with the liberal and social democracy of
the Citélibristes than with traditional French-Canadian nationalism.[63]

TRADITIONAL NATIONALISTS
COUNTER-ATTACK

Ideological developments within Quebec society after 1956 did, in fact,
force proponents of neo-nationalism and those of liberal and social democracy to put an increasing emphasis on the common aspects of their respective
ideologies rather than continue to stress "irreconcilable" differences. One of
the important factors in the attempted reconciliation was the counter-attack

of the traditional conservative forces that was initiated with the publication of Robert Rumilly's polemical attack on the Citélibristes and the neo-nationalists in December 1956. His pamphlet was entitled *L'infiltration gauchiste au Canada français* and it began with a condemnation of the "left-wing Catholics" of France and their close alliance with the French communist movement. He implied that French-Canadian "left-wing Catholics" were similarly sympathetic to socialism. Rumilly, a nationalist historian, had become a firm defender of Maurice Duplessis and the Union Nationale regime and disapproved vehemently of *Le Devoir*'s incessant criticism of the premier's defensive approach to the question of provincial autonomy and his conservative socioeconomic policies and programs.[64]

Rumilly focused his attack on the "anticlerical," "antinationalist," and "communist sympathizers" of *Cité libre* but he also attempted to discredit the neo-nationalists by associating their ideas and activities with this group. Because of their close association, argued Rumilly, "the leftists are de-nationalizing our youth. In the struggle for the defence of provincial autonomy, the leftists act like a fifth column in the service of our enemy."[65] The enemy, it went without saying, was English Canada and the centralizing Ottawa government.

Rumilly was soon joined by Léopold Richer, the editor of the Union Nationale's organ *Notre Temps*, and by Anatole Vanier, one of the diehard conservative nationalists remaining on the board of the Ligue d'Action nationale. Their call for a resurgence of traditional nationalist forces produced some results by 1957, when two periodicals were created to defend the doctrines of traditional French-Canadian nationalism. The first, *Tradition et Progrès*, was edited by Albert Roy and served as a forum for those French Canadians who rejected the solutions being proposed by Quebec's left-wing intellectuals to the problems created by the industrial revolution.[66] The second, called *Laurentie*, was the organ of L'Alliance Laurentienne, a movement founded in 1957 by Raymond Barbeau. The movement and its leaders preached the need for a politically independent French-Canadian nation infused with traditional religious and social values inspired by the social teachings of the church and Salazarian corporatism. In other words, the movement was a throwback to the separatist movements of the 1930s. Many of L'Alliance Laurentienne's members ended up as militants in the Rassemblement pour l'indépendance nationale (RIN) after its formation in September 1960.[67]

The cleavage between traditional nationalists and neo-nationalists became public knowledge in the months following the June 1956 provincial election when the Union Nationale was returned to power with a comfortable majority despite the vigorous opposition of *Le Devoir*, the unions, and the Liberal party. Prior to the election an editorial in *L'Action nationale* had indicated that the Ligue d'Action nationale was initiating a systematic rethinking of

French Canada's major problems such as language, economic development, education, and social programs. This modernizing process would be based on the premise that "'nationalism' and 'social justice' had a great many things in common."[68] Jean-Marc Léger, embittered and disillusioned by the election results, declared in no uncertain terms that the neo-nationalists had to break all ties with traditional nationalists who persisted in supporting a retrograde and antinationalist government. "Against an attitude," wrote Léger,

which denigrates the notion of the "left" and of social progress, neo-nationalists must make it very clear that nationalism, once associated with the advancement of the complete French-Canadian man as well as the entire liberation of the French-Canadian people, is first and foremost a revolutionary undertaking. It must be understood that those people who persist in labelling themselves nationalists while continuing to practise reactionary behaviour must be denounced as the most dangerous enemies of a true French-Canadian nationalism.[69]

The die had been cast. Traditional nationalists who opposed the redefinition of French-Canadian nationalism and continued to support the Duplessis regime were denounced and castigated as traitors to the cause of the nation.

The reaction of the traditional nationalists to this charge of treason was both emotional and ideological. Following Rumilly's lead, they immediately set out to discredit the neo-nationalists by associating them and their ideas with the ideologies of socialism and communism, both of which, they claimed, were antinationalist, anticlerical, and fomenters of class conflict.[70] Anatole Vanier denounced Léger's so-called "true nationalist left-wing movement" as a fraudulent attempt to mislead the French-Canadian people. He enjoined him to disseminate his propaganda elsewhere than in the pages of *L'Action nationale* and proclaimed as the real traitors those pseudo-nationalists who worked to destroy the traditional sociocultural values and institutions of their own society.[71]

Rumilly, for his part, charged *Le Devoir* with being soft on the persecution of Catholics in Iron Curtain countries and with giving extensive and sympathetic coverage of Trudeau's 1952 trip to the Soviet Union. Filion and other staff members of *Le Devoir* were denounced for having visiting the People's Republic of China and for advocating Canadian recognition of this regime. The root of *Le Devoir*'s "left-wing ideas," argued Rumilly, resided in the fact that its director and managing editor had erroneously accepted the socialist and anticlerical ideas of French left-wing Catholics as expressed in periodicals like *Esprit*, *La Vie intellectuelle* and *Témoignage chrétien*, and the daily *Le Monde*.[72] In effect, neo-nationalists were viewed as "left-wing ideologues" in disguise, who actively supported the anticlerical and anti-nationalist organizations and activities of the Citélibristes – namely, the

Institut canadien des affaires publiques and the *Rassemblement*.[73] The term "left-wing" was a euphemism for socialism and the traditional nationalists probably hoped that this charge would bring the wrath of the church down upon the neo-nationalists, thereby coercing them back into the fold.

On the ideological level, traditional nationalists made a concerted effort to dismantle the synthesis of national and socioeconomic objectives that had been carefully elaborated by the neo-nationalists. Léopold Richer, Robert Rumilly, Albert Roy, and Raymond Barbeau all contended that a left-wing nationalism was a dangerous and revolutionary ideology that had been concocted by a group of intellectual zealots who wanted to exploit simultaneously nationalism and socialism, two ideologies that were inherently and historically contradictory.[74] "True nationalism," wrote Barbeau,

and true left-wing ideologies are as incompatible as fire and water. The first, contrary to what one hears, is creative, noble, proud, ambitious and honest. Nationalism does not blush when it enters the spiritual realm or when it imbues even its smallest gestures with spiritual concerns. Such gestures take on an eternal value and this is in conformity with the doctrine of the church which places the Sovereign Creator (the people have never been sovereign over anything) at the very foundation of society. All legitimate authority, consequently, flows from the Sovereign Creator. Left-wing ideologies are all man-centred and place in him all authority, value, and hope.[75]

The neo-nationalists in their rejection of the forces of conservatism – history, spiritual and profane traditions, a mission of cultural superiority, the family, and the parish – were destroying "the vital and living dimension of nationalism" and would be held responsible for the collective suicide of the French-Canadian nation.[76]

One of *Tradition et Progrès*'s most faithful contributors, Jean Deslauriers, reminded neo-nationalists that a mixture of socialism and nationalism had resulted in fascist regimes in many European countries. While there was room in French Canada for a right-wing movement, Deslauriers argued, it was hypocritical to camouflage such a movement as "one of 'left-wing nationalism'."[77] He also questioned the neo-nationalists' assumption that the francophone working class was synonymous with the French-Canadian nationality. The industrialization of Quebec had, he perceptively noted, simply substituted a new urban middle class for a traditional rural middle class, and no working-class political party was going to gain power and challenge the position of the new urban petty bourgeoisie.[78] Finally, if the neo-nationalists were sincere in their desire for the socioeconomic advancement of the French-Canadian people, then there existed no real conflict between social and national objectives. In Deslauriers' view it was imperative that Quebec's nationalists, before they started demanding socioeconomic reforms from their own government, undertake to ensure the survival of the

Quebec state. This could be accomplished in either of two ways. French Canadians could insist on the decentralization of the existing federal system or, if that was not acceptable to English Canadians, they could work for the complete political independence of their homeland. As for Deslauriers, he had already made his choice in favour of separation, based on the argument that

Quebec's weaknesses in the "socioeconomic" domain are inherent in its position as a member state of a federation. "Left-wing nationalists," if they want to be consistent with themselves, if they demand genuine Québécois social and economic policies, will accept, as the prerequisite, a SOVEREIGN AND FREE STATE. If we accept the maintenance of the federal state, we condemn Quebec, by force of circumstances and not of men, to highly restrictive social and economic policies.[79]

The editorial group of *Tradition et Progrès*, strongly influenced by this and other arguments, decided to publish a separatist manifesto in the summer of 1960. An independent Quebec state was seen as the only remaining instrument capable of retaining intact the traditional French-Canadian socio-cultural values and of ensuring the survival of such institutions as the Catholic church as a dominant force in that society.[80] The traditional nationalists' reaction to the rapid disappearance of the rural and Catholic society they knew and loved so well was to clamour for the creation of *la patrie* prescribed by Jules-Paul Tardivel at the turn of the century and the Ligue Action nationale in the 1920s and 1930s.

CONCLUSION

One of the most exciting and significant developments in Quebec during the 1950s was the shattering of the dominant ideological outlook of that society's intellectual élite. The stranglehold in which clerical and petty bourgeois professional leaders had held the nationalist movement, and consequently its character and objectives, had finally been challenged successfully by a group of young liberal-minded intellectuals centred around *Le Devoir* and *L'Action nationale*. Traditional nationalists could no longer make the claim that they, and they alone, had a mandate to define the parameters of French-Canadian nationalism and to defend the rights of French Canadians to survive as an autonomous collective entity.

The development of a highly centralist form of federalism evoked a resurgence of nationalism in Quebec during and after the war, but it was a new round of industrial expansion that brought on the internal crisis in French-Canadian nationalist thought. The traditional nationalists decried the demise of the rural society with its familiar sociocultural values and fairly rigid social structure. They also considered the secular values and institutions created by a rapidly expanding industrial and urban society to be detrimental to the survival of the French-Canadian nation and the predominant role of the Catholic church within it. The struggle against Ottawa for the preservation and expansion of provincial prerogatives and the anxiety over the kind of socioeconomic values and institutions being offered to French Canadians by the neo-nationalists, as well as by the liberal and social democrats, eventually prompted some of these traditional nationalists to declare themselves in favour of a separate Quebec state.

The neo-nationalists were not confronted with this dilemma. They did not feel that they had their backs to the wall. This was primarily because they had come to accept the urbanization and industrialization of their society as inevitable and, for the most part, beneficial. What they did deem crucial was the need for French Canadians themselves to play an ever-increasing role in the modernization of Quebec's economic, social, and political structures. French Canadians had to use their creativity and energies to make modern technological developments work to the benefit, rather than the detriment and eventual destruction, of the French-Canadian nationality. In an increasingly secular society dominated by the need for continued economic development and widespread social services, the neo-nationalists came to view the Quebec government and not the Catholic church as the primary instrument in the survival and *épanouissement* of the French-Canadian nationality in Quebec and in Canada. The state of Quebec alone could finance and administer a fully democratized educational system and provide the numerous social services required in a society containing a new majority, the industrial working class.

It was the full acceptance of an increasingly secular, democratic, and open society that forced neo-nationalists to redefine nationalism as an ideology of socioeconomic change and of individual and collective liberation for the French-Canadian people. If class interests were not to clash head-on with national interests, if the working-class majority was to remain French in its aspirations and activities, it was important that Quebec's political and economic leaders provide the services and institutions deemed essential for the well-being of all French Canadians – habitant and industrial worker alike. French Canadians from all walks of life had to feel that their culture was valid and relevant in a rapidly changing world and that to remain French did not constitute a barrier to individual and collective social and economic advancement. This could be achieved, according to the neo-nationalists, if French-Canadian nationalism, rather than harp on the "spiritual" superiority of a Catholic and rural society, championed instead the need for "secular" superiority in the realms of social, cultural, and economic development. French-Canadian nationalism had indeed, in the hands of the neo-nationalists, undergone a significant transition in the late 1940s and throughout the 1950s. Little was it realized where a third generation of French-Canadian intellectuals would take this fully secularized, liberal-oriented neo-nationalism in the 1960s. Nor was the reformulation of traditional nationalism the only significant ideological development of the postwar years. The long-eschewed ideology of liberalism, relegated by Bishop Bourget and his ultramontane clerics to the very fringes of the professional petty bourgeoisie, reemerged in the *Cité libre* movement and the unions. This modern welfare state liberalism, riding tandem with a fledgling social democratic movement, would challenge both old and new nationalisms for the support and allegiance of French Canada's emerging bureaucratic middle class as well as of the urban working class.

CHAPTER FOUR

Cité libre *and the Revolution of Mentalities*

In a province where an intellectual is presumed, *juris*, and *de jure*, to be an orthodox Catholic, where a certificate of doctrinal allegiance takes the place of a genuine diploma of culture, how can the development of an audacious and autonomous mind not be impeded by the formidable pressures of clerical caesarism?[1]

The existence of a vibrant and politically influential liberal intelligentsia had all but collapsed with the demise of the Institut Canadien and the Rouge movement in the late 1860s. A small minority of anticlerical liberals such as Godefroy Langlois, Jean-Charles Harvey, and T.D. Bouchard hammered away at the official orthodoxy of traditional clerical nationalism. Despite the fact that liberal values and norms, and North American forms of progress and material expansion, thanks to the secularizing pressures of urbanization and industrialization, already permeated much of urban Quebec by the 1920s, no petty bourgeois liberal intelligentsia emerged in any organized fashion until the 1950s. Until then, Quebec's lay and clerical intelligentsia shunned and denounced all forms of social, economic, and political liberalism and preached a religiose nationalism which emphasized highly conservative rural social values and behaviour, deference to all authority, and the sanctity of private property and free enterprise. By the 1930s this nationalist intelligentsia had turned to social corporatism and limited state intervention as a means of restoring the organic nature of social relations and of undermining the abuses of foreign-dominated monopoly capitalism.

Postwar urban and industrial expansion coincided with the emergence of a new generation of young French Canadians who had experienced firsthand the shock of the depression and the inability of the ruling élites and supporting intelligentsia to deal with widespread socioeconomic dislocation and rising expectations. In the early 1950s, Montreal became the centre for a movement of French-Canadian intellectuals and sociopolitical *animateurs* dedicated to the elaboration and dissemination of the ideology of political and social liberalism and its concomitant secular and humanist world-view or "ethos." This liberal intelligentsia found its home and forum in a small but outspoken, iconoclastic, polemical, and highly influential periodical entitled *Cité libre* which first appeared in the summer of 1950. The periodical never had a large circulation (200–500 copies) but its contributors were often invited to express *Cité libre*'s ideology on the airwaves and television screens of Radio Canada as well as in the pages of *Le Devoir* and other Quebec dailies. Two of the leading figures in this movement were *Cité libre*'s co-editors, Pierre Elliott Trudeau and Gérard Pelletier. A close scrutiny of their formative years reveals much about the nature and thrust of the ideological assumptions and content of the *Cité libre* movement. The catalyst underlying the emergence of *Cité libre* was the growing awareness of the religious and spiritual crisis confronting the editors' generation, a crisis that had its origins in the depression decade and had grown deeper and more troublesome as the search for solutions produced more questions than answers. In the words of Maurice Blain, "This generation without masters is seeking a humanism and is anxiously asking on what kind of spiritual foundation this humanism should be based."[2] For over a century, Catholicism and the Catholic church had functioned at the very heart of what was perceived as the identity of the French-Canadian community. This strong presence had determined the attitudes, values, aspirations, and behaviour of all social classes but was especially influential in the case of the clerically educated professional middle class and its ideologues. The emergence of *Cité libre* with its unbridled determination to develop an incisive but constructive critique of French-Canadian Catholicism marked the emergence, ideologically and sociologically speaking, of modern French Canada. *Cité libre* came to symbolize "the revolution of mentalities," in that its militants proposed the creation of a secular and humanist "Cité libre" to serve French Canada's material as well as spiritual needs. French Canada, the Citélibristes maintained, in order to survive and expand had to abandon a religious ethos and societal model based primarily on the pursuit of eternal salvation in the hereafter.

CITÉ LIBRE'S FOUNDERS

Cité libre was founded in the spring of 1950 by a group of young French Canadians including Gérard Pelletier, Pierre Elliott Trudeau, Charles Lussier, Maurice Blain, Guy Cormier, Réginald Boisvert, Jean-Paul Geoffroy, Pierre Juneau, and Roger Rolland, each of whom put up thirty dollars to defray the printing costs of the first issue.[3] Others, including Jean Le Moyne, Pierre Vadeboncoeur, Marcel Rioux, Fernand Dumont, Jean-Charles Falardeau, Léon Dion, and Jean Pellerin joined the editorial committee and/or contributed significant critical and interpretive essays to the magazine. Pierre Trudeau and Gérard Pelletier, the magazine's co-editors, quickly established themselves as the guiding forces behind the group. Any full understanding of the ideological thrust of *Cité libre* and the significance of the Citélibristes is dependent upon some insight into the character and background of the magazine's co-editors.

Of the two individuals, Pierre Elliott Trudeau was and has remained the more elusive and complex. Born on 18 October 1919, Pierre Trudeau was the product of a small but growing French-Canadian business-oriented upper bourgeoisie. His father, Charles-Emile, who died prematurely in 1935, was a farmer's son who made good the transition from habitant to petty bourgeois lawyer to upper middle-class businessman in one generation. His shrewd investments in the service station business, real estate, stocks, and sports entertainment left the family independently wealthy and ensured the future of his three children. Their mother, Grace Elliott, of Scottish and French-Canadian parentage, inculcated in the family a love of culture and the fine arts and gained the esteem of her children by respecting their freedom and individuality. Pierre took full advantage of the opportunities thus provided and developed a deep love of the arts and the wilderness, making several canoe and portage excursions through northwestern Quebec to James Bay.[4]

By the standards of his day Trudeau's formal education was, in both range and depth, quite impressive. On the surface, the nature of his secondary education is deceptive. He completed an eight-year classical college program at one of Quebec's most prestigious, traditional nationalist colleges, Jean-de-Brébeuf, located not far from his Outremont home. There he had the good fortune of having as his professor of belles-lettres not the traditional nationalist cleric encountered by most college students, but rather an exceptionally liberal-minded French-Canadian priest from Manitoba, Father Robert Bernier. Trudeau freely acknowledges that Father Bernier introduced him to the precepts and significance of social and political democracy. It was also due to Father Bernier that Trudeau came to perceive federalism as the political system of the future because it allowed the achievement of political unity without undermining the existing cultural, religious, and ethnic differences in the country.[5] A strong democratic spirit and a healthy federalism were the two major prerequisites for modern, pluralistic, industrial, and urban societies. Another teacher encountered by Trudeau during his Brébeuf days was Rodolphe Dubé, better known as François Hertel, a literary figure who by the 1940s was highly critical of the cultural and social "backwardness" of French-Canadian society. As shown earlier, François Hertel was a strong and active proponent of French Catholic personalist thought. He was, no doubt, instrumental in instilling in Trudeau the tenets and precepts of liberal Catholicism as expressed by Maritain, Mounier, Gilson, and others. Trudeau and his *Cité libre* colleagues were somewhat dismayed when Hertel decided, in 1949, to leave Quebec and the priesthood and settle in Paris to write poetry and novels. He was driven out by what he believed to be a lack of intellectual maturity and freedom of expression in Quebec.[6] In effect, Hertel's decision played a small role in inducing some of his students and disciples to speak out against the stifling sociocultural conditions which had brought about his exile. Finally, while at Brébeuf, Trudeau encountered Father Richard Arès, a French-Canadian nationalist who perceived the intrinsic merits of federalism for national minorities. Arès was the editor of the Jesuit periodical *Relations* until he was removed for his overly sympathetic attitude to the working class, especially organized labour.[7]

Trudeau filled the vacuum of the war years by obtaining a law degree with honours from the Université de Montréal. His thirst for intellectual challenge and a strong political instinct, aroused by the undemocratic nature of wartime politics and the conscription crisis of 1942, then led him towards a career in the social sciences. He might well have chosen to enrol at Laval's recently established Faculty of Social Sciences but clerical domination of the university and the parochial nature of Quebec City forced him to look elsewhere. Unlike most of Laval's social science students, Trudeau could afford to pursue graduate studies at any one of North America's leading universities. He chose Harvard, where he completed a master's degree in political economy under the tutelage of Louis Hartz, a critic of the American liberal tradition, and Adam Ulam, a budding sovietologist. Next came the Ecole des sciences politiques in Paris in 1946 and then on to the London School of Economics where he began but did not complete a doctorate under the Fabian socialist and Labour government supporter Harold Laski.[8]

When asked in 1969 to assess the comparative influence of various writers upon the formulation of his social and political thought, Trudeau responded that while he had been favourably impressed by Laski, no single political or economic theorist, including Plato, Acton, de Tocqueville, Montesquieu, Keynes, Mill, and Marx, had provided him with a comprehensive insight into the problems of the modern world. His interests were indeed, as he always claimed, eclectic. A great many of his ideas emerged from his close reading of modern novelists and his prolonged travels – referred to as "cours pratiques" by Pelletier – in Western and Eastern Europe, in the Indian subcontinent, and in Southeast Asia in the late 1940s and throughout the 1950s.[9] To be sure, Trudeau's political and social ideas had not fully crystallized by the time he helped to establish *Cité libre* in 1950. Yet Pelletier has remarked that at the initial planning sessions for the magazine he quickly discovered Trudeau's "ability to communicate his knowledge and ideas to others. He had such a natural superiority over all of us in the international field, and we also discovered how far he had gone in evolving political ideas for French Canada – and for the rest of Canada."[10]

Much of the same sort of assessment can be made of Gérard Pelletier. By

1950 Pelletier, who had come to know Trudeau during the war years and in Paris in 1946-7, had reached a similar level of intellectual maturity via a very different set of circumstances and experiences. In family background, temperament, and education, both formal and informal, Pelletier differed in degree and kind from his colleague. One of eight children raised in the large Victoriaville family of Achille Pelletier and Léda Dufresne, he was born on 21 June 1919. Despite the fact that his father was only a railroad worker of modest means, Gérard's intellectual curiosity and promise led him through the seminary at Nicolet, Collège Mont-Laurier, and eventually on to the Université de Montréal during the war years.[11]

Pelletier, who readily confirms that religious thought and concerns dominated his preoccupations during these formative years, followed his belief that thought, to remain vigorous and healthy, must endure the test of action. He agreed to become national secretary of Quebec's Catholic Action movement for students, the Jeunesse étudiante catholique.[12] Along with several others, including his wife, Alexandrine Leduc, Pelletier was responsible for transforming a faltering JEC into a dynamic and progressive organization that instilled in a whole generation of college students a renewed and intellectualized Christian humanism and a deep collective sense of their social responsibilities as lay Catholics. The services offered to students – discussion courses on various themes, periodicals, athletic committees, student co-ops, and "caisses populaires" – served also as an excellent practical introduction to civic and democratic values.[13]

In 1945, Pelletier left the JEC to become the itinerant secretary for the Fonds national de secours aux étudiants. After twenty months of touring postwar Europe, he and his wife decided to visit South America, where they were profoundly struck by the extreme poverty of the masses and the unbelievable wealth of the small but thoroughly entrenched ruling élites. Gérard was offered a position in UNESCO, but he and Alex chose instead to return in 1948 to Canada, where they wrote scripts for Radio-Canada until Gérard was hired as a reporter at Le Devoir.[14] For a while, he edited the youth page and wrote a column in which he tried to instil in his generation a sense of urgency regarding social and political change. He was critical of the traditional political parties for their eternal ability to destroy the vigour and idealism of successive generations of French Canadians and he chastised Paul-Emile Borduas for his existentialist manifesto – Refus Global – because it proposed no concrete plan of action.[15]

Pelletier made his mark as a strong investigative reporter when Le Devoir assigned him the task of reporting, on the scene, the day-to-day developments of the prolonged and bitter strike that erupted in Quebec's asbestos mining industry in February 1949. It was on the streets of the grim company town of Asbestos that Trudeau renewed his acquaintance with Pelletier after his return to Canada in May 1949. The strike was a turning point for both of them, although for different reasons and in different ways. It confirmed Pelletier's career as a labour journalist when he accepted an offer from the CTCC to direct and edit its union newspaper *Le Travail*. The intense drama of the whole affair – both Trudeau and Pelletier were apprehended by the provincial police when they ventured too close to the picket lines – confirmed for Trudeau the undemocratic and oppressive nature of the Duplessis regime, especially when it was confronted by the increasing class-consciousness of the French-Canadian urban proletariat. Sensing that the asbestos strike of 1949 marked a fresh new departure in Quebec's social development, Trudeau, Pelletier, and several others decided to undertake on the ideological level the struggle for individual and class rights and human dignity that the five thousand courageous asbestos miners had launched in the workplace. After several months of deliberation and discussion, the group decided that what Quebec required was a provocative, educational, and independent journal of opinion and ideas in which writers would be asked to dissect critically all areas of Quebec's social and political life and recommend the appropriate reforms. The challenge was enormous, but as events were to prove, the climate was appropriate and the Citélibristes had the courage, skills, and human resourcefulness to measure up to the task.

The social, educational, and occupational backgrounds of the remaining Citélibristes were as varied and as interesting as those of Trudeau and Pelletier. Charles Lussier was a classmate of Charles Trudeau, Pierre's elder brother, at Collège Jean-de-Brébeuf. He received a law degree from the Université de Montréal in 1945 and went on to do postgraduate work at McGill in 1945-6. There he encountered Frank Scott, a constitutional lawyer and ardent civil libertarian. After the war he practised labour law and became an organizer for the Quebec wing of the CCF party. Both occupations, he recalls later, were extremely frustrating but rewarding. He was able to witness Duplessis' hostility toward organized labour, while within the CCF he met many like-minded French- and English-speaking Canadians who encouraged his left-wing tendencies. He left Quebec in 1956 to become director of La Maison des étudiants canadiens at the Université de Paris. He returned to Canada in 1960 and became an assistant secretary of state in Ottawa during the late 1960s.[16] Roger Rolland, a writer and a critic, was a very close Montreal school friend of Trudeau's and shared accommodation with him during Trudeau's stint at the Ecole des sciences politiques in Paris. Jean-Paul Geoffroy was a technical adviser for the CTCC and had been, along with Jean Marchand, a "strike director" for the Asbestos Workers' Federation during the prolonged and bitter asbestos strike in 1949. He eventually left the CSN in 1966 to become a federal civil servant in the immigration division.[17] Réginald Boisvert came to *Cité libre* with little formal education and plenty of working-class experience. He developed his talents as a journalist in the JEC and as editor of the *Front ouvrier*. He then turned his attention to the creation of television scripts dealing with the social and political problems of working-class families. His beliefs evolved in the direction of democratic socialism and he was, for a brief period in the early 1960s, a member of the national council of the NDP.[18] Pierre Juneau, a junior member of the National Film Board in the 1950s, became one of French Canada's most accomplished film and television critics, and his articles added a strong cultural emphasis to *Cité libre*'s otherwise predominantly political orientation. Maurice Blain, a notary and literary theatre critic, and Guy Cormier, a journalist, contributed occasionally to the magazine. Both later accepted and encouraged the alliance of democratic socialism and neo-nationalism that became increasingly popular in Quebec during the late 1960s.[19]

Other occasional contributors who followed the same intellectual evolution were Pierre Vadeboncoeur, Marcel Rioux, and Fernand Dumont. Vadeboncoeur, like Trudeau, came from an affluent bourgeois Outremont family. He started his classical education at Collège Sainte-Marie where his professors considered his socialist ideas far too radical. He enrolled in the Faculty of Law at the Université de Montréal in 1942 but withdrew in January of his second year. His rejection of this bourgeois profession was symbolized by his releasing into the air some 3,000 pages of notes he had collected. He did some work for the Canadian Press and the Chambre de Commerce but did not settle into a career until 1950 when he became a grievance counsellor for the CTCC. His lifelong commitment to working-class causes had begun with the asbestos strike and was formalized by his adherence to the CCF in 1954. By the early 1960s Vadeboncoeur had broken with the NDP, joined the Parti socialiste du Québec, supported the young marxists of *Parti pris*, and finally, renouncing his virulent opposition to nationalism, ended up joining the neo-nationalist and neo-marxist political movements favouring independence for Quebec.[20] The intellectual evolution of Marcel Rioux, an anthropologist with the National Museum of Canada until he became a member of Montreal's Faculty of Social Sciences in 1958, and Fernand Dumont, a sociologist at Laval since 1955, followed a similar pattern to that of Vadeboncoeur. They too overcame their initial rejection of nationalism and became ardent supporters of the Parti Québécois after 1968.

What common denominators, what motivations, what aspirations brought these Citélibristes together in 1950? This under-thirty generation of brilliant and high-spirited francophones shared, in varying degrees, three points of view. First, they were all deeply influenced by the Great Depression. They had all witnessed the failure of traditional ideologies and their spokesmen to understand the crisis and to discover remedies to resolve it. Given the congenital absence of inspired leadership from the traditional intellectual élite, *Cité libre* was created to serve as a forum in which a group of committed, socially minded francophones might freely express their thoughts, reveal their anxieties, put forward new ideas, ask difficult questions, and propose original solutions to old and new problems alike. In so doing, the Citélibristes believed they would serve as leaders and social models for the postwar generation.[21]

Second, Citélibristes were drawn together by a shared world view or "ethos" which emerged in the 1930s and took definite shape in the war years. Some, like Jean Le Moyne and Robert Elie, had contributed to *La Relève*'s questioning of French-Canadian Catholicism and traditional nationalism. They supported *La Relève*'s acceptance of a more universal, left-wing Catholicism as expressed by the French personalist movement of Mounier, Maritain, and Gilson. Still others, like Gérard Pelletier, absorbed a philosophy of progressive Catholic social action through their participation in the Jeunesse étudiante catholique.[22] It was in this movement that Pelletier began to question the highly restricted role of Catholic laymen in the church. For Pelletier, any effective Catholic social action would have to be undertaken by laymen or not attempted at all.[23] French Catholic personalist philosophy taught Citélibristes to reject the *a priori* dogmatism and excessive idealism of right- and left-wing ideologies. Their role was to emphasize that preservation of individual rights and personal self-realization were paramount. Most importantly, these two objectives could be achieved, not at the expense of, but through the pursuit of collective goals such as greater equality of economic condition between classes and a more democraticized political culture and socioeconomic institutions, as well as the enhancement of collective tools, in particular, an interventionist and pluralistic nation-state. Furthermore, *Cité libre*'s deliberate public identification with French left-wing social Catholicism helped it to legitimize for French-Canadian Catholics many Citélibriste ideas and proposed reforms, especially those entailing a marked discontinuity with the past.[24]

Finally, most Citélibristes shared a knowledge of the modern social sciences and all of them accepted the secularist and rationalist values and assumptions inherent in the study of social science methodology and its application to contemporary problems. *Cité libre* supported the development of the secular social sciences in Quebec's francophone universities. Several professors from Laval's Faculty of Social Sciences – Jean-Charles Falardeau, Léon Dion, and Fernand Dumont – contributed significant essays and, after 1955, participated in the editorial discussions of *Cité libre*'s themes and ideas.[25] Furthermore, a number of Citélibristes used their social science training to advise Quebec's labour movements, the CTCC and the Fédération des unions industrielles du Quebec (FUIQ), the provincial central for Canadian Congress of Labour unions after 1952.

Cité libre challenged young French Canadians to initiate an ongoing serious debate that would serve to distinguish their society's real problems from its false ones and eventually lead to an agreement on some common goals and an appropriate course of action. Reflecting a deep mistrust of *a priori* reasoning and *parti pris* proselytizing, *Cité libre* shunned the strategy, all too common among the nationalists, of issuing wordy manifestoes replete with good intentions and ready-made idealistic solutions to Quebec's deep-seated and complex problems.[26] Trudeau expressed the group's basic philosophy with much incisiveness and wit when he wrote:

We want to bear witness to the Christian and French fact in America. Agreed; but we must also throw everything else overboard. We must systematically question all political categories bequeathed to us by the intervening generation. The strategy of resistance is no longer useful for the growth and maturation of the City. The time has arrived for us to borrow from architecture the discipline called "functional," to cast aside the thousands of past prejudices which encumber the present, and to build for the new man. Overthrow all totems, transgress all taboos. Better still, consider them as dead ends. Without passion, let us be intelligent.[27]

French Canada lacked a philosophy of positive action based on a secular, rationalist, and scientific scrutiny of all its important problems and traditionally unquestioned values and institutions. Boisvert described his fellow Citélibristes as artisans of social renewal and *Cité libre* as "a place of reflection and interchange of ideas" where a group of young French Canadians were assuming their adult, that is to say, their social, responsibilities.[28] Indeed, *Cité libre* was intended to be more than a debating society. Pelletier, under the influence of the ardent French social Catholic Emmanuel Mounier, firmly believed that a "community of thought and ideas demands a community of action . . . modest, threatening but determined action."[29] Yet Pelletier was honest enough to admit in 1951 that while the Citélibristes shared a general feeling of discontent, malaise, and a very vague sense of revolt, "we often give the impression of a unanimous agreement on the ends to be pursued, when in reality this unanimity does not exist."[30] Contrary to a later allegation that Citélibristes were "essentially individualists,"[31] the group managed to develop a strong team spirit and in effect had hammered out a coherent set of assumptions and ideas by the mid-fifties. This was the result primarily of fortnightly gatherings during which commissioned articles by one or more of the group's members were scrutinized and criticized thoroughly by all present. It was not long before a fruitful cross-fertilization of ideas and a shared outlook was achieved. *Cité libre*'s articles, though issued under the signature of individual authors, reflected by and large the perspective and ideas of the entire group.[32] This team approach was particularly effective in *Cité libre*'s critique of French-Canadian Catholicism and the role of the Catholic church in Quebec society.

THE BATTLE AGAINST
CLERICALISM

Catholicism is not proposed or taught but rather imposed, inflicted, and driven home. God, that all-loving being who must be approached in the full freedom of one's heart, is injected like a serum. "Believe or die": that is still our present situation. If before the divine mystery anyone hesitates slightly, trembles, or dares to think, he is declared guilty of acting in collusion with Satan.[33]

The Catholic church remained, even in 1950, one of the most powerful social institutions in Quebec, sharing power with the predominantly anglophone commercial and industrial institutions and the francophone-dominated political institutions. Through its diocesan and parish administrations, educational institutions at all levels, farmers' amd workers' organizations, social service institutions, national associations of every variety, and its enormous fiscal power, the Quebec Catholic church permeated all of the conscious and unconscious social, cultural, and political behaviour of the vast majority of French Canadians.[34] Many individuals had, since the turn of the century, denounced this all-pervasive power and influence but to no avail. It was under these circumstances that *Cité libre* undertook a provocative, incisive, and constructive critique of the Catholic church in Quebec. They were to succeed where others had failed because the conjuncture of circumstances was appropriate to their cause. Furthermore, they argued their case from the perspective of sincere and dedicated Catholics wishing to renew and reinvigorate rather than diminish the spiritual dimension of Catholicism. Their mentors, in this respect, were the French liberal Catholics who sought to make their religion a vital and influential force in an increasingly impersonal and materialistic world.

The essence of *Cité libre*'s condemnation of the Catholic church was that it preached an overly theocratic social and political philosophy which had spawned a corrupting form of clericalism. Jean Le Moyne described the religious atmosphere reigning in Quebec in the early 1950s in an essay that was so provocative, so iconoclastic, that the author and the editorial committee deemed it necessary to delay its publication until 1955. Comparing modern Quebec with modern France, Le Moyne found French-Canadian Catholicism severely truncated and immature.

Originating from the same Catholicism which, since the Ancien Régime, has survived in France in pious enclaves in the provinces, our religion is today highly characterized by clericalism. It has the advantage of its glorious and sombre ancestor in being the only form of religion in Quebec. Our French coreligionists enjoy the radiant presence of a metropolitan Catholicism which is the honour and light of the contemporary church and which can be for them a free incarnation, a normal state of salvation.

They also have at their disposal a revolutionary tradition which has given them a right of seniority over other European peoples and which in itself is a very noble human condition. Here at home, we have no living and positive counterpart to the dominant doctrines. Even outside our archaic Catholicism there is nothing habitable. One must choose between an amorphous Protestantism and a niggling atheism. Even if only for the sake of drama, we decided to take refuge in Spanish or even Italian Catholicism. This would be a vast improvement! Unfortunately the question is never raised.[35]

Maurice Blain had composed a similarly provocative and iconoclastic critique of Quebec Catholicism in 1952 but the article was published in the French personalist periodical *Esprit*.[36] In this way *Cité libre* would not receive the brunt of the church's counter-attack, while still making the point that Quebec required an urban, liberal Catholicism. Indeed, the Citélibristes feared that Quebec had become so thoroughly imbued with clericalism at all levels that the society had virtually abandoned its quest for an autonomous secular intellectual life. Paradoxically, without the counterbalance of this latter phenomenon Quebec society was also on the verge of ceasing to be truly and effectively Catholic.

Cité libre's members arrived at these startling conclusions primarily from personal experience of the spiritual and religious crisis permeating their society since the depression. "Their Christianity, often traditional and implicit, has declined dramatically. From a state of conscience that was tranquil, somnolent, or only preoccupied with personal faults, they have suddenly entered a state of vigil, of doubt, and sometimes revolt," wrote Pelletier in 1951 of himself and his colleagues. Pelletier recounted an extra-ordinary personal incident which made him and several other young college students realize how sterile, meaningless, and ritualistic the Catholic faith had become for the majority of young French Canadians. A young, soft-spoken lay student, visiting their college, had challenged them to choose the road of sainthood, to understand that only one thing explains and animates the life of a true Christian. That was "a loving tendency towards perfection."[37]

Why had this proposal to seek perfection in their lives so impressed Pelletier and his friends? Was it their susceptible age? No, replied Pelletier. The shock resided in the fact that it was the first time that he and his colleagues had ever been offered the challenge. "Sainthood, in effect," recalls Pelletier, "was never a living ideal for the adolescents that we were. It did not even appear as a form of heroism to which we might aspire. On the contrary, we saw sainthood as a secret kingdom into which certain men, arbitrarily chosen, one day found themselves precipitately introduced."[38] The saints remained forever a part of the myths and legends of their child-hood and were never personified as real human beings capable of motivating others to seek perfection. Christian dogma was presented to the students through a dull and negative moralistic education; through the preaching of an edited gospel (students were never introduced to the complete text), stripped of its forceful language, its implied demands and expectations, "and the revolutionary action which underlaid it."[39] The teachings of the church and gospel were reduced to a suffocating moralism devoid of the personality of Christ and the sense of love that motivates a mature and true Christianity. The Bible had, in fact, become identified with Protestantism in the minds of most French Canadians. "The dizziness of solemn communions (oh! the eucharistic nausea . . .), the torture of processions, time held in suspense, the distracting hypnosis of litanies"[40] constituted Jean Le Moyne's memories of boring, romanticized, and sensualized religious ceremonies and rituals. As far as he was concerned there existed no relationship between the cult and daily reality. The most obvious result of these "pious orgies" was to dissociate completely "the vital act from the religious act."[41]

Taking the bull by the horns, many Citélibristes had tried to confront the crisis from within the church by joining Catholic action movements such as the JEC. The result was increased frustrations, unresolved personal crises, and eventual abandonment of these movements in the 1950s.[42] This catastrophe convinced the Citélibristes that any meaningful and successful critique of the Quebec Catholic church would never take place under the aegis of the hierarchy. An independent, secular, and lay-controlled medium of expression was the only strategy possible. Citélibristes, Maurice Blain informed his French readers, were convinced "that our clerical Catholicism is unfortunately powerless to propose anything of value for the mind. Some of us believe that the scandal must occur, the scandal of a Catholicism renewing the tradition of a liberal humanism and an autonomous culture. The scandal of a church in which the real distinction between the spiritual and temporal spheres is re-established. The scandal of a spiritual freedom without any other condition but respect for the individual conscience."[43] The challenge was defined, the risks were weighed, and the Citélibristes drew upon their courage, tenacity, superb intellectual and writing skills, and a strong sense of humour to initiate, develop, and refine a devastating but constructive critique of French-Canadian Catholicism and its institutional framework.

The approach chosen by the group was relatively straightforward but highly effective. The nature of the problem was defined. Then the ravages that excessive clericalism had created were described with a great deal of precision, wit, and effectiveness, after which broad concrete solutions were proposed. Considering that many of the group were social scientists, it is ironic to note that so few of the articles used rigorous historical or empirical evidence to support their allegations. The style was primarily intuitive and the editors preferred articles that would provoke, shock, and, it was hoped, serve as a catalyst to stir public debate on issues they felt were significant and needed urgent attention.

The charge of clericalism was comprehensive. But the Citélibristes were honest and sensitive enough to realize that there existed concrete historical and continuing reasons to account for the immature nature of Catholicism in French Canada. The survival of the French-Canadian culture after the Conquest of 1760 was due, in large measure, to the foresight and courage of the clergy who constituted the only remaining educated élite in the colony.[44] The only problem, as Le Moyne saw it, was that, in the absence of any other effective centres of power, the Catholic church presented itself as the only institution capable of ensuring the precarious survival of the French-Canadian nation. "It is a fact that the church constituted everything. It is another fact," wrote Le Moyne, "that we owe it everything and the church doesn't know how terrible this reality is for it."[45]

In fact, argued the Citélibristes, the ravages of urbanization and industrialization in their initial stages, at least, had reinforced the authority of the church. This was so because the clergy constituted the only educated class capable of fulfilling in the short term the growing demand for social services and education. Furthermore, each successive generation of French Canadians had a church which mirrored the existing cultural and social values and, to that extent, the clericalism was not a consciously reflected phenomenon, but rather associated with prolonged cultural immaturity and homogeneity.[46] It was readily admitted that the life of a cleric in a society undergoing rapid socioeconomic metamorphosis was a frustrating and confusing experience. If the priest restricted himself to administering the sacraments and guiding the consciences of his faithful and remained totally aloof from temporal matters he risked falling out of touch with reality. On the other hand, if he chose to participate in the temporal sphere the cleric risked transferring the authority he retained in the spiritual sector to the temporal realm of society, hence the accusation of clericalism.[47]

Clericalism in Quebec expressed itself in two forms. The first involved the invasion of intellectual and cultural life by religious dogmatism. The second pertained to the control of secular institutions by ecclesiastical power and personnel. *Cité libre*'s members directed their attack against both forms. To some extent, they were the first critics to perceive accurately the all-pervasive consequences of intellectual and cultural clericalism which was an outgrowth of institutional or sociological clericalism. It was, the Citélibristes contended, intellectual clericalism which menaced most directly the freedom of the spirit. In the words of Maurice Blain, this historical fusion of the profane and the sacred "appears as a phenomenon of cultural alienation to the benefit of theology, a subtle undermining of human values at the expense of divine values ... The annexation of intellectual life by religious dogmatism submitted freedom to the immediate sanction of clerical absolutism. It is therefore logical today that the exercise of oppression is confused with the apologia of Catholic doctrine and morals."[48]

The psychological consequences of this intellectual and cultural clericalism were devastating. For the believing conformist, the possession of theological truth stifled intellectual curiosity and the quest for secular knowledge and human truths. Those who refused to succumb to this suffocating and oppressive orthodoxy lived in a world of fear, guilt, and confusion, torn between the contradictory demands of their faith and their reason. On occasion, an individual crumbled under the enormous pressures and committed suicide. Gérard Pelletier, using the literary device of a dialogue between a monk and a journalist, sought a *rational* explanation for the loss of a close friend by suicide. Solid reasons were needed to explain the frustrations, anxieties, and despair that drove a young and healthy French Canadian from a good bourgeois family to take his own life. Pious explanations emphasizing the will of God were totally unacceptable. What the tense and, at times, difficult dialogue between the monk and the journalist revealed was that the suicide victim had lost his Catholicism and consequently had been completely ostracized by the French-Canadian cultural community. Because of the intense historical relationship that had been forged between Catholicism and the French-Canadian people, a non-Catholic French Canadian experienced less tolerance from his own people than would an English Protestant.[49] French Canadians were "a people with a single faith where nonbelievers are considered errants who have abandoned their caravan."[50]

Further insights into the deep despair suffered by non-Catholic French Canadians were provided by Le Moyne, Father Ernest Gagnon, and Robert Elie, a novelist. For these authors, the two most powerful mechanisms of social control in Quebec society were those of fear and guilt, two qualities that continually reinforced each other and which were instilled from birth in the subconscious of every French Canadian. Life was a continual struggle against a long list of sins defined in rigid black and white terms with no gradations of right and wrong, no grey areas. Straying from the rigid and narrow path of righteousness led not to self-discipline and moral regeneration, but rather to neurotic and despairing guilt which in turn reinforced an obsessive need to make amends and a fear of authority.[51] Little wonder there were so few avowed non-Catholics among French Canadians in 1955. The costs, in psychological, social, cultural, and even political terms, were simply far too enormous.

The sociological aspects of clericalism, that is, the presence of large numbers of clerics in secular occupations and the control of the church over entire temporal fields, was highly visible and easy to confront. Ecclesiastical authority, thanks to its historically privileged situation, had acquired immense power in the temporal sphere because of its wealth of human and capital resources – real estate, churches, convents, schools, hospitals, colleges, universities – and liquid assets in shrewd portfolio investments. The Catholic church fulfilled a whole range of educational and social welfare functions.[52] Both the immense wealth and the secular administrative functions threatened, in Pelletier's view, to compromise severely the church's spiritual mission. The growing need for funds was forcing church officials to get involved in clandestine backroom politics. The entire procedure whereby the church obtained subsidies to carry on what were essentially temporal functions was questionable and highly undemocratic from the public's point of view. Furthermore, the procedure, if prolonged, threatened eventually to undermine permanently the church's prized independence.[53]

A further consequence of the church's involvement in secular matters was ecclesiastical sensitivity to what normally would be considered responsible criticism. Church officials used their ecclesiastical authority to censor any sort of critical debate involving areas in which the church had vested interests, such as education and social welfare. *Cité libre* members, Roger Rolland and Pierre Trudeau, found themselves the victims of clerical wrath for having transgressed certain unwritten but important rules. Rolland was chastised by Father Marcel de Grandpré in *Le Devoir* for having had the audacity to criticize publicly the classical college system and its educators. Rolland had to remind de Grandpré that as a citizen he had the right and the responsibility to criticize secular institutions. Furthermore, such criticism should not be interpreted as an attack upon the church or its staff.[54] Unfortunately for the democratic rights of French Canadians, many clerics continued to contend that laymen had no business questioning areas of church jurisdiction, be they spiritual or secular.

One such incident occurred when an Assumptionist priest, Father Léopold Braün, charged Trudeau with being a communist sympathizer. The grounds for the charge were that Trudeau had visited Moscow and other parts of Russia, allegedly as a delegate to a world economic conference in 1952. Moreover, Trudeau had written a series of articles on his trip for *Le Devoir* which, in Braün's view, were excessively sympathetic to the Kremlin and failed to raise the issue of the Communist regime's suppression of Catholics and the Catholic faith in Iron Curtain countries. In fact Trudeau, while keeping an open mind as to the Soviet Union's prospects for progress and development, had brought to light several of the shortcomings and paradoxes of a society that was theoretically egalitarian and democratic.[55] Given his critical perspective, Trudeau's vehement countercharge of clericalism was understandable. Father Braün and the editors of a Quebec Catholic newspaper, *L'Action Catholique*, Father J.-B. Desrosiers and Louis Philippe Roy, who had reprinted the charges, could have been taken to court on a libel charge had Trudeau not felt he would have been run out of the province as an irresponsible communist sympathizer and an irrepressible anticlerical. What he found most distasteful was that these individuals, none of whom were competent as economists or political scientists, had hidden under the cloak of the Catholic church to denounce his views concerning purely secular matters. That, Trudeau felt, was taking clerical privilege to its most nefarious and undemocratic extreme.[56]

In pursuit of a Catholic renaissance the liberal-minded social Catholics in *Cité libre* were also critical of clericalism within Quebec's Catholic church. The church, they contended, was not strictly a preserve of clerics, but belonged to all the faithful. What infuriated many laymen, Citélibristes included, was the church's firm, but ever-so-diplomatic refusal to allow laymen to participate in the policy and decision-making processes of the Catholic church. The status and role of the laymen in the society was that of second-class citizens. Pierre Dansereau, a natural science professor at the Université de Montréal, upon losing one of his most promising graduate students to the priesthood, expressed his bitter resentment at the church's attitude towards even the highly qualified laymen in the society. He decried the continuation of a rigid hierarchy of values which placed metaphysial and philosophical inquiry at the summit and degraded all inquiry which was empirical in nature. Only the theologian and the philosopher contributed to the cause of Christianity. "Nobility and piety are theirs alone," wrote Dansereau to his former student, "while humble labour, *profane* and unconscious of itself, is for us. There is no piety except their kind, which is often in our view pompous and verbose."[57]

When this mentality was pushed, as it often was, to its extreme logical limit in the day-to-day activities of church administration, the end result was an authoritarian, paternalistic, and totally undemocratic institution. While commerce and industry had invented "le cochon de payant," the church, wrote Jean Le Moyne with intense bitterness and sarcasm,

created for itself "le cochon de laic," a man without a mind, the Christian from the backward church, the deplorable believer whom, with the insensitive arrogance of purists on high, the church watches floundering in the "decay" of the century. To amuse him and to make him inform on himself, the church identifies him publicly as a special type of imbecile, thanks to the miraculous institution of "committees." The layman being essentially interpretable, the church reinterprets him constantly. It organizes for the layman at great cost (which is defrayed by him) "spontaneous" devotions and, under the pretext of being at his disposal, the church speaks to him in a facile and dishonourable language of foolishness, confusing this approach with simplicity, without realizing that it is thereby reducing to zero the spiritual dimension of the Holy Word.[58]

It was this continued reluctance of the Quebec Catholic church to grant an increasingly larger group of highly educated laymen any meaningful responsibilities which prompted committed lay Catholics like the Citélibristes to question the sincerity and maturity of church leaders.

What solutions were advanced by *Cité libre* members to rid their society of intellectual and sociological clericalism? One thing was clear. Religion was too important to be left to a self-serving clerical elite. "The clerical problem is the responsibility of laymen," wrote Dansereau; "the excessive power of one group always resides in the consent, if not the complicity, of all the other groups."[59] While the Citélibristes envisaged a severe curtailment of the church's power in the secular field they also strongly favoured a renewal of its spiritual effectiveness in the French-Canadian community. A sterile, conservative, petty bourgeois Catholicism had to be challenged and eventually replaced by a modern, progressive social Catholicism similar to the variety that had taken root and flourished in France, thanks to committed Catholic intellectuals such as Jacques Maritain and Emmanuel Mounier. As Gérard Pelletier readily admitted, "even if we wanted to, we could not succeed in denying the influence of Mounier."[60] Yet the Citélibristes were realistic enough to understand that French social Catholicism could not and should not be transplanted unaltered to Quebec. The French experience merely served as an excellent example of what could take place if courgeous Catholic laymen understood their responsibilities in the elaboration of a vital and dynamic Catholic church and Christian society. Such was the nature of the challenge proposed to *Cité libre*'s readers.

A renewed Catholicism implied a substantial revision in the Catholic's perception of his role as a temporary, but crucial, participant in the development and perfection of mankind. A revitalized Catholicism needed to be founded on a premise more enlightened, more creative, and more challenging than "the rigid behaviourism of the moralist tradition which takes as given an irreparable, old, and finished mankind, one totally removed from any possible progress and achievement." The "earthly promises" had not been abolished by the Fall. Twenty centuries after the coming of Christ, modern man still had a tremendous distance to travel before fulfilling his mission of occupying the earth, cultivating its immense agricultural and mineral resources, naming its creatures, and, in general, exercising a rational and benevolent domination. "Christ," suggested Le Moyne, "did not come to remove us from this world; rather He placed us at the very centre of that world . . . According to our various capacities, taking into account the limits created by original sin and the obstacles of the mystery of inequality at work among us, we must go to the limit of the perfection of Christ, to the extreme of his human implications."[61] This was precisely the perspective advanced by the French Catholic personalists and described so well by Maritain in his *Humanisme intégral*. Maritain had argued that true Christians had a responsibility to participate in the transformation of the existing social order. Catholics could achieve salvation – perhaps even sainthood – by participating in the renewal and revitalization of society's temporal institutions so that these institutions could better serve the communal-personalist needs and aspirations of every individual.[62]

French-Canadian Catholics must therefore come to accept the fact that they functioned no longer in a "sacralized" society but rather in a secular world in which the relationships between human beings were just as significant as the relationship between man and his Creator. A renewed faith in God had to be supplemented with a strong faith in Man. "An analysis of the dominant characteristics of our present cultural conditioning," concluded Vadeboncoeur,

demonstrates to us the need to introduce in our general philosophy an idea, regarded unfortunately as secular, but which cannot be rejected without willing oneself to destruction: the "myth" of Man. Without renouncing God, our society must now turn toward Man, and contemplating the work of those who, since the French Revolution, have under the aegis of humanity gained large areas for civilization, for law, for knowledge, for art and technology, it must seek out these developments with determination. This is not to obliterate the image of God, but rather to be certain to deal with that image with the same zeal and generosity as do those who believe in that image exclusively.[63]

To be modern signified for Citélibristes to be deeply engaged in the struggle of man, to see man as the central figure in this Promethean endeavour to vindicate and establish political equality and economic abundance and to develop the social and natural sciences, making it possible to change nature and to organize the political basis of a human fraternity. In brief, their objective was the creation of the *temporal City*, recognized not by its confessional character but rather by a certain harmony, a certain equilibrium, enabling man to achieve both temporal and eternal salvation.[64]

IMPLEMENTING THE
REVOLUTION OF MENTALITIES

Citélibristes recommended four essential steps in their quest for a Christian and Catholic humanism and the creation of the true *Cité libre*. All entailed and would produce a substantial shift in mental outlook. First, cultural and intellectual thought must regain its autonomy from theology and religious dogmatism. Second, French Canadians must attain their fundamental rights of freedom of thought and expression and the freedom of selecting and living openly the faith of their own choice. Third, the Catholic church must withdraw from administration of secular concerns like eduation and social services. Finally, Catholic laymen should acquire greater responsibilities and say in the internal affairs of the church.

Undoubtedly hoping to attack the problem of clericalism at its origins, the liberal Catholic laymen of *Cité libre* emphasized strongly this fourth recommendation. They were unanimous in their call for a democratization of the policy and decision-making processes within the Catholic church of Quebec. An institution as large and as important as the church had to reflect the values of the society in which it functioned and in which it hoped to exercise a fair degree of spiritual guidance and moral persuasion on major issues. Trudeau drew the attention of the traditionalists to a 1946 speech in which Pope Pius XII had declared that laymen should be fully conscious not only of belonging to the church but of being the church.[65] If the French-Canadian laity continued to visit and not inhabit the church, to desert it in increasing numbers, then both the church and the laity would suffer. Laymen had to be treated as mature educated adults. They had to be encouraged to participate so that they could feel the Catholic church was an essential aspect of their daily lives. "If the layman begins to speak out, if he manages to impose some of his traits on the face of the church, the church will belong to him as he belongs to himself. A true measure of how deeply the layman can penetrate the church will be whether or not the layman can save himself while contributing to the mission of the church at the same time."[66] The basis for an open and mature dialogue could be achieved if church spokesmen accepted Citélibristes as ardent and sincere Catholics and understood that laymen and clerics need not necessarily agree on all matters. Only an open, honest, and public debate, Pelletier was convinced, would help to dispel the growing tensions and animosities developing between clerics and the rapidly expanding, educated middle-class sector of the Quebec community.[67]

"Crisis of authority or crisis of liberty?" was the question Pelletier put to Cité libre's readers in 1952. The query was prompted by an abbé who charged the group with feeding and reflecting the crisis of authority which, he claimed, permeated Quebec society. Pelletier agreed that attitudes and values were evolving, that the authority of the bishops and the church councils was being questioned by concerned laymen. This development was the natural outcome of a society in the adolescent stage seeking an adult equilibrium. The crisis was acute because the church's authority had, for a long time, been solidly entrenched in nearly every important sector of the national life of all French Canadians. The crisis, argued Pelletier, was a healthy one and, if allowed to follow its natural course, would enable the community to acquire a sense of maturity and reestablish the respect of French Canadians for their church and its personnel.[68]

What seemed less certain was whether the struggle against cultural and intellectual clericalism was going to be resolved as easily as the sharing of religious responsibilities. Indeed, during the 1950s most traditional Catholics continued to believe that Catholic intellectuals had no right to participate in a discussion in which everything, including the premises of their own faith, was questioned. Citélibristes, supported by Father Louis O'Neill of Laval, disagreed strongly. "The path to truth appears to me," wrote Robert Elie, "increasingly each day as a renewed search pursued not in isolation but rather through dialogue, through an incessant exchange of questions and provisional answers. I believe that it suffices to be man in order to have not only the right, but the duty to undertake this search with the greatest of zeal while accepting all the risks of a voyage in unknown territory."[69] *Cité libre* questioned why the departments of philosophy at Laval and the Université de Montréal continued to function on the premise that theologically trained clerics were inherently better qualified to teach a secular subject like philosophy than laymen holding doctorates in the field. As long as philosophy, a discipline which by its very nature demanded complete intellectual freedom, remained an exclusive preserve of clerics and hence a branch of theology, full-fledged critical thought and expression would never take root in Quebec.[70]

The acceptance of full intellectual freedom and religious pluralism remained paramount objectives of the group. Maurice Blain proposed in the strongest terms possible that the Centre des intellectuels catholiques canadiens abandon its confessional character and thereby enable its annual conference, known as Carrefour, to become a dynamic and stimulating intellectual experience, rather than degenerate as it had for many years into a moralizing of issues, or as Blain preferred to call it, "a dialogue of the deaf."[71] Citélibristes had, in fact, boycotted Carrefour and with the help of several university people, including Léon Lortie and Jean-Charles Falardeau, founded the Institut canadien des affaires publiques (ICAP) in 1954. The organizers invited renowned French-Canadian and foreign intellectuals to give their perspectives on such subjects as freedom, education, federalism, and the Third World, at annual conferences in the Laurentians. The full proceedings were aired over Radio-Canada.[72] The forum was adopted to encourage public debate on important secular and religious issues and to encourage French Canadians to be open to new ideas and original points of view. Despite the outburst of opposition from traditional nationalists, spearheaded by Robert Rumilly and his 1956 polemic *L'infiltration gauchiste au Canada français*, the annual ICAP sessions reached a large and receptive audience, much to the chagrin and dismay of traditional nationalists and politicians.

The Citélibristes contended that French Canadians, as Christians, had to develop a deep respect for liberty, a privilege which mankind alone shared with God. Confronted with all forms of modern totalitarianism, and the growing oppression of the materialist ethic, it was imperative that Christians be in the vanguard of the struggle for freedoms of every nature.[73] The slogan which best incarnated the *Cité libre* spirit of pluralism was "*feu l'unanimité*," that is, to heck with unanimity. This battle-cry was Pelletier's response to a suggestion that French Canada was quickly losing its unanimity on questions such as divorce and censorship. It was also Pelletier's response to a personal letter in which he was charged with – and, so to speak, excommunicated for – corrupting the minds of a whole generation of young French Canadians with his radical ideas. The lack of unanimity, responded Pelletier, was merely a reflection of the altered social realities of contemporary Quebec. Regardless of how far church officials and their self-appointed spokesmen strained the evidence to deny that hundreds of French Canadians were losing their faith and leaving the church, the phe-nomenon was real, irreversible, and had to be acknowledged. A good deal of tension and animosity could be avoided, in Pelletier's view, if this new religious pluralism and intellectual freedom were accepted and a dialogue established between the believers and nonbelievers.[74] Was the Catholic French-Canadian majority mature enough to take up the challenge? Cité-libristes felt it was. Acceptance of religious differences and open dialogue were the only Christian responses possible.

Inherent in all reforms discussed above and, in fact, a prerequisite to their fruition was the demand by the Citélibristes for a quick, comprehensive, and irrevocable separation of church and state. Continuation of the church's participation in secular affairs would lead to further denial of the democratic rights of French Canadians. The church found its role as a moral critic of politics and politicians severely curtailed because it had become increasingly dependent upon those politicians and the political system to subsidize the church's administration and financing of the rapidly expanding educational, health, and social services required by a modern industrial society. The church hierarchy turned a deaf ear to charges of widespread political corruption, misuse of public funds, conservative social and economic policies, and the physical and legislative oppression of workers' organizations for fear of arousing the wrath of the government.[75] The only effective remedy to this nefarious situation was for the church to withdraw entirely from secular functions, thereby regaining its full measure of independence.

This separation of church and state did not mean that clerics need lose interest in secular affairs. In Trudeau's view, an effective priest was one who retained an open mind toward all of man's problems, who understood the dynamics of his era, denounced its flagrant shortcomings and abuses, and knew how to love all individuals and mankind. If a cleric chose to participate in a discussion of the administration of temporal affairs he must do so as a common citizen, totally divested of his prestige and authority as a cleric.[76] "If it was well understood by everyone," wrote Trudeau with his usual flair, "that to solve purely temporal problems, a cassock did not provide any special support, that being tonsured did not provide any immunity before the law or public opinion, and that a doctorate in theology was not a certificate of universal and infallible competence. If it was well understood that a priest who chooses to serve secular forces has no more knowledge or authority than any other citizen, then clerics and laymen might be able to collaborate more serenely in the building of a church and a society that are truly Christian."[77]

CONCLUSION

Cité libre's acute awareness of the religious crisis confronting a growing number of educated, middle-class French Canadians prompted an incisive and devastating critique of French-Canadian Catholics and the Catholic church. Conveniently armed with the "radical" ideas of the French Catholic personalists, the Citélibristes called for an end to all forms of clericalism and the creation of a more militant, democratic, reform-oriented, and communal-personalist inspired Catholicism. In short, a response by the Catholic church to the material as well as spiritual needs of an urban-industrial society. Indeed, were sufficient numbers of French Canadians to abandon their "theocratic" ethos in exchange for the secular homocentric perspective proclaimed essential by *Cité libre*, their society would undergo fundamental changes. This "revolution of mentalities" would bring about a dramatic shift in power from the church to the state, from clerics to the new middle class. Religion would be relegated to the private world of the individual. French Canada would remain a Catholic society but would cease to be a clerical society which stifled the development of the full human potential and prevented French Canadians from coming to terms with the modern world.

Measured in terms of the ensuing intellectual debate – a debate not always characterized by rationality – *Cité libre*'s plea for a fundamental shift in the attitudes and mental outlook of French Canadians proved to be remarkably successful. The vast majority of enlightened lay leaders and intellectuals concurred with *Cité libre*'s condemnation of clericalism in all its forms. It was becoming increasingly evident that the time was ripe for a redefinition of the role of the church in francophone Quebec. A new entente needed to be forged between the clerical élite representing a prestigious and influential institution, the Catholic church, and the new and old élites representing the secular interests of francophones as individuals and as members of a beleaguered collectivity. By the late 1950s enlightened members of the Catholic hierarchy, including Cardinal Léger, realized the full import of the socioeconomic changes sweeping the province. As pressures for change mounted, it became apparent that leading clerics were generally less hostile to new arrangements than most members of the traditional élites.[78] *Cité libre*'s struggle against clericalism had been timely. It succeeded where countless others had failed. The Catholic church was no longer to function as a powerful public institution moulding the collective psyche and actions of Quebec's francophone society. When this transition took place in

Western Europe, beginning in the late eighteenth century, the decline of religion was accompanied by the rise of secular ideologies, the most powerful and prominent being nationalism. Citélibristes, determined that Quebec was going to avoid the cataclysmic consequences of this historical pattern, undertook a comprehensive critique of French-Canadian nationalism and nationalists.

CHAPTER FIVE

Cité libre *and Nationalism*

Delivering oneself from traditionalism entails the suppression of clerical oppression and of nationalism which have until now prevented or impaired the emergence of a fruitful liberty.[1]

The liberal and social democrats in *Cité libre* were convinced from the outset that the greatest obstacle to the modernization of French-Canadian society was the omnipresence of a paranoid and distorted traditionalism. Originally, this traditionalism had the laudable mission of preserving intact the values of French culture and civilization. But with the growing threat of contamination by Anglo-Saxon values this traditionalism adopted a state of siege mentality which had the nefarious effect of immobilizing "in history the dynamism of the culture and of exhausting the creative energy of civilization."[2] This siege mentality, reinforced by clericalism, served primarily the interests of the church. More important, however, was the fact that a corrupted traditionalism inspired the emergence of the ideology of nationalism. Citélibristes readily accepted Maurice Blain's assertion that since the turn of the century "the demagoguery of various schools of nationalists, and particularly of nationalist history, perhaps has done more to provoke the stiffening of intellectual traditionalism and to precipitate the decline of the culture than the church had accomplished in an entire century."[3] This perception of nationalism was going to draw the Citélibristes into undertaking a severe critique of French-Canadian nationalism, its major assumptions, aspirations, and specific proposals. As a result of this critique, they were charged with being not only antinationalist but anti-French-Canadian, in short, traitors to their own cultural community. Citélibristes, except for pessimists like Pierre Vadeboncoeur, were not anti-French-Canadian. In reality, they were driven by a deeply rooted belief in the survival and *épanouissement* of the francophone culture in Canada and North America. They disagreed fundamentally with traditional French-Canadian nationalists about the nature and aspirations of what they considered to be a viable, modern French-Canadian society. Citélibristes were antinationalists because they believed sincerely that nationalism, like clericalism, had prevented the emergence of a dynamic, creative, indigenous, French-Canadian culture and society rooted in North America. French-Canadian society would survive and flourish, not because of any nationalist doctrine, but by maturing into an open, democratic, pluralistic, secular, urban-industrial society in harmony with, yet distinct from, that of the rest of North America.

THE CRITIQUE OF NATIONALISM

For some Citélibristes their distrust and scepticism of nationalism predated the founding of the movement. For Pierre Vadeboncoeur a national revolution was "generally a failed opportunity to tackle an international problem which is that of mankind."[4] Marcel Rioux, while stating his confidence in the continued survival of nations as viable and necessary cultural entities, concluded that "the rights to survival, to individual and religious freedom, to property, to work and social security, are all rights of everyone living in society," and thereby had priority over national rights.[5] Guy Cormier complained bitterly that nationalism had never served the interests of the working class in Quebec and consequently the proletariat had no use for an ideology which stressed autonomy for the nation at the expense of autonomy for the individual.[6] Trudeau also revealed his distaste for the ideology when he rejected Filion's call for the creation of a republican and social movement to replace the moribund Conservative party. Trudeau preferred a new political movement based strictly on a platform of social democracy. The achievement of an independent Canadian Republic, while important, could wait until later.[7] The *Cité libre* group was thus well disposed to undertake a critical analysis of traditional French-Canadian nationalist thought. Events of the 1950s only reinforced their initial scepticism and impelled some members to question the viability of a society that had fostered and nurtured what they perceived as a highly conservative and at times reactionary ideology and culture.

The demise of the Bloc had prompted the young postwar nationalists to question the attachment of the French-Canadian working class to its cultural milieu. Neo-nationalists were provoked into a reassessment of traditional nationalism. The famous five-month strike in the asbestos mines in the Eastern Townships in 1949 served as a major catalyst in the formation of the *Cité libre* movement. The strike led the Citélibristes to question the nationalist ideology that, in their view, had given birth to the antisocial and antilabour Duplessis government during the depression and had returned it to power in 1944. The Duplessis regime was the incarnation of the petty bourgeois and clerical nationalism formulated in the pages of *L'Action française* during the 1920s and *L'Action nationale* in the 1930s and 1940s. The nationalists had clamoured for a French-Canadian republic on the banks of the St Lawrence. "But," wrote Guy Cormier with a cutting sense of sarcasm, "in this little republic which Mr Duplessis has given you (with a nice flag to boot), there are no republicans ... The People, Mr Duplessis has sent to college. 'The People are in college and strikes are its holidays.' Mr Duplessis is the usher, the professor, and the spiritual guidance counsellor (Gospel in hand!)." As a result, the French-Canadian people were living a disguised separatist existence distinct from that of the rest of Canada and the international community. This led Cormier to ponder aloud whether the French Canadians would soon wake up one morning as citizens of a newly proclaimed fascist state! While his fears certainly were exaggerated, it was clear that *Cité libre* had opted for a society which placed a priority on the defence and development of civil rights and individual liberties rather than "a political and religious state which oppresses consciences" in the name of an ideology called nationalism.[8]

According to the *Cité libre* interpretation, expressed by Trudeau, the asbestos strike occurred, in part, because the industrial workers of Quebec were suffocating in a society "overburdened by inadequate ideologies and oppressive institutions."[9] How had these two distinct yet related developments taken place? What did Citélibristes mean by the term "inadequate ideologies"? Several members of the group, including Trudeau, Jean-Guy Blain, Vadeboncoeur, Dumont, and Rioux, contributed lengthy and revealing essays on this question. The central thesis and conclusion of all these essays was that an expanding gap had been allowed to develop between the socioeconomic and cultural realities of modern Quebec and the unchallenged clerical and petty bourgeois ideology of nationalism that had been widely promulgated since the late nineteenth century.[10] French-Canadian social and economic thought had, as a result of historical events particular to French Canada, become synonymous with the prevailing nationalist thought. It thereby carried the burden of ensuring the survival of the French Canadians as a distinct collectivity. A heavy responsibility indeed.

It was this rigid identification of all French-Canadian social thought with nationalist thought that, in the view of the *Cité libre* group, created the dual sociocultural and intellectual crisis confronting French Canadians in the 1950s. Nevertheless, the Citélibristes wanted it made clear that their critique of traditional nationalist thought should not be interpreted as an attack upon the integrity of the nationalists themselves. The latter, argued Trudeau, merited full respect for they lacked "neither creativity in their intentions, nor courage in their undertakings, nor firmness in their proposals, nor inventiveness in their resolutions." Trudeau merely wanted to "rid nationalist thought of the aspects which above all obstructed the present and prevented free and direct action."[11] These nationalists, responding intuitively, had elaborated a security system to ensure the survival of a people that had been conquered, occupied, decapitated of its élites, forced out of the commercial sector and the urban centres, and reduced to the status of a minority with little influence in a country French Canadians had discovered, explored, and colonized. Nationalists and their doctrines, it was acknowledged, had played a role in saving French-Canadian culture and civil and religious liberties.[12] The point that Citélibristes hoped to make was that traditional nationalist doctrines simply had outlived their historical usefulness and had become burdensome intellectual anachronisms.

The major shortcoming of traditional nationalist thought was its excessive idealism. French-Canadian culture lacked an aspect fundamental to all dynamic cultures – an intimate contact with reality. Vadeboncoeur expressed the crisis confronting French Canadians in these harsh terms.

We are nourished by myths, by ideals, whose relationship to reality are at the very best highly vague; this is a most irritating characteristic of our culture. This situation is quite evident in politics, for example. We envisage a highly patriotic national project without ensuring that an exciting and imperious reality provide the essential elements of a dynamic policy that is capable of being fulfilled. Our national mystique therefore remains necessarily sentimental and idealistic. It is not founded on a power base, it is not at the cutting edge of reality, because that reality is solvent. Our national mystique is based on an antiquated reality, fixed in tradition, which reached its zenith perhaps in the middle of the last century. This reality was for us the plausibility of becoming a small nation in the nineteenth-century conception of that term.[13]

What were these myths, these ideals, that inspired and motivated several generations of well-intentioned but naïve nationalists? In the *Cité libre* view of things, French-Canadian nationalists had constructed an ideal society that was totally unprogressive, antimodern, and destructive of the individual. French-Canadian nationalism, suggested Rioux, "has always had the tendency to define a French Canadian not in his own terms but rather by what he was in relation to other groups. While the efforts of educators in other western societies concentrated on democracy, freedom, intellectual and scientific knowledge, the imperatives of our ideology were drawn from three characteristics which differentiated the French Canadian from his neighbours: minoritary, Catholic, and French."[14] Clerical and petty bourgeois nationalists persisted in selling the virtues of a society which emphasized the superiority of spiritual and moral integrity to the fulfilment of mankind's material and social needs, a society which had as its mission the preservation and diffusion of Catholicism and the French culture on a continent dominated by secularism, materialism, and Anglo-Saxon values and institutions.[15]

Traditional nationalism was characterized by a "mythical" and "historicist" mentality which made a cult of differences and the past and took account of a forbidding and treacherous present only in terms of its relationship to an idealized past and never to the future. This "mythical" and "historicist" mentality had rendered French Canadians prisoners of their past. It had made them incapable of assimilating the two major developments of the twentieth century – industrialization and urbanization.[16]

The psychological, intellectual, and institutional consequences of this monolithic, unrealistic, and doctrinaire nationalist system of thought were devastating and pervasive. Trudeau effectively demonstrated in his lengthy introduction to *La grève de l'amiante* how doctrinaire nationalist ideology had prevented French-Canadian intellectuals from drawing upon creative and novel developments in the modern social sciences. It had also brought about, in Trudeau's estimation, a reactionary interpretation of the social thought of the Catholic church. On the political level, the nationalist influence made it virtually impossible for francophone politicians to implement socioeconomic programs that had proved successful for the Protestant and materialistic English-speaking Canadians. Furthermore, the clerical nationalists' equation of state intervention with communism and socialism had made the implementation of meaningful provincial autonomy impossible, thereby impeding the growth of a democratic concept of authority and the role of the state. The five concrete solutions proposed by the nationalists – return to the land, support for small business, cooperatives, Catholic unionism, and Christian corporatism – were all, in *Cité libre*'s view, conservative, reactionary programs intended to impede the secularization and democratization of the society's values and institutions.[17]

Unfortunately, many of French Canada's important institutions – the Société Saint-Jean-Baptiste, the Ecole sociale populaire, *L'Action nationale*, the classical colleges and the universities, the church and the Catholic unions – had been thoroughly imbued with this clerical-nationalist ideology, making their transition to a modern secular world difficult, if not virtually impossible. "Our ideologies," concluded Trudeau in somewhat overstated terms,

full of mistrust of industrialization, clinging to a desire for isolation and rural nostalgia, no longer corresponded to our ethos, thrown into disarray by anonymous capitalism, swayed by foreign influences, and transported without baggage into a modern *capharnaüm* where the family, the community, the parish – traditional bulwarks against chaos – no longer offered the same security. In an industrial society, such as developed by capitalism, other remedies were required to deal with illness, accidents, and old age, than the parish school, good neighbours, individual charity, and private initiative. But our social thought had imagined such inadequate solutions to these problems that it had managed to take root only in the written programs of artificial, useless, and debilitating associations. Meanwhile our living institutions, those whose very existence required them to remain in touch with reality, had to renounce all ideology or see their dynamism sacrificed.[18]

In his introduction to *La grève de l'amiante* Trudeau demonstrated effectively, to the satisfaction of his *Cité libre* colleagues, what Maurice Blain had claimed in 1952. That is, that various schools of nationalists had since 1900 contributed as much if not more to the dissemination and entrenchment of a rigid, authoritarian intellectual traditionalism than the oppressive clericalism of the Catholic church had achieved in well over a century.

These harsh and extreme allegations by Citélibristes constituted, in effect, a form of secular moralizing. There were, undoubtedly, factors other than nationalist ideology which accounted for the lack of political and social modernization of French-Canadian society but the Citélibristes paid no attention to these. This narrowmindedness led a couple of Citélibristes to question seriously the future of French-Canadian society, its culture, and language. Pierre Vadeboncoeur, the most pessimistic *Cité libre* member, questioned the prospects of renewal for the French-Canadian society. Could a culture which be characterized as sterile, negative, passive, and authoritarian save itself from total decay and collapse? He concluded that French Canada's future was bleak indeed.[19] It was psychologically impossible, he argued, for a culture based on the idea of "survival" to grasp the internal dynamic of its decadence because serious intellectual self-criticism of the essentials was considered taboo. Literary criticism, for example, was limited to secondary external problems – economic inferiority, failure of nationalist politics – "but the soul of the people, and in particular the soul of the individual, his level of energy, of courage, of independence, of intolerance, of injustice, of confidence, of liberty, and of the exercise of liberty, of intellectual toughness, of personalism, of internal autonomy, of determination, of spirit, of conquest, of passion, did not constitute subjects of analysis and certainly did not furnish the themes of major ideological movements."[20] The signs of moral and cultural decay and popular inertia had never provoked nationalist intellectuals to revolt against the reigning culture or to examine it critically, but rather had led them blindly to reaffirm their faith in that culture and the institutions associated with it. Vadeboncoeur's pessimism and Rioux's scepticism stemmed from their conviction that traditional nationalist thought barred all original and creative revolutionary action without which, in their estimation, any modern society was doomed to disappear.[21] While Vadeboncoeur felt nothing could be done to revive the dying corpse of French-Canadian culture, all other Citélibristes, including Rioux, believed in the possibility of a modern, secular, democratic, and pluralistic French-Canadian society emerging if the appropriate strategy of thought and action was undertaken.

CITÉ LIBRE'S ANTIDOTE TO NATIONALISM

How was the crisis to be resolved? *Cité libre*'s first suggestion was to invite French Canadians to examine objectively their culture, to assess its relative strengths and weaknesses, to attempt to close the gap between the definition of the collective self-image and the realities of the socioeconomic world in which their society functioned. Using arguments first developed by Maurice Tremblay, a Laval sociologist, Marcel Rioux contended that a national élite should not base its ideology on particularist and provincial elements or narrow class interests. An authentic national élite had the responsibility to use its prestige and influence to break "the narrow circle of national egoism and to apply itself continuously to the purging and the surpassing of ethnic particularism, especially by working for its development and maturation through an enriching contact with foreign cultural values susceptible of being assimilated."[22]

Again, following Tremblay's suggestion, *Cité libre* members questioned the traditional nationalists' definition of their culture as "minoritary, Catholic, and French." The majority of the French-Canadian people did not perceive themselves as members of an inferior minority, neither were they excessively nationalistic. Freed from the strait-jacket of nationalist doctrines, the majority of French Canadians, Rioux felt assured, would express their dynamism, confidence, and creativity. They would, in short, take their rightful place alongside other citizens of the world. Moreover, Catholicism in Quebec was not its highest and purest form, but rather a very specific French-Canadian Catholicism and in no way inherently superior to English-Canadian Protestantism. The Catholic French-Canadian culture could not claim to draw its distinctiveness from a theoretical moral and spiritual superiority. What counted was how French Canadians lived their Catholic beliefs.[23] Neither could the nationalists lay claim to defending the French culture and language in North America. Those elements, argued Rioux, had undergone a tremendous metamorphosis since the early days of New France. A specific French-Canadian culture and related language had taken root in Quebec and these should not be confused with the culture and language of modern France. French-Canadian literature was essentially North American literature of French inspiration. For nationalists to equate their culture with that of modern France was dishonest and misleading. The confusion prevented French Canadians from defining and coming to grips with the shortcomings of their own specific culture and language. The essence of the French mentality – a critical mind, a love of liberty, and a desire for creativity – had found refuge in a small group of French Canadians forced to live intellectually and psychologically, and in some cases physically, outside the mainstream of their own society.[24]

Vadeboncoeur, none the less, resigned himself to the eventual demise of the French-Canadian culture, a culture which lacked ambition, a sense of power, and the will to follow a cause to victory. French-Canadian politics and politicians were far too élitist, authoritarian, and nationalistic to fulfil in a revolutionary way the real needs of the people. Nationalism in a world dominated increasingly by the unifying and levelling forces of technology and economic development was a reactionary and anachronistic ideology. To believe in the importance of preserving national entities was futile, a pure waste of energy, and a sure sign of misinterpreting the forces of the modern world.[25] Working from a Marxist theory of superstructures, Vadeboncoeur suggested that French Canadians, if they wished to partake of the fruits of the modern world, follow existing socioeconomic and geographic imperatives to their logical extreme.

... a people of sparse population inhabits an immense territory, full of natural resources, neighbour of a nation which is in the process of engulfing the entire continent with its machines. Everything will be industrialized; wealth will create industry; industry will fully populate what is still a savage land. It is not we who will create the country but the machine and the foreigner. We have a political national vision, in tune with the rhythm of nature, with the natural increase of population, supported by the classical defences of distance and isolation in virgin territory, enjoying, in short, guarantees which are no longer in vogue. It is naïve to focus our attention on this national vision or to use it as an inspiration for our lives because it is no more than the ideological photograph of a situation whose conditions are in the process of disappearing. It is antidialectical to view our political situation first and to reason on the basis of the forces and an outdated situation that were able to provide us with some consistency. It is not this result which determines history, nor is it the ideal that these conditions created. What determines history are the actual forces at work – such as industrialization, our natural resources, the population those resources will attract, American expansion, progressive universal uniformization, the influx of high levels of foreign cultures, the forced contamination of our language, the general substitution of American values for ours – which are invading us on all sides and undermining us. To be dialectical is to perceive that these hidden forces constitute the essentials.[26]

The majority of Citélibristes were not amused. While accepting Vadeboncoeur's diagnosis they rejected his antinationalist Marxist cure. They spurned his overly pessimistic economic determinism and refused to despair of the survival of the French-Canadian society. Pelletier, expressing the group's strong dissent, quoted the French author André Malraux to the effect that "For better or for worse, we are tied to the homeland ... The revolutionary who does not possess a sense of faithfulness will become despite himself a Fascist."[27] The *Cité libre* group wanted the French-

Canadian collectivity to strive to become an open, democratic, pluralistic, and humanistic society adjusted to the realities of the present and capable of confronting all reasonable challenges. Citélibristes firmly rejected a societal model based on mere survival or the nationalist imperative – *L'Etat français* – which according to Canon Groulx had to be imposed upon the history of North America. On the other hand, neither could they condone the argument that a collectivity, merely because it was weak and poor, should have to cut itself off from its past voluntarily by encouraging and collaborating with the unifying and levelling forces of technology, economic development, and American imperialistic nationalism. "On the verge of the abyss," countered Pelletier, "I do not accept suicide. That the abyss kills us, this we cannot control. That is its business, not ours. It does not need our collaboration to carry out its task."[28]

Fernand Dumont, agreeing wholeheartedly with *Cité libre*'s dissenting opinion, provided a solid sociological argument for the perpetuation of distinct cultural entities. From a sociopsychological perspective, he argued, the achievement of self-awareness constituted the deepest form of intellectual revolution. This self-knowledge was not attained through contact with a theoretical universal humanism, but rather by living and understanding one's own culture. Any attempt at short-circuiting the process would lead to an ideological outlook divorced from the realities of one's own society. Such had been the fate of traditional nationalism, which emphasized the attainment of self-awareness through the discovery of a mythical and systematized past interpreted so rigidly that it offered no options for future behaviour. In this framework the only alternatives were acceptance or rejection, neither of which led to a creative pursuit of humanist values. The homogeneous, petty bourgeois interpretation of French Canada's past had to be supplemented by a pluralistic account which considered the perspective and role of all classes, especially the working class. Only a new, more realistic, collective self-image, which took into consideration all social classes and contemporary socioeconomic conditions, could ensure that French-Canadian culture possessed "a destiny and a choice."[29] In sum, French Canada needed a new history, or better still, a series of histories affirming the pluralist nature of its past.

Yet French Canada required more than a pluralistic interpretation of its past. What was also urgently required, according to the Citélibristes, was a strong and viable French-Canadian left-wing intelligentsia to serve as an ideological counter-force to the all-pervasive nationalist right. Nationalism and nationalists were, in the *Cité libre* perspective, inherently conservative, concerned with preserving and transmitting, with seeing the world strictly from a particularist, provincial perspective.[30] A strong and influential left-wing intelligentsia, however, could challenge the established order and work to establish a new social order based on Catholic personalist philosophy, secular humanism, and North American liberal and social democracy. Speaking for all Citélibristes, Marcel Rioux rejected the intense, sincere pessimism of Vadeboncoeur and opted for the creation of a "gauche cana-dienne-français" which would, in due course, bring about the integration of a revitalized and dynamic French-Canadian society into the mainstream of North America.

Far from despairing about the future of the French Canadians, the Left will know how to place them in the mainstream of history. At a time when the ideology of the Right is demonstrating its pessimism and wonders how many years the "race" will endure, it is time to show confidence in one's people and to contest the ideology that has oppressed them for two centuries. The term leftist must not scare enlightened Catholics; to fight ignorance, narrow-mindedness, and caste interests is not doing the work of perdition. To rise against the stagnation and the unrealism of a fossilized ideology is to have faith in man, it is to rely upon the desire for improvement which appeared on earth with man and which is one of his highest and noblest charac-teristics.[31]

Subsequent chapters will delineate the nature and contours of the liberal ideology proclaimed essential by Citélibristes to counterbalance the conser-vative and ethnocentrist thrust of traditional French-Canadian nationalism and to create a modern, secular, liberal society.

THE NATIONALISTS REACT

Naturally *Cité libre*'s strong critique and condemnation of traditional na-tionalist thought provoked a hostile reaction from its lay and clerical expo-nents. Father Marie-Joseph d'Anjou, the editor of the traditional nationalist Jesuit periodical *Relations*, denounced the group as irrepressible anticlericals and suggested a ban on *Cité libre*.[32] In fact, *Cité libre* was banned in some classical colleges and when Pelletier and Trudeau approached Bishop Léger they received a cool reception and no assurance that college rectors would be requested to lift the ban.[33] The event that sparked a concerted traditional nationalist counter-attack was the appearance in 1956 of Trudeau's compre-hensive and devastating critique of French-Canadian nationalism in his introduction to *La grève de l'amiante*. Robert Rumilly was infuriated, and he immediately set out to unmask and denounce what he considered to be a left-wing or socialist conspiracy to destroy the French-Canadian Catholic nation of Quebec. As stated earlier, Rumilly considered French left-wing Catholics to be allied with what he regarded as anti-Catholic forces, namely, France's Socialist and Communist parties. The periodical *Esprit*, founded by Emmanuel Mounier in 1932 and taken over in 1952 by Jean-Marie Domenach after the former's death, was considered by Rumilly to be in the vanguard of an influential movement of left-wing Catholics trying to "humanize" socialist and communist doctrines to make them acceptable to a majority of Catholics.[34] *Cité libre* and its members, in Rumilly's view, were attempting to achieve the same objective in Quebec with the full support of Radio-Canada and the "leftists" at *Le Devoir* and *L'Action nationale*, in the labour movement, and in the CCF.[35]

One forceful critic of Trudeau's and *Cité libre*'s condemnation of French-Canadian nationalism was the Jesuit Father Jacques Cousineau. As a member of the Commission sacerdotales d'études sociales and moral councillor of the Conseil central des syndicats de Montréal, Father Cousineau participated in the Catholic church's eventually successful endeavours to resolve the asbestos strike in 1949. Cousineau charged that Trudeau's introduction to *La grève de l'amiante*, by denigrating French-Canadian nationalist thought and ignoring the important role of the church in the resolution of the strike, "empties of its essential meaning an important and painful event of our social life."[36] Cousineau rejected Trudeau's interpretation that the asbestos strike was a break with the past because the asbestos workers, rejecting Catholic social doctrine and nationalist myths, had undertaken French Canada's first real movement of socioeconomic emancipation. The strike, asserted Cousineau, marked the maturation and dynamism of the Catholic and national labour movement and was an expression of "our" Catholic social doctrine.[37] Trudeau had idealized and mythologized the asbestos strike because such an interpretation reinforced his hypothesis that a monolithic, idealistic, and backward-looking nationalist creed had retarded the political and social modernization of French Canada. Trudeau's description and analysis of twentieth-century French-Canadian social thought was, in Cousineau's view, false because it was incomplete, methodologically flawed, and distorted by his personal doctrinal prejudices. "His value judgments," concluded Cousineau, "are based upon well-known norms, those of the CCF and PSD programs, both characterized by a rigid and passionate idealism bordering on utopianism."[38] François-Albert Angers, promoted to the post of editor of *L'Action nationale* after the neo-nationalists had abandoned its editorial board in 1956, published a six-part diatribe against *Cité libre* focused on Trudeau's critique of French-Canadian nationalism.

Angers attempted to discredit the Citélibristes by denouncing what he called the "libellous," "socialist," "revolutionary" overtones of their exaggerated declarations concerning French-Canadian nationalism and its adherents. "In wanting to build from scratch a new society without using the materials or the methods of the old society," *Cité libre*, contended Angers, "was assuming responsibility for a society which will not be ours. It will be so similar to the Anglo-Canadian society which dominates Canada that, failing to distinguish themselves, both societies will almost inevitably assimilate one another."[39] Taking his analysis one step further, Angers argued vigorously that the *Cité libre* interpretation of French-Canadian nationalism, like a house of cards, was built on a shaky foundation. *Cité libre*'s fatal hubris resided in the fact that its members were all unconscious prisoners of the corrupted sense of objectivity inherent in Marxist methodological concepts.[40] In short, educated French Canadians need not waste their time reading *Cité libre*. The assumptions and methodology of its authors were seriously in doubt, and consequently, little of intellectual value could flow from their pens! More importantly, *Cité libre*'s misguided antinationalism would only serve to bring about the assimilation of French Canadians by the English-Canadian majority.

Trudeau ignored F.-A. Angers' diatribe because he had always considered him to be extremely right-wing. He was, however, disturbed by Father Cousineau's critique, especially when it appeared in pamphlet form under the auspices of the Institut social populaire and was circulated widely throughout the province under the imprimatur of the church. What made Trudeau even more upset was Father Richard Arès' refusal to publish either Trudeau's "Critique d'une critique" or his short letter drawing the attention of *Relations'* readers to his assessment of Cousineau's critique. In his "Critique d'une critique" Trudeau reasserted his interpretation of the absestos strike by poking holes in Cousineau's counter-interpretation and by pointing out the contradictions, errors, slanders, distortions, sophisms, and sloppy methodology in Cousineau's attempt to undermine his critique of French-Canadian nationalism. Trudeau remained convinced that *La grève de l'amiante*, despite its faults, had begun the process of demystifying the past and had laid the foundation for elaborating a clearly defined social philosophy, one capable of meeting the challenges of the industrial revolution.[41]

The neo-nationalist response to *Cité libre*'s critique of nationalism was, as we have seen, somewhat ambivalent. After all, neo-nationalists themselves had roundly condemned what they termed the excessive idealism of traditional French-Canadian nationalism. What made them feel uncomfortable with the *Cité libre* critique of French-Canadian nationalism was its authors' belief that all forms of nationalism were inherently unprogressive, undemocratic, and antimodern. Jean-Guy Blain questioned Trudeau's use of a single historical event to explain French Canada's isolationism and the inertia of its social values and institutional structure. "This situation was due less to nationalist doctrine which, as compensation, served us as ideological fodder, than to an ethnic handicap which only history could explain fully."[42] Pierre de Grandpré wondered how traditional nationalism, an ideology that was consciously opposed to secularism and industrialization, could reflect the socioeconomic realities of such a society.[43] Trudeau's essay, responded Laurendeau, was excellent polemic but unjust and inaccurate history. Nevertheless, his denunciation of nationalist thought for failing to recognize the inevitability of the industrial revolution was, in Laurendeau's view, quite valid. Trudeau had outlined the problem – the excessive idealism of nationalist thought – and described its practical consequences with great precision and scathing wit. What he had failed to do satisfactorily was to elucidate the "why?", that is, the complex of historical reasons – social, cultural, economic, and political – that had fostered and nurtured the ideology. Despite Trudeau's polemical approach and oversimplified generalizations, Laurendeau willingly acknowledged that the essay revealed new insights, new truths. "What is best in Trudeau, other than this technical competence, is his love of liberty; he welcomes its risks as well as its advantages. A remarkable personality is being revealed."[44] The road for compromise and further discussion had been consciously left open by the neo-nationalists.

CONCLUSION

Cité libre's opposition to nationalism was both ideological and political. As Christian humanists and liberal and social democrats, the Citélibristes considered nationalism to be irrevocably and inherently conservative, anti-democratic, and reactionary. Nationalism placed a priority on collective values and interests at the cost of neglecting and, on occasion, opposing universal human values, such as freedom of expression, freedom of creed. Furthermore, nationalists seldom gave the appropriate priority to the socio-economic advancement of the individual or the weaker groups and classes in society. On the political level the ruling Union Nationale party and its astute and wily *chef*, Maurice Duplessis, used nationalist rhetoric to retain office and prevent the modernization of Quebec society. In short, nationalism and nationalist programs, when they were implemented, served the vested interests of the established secular and clerical élites, anglophone and francophone, at the expense of the needs of the Quebec people. Nationalism, by camouflaging the real interests and ambitions of its advocates, distorted the true meaning and operation of parliamentary democracy. All in all, there was little in the *Cité libre* analysis to endear the group to either traditional or neo-nationalists. A close scrutiny of how both groups approached certain fundamental issues, such as the role of the modern state, will illustrate the basic divergences between their respective ideologies.

CHAPTER SIX

The Nationalist versus the Liberal State

French Canadians will remain drawers of water and hewers of wood, small shop-keepers and small-time investors, with a few millionaires here and there, as long as they do not learn to use the only government at their disposal to elaborate and carry out a grand economic strategy.[1]

It is now well established and readily accepted that Quebec under the regime of Maurice Duplessis's Union Nationale experienced a considerable lag in political modernization. More specifically, the growth of an active, interventionist state did not follow the rapid social and economic developments experienced since 1940.[2] Under these circumstances both neo-nationalists and Citélibristes turned toward the state as the major key to achieving the modernization of Quebec society. The groups did so for different motives and from divergent ideological perspectives and societal models. Neo-nationalists became ardent proponents of an activist and inter-ventionist Quebec state to redress what they had come to perceive was the dominant threat to the continued survival of their nation, that is, the growing economic inferiority of French Canadians as individuals and as a collectivity. French Canadians had to become economic as well as political masters in their own house – *Maîtres chez nous* became the neo-nationalist motto – if they were going to create a modern, dynamic, secular French-Canadian society capable of resisting the powerful assimilationist pressures of English-speaking Canada and North America. Nationalism, which for so long had played a role in undermining the growth of the Quebec state, now became a powerful tool in the hands of neo-nationalist state-builders. Citélibristes also strongly believed in the need for a dynamic, interventionist Quebec state, but only if such a development had as its prime objective the expansion and fulfilment of individual rights through increased political and social democracy. The neo-liberal state must endeavour to provide its citizens with greater equality of opportunity and an enhanced equality of condition.

The neo-liberal state must not champion the collective rights of one ethnic group or class at the expense of other ethnic groups, classes, or individuals.

OPPONENTS OF
STATE-BUILDING

There are a number of explanations for the long-standing and effective opposition to the creation of a powerful and dynamic Quebec state. Both neo-nationalists and Citélibristes had pointed to the influence of traditional French-Canadian nationalism preached by the dominant majority of Quebec's intelligentsia, namely, the clerical and lay professoriat and some liberal professionals. Having defined French-Canadian society as fundamentally spiritual, personalist, decentralist, and pluralistic, these spokesmen for traditional nationalism, Father Richard Arès, François-Albert Angers, and Esdras Minville, reiterated constantly that statism, *dirigisme*, and all forms of socialism constituted the gravest threat to the continued survival of French Canada. These forms of political and economic organization would produce a society resembling that of English Canada, a society characterized by materialism, centralization, secularism, and homogeneity.[3] These lay and clerical nationalists believed sincerely in their vision of French Canada but it is also clear that they propagated this anachronistic vision because it served to maintain their vested interests. This was particularly evident in the case of the Catholic church. Its leaders wielded an enormous amount of prestige, social control, and economic power through their pervasive control of social welfare, health, and educational services in the province. Administrative and management skills acquired in these areas could and were applied to the operating of parish and diocese structures on a more professional and business-like basis. The power and prestige involved undoubtedly enhanced the recruitment of many of French Canada's brightest young men and women into the multitude of religious orders and communities. While the remunerative benefits were slim, virtual job security and care in old age were guaranteed.[4] The most comprehensive synthesis of the traditional nationalist viewpoint on the question of the role of the state can be found in the 1956 report of the Tremblay Commission set up to inquire into all aspects of Quebec's role in the Canadian constitutional system. Arès, Angers, and Minville all played leading roles in the commission and determined the thrust of its views on the role of the state in such areas as health and social welfare. The Tremblay commissioners contended that the "French-Canadian conception of social assistance based on the triple foundation of the family, voluntary associations, and the church has been sufficiently flexible to respond to the needs created by the successive emergence of the pioneer, rural, and urban types of family and, with the aid of the state, to the new situations born of industrialization and urbanization."[5] The Tremblay commissioners concluded that the state should play only a minor, supportive role in health and social welfare programs.

The second impediment to the growth of the Quebec state came from the deeply entrenched laissez-faire economic philosophy of business circles, both anglophone and francophone. Even the beleaguered French-Canadian business community, located primarily in the retail trade and service industries and expressing its views through the local, regional, and provincial chambers of commerce, remained in the 1950s firmly wedded to the precepts of free enterprise. French-Canadian advocates of strong economic nationalist measures, such as Olivar Asselin, Dr Philippe Hamel, and the Bloc Populaire Canadien, received little if any support from the French-Canadian private sector. In fact, traditional nationalists like F.-A. Angers and Esdras Minville had considerable influence on the Montreal Chamber of Commerce in the 1950s and they helped to prepare its submission to the Tremblay Commission in 1955. The thrust of the business community's argument against a strong and active state was that, given the appropriate legislative measures and taxing policies, French-Canadian businessmen would be able to gain for themselves a greater degree of control over the development of Quebec's economy. In what appeared to be an endlessly expanding economy, French Canada's business community felt confident that it could compete successfully with English-Canadian and foreign business if it mastered modern business techniques and reorganized its sources of financing. In short, if French-Canadian businessmen emulated successfully their English-speaking competitors they would, in due course, come to play a larger role in Quebec's booming economy.[6] Only in the late 1950s when Quebec began to suffer the effects of a growing recession would French-Canadian business leaders begin to perceive the benefits of increased state participation in the economy.

In the end, however, the most effective opponents of political modernization were Premier Maurice Duplessis and the Union Nationale. It has been well documented that Maurice Duplessis was a deeply conservative, cautious man, especially after the humiliating defeat of his party in the 1939 provincial election at the hands of Quebec's anglophone economic élite and the federal Liberal party.[7] Determined to prevent his government from becoming too dependent upon the anglophone financial and industrial élite which dominated Quebec's economy, Duplessis rejected a policy of large public borrowing and relied on current revenues to finance capital projects.[8] This policy, of course, obstructed any new state initiatives because these required immediate tax increases to ensure a balanced budget. Duplessis was by nature, and ideological conviction, a powerful advocate of free enterprise. He made it very clear in the 1948 throne speech that the role of government was not to control the economy. "We are of the opinion that state paternalism is the enemy of all real progress. We believe that the province of Quebec will be developed more rationally and more rapidly by sound and fair private enterprise."[9] Little wonder that Duplessis looked up to and befriended a number of English-Canadian and American corporate barons, namely, the Cleveland industrialist Cyrus Eaton, R.E. Powell of the Aluminium Company of Canada, J.W. McConnell of the Montreal *Star*, and Jack Bassett of the Montreal *Gazette*. Ironically, Duplessis' commitment to classical free enterprise was stronger than their own. When they tried to encourage the premier to expand Hydro-Quebec so as to attract more high-energy consuming industries such as steel-processing, aluminium refining, and petrochemicals he refused for fear that taxes would have to be increased.[10]

Even if Duplessis had agreed to nationalize Quebec's private hydroelectric companies it is very doubtful that his cabinet or caucus would have supported him. The 1936 victory of the Union Nationale, according to Robert Boily, marked the arrival of a professional political élite which he terms "la partitocratie," that is, an élite of career politicians devoted to the well-being of the party that kept them in power. These professional politicians, drawn from the ranks of the lower middle class of "small traders, merchants, and local administrators," owed their political success not to the traditional source of social and economic power, the "upper bourgeoisie," but rather to the party, its leader, and its organization. Twelve of Duplessis' thirty-four cabinet ministers came from this lower middle class which accounted for a third of the members of the legislature.[11] Furthermore, the fact that the vast majority of Union Nationale legislators – 90 per cent in 1952 and 85 per cent in 1956 – represented constituencies outside the metropolitan regions of Montreal and Quebec City explains why this professional élite which dominated the Union Nationale caucus and cabinet experienced little or no pressure from its constituents to modernize the political process and the political and governmental institutions of Quebec. Nor did Union Nationale politicians wish to see their power base in the legislature eroded by the more highly educated and skilled bureaucracy that would be required by an active, expanded state.[12] It was in this context that neo-nationalists and Citélibristes hammered out their respective approaches to the role of the state in modern Quebec.

THE ROOTS OF ECONOMIC INFERIORITY

Undoubtedly the most significant ideological impact of the renewed industrialization and urbanization of Quebec after 1940 was the realization by most elements of the French-Canadian intelligentsia of the devastating effects of economic subservience and the extraordinary potential of economic power. Buried once and for all was the long-standing myth that the economy of Quebec was backward, that the province lagged behind in the development of its natural and human resources. This argument had been used all

too frequently and effectively to rationalize and justify the economic inferiority of the French Canadians as individuals and as a collectivity. The fact
that the Anglo-Saxon, Protestant minority prospered in this "sea" of economic backwardness only served to reinforce the oft-repeated cliché that
anglophones were inherently suited to the pursuit of the almighty dollar no
matter what the obstacles were.

"Let us be wealthy or we will perish," was Pierre Laporte's summons to
his compatriots celebrating the Saint-Jean Baptiste national holiday on 24
June 1956.[13] By the mid-1950s what set neo-nationalists clearly apart from
their clerically minded, conservative predecessors was the firm conviction
that "spiritual and cultural values have to be buttressed by economic realities, that is, they must reside on solid material foundations."[14] Neo-nationalists were all keenly aware that Quebec's economy was undergoing a vigorous expansionary thrust in nearly all areas except agriculture. The print and
electronic media issued daily reports of new and projected investment in all
the resource industries as well as in residential, commercial, and public
construction projects. While not a phenomenal boom, the growth of the
Quebec economy in the decade and a half after the war was steady and
relatively uniform. The vast majority of the province's inhabitants experienced a modest improvement in their standard of living, while a minority,
through luck and skill, found their way into the ranks of a regenerated
plutocracy without the appropriate social and cultural values and behaviour
to match their new-found wealth and status. While the standard of living in
Quebec could not match that of Ontario or many regions of the United
States, the vast majority of Quebec families by the late fifties had electric
refrigerators, telephones, and radios, while many could boast of an automobile, television, and perhaps a summer cottage.[15]

Ironically, it was this increasing material prosperity which complicated
the neo-nationalists' task of convincing the francophone community at large
that its collective economic situation was deteriorating at an alarming rate.
Taking stock of the situation in May 1954, Gérard Filion concluded that in
the proper definition of the term there simply did not exist in Quebec a
French-Canadian capitalist economy.

French-Canadian industry is backward. It is virtually absent from the exploitation
of the natural resources which are at the heart of the economic prosperity of the
North American continent. It is barely present in the pulp and paper industry; it is
represented by only a handful of companies in the mining field; only a small number
of secondary hydro-electric companies belong to French-Canadian industrialists.
French Canadians are better represented in high finance yet the powerful corporations still do not belong to them. In the manufacturing sector, French Canadians are
absent in the aircraft, the railroad rolling stock, the automobile, the chemical, and
the electrical appliance industries, to name only a few. It is only in the construction,

the shoe, and the textile (other than cotton) industries that French Canadians really play a strong role.[16]

Nor was there, even in embryonic form, a French-Canadian financial and industrial bourgeoisie. French Canadians sitting on the boards of directors of large corporations were integrated with an Anglo-Saxon and North American capitalist structure. Most retained their positions because of their personal qualities or because of the political services they rendered these corporations vis-à-vis various levels of government in Quebec. In no case were these francophones representative of an indigenous and autonomous French-Canadian capitalist economy which they could claim to own and direct.[17]

In May and June of 1956, Jean-Marc Léger, while in the employ of *La Presse*, made a close assessment of the economic situation of French-Canadian society and his conclusions were as alarming as those of Filion. French Canadians were simply, Léger wrote, "at the moment of the technological revolution, of automation, of corporate concentrations, in sum, at the moment when the economic landscape of the country was changing at an unprecedented rate, the beneficiaries, the parasites, of prosperity created by others, . . . simply put, better-paid servants because their masters were better off than before."[18] The initiative, the capital, the administrative and financial talent, and the technological know-how for the renewed expansion of Quebec's economy since 1940 had come not from French-Canadian corporations but almost exclusively from American, British, Anglo-Canadian, and Eastern European firms. These firms were only too eager to exploit Quebec's immense natural resources, abundant hydro-electric energy, and relatively cheap labour to produce commodities for the North American and international markets. By 1957, 25 per cent of Quebec's manufacturing production came from American branch plants, most of it destined for American consumers. Only a handful of French-Canadian firms had managed to build up markets outside the province. In the area of finance, two French-Canadian banks retained only 7 per cent of the total active assets held by Canadian banks, while in the province of Quebec less than 10 per cent of all life insurance sold was underwritten by French-Canadian companies. Except for a few small bus and trucking companies, French Canadians were conspicuous by their absence from the fields of transportation and communications. A clear indication that French-Canadian enterprises had not made the shift to big corporate business was revealed daily by the fact that only 1 per cent of the active stocks listed on both Montreal stock exchanges belonged to French-Canadian firms. Furthermore, only 5 per cent (400) of the 8,000 company directors listed in the 1954 *Directory of Directors* were French Canadians. Little wonder that the French-Canadian people, nearly 30 per cent of the Canadian population, could lay claim to only 7 or 8 per cent of the country's wealth, while in Quebec where they constituted 80 per cent of the population their share of the wealth amounted to little more than 25 per cent.[19]

Contacts between English and French Canadians on the professional and economic levels were numerous and constant. But unfortunately these contacts were characterized not by equality but rather by subordination. The economic life of the province was dominated by English-speaking Canadians and Americans who conducted their business on a national and international basis with little reference to the socioeconomic needs of the Quebec region. French-Canadian subordination in the economic sphere was partly responsible, in Parenteau's view, for the limited contacts between the two ethnic communities in other spheres of activity such as politics, education, the arts, leisure, and family life.[20] The "two solitudes" persisted and, all in all, little progress had been accomplished since the turn of the century when Errol Bouchette had summoned and cajoled his people to pursue aggressively majority control of all sectors of their economic life, including the all-important industrial sector.[21] The gap between the two communities had indeed widened, thereby setting off a search for more fundamental causes to help the increasingly frustrated French-Canadian middle-class spokesmen explain their and their nation's continued subordination in the economic realm to the anglophone minority.

By the end of the 1950s no stone had been left unturned or dark corner unlit in the process of trying to explain this state of subordination. All possible cultural reasons – educational, psychological, sociological, religious, and ideological – had been duly and appropriately scrutinized and the French Canadians had been found wanting on all accounts.[22] In general, the neo-nationalists supported the critical examination of the francophone collective mentality by Quebec's first generation of social scientists. While consistently seeking more satisfactory explanations, they rejected neither the importance nor the persistence of a wide range of internal cultural and ideological impediments to the economic advancement of their people.

Thanks to the work of economists like Albert Faucher, Jacques Mélançon, and Roland Parenteau, it was generally conceded that French Canadians could no longer plead an absence of capital as a means of rationalizing their nonparticipation in big business. French Canadians, it was demonstrated, were ardent savers. While a good proportion of these savings found its way into English-Canadian banks and financial institutions, over $2 billion was held by French-Canadian banks and financial institutions in 1956. Neither could the standard cliché that French Canadians were inherently unsuited to business activities hold water. The vast majority of small and medium-sized Quebec firms were owned and operated by French Canadians, and these firms represented about 50 per cent of the total number.[23] Having debunked these long-standing explanations, francophone economists and political economists focused serious attention on the behavioural patterns and educational background of French Canadians active in commerce and industry. The Achilles heel of French-Canadian businessmen, concluded these specialists, was their inability and/or unwillingness to move beyond the middle stage of family-run and financed enterprises into the realm of large, anonymous, public-funded corporations wherein managerial, technical, and administrative skills were clearly defined and segregated from the financial aspects of doing business. French-Canadian commercial and industrial capitalism remained, at mid-century, almost exclusively familial in structure and mentality.[24] Little consideration was given as to why this was the case, but when pushed to the wall for answers these economists usually referred to cultural and ideological factors rather than political ones.

The neo-nationalists, especially the business-minded Filion, readily agreed that the French-Canadian businessman's obsession with family ownership was preventing the formation of powerful francophone corporations and acquisition of a twentieth-century capitalist mentality.[25] Large corporations were quickly becoming the norm and the creative force in the economy. It was high time that French Canadians, wrote Filion, "stop living as small investors satisfied with placing their savings in state funds or parish and religious community debentures. Everything considered, it would be a hundred times better to place these debentures in New York or Toronto and to use our own capital to finance commerce and industry. Because in the modern world it is economic activity, it is dams, factories, stores, hotels, transportation companies which are the indicators of a people's true strength."[26] French-Canadian capital resources had been used by the English-Canadian financial institutions to guarantee anglophone control over the most important sectors of Quebec's economy. In effect, French Canadians, through their conservative investment habits, had contributed to their position of economic inferiority vis-à-vis the anglophone minority.[27]

When, by the mid-1950s, it became increasingly clear that changing the mental outlook of both French-Canadian businessmen and French-Canadian investors was simply not going to create, in itself, a dynamic and influential francophone-dominated private sector, the neo-nationalists began to look for alternative explanations and solutions. It was at this point that the neo-nationalists became increasingly receptive to the political interpretation being elaborated by the Montreal school of neo-nationalist historians, namely Michel Brunet, Maurice Séguin, and Guy Frégault. An intense personal commitment to the development of a modern, secular nation whose economy would be controlled by an indigenous francophone financial and industrial bourgeoisie motivated these professional historians in their reinterpretation of French Canada's past.[28] All three practised a "functionalist" conception of history and like their clerical nationalist precursors perceived their discipline as a nationalist vehicle for creating "a growing awareness that will lead to a more realistic and effective form of collective action."[29]

It was Maurice Séguin's 1947 doctoral analysis of the post-Conquest agricultural economy of Lower Canada which prompted a reinterpretation of the socioeconomic and governmental structures of New France and a revaluation of the impact of the Conquest itself on the French colony established along the banks of the St Lawrence.[30] Rejecting the accepted interpretation, Séguin argued that the serious crisis in Lower Canada's agricultural economy was structural in nature. That is, it was caused by the continued lack of stable external markets and the overly competitive position of cheaper wheat from Upper Canada and the American Midwest. Consequently, Lower Canadian society turned to the development of a strong commercial economy based on the production and transportation of staples such as timber and wheat, the latter primarily from Upper Canada and the American Midwest. Rural depopulation, then, while aggravated by poor agricultural techniques, subdivision, and shortages of good arable land due to speculation by the Chateau clique, was inevitable and normal given the economic imperatives of the region. The real question to ask, claimed Séguin, was why French-Canadian society had become so closely identified with an agricultural way of life from which its members could only escape through the church, the liberal professions, and working-class occupations, while the fields of commerce, finance, and industry remained virtually closed to French Canadians.[31]

Contrary to the teachings of the clerical-nationalist historians like Groulx, who stressed that New France constituted "an essentially Catholic and Latin society" dominated by "a contented agricultural class,"[32] the Montreal school elaborated a secularist picture of a "normal" colonial society in which no single occupation was closed to the ambitious habitants and the economy was dominated by a commercial bourgeoisie, the real motor force of the colony. Taking his cue from Séguin, Guy Frégault, in a 1954 pamphlet entitled Canadian Society in the French Regime, secularized completely his earlier interpretation. He wrote in part:

Titled or not, the lesser nobility or the upper middle class, the upper stratum of society, enriched by commerce, set the tone of Canadian society. It constituted an oligarchy which shared the trading posts, occupied most of the public offices, and distinguished itself in military expeditions. In fact it was that group which had built up Canada, the Canada which disappeared in 1760, by developing its economy, directing its territorial expansion and inspiring its politics . . .

Such seemed to be, around 1750, the social structure of Canada. At the bottom, the peasants on the seigneuries and the artisans in the towns; above, the commercial groups, including a middle class and an aristocracy in which were included the civil and military officers, who, having control of affairs, had the destiny of the country in their hands.[33]

In the mid-1950s this revisionist view became the officially sanctioned historical version duly preached by the Société Saint-Jean-Baptiste de Montréal. Michel Brunet, the author of the Société's brief to the Tremblay Commission, claimed that toward the end of French colonial rule in North America, Canada possessed nearly forty millionaires. "These directors of the Canadian economy constituted a true capitalist bourgeoisie, a class of entrepreneurs required by societies in order to develop normally and progressively."[34] In brief, the French had colonized New France in the fullest sense of the term, exploiting to the greatest extent possible at that time all commercial, industrial, and human resources at their disposal.

What cataclysmic event or series of events could explain the absence of a French-Canadian commercial and financial bourgeoisie in the mid-nineteenth century and, more closely related to the contemporary concerns of the Montreal school, the virtual nonexistence of a vibrant French-Canadian industrial bourgeoisie in the mid-twentieth century? Reflecting his secular nationalist assumptions, Maurice Séguin signalled out one historical event, the military conquest of the French colony by the British forces in 1759–60, to explain his people's inability to continue to colonize in the integral sense of the term.[35]

Both Guy Frégault and Michel Brunet concurred in this interpretation and neither felt the need to qualify with a single reservation this thesis.[36] In fact, the Conquest thesis gained strong momentum along with the turbulent career of the historian Michel Brunet, who devoted his available research time to assembling "irrefutable" evidence documenting the short- and long-term consequences of Wolfe's victory over Montcalm on that fatal September day in 1759. The immediate impact of the Conquest had involved the emigration of New France's governing élite of administrators, military leaders, and entrepreneurs back to the metropolitan centre, France. What remained of the commercial élite was too small and weak to compete successfully with the British merchants who received the lion's share of government contracts and had advantageous ties with supply houses and credit firms in the new metropolitan centre, England. As a result, French Canadians within a generation lost financial control over the fur trade and transatlantic commerce. Out of necessity and drawn by an innate impulse for survival, French Canadians withdrew almost exclusively into agriculture, local trade, and related crafts.[37] "The Canadian nationality," wrote Brunet in 1955,

no longer possessed, thirty years after the Conquest, the cadres necessary for a society of the Atlantic world to develop beyond the point it had reached at the time of the Conquest: a sociological phenomenon not due to the malice of man. This colonial society had prematurely lost its metropolitan tie. Forced to rely upon its own resources, it was doomed to an anaemic collective survival. It could no longer benefit from the enlightened and dynamic leadership of an economically independent bourgeoisie, devoted entirely to the community's interests as an ethnic group and capable of building a political, economic, social, and cultural system exclusively in its service.[38]

The possibility of New France evolving into a "normal" North American industrial society with the majority nation of French Canadians at the helm of the Quebec state had been vitiated by the Conquest of 1760.[39]

Moreover, the Conquest, contended Michel Brunet in a provocative 1957 essay, had led to the domination of French-Canadian social and national thought by agriculturalism, antistatism, and messianism. Choosing his sources selectively, Brunet demonstrated to his satisfaction the restrictive and monolithic nature of French Canada's socioeconomic thought, which for over a century and a half had continually preached the virtues of the rural way of life, a hands off policy for the Quebec government in all social and economic matters except agricultural subsidies, and the firm conviction that the French-Canadian nation was inherently superior both spiritually and intellectually and therefore had a divine mission to disseminate its Catholicism and French culture to a predominantly Protestant, Anglo-Saxon, and materialist North American society.[40] In short, French Canada's clerical nationalist intelligentsia had rationalized the economic superiority of the anglophone minority by elaborating a nationalist ideology which emphasized noneconomic objectives, thereby concealing the true source of continued economic inferiority, the political domination of the minority nation by the majority nation.

Most neo-nationalists welcomed the strategic importance of, and the psychological relief afforded by, this shifting of responsibility for franco-phone economic inferiority from cultural, geographic, and economic factors to the political factor. They supported Brunet's critique of the conservative social thought and programs of the traditional nationalists because it con-firmed their own views. Referring to the Ecole sociale populaire and its incessant dissemination of the social doctrine of the Catholic church, Filion questioned its practicality and its excessive conservatism. "Probably very few people as underdeveloped as French Canadians have been reminded so often of the sacred nature of free enterprise," declared Filion during one of the recurring debates over the importance of the social doctrine of the Papal Encyclicals.[41] The neo-nationalists incorporated the Conquest thesis into their analysis of modern Quebec and it helped shape, to a considerable degree, the solutions they recommended in order to guarantee that, once and for all, the "iron curtain" surrounding the francophone community would be broken.[42]

THE STATE OF QUEBEC: KEY TO
ECONOMIC LIBERATION

Once neo-nationalists were convinced that the root cause of French-Canadian economic subservience was essentially political, that is, the Conquest of 1760, then it was inevitable that they would turn to a political solution. The step was not a difficult one to take. Laurendeau and Filion had, as members of the Bloc Populaire, supported the concept of *l'Etat du Québec*, that is, the creation of an aggressive, interventionist, social welfare state willing and capable of nationalizing key sectors of the economy. Furthermore, by the mid- and late fifties neo-nationalists realized that French Canadians were not, of their own accord, going to penetrate the realm of the industrial, financial, and commercial giants. The francophone private sector lacked technological expertise, unlimited capital resources, and trained personnel. Neither were sufficient numbers of francophones being allowed into the top echelons of the existing Anglo-Canadian, British, and American firms. The phenomenon of ethnic discrimination simply was too deeply entrenched to expect any progress from the anglophone-dominated private sector.[43] The only effective alternative open to French-Canadian society and its rapidly expanding new and old middle classes was the creation of a dynamic, interventionist Quebec state. This political instrument would enable French Canadians to become masters in their own house. To deny them this alternative, the neo-nationalists warned, was to feed the dangerous fires of social and political revolution.[44]

French Canadians, argued neo-nationalists with force and conviction, had to abandon their fear of the state and put their government to work for them as individuals and as a collectivity. They must overcome the church's fear of secularization and socialism and the petty bourgeoisie's blind adherence to the doctrines of laissez-faire capitalism.[45] No contemporary industrial society, argued the neo-nationalists, could survive for long if it continued to rely strictly on the private sector to furnish the socioeconomic and cultural needs of its citizens. In 1867 French Canadians, for the first time since the Conquest, had regained majority political control over the province of Quebec. This province, like the other three English-controlled provinces at that time, had been granted exclusive control over education, natural resources, civil law, and social legislation. "Was anything more required by Quebec to allow it to mould the population that inhabits its territory according to a certain conception of man and society?" asked Filion in 1960. Areas of federal jurisdiction such as international commerce, monetary policy, transportation and communications, national defence, and foreign relations demanded heavy taxes but did not affect in normal times the day-to-day lives of Quebec's citizens in a direct way. The Quebec government had sufficient constitutional jurisdiction over all matters which related directly to the socioeconomic and cultural spheres of activity to create within certain limits the kind of society its citizens wanted.[46] Summarizing the neo-nationalist policy on the role of the state, Gérard Filion declared to Les Amis du Devoir in 1960 that while he did not believe the state could or should do everything,

nevertheless there are a certain number of accomplishments that only a modern state can fulfil, especially when it has the responsibility of seeing to the common good of an underdeveloped community. A system of natural resource exploitation, a policy of energy utilization, the protection of manpower, the participation of nationals at all levels of business and industry, the control over certain large areas of public service, respect for language and culture in the making of social choices and in public relations, these are some of the many functions that a state which recognizes its responsibilities and is convinced that it is there to govern and not to be tossed about should not hesitate in undertaking. If the Quebec state one day decided to use its powers to direct, contain, and discipline the economic life of the province, to force foreigners to respect the people who live here, the strength and influence of the entire country on this side of the Ottawa River would be completely transformed within a half century.[47]

This revisionist approach to a long-standing unresolved issue acted like a front of cold northerly air sweeping across the province and, contrary to the claim of one Citélibriste critic, it was fundamentally regenerative in its impact. The transfer of responsibility from the individual level, where moralizing often prevailed, to the collective level made the introduction of objective secular proposals for reform possible and predictable. In short, the neo-nationalist approach to the question of economic inferiority proved to be basically regenerative and optimistic, not pessimistic as Léon Dion claimed in 1957. In his view, that pessimism originated not in the neo-nationalists' newly acquired secular perspective itself, which he welcomed, but rather in the combination of that secular outlook with the ideology of nationalism. Quebec's neo-nationalists, following the pattern of all modern secular nationalists, had come to perceive the homogeneous nationalist state as the final and perfect expression of the nation, as the normal objective of the thought and action of modern man.

In this context we can understand the significance of the neo-nationalists' pessimism regarding the French-Canadian reality: the nation has no framework or support to achieve the dream of a national state; as Frégault makes clear in the introduction to his magnificent *La guerre de la Conquête*, there is no "Canada" for the "Canadiens": the neo-nationalists are confronted with an impossible dream . . . Finally, the pessimism of the neo-nationalists emerges from the fact that, realizing the absence of the nation as they conceive it, they become aware of their uselessness.[48]

What Léon Dion was referring to, of course, was his belief that the neo-nationalists were losing the support of the traditional nationalists in the church and the liberal professions, while at the same time finding it virtually impossible to rely upon the support of a "nonexistent" francophone upper bourgeoisie which they claimed was essential but which the Conquest had destroyed. What he did not perceive was the potential support of the new bureaucratic middle class for this new nationalism.

Defined in this clear-cut hypothetical fashion, Dion's analysis appeared, on the surface at least, to be a reasonable assessment of the neo-nationalists' dilemma. In practice his critique proved less damaging for a couple of reasons. The majority of the neo-nationalists, with the exception of the separatist-minded Maurice Séguin[49] and Jean-Marc Léger, were sufficiently realistic to understand politics as the art of the possible and therefore adjusted their reform proposals to the socioeconomic and political realities of the Canadian federal national state. Furthermore, the broadening of the francophone middle class to include, in rapidly increasing numbers after 1950, scientists, social scientists, technicians, and managerial and administrative personnel created a new and more receptive environment in that class for the acceptance of neo-nationalist reform proposals. The central goal of the neo-nationalists was the implementation of a fully modern Quebec society in which all sectors, including the economic sector, were firmly in the control of the French-Canadian majority. A wide range of reforms were proposed in the 1950s to make this goal a reality.

THE NEO-NATIONALIST STATE AT WORK

The neo-nationalists' decision to embrace the interventionist state as the pivotal key in their battle for economic autonomy was not inspired strictly by abstract intellectual arguments. As sensitive and perceptive journalists attuned to the ever-changing socioeconomic realities, they soon came to realize in the early fifties the striking inability of the francophone private sector to compete successfully, if at all, with the anglophone private sector. They also came to understand, although somewhat more slowly and grudgingly, the serious limitations of church-owned and administered educational, health, and social service institutions. In effect, it was the reinforcing symbiotic relationship between ideas and concepts and changing socioeconomic realities which drew neo-nationalists inexorably to champion the development of a dynamic, francophone-inspired secular state in Quebec.

Despite the Bloc Populaire experience, the neo-nationalists' commitment to a fully developed and activist government in Quebec still remained qualified in the early 1950s. Direct provincial initiatives in low-cost housing and other social services were shunned. Instead, neo-nationalists called for municipal programs funded in part by the province and Ottawa if necessary. For example, immediately following the war they strongly advocated tri-level government participation in the residential construction industry and urban renewal. The postwar housing shortage was particularly acute in Montreal. The city's population was growing very rapidly because of internal migration from farm and rural communities and external migration. Rents were exorbitantly high and the vast majority of French-Canadian working-class families lived in condemned and unhealthy houses or tenements built at the turn of the century. Aware of these hardships, neo-nationalists called repeatedly for a provincial urban credit program similar to the rural credit scheme already in place. Such a program would enable working-class families or cooperative associations to build reasonably priced housing at low interest rates.

Le Devoir concluded that the private sector was unable and/or unwilling to undertake a program of urban renewal in Montreal and therefore the city had the right and the responsibility to initiate and administer programs of urban renewal and the construction of publicly funded low-cost housing projects. The Duplessis government was denounced on numerous occasions for its failure to underwrite municipal financing of such schemes, while at the same time preventing the transfer of available federal grants to the municipalities for these purposes. The slums in east- and west-end Montreal were, in *Le Devoir*'s eyes, a serious blight on the province and a prime source of political and social unrest. Continued provincial and municipal inaction in the housing field would result in a combined social and national disaster for the French-Canadian community. The working class would, with good cause, eschew nationalist arguments and objectives. They would, in frustration, turn to Ottawa for concrete solutions to their problems and provincial autonomy would be considerably undermined.[50]

The area concerning which the neo-nationalists had absolutely no qualms about advocating government intervention and control was that of natural resource development. They carried on an incessant, hard-hitting campaign for the exploration and development of Quebec's natural resources by French Canadians for French Canadians. Barely a week passed by without a biting editorial denouncing the Duplessis regime for its laissez-faire, antisocial, and antinational resource development policy. Gérard Filion expressed, in rhetoric common to the sixties, the neo-nationalist strategy for economic liberation.

It is through the exploitation of natural resources that a nation affirms its personality and assures its independence. When a nation seeks to free itself from the economic domination of foreign capital, it starts by regaining control over its natural resources. This was the case of Mexico twenty years ago; this is presently the strategy of Bolivia; the Nehru government of India is doing the same thing and the deposed prime minister Mossadegh is being tried before a military tribunal for having failed in the essential plan of developing for the benefit of Iranians the petroleum deposits and natural gas refineries of Abadan.

If, one day, the nation of Quebec wants to overcome its impediments and become master of its own destiny once again, it must start by regaining control over the natural resources which improvident governments handed to foreign capitalists.[51]

Neo-nationalists stressed greater government control over and, if need be, participation in the development of Quebec's renewable resources like hydro-electricity and pulp and paper. The province of Quebec could, through appropriate legislation, ensure that the majority of stockholders and administrators of all companies exploiting natural resources be Canadian citizens, that the percentage of foreign investment be closely regulated, that French-Canadian technocrats and administrators be hired in appropriate numbers and be allowed to work, when possible, in their own language, and that the province retain an equitable return for its citizens from the sale and lease of these resources.[52] *Le Devoir* supported the formation of production co-operatives, for the cutting of timber, being organized by the forestry service of the UCC. Co-ops would assure the workers of fair wages and improved working conditions and, it was hoped, improve forest management and conservation programs. When, in the mid-fifties, the paper companies announced unilateral and uniform price increases which directly threatened small dailies like *Le Devoir*, Filion called for government imposition of a two-priced system. Failing cooperation from the companies in this solution, the government should proceed quickly with a vast program of nationalization.[53] When, in the spring of 1957, Hydro-Quebec announced the sale of its entire production and distribution system of natural gas, the neo-nationalists were furious. They argued that the only method of undermining the private sector's attempts to swamp Hydro-Quebec was to nationalize all of the private hydro production and distribution companies in Quebec. The province would reap three immediate benefits besides control over a crucial resource. First, French-Canadian scientists and technocrats would acquire an enormous public corporation in which they could exercise their skills in their own language, an unquantifiable social and national benefit. Second, the provincial government could recoup over $12 million in tax revenue paid to Ottawa by these private companies. This economic windfall could help finance Hydro-Quebec's expansion or be channelled into necessary social programs. Finally, the power of the Quebec government would be enhanced and provincial autonomy reinforced.[54] These would be very powerful arguments once the Liberal party, urged on by René Lévesque, its natural resources minister, decided in 1962 to proceed with the nationalization program.

Many of the same arguments were made, and often more forcefully substantiated by solid investigative reporting, for full provincial regulation and development of the vast iron-ore deposits in the Ungava region of Quebec near Shefferville. From the inception of the project in April 1946 the neo-nationalists focused their attention on the huge deposits in Ungava and the intimate relationship between the Duplessis government and the Iron Ore Company, a consortium of five American steel companies headed by George W. Humphrey, and Labrador Mining and Exploration, a subsidiary of Hollinger Mines, presided over by Jules Timmins, the mining baron of Northern Ontario. According to the terms of the 1946 "Loi pour faciliter le développement minier et industriel dans le Nouveau-Québec" (10 Geo. 6, c. 42), the Duplessis government granted the Hollinger North Shore Exploration company the right to 300 square miles of choice deposits in the Ungava region. The exploration permit cost $10,000 initially and $6,000 for each subsequent year. When operations came on stream the company agreed to pay $100,000 a year in fixed royalties to be revised every ten years beginning in 1968, as well as the appropriate corporation taxes on profits as stipulated in section III of the "Loi des mines du Québec."[55] The company forged ahead with the railroad and extraction facilities and began to ship iron ore down the St Lawrence in 1954.

On the surface the deal seemed fair enough, considering that the project required the company to construct a 330-mile, $300 million railroad from Sept-Iles north to Shefferville. Yet the neo-nationalists condemned the deal on several grounds and their constant criticisms of the government and the mining company turned the Ungava affair into a major national scandal. Ungava became the classic example of how Quebec's natural resources should not be developed. Neo-nationalists maintained that the government had been duped by the predominantly American corporation into selling out the iron ore deposits at a ridiculously low return for Quebec's citizens. By 1957 the company was producing well over ten million tons of ore annually. It was well documented that the government of Quebec received approximately an eleven cent per ton royalty compared with a royalty of fifty-two cents a ton collected by the State of Minnesota. Including all taxes and gifts, Quebec citizens gained thirty cents a ton compared with approximately $1.25 a ton received by the State of Minnesota! In sum, the province had tied itself into a bad financial deal, considering the projected shortage of known deposits in the United States in 1946, and should reopen the contract in order to negotiate a better fiscal deal for its citizens.[56]

What upset the neo-nationalists even more was the fact that the resource was being developed strictly to serve the needs of the American military-industrial complex. French-Canadian society stood to gain very little. Few

French Canadians were hired at the administrative and technical levels in the corporation. Furthermore, despite positive sophisticated studies by specialists at Laval, the Duplessis government and company officials persistently denied that processing and refining of the iron ore in Quebec was financially feasible. The ore was destined for the American steel corporations. In fact, the development of the St Lawrence Seaway project with United States government cooperation was made possible because the lobby of the huge and powerful American steel corporations was finally able to overcome the eastern seaboard vested interests. Only the creation of a provincially owned steel corporation could, in the view of the neo-nationalists, offset the disastrous mistakes made by the Duplessis government in the development of the vast Ungava deposits.[57] Only a dynamic activist state could negate the nefarious socioeconomic and cultural consequences of the actions of large multinational corporations which had no more concern "for the white niggers of Quebec than for the Blacks of South America."[58]

The area in which the neo-nationalists were initially very cautious and reluctant to advocate increased government intervention and direct involvement was that of social services and health care. While quick to admit that the urban family urgently required new supportive services to ensure its moral and physical well-being, the neo-nationalists persisted in believing, until the mid-fifties, that those new services could best be provided by the private sector rather than the state. Filion and Sauriol, Le Devoir's social policy specialist, favoured pension schemes and medical insurance programs that were organized and administered by the unions in conjunction with industry and business. The state's responsibility should be restricted to providing social services and health insurance to the poor, the indigent, and the handicapped. All universal, comprehensive, and tax-supported schemes were shunned.[59]

The reasons for taking this conservative position were religious and nationalist – but also political. The neo-nationalists did not want to alienate the church and have it oppose necessary reforms in other more pressing areas such as education. Until the late 1950s the neo-nationalists never questioned the church's continuing role in the fields of hospital care and social services. As long as these services were efficient and available to all there seemed little reason to alter a situation where the church's work had long been accepted and highly beneficial. The care of the body was merely an extension of the care of the soul. The two should not be segregated. Filion sincerely believed that universal, comprehensive, tax-supported schemes encouraged irresponsibility in the individual and therefore should be avoided at all costs. Moreover, the province of Quebec had for over two centuries developed a structure of social services and health care that was distinctly French-Canadian and therefore, as such, marked Quebec society off from the rest of North America and from English Canada in particular.

The government of Quebec was encouraged to resist federal encroachment upon social services and health care by ensuring that Quebec's system was properly administered, well funded, and reformed where needed but always keeping in mind French-Canadian social and cultural values.[60]

The neo-nationalists found support for this position in the 1956 *Tremblay Report*, but shortly thereafter began to modify and attenuate their opposition to government intervention.[61] Renewed pressure on the federal government for a national health care program, combined with strong support from organized labour for a national medicare scheme administered by the provinces, made neo-nationalists realize that the writing was on the wall.[62] If universal, tax-supported schemes run by the state were inevitable, it was preferable to see the provincial governments rather than the federal government in the driver's seat. Once again a combination of social and nationalist imperatives, but primarily the latter, impelled neo-nationalists to advocate a strong interventionist state as the primary instrument of the modernization of French-Canadian society. Influenced by economists at the Ecole des hautes études commerciales, namely, F.A. Angers and Roland Parenteau, the neo-nationalists became ardent proponents of what the French call *dirigisme*, that is, overall government socioeconomic planning with well-defined priorities and objectives and with political and administrative strategies to achieve those objectives. The provincial government was urged to hire a wide range of economic and social planning specialists to begin the elaboration of a coherent set of social and economic policies which would guarantee the development of the French-Canadian collectivity. It was high time, wrote Paul Sauriol, that French Canadians began "a peaceful offensive to assume control and management of their provincial patrimony, to undermine gradually the foreign economic occupation which has endured since the Conquest."[63] For neo-nationalists the state had replaced the church as the dominant institution in the survival and modernization of French-Canadian society.

THE NEO-LIBERAL STATE

Citélibristes also participated in this debate on the economic inferiority of French Canadians and the French-Canadian community. They, too, came to advocate the creation of a dynamic, interventionist Quebec state but with somewhat less zeal and greater reservations than the neo-nationalists. As committed federalists the Citélibristes believed that the responsibilities of the state should be divided according to "functionalist" principles between the national and provincial governments and bureaucracies. As committed democrats, they feared handing over too many responsibilities and powers to the Quebec state until democratic principles were accepted by it as something to be valued in their own right. This meant, of course, that the growth of the Quebec state would have to await the defeat of the autocratic and undemocratic Union Nationale government of Maurice Duplessis. Cité-libristes therefore supported state-building, but with democratic rather than neo-nationalist goals and aspirations in mind.

To begin with, Citélibristes rejected the neo-nationalists' reinterpretation of French-Canadian history whereby a political/military event, the Conquest of 1760, was considered to be the exclusive cause of the economic inferiority of French Canadians and the absence of a modern, dynamic francophone industrial bourgeoisie. Citélibristes were not willing to absolve their society of responsibility for these phenomena. They preferred to perceive the "backwardness" of French-Canadian society as resulting from a complex conjuncture of cultural, ideological, religious, and economic factors rather than a single historical event such as the Conquest of 1760. Like the neo-nationalists, the Citélibristes had their own school of historical thought to draw upon to reinforce their point of view. The Laval school of historians, made up of Marcel Trudel, Jean Hamelin, and Fernand Ouellet, rejected the traditional and neo-nationalist interpretations of French-Cana-dian history. Its members attempted to provide a more objective and realistic assessment of the evolution and development of French-Canadian society. Marcel Trudel contended that the economic weaknesses of post-Conquest French-Canadian society, as he would later document in his multivolumed *Histoire de la Nouvelle-France*, had their origins in the immature, under-developed colonial society of New France.[64] Jean Hamelin, in a careful study of the economy of New France prior to the Conquest, concluded that, contrary to the claim of the neo-nationalist historians, there was no dominant French-Canadian bourgeoisie present at the time of the Conquest because the economy of New France had remained firmly in the hands of the metropolitan bourgeoisie which exploited the colony for its own benefit.[65] However, it is Fernand Ouellet who has gone to the greatest lengths to destroy the neo-nationalist Conquest thesis. Like his colleague Hamelin, Ouellet questioned seriously the existence of a true capitalist bourgeoisie in New France. *Ancien régime* values, coupled with extensive state intervention, he argued, had effectively prevented the creation and expansion of a self-perpetuating middle class imbued with a bourgeois-capitalist mentality and behavioural patterns.[66] This mental outlook and the rise of French-Canadian nationalism engendered and fed by a new, professionally dominated, con-servative middle class, Ouellet contended, were responsible for the economic inferiority of French Canadians. Nationalism, the perpetuation of an ancien régime mentality, and the rise of clericalism, not the Conquest, prevented after 1800 the restructuring of French Canada's social, economic, and polit-ical institutions in accordance with the imperatives of nineteenth-century commercial capitalism.[67]

As was the case with the neo-nationalist historians at the Université de

Montréal, members of the Laval school were motivated by their concern over contemporary developments in French Canada. They shared the Cité-libristes' vision of a modern, secular, and democratic French-Canadian society and believed that nationalism and clericalism were conservative regressive forces preventing the modernization of Quebec.

Citélibristes also drew upon the work of Maurice Tremblay, a Laval sociologist. In a 1952 symposium on industrialization and French Canada, Maurice Tremblay argued forcefully that the social thought of French Canada, as it was elaborated by the clerical and nationalist élites after the conquest, stressed almost exclusively "the agricultural vocation of the French-Canadian nationality," or what was generally referred to in spiritual terms as "loyalty to the land." The Catholic church, with no strong French-Canadian state to oppose it, became the dominant institution in the lives of French Canadians and created or fostered institutions such as the parish, the classical colleges, colonization societies, and the family, to perpetuate a basically rural and Christian society. French culture, which was idealist and universalist in orientation, coupled with the Catholic philosophy of life which placed a higher priority on contemplative as opposed to active careers, made it virtually impossible for French Canadians "to compete on an equal footing in the higher echelons of economic activity with our Anglo-Protestant fellow citizens."[68] Maurice Tremblay was roundly denounced in traditional nationalist circles for his "anticlericalism," while the neo-nationalists felt he had not pushed his analysis far enough.

Trudeau, picking up Tremblay's approach, pushed the analysis further and developed what could be termed the "mentalité" hypothesis to explain the economic inferiority of the French-Canadian people. Quebec's economy was controlled and directed almost exclusively by Anglo-Canadian and American managerial and financial élites for the simple reason that the religious and secular ideologies propounded by French Canada's clerical and lay leaders were inherently anti-industrialist and antipluralist. Confronted with a culture that was English, Protestant, democratic, materialistic, commercial, and later industrial, French-Canadian nationalist thought created a state-of-siege mentality emphasizing all the contrary qualities and forces: the French language, Catholicism, authoritarianism, idealism, the rural way of life, and, in periods of crisis, a return to the land.[69]

Furthermore, according to Trudeau's reading of the past, the social doctrine of the Catholic church, unlike the experience of many Western European countries, did not fill the vacuum created by the prolonged rejection of the secular social sciences. The francophone petty bourgeois intelligentsia, unable to accept or understand the phenomenon of industrialization and the proletarization of the masses, exploited papal authority and the encyclicals for the benefit of French-Canadian nationalism and their own position of authority. While Leo XIII and his successors denounced the capitalist system because it held the proletariat in an abject state of poverty and impeded in the individual the development of truly human values, the French-Canadian clerical nationalists denounced the same system because it held French Canadians in a state of economic colonialism and impeded the development of truly nationalist values.

This clerical and nationalist thought, contended Trudeau, made it impossible for the French Canadians to modernize their society. Because the ideology of nationalism led to the rejection, on principle, of any and all reforms proposed by English-speaking Canadians, such as state-funded and administered social security programs, it perpetuated an authoritarian and undemocratic conception of the political process and the role of government. Consequently, French-Canadian nationalists had burnt their bridges and backed themselves into a set of unrealistic and reactionary solutions involving the back to the land movement, small business, cooperatives, Catholic unionism, and, to round them out, a corporatist social structure. The end result was that French-Canadian leaders had failed, time and time again, to acquire majority control over the economic institutions governing their lives or to create new social and economic institutions, private and public, to serve the needs of their vastly altered society.[70] The Trudeau analysis, on the surface at least, seemed attractive in that it provided a fairly simplistic but comprehensive explanation. What Trudeau, the polemicist and antinationalist, failed to point out was that there existed real political and economic constraints which hindered putting into place institutions at variance with the economic and social values of the very powerful Anglo-Canadian minority in control of the Quebec economy and the political process. Even had those nationalist-inspired institutions been modern, secular, and social democratic in nature, the problem of having them accepted by the dominant economic class would still have remained an important element in the equation.

The neo-nationalists' growing commitment to an aggressive interventionist Quebec state received cautious and somewhat ambivalent approval from the Citélibristes. Quite clearly, Citélibristes and the union centrals they actively supported – the CTCC and FUIQ – favoured the concept of a strong and active government in the province. Yet they differed among themselves on just how interventionist the state should be. Trudeau favoured a severely circumscribed and controlled capitalist economy with active state participation introduced in key areas when such action proved technically and politically feasible.[71] On the other hand, FUIQ leaders, in their May 1955 *Manifeste politique*, called for the immediate implementation of a social democratic state in Quebec capable of socializing all natural resources and public services and creating a full range of social security programs. These programs should be national in scope if possible but if no cooperation was forthcoming from Ottawa and the other provinces then Quebec should proceed alone. The position of the CTCC and its secretary-general, Jean Marchand, resembled more closely that of Trudeau than their rival FUIQ, at least in the period prior to 1960.[72] On the crucial question of greater franco-phone control over the province's natural resources, the neo-nationalists received the full and unwavering support of the CTCC and FUIQ. These unions and their Citélibriste advisers attributed Quebec's lower salaries and higher levels of taxation vis-à-vis Ontario to the lack of sufficient heavy industry in the province and the government's unwillingness to demand a greater return on the development of the province's natural resources. In-creased processing within the province of its natural resources would remedy the structural weaknesses while at the same time improving the salaries of the workers and providing a greater number of skilled jobs. A strengthened economy would enhance the revenue of the provincial treasury, thereby making available funds for more improved social programs and a reformed education system. There was little to lose but a colonial mentality and much to gain in terms of economic self-sufficiency. Less rhetoric and quick action, according to the CTCC, was the remedy for Quebec's social and economic inferiority.[73]

CONCLUSION

The 1950s marked a turning point in the development of political economy as an important element in the social thought of Quebec's francophone intelligentsia. The period was characterized by a broadening and deepening of the debate on the question of the economic inferiority of French Cana-dians as individuals and as a group.

In the course of the debate several new developments took place. The notion that the Quebec economy seriously lagged behind that of the rest of Canada was duly and appropriately disregarded, although economists like Pierre Harvey and André Raynauld noted important qualitative and struc-tural differences in the Quebec and Ontario economies.[74] In fact, these differences were often referred to by the advocates of state intervention to substantiate their support for such a policy. Yet the most significant and novel aspect of the debate was that it was taken out of the realm of individual responsibility and moral exhortation into the field of the social sciences where secular, rational, and collective solutions could be arrived at and discussed. This did not mean that the debate was any less intense or emo-tional, or that the solutions proposed in some cases were less categorical. What it did mean was that for the first time the political factor, namely, the Conquest and its concomitant, English majority rule, came in for close scrutiny by the neo-nationalists. This approach predicated to a considerable degree their proposed solution and strategy of action.

That solution was to advocate the creation of a strong and active Quebec state, the only one over which French Canadians held majority control. The Quebec state was to become the central motor force in the modernization of French-Canadian society while ensuring that well-educated and skilled middle-class French Canadians gained access to, and eventual control of, the main instruments of economic, social, and political power. For neo-nationalists, state intervention was at first restricted to matters of economic development. But by the mid-fifties it came to include the field of education, and by the late fifties, the heretofore sacrosanct areas of private initiative, social services, and health care were deemed appropriate areas of activity for the modern state. The neo-nationalists' concern for the preservation and modernization of French-Canadian society as well as their desire to acquire social, economic, and political leadership in this modernized society were the primary motivating factors behind the decision to advocate the creation of a modern secular state.

Citélibristes, in contrast, approached the issue of the role of the modern state as liberals and social democrats. The prime function of the "servant" state was to create the conditions and institutions necessary for the protection and advancement of all its citizens regardless of their race, language, colour, or religion. Furthermore, the modern state should encourage the widespread participation of its citizens in the decision-making process – political democracy – and work incessantly toward a fairer distribution of the society's wealth and resources – social democracy. The achievement of these objectives, claimed Citélibristes, would ensure, in due course, control of Quebec's political, social, and economic institutions by the French-Canadian majority. To place nationalist concerns ahead of democratic and social objectives was, in the Citélibristes' view of the world, placing the cart before the horse and eliminating *a priori* the required flexibility in the choice of strategy and modes of action. In short, for the Citélibristes, the individual had primacy over any group, whether national or social, and the role of the state was to serve the former and not the latter. The neo-nationalists claimed that the state could reconcile service to the individual with service to the collectivity.

What was interesting and important for future developments was that both neo-nationalists and Citélibristes, while working from different ideological assumptions, had arrived at the same conclusion – the need for a modern secular interventionist state in Quebec. The values and objectives emphasized by such a state would depend entirely upon which political party held the reins of power in Quebec City. It was in the light of this realization that the neo-nationalists and Citélibristes, followed by increasingly large numbers of young Québécois, turned their attention and energies to the politics of organized labour and, later, political party action, with the eagerness and dedication of young neophytes.

CHAPTER SEVEN

The Role of Organized Labour

One of the most vocal and effective extraparliamentary forces in Quebec during the 1950s was organized labour, especially the Confédération des travailleurs catholiques du Canada (CTCC) and the Fédération des unions industrielles du Quebec (FUIQ). Both Citélibristes and neo-nationalists came to perceive organized labour as a central tool for the attainment of their respective ideological and social objectives. In the absence of a viable third party Citélibristes, in the early 1950s, looked to organized labour as the only democratic and liberalizing force in French-Canadian society. *Cité libre*'s members believed that a united, democratic, and politically active labour movement could break the unholy alliance between the Duplessis government and foreign-controlled big business. A dynamic and democratic labour movement would become a major force in the struggle to modernize Quebec society at all levels. Neo-nationalists supported this strategy but maintained one very significant ideological difference. Working-class franco-phone institutions and organizations, especially the Catholic labour move-ment, had a responsibility to seek to fulfil the collective as well as the individual goals and aspirations of their members. Organized labour's battle for greater equality of opportunity and living conditions for working people was essential. But according to the neo-nationalists this battle must be pursued simultaneously with the struggle for socioeconomic equality and greater political autonomy for the French-Canadian nation. Liberal and nationalist "revolutions" had to coincide. The former could not be achieved at the expense of the latter.

The commitment of Citélibristes to a dynamic, democratic, and politically active labour movement was both ideological and personal. Many of them worked in some capacity as technical advisers, lawyers, journalists, and resident ideologues and critics for the CTCC and FUIQ. Some years later Pierre Vadeboncoeur recalled that:

For several years we believed that the union movement, especially the CTCC would, by a series of social upheavals and increasingly militant union action precipitated by a more and more audacious interpretation of these events, impose with the support of its several thousand members a revolutionary consciousness which would expand indefinitely. In fact, from 1949 to 1954, the CTCC, for one, attacked certain enemies of the people with such force and tenacity as to qualify as revolutionary. In a crafty and corrupt society we were finally beginning to hear the sound of freedom. The CTCC was creating class divisions, that is, strongly rejecting disorder for the sake of disorder, capitalism for the sake of the exploiters, while developing an unequivocating body of militia. Its positions, even when left unstated, were nonetheless clear.[1]

While neo-nationalists were not involved directly with any of the labour centrals, *Le Devoir* devoted extended coverage, via its full-time labour correspondents, to the full range of union activities in the province and, on occasion, in other parts of Canada. All the major labour conflicts, especially those involving the CTCC, were covered in depth. Furthermore, the CTCC's annual congresses and its numerous briefs to all levels of government and special commissions were given full play in *Le Devoir*. In return, the neo-nationalists took on the role of sympathetic and constructive critics of the CTCC and its leadership. On occasion they cautioned the CTCC against excessive militancy, as was the case in 1952 when *Le Devoir* vigorously opposed talk of plans for a general strike to protest police brutality during the textile plant strike in Louisville. On the whole, however, neo-nationalists supported and continually reinforced the growing militancy, the secular orientation, and the dynamic leadership of the CTCC.

THE LABOUR SCENE

To astute observers, it was clearly evident by the 1950s that organized labour represented and symbolized, better than any other movement, the pressing realities and aspirations of the new industrial order. Physical aggressiveness and ideological militancy, engendered by the expansion of industrial unionism and the bitter interunion rivalry of the war years, and the desire of public and para-public employees to gain the right to collective bargaining, became the hallmarks of unionism in Quebec by the mid-1940s.[2] In the decade and a half following the war, Quebec's three union centrals, the CTCC, FUIQ, and the Fédération provinciale du travail du Québec (FPTQ), worked diligently to expand their respective memberships and reorganize their internal structures so as to serve their locals and regional councils better. Despite an era which one author characterizes as "an era of the most ferocious repression," union membership rose from 179,763 or 19.6 per cent of Quebec's labour force in 1945 to 341,151 or 28.7 per cent in 1955.[3] Unions affiliated with the Trades and Labour Congress accounted for

130,000 members in 1955, yet only 25 to 30 per cent of these members belonged to unions which cared to affiliate with the FPTQ. Consequently, the latter central was weak, administratively and financially, and exercised little control over TLC locals in the province, 50 per cent of which were located in Montreal and Quebec City. TLC leaders in the province were cautious and conservative, staunchly anticommunist, and strong adherents of the Gomperian doctrine of nonpartisanship in politics. They preferred a policy of cooperation with the Duplessis government and in return experienced little trouble in getting their unions certified and arbitration proceedings settled quickly.[4] Union locals affiliated with the more militant industrial-oriented Canadian Congress of Labour accounted for only 45,000 workers in Quebec in 1955, 65 per cent of them located in Montreal and Quebec. Over 70 per cent of these CCL members were affiliated through their locals with the FUIQ, the highly vocal, highly active, and dynamic provincial central created in December 1952. FUIQ leaders and organizers, following the tradition created by the CIO and the CCL, were committed to more than bread and butter unionism. Through worker solidarity, militant unionism, and political action, the FUIQ strove to obtain greater economic, social, and political justice for the working classes. The FUIQ supported the provincial and federal wings of the CCF and cooperated closely with the CTCC in opposing the antisocial, antilabour, and undemocratic tactics and legislation of the Duplessis government.[5]

What differentiated the Quebec labour scene from that in other provinces was the presence of the CTCC. The Catholic labour movement, founded in 1921, had remained during its first decade and a half ideologically differentiated from Quebec's international unions. The CTCC, recalled Jean Marchand in 1961, "was definitely nationalist, confessional, pro-corporatist, and the chaplains played a dominant role. Often Catholic action took priority over professional and purely union action. Industrialization was viewed with suspicion and we produced resolutions, during our early congresses, against rural depopulation and for a return to the land."[6] The primary function of the CTCC, as perceived by its clerical founders, was the defence and perpetuation of the Catholic faith and the French-Canadian cultural heritage and language of the francophone working class.

Despite this professed ideological orientation, the CTCC, its federations, and locals were forced to adopt during the 1920s the same collective bargaining tactics and strategies as those used by the internationals. As a result, a gap developed between the Catholic labour movement's official ideology and its concrete actions.[7] This process was accentuated during the 1940s with the emergence of industrial unionism and the rise of a new generation of secular leaders. Furthermore, the CTCC's leaders and militants began the process of modifying the movement's ideological conception of the role and aspirations of organized labour with the support and encouragement of both Citélibristes and neo-nationalists. As a result, the CTCC became a modern industrial union central dedicated to serving the secular socio-economic and political needs of Quebec's blue- and white-collar workers. Religious and nationalist preoccupations were relegated to a secondary level, the former disappearing almost entirely by 1960. Nationalist concerns, as we shall see, reemerged in a much altered form by the late 1950s as the CTCC began to reflect and channel the neo-nationalist aspirations of a fully secularized and modernized French-Canadian society. As a result of its new ideological orientation the CTCC became the fastest-growing union central in the province between 1947 and 1955. In less then a decade its membership rose by nearly 30 per cent from 70,176 to 97,173, represented in 450 locals, 16 federations, and 16 regional councils. The CTCC was the most dynamic and most deeply rooted of the three provincial centrals. None the less, it remained weak in metropolitan Montreal and lacked the fiscal resources to back up its newfound militancy. Unlike its competitors, it had no pan-Canadian central to fall back upon.[8]

The debate surrounding the role of organized labour found a focus in five issues. The first involved the asbestos strike of 1949 and the divergent interpretations assigned to it by Citélibristes and neo-nationalists. The second was concerned with the role of the state in labour-management relations. The third theme centred on labour's role in humanizing capitalism and overcoming the economic inferiority of French Canadians. The highly sensitive question of the CTCC's potential merger with the CLC emphasized the divergences between liberals and nationalists within and outside the labour movement. Finally, organized labour's role in active politics became a subject for heated discussion as reformers of all schools searched for a ready-made constituency upon which to build an effective third party.

THE ASBESTOS STRIKE

Pressured by a frustrated and militant work-force and encouraged by the new leadership of the CTCC, the Fédération des syndicats de l'amiante called a wildcat strike in 1949 of all the miners in Asbestos and Thetford, two small Eastern Townships communities. The asbestos mining industry was dominated by the powerful building materials firm, the Canadian Johns-Manville corporation, a branch plant of its much larger United States parent company, and the Asbestos Corporation, an independent mining company. At issue was the workers' demand for union recognition in practice as well as in principle, better wages and fringe benefits, vastly improved working conditions, and some say in such matters as promotions, transfers, and firings, areas traditionally associated exclusively with management. After six months on the picket lines, involving frequent conflict with the provincial police in Asbestos, the strike ended in a draw. The workers returned to work with a promise of no recriminations and, if necessary, arbitration of a collective agreement on wages, fringe benefits, and working conditions. The latter was achieved in January and February of 1950, but few real gains were made by the miners. Nevertheless, the CTCC did come out of the bitter and prolonged strike with a substantially altered public image. It could no longer be castigated by international organizers as a tame and docile tool of traditional French-Canadian political and clerical élites and employers. It was henceforth a potent autonomous force to be contended with by all parties involved in labour matters, the companies, the government rival unions, and the church.[9]

The rise of secular, university-trained leadership in the CTCC, represented by Gérard Picard as president and Jean Marchand as secretary-general, coincided with the arrival of Filion and Laurendeau at *Le Devoir* in 1947. The coincidence was highly fortuitous. The new director and refurbished editorial team were quick to welcome and actively support the increased militancy and socioeconomic orientation of the CTCC.[10] It was hoped that militant organizations like the CTCC, the cooperative movements, and the Union catholique des cultivateurs would fill the void left by the demise of the Bloc Populaire. The CTCC's new orientation was also welcomed because it helped to take the hard edge off Laurendeau's belief that the francophone working class was the least nationalist-minded class of French-Canadian society. The CTCC's commitment to cultural survival was well recognized. Perhaps it could rekindle the nationalist spirit among the workers by looking after their secular as well as their moral and spiritual needs. In sum, the conjuncture of circumstances and aspirations was such as to attract neo-nationalists to organized labour, especially the Catholic labour movement.

Le Devoir took this newfound commitment to organized labour to heart when it threw its full weight solidly behind the 5,000 asbestos workers in their 1949 wildcat strike. As noted earlier, Filion quickly commissioned one of his young reporters, Gérard Pelletier, to provide *Le Devoir*'s readers with daily on-the-scene reports of the strike as it unfolded. This unflinching commitment helped to galvanize the support of the general public, rival unions, and the Catholic church in favour of the strikers, who were, in fact, breaking the law. The forthcoming food, clothing, and rent monies helped maintain high morale among the workers and made it feasible for them to prolong the battle against the companies, one of which threatened to evict the workers and their families from company-owned accommodations.

The strike was important because it revealed the divergent ideological perspectives that were to become the hallmarks of neo-nationalists and Citélibristes, the latter group an indirect product of the strike itself. Neo-nationalists interpreted the strike as both a nationalist and a socioeconomic struggle, with the latter dimension welcomed as a long overdue development. For them, the originality of the strike lay in the fact that the Catholic labour organization had championed the priority of secular socioeconomic objectives such as union recognition, improved wage and fringe benefits, industrial hygiene, industrial democracy, and the creation of a social conscience in the labour movement and the community at large. In their view, a major catalyst in the situation was a growing sense of working-class consciousness and the perception by French-Canadian labour leaders that they had to serve the material as well as the national and spiritual needs of their membership.[11]

Yet the neo-nationalists also made it very clear that they considered the strike to be a major nationalist struggle. It was a struggle to ensure the survival and expansion of a crucial French-Canadian institution, the CTCC, against the combined onslaught of a reactionary anti-union government and foreign capitalists who easily manipulated that government. The Duplessis government had failed not only to grasp the justification for the demands of the asbestos workers, but had lost sight of the collective interests of the French-Canadian people. By encouraging and cooperating with the American branch plant managers in their undemocratic, antisocial, and anti-French-Canadian behaviour, the Duplessis government had threatened the survival and development of the CTCC and thereby had risked leaving the field wide open to the international unions. The real losers in the asbestos strike were the workers, who were forced to accept less than they deserved, and the French-Canadian nation at large. If unions affiliated with the CTCC were not successful in looking after the interests of their members, then those workers would have every right to look elsewhere. French Canadians would then cease to have at their disposal a strong and viable indigenous institution.[12] As Fernand Dansereau put it some time after the strike, foreign domination of the rapid industrialization of Quebec's economy resulted in the subordination and exploitation not only of the French-Canadian working class but also of the old and new middle classes. "In reality, an entire people is becoming a labour-class. An entire people is being reduced by force of circumstances to the condition of an exploited class."[13] Given the lack of any other viable instrument, French Canadians, working class and new middle class alike, had turned to unionism as the potentially liberating force for both the individual and the collectivity.

The *Cité libre* team offered a much different interpretation of the asbestos strike. Its members perceived the role of unions as a vehicle of greater socioeconomic and political equality for the working classes. As liberals and social democrats, Citélibristes maintained that class distinctions, not cultural and religious differences, were responsible for their society's disparities. All French Canadians had to be brought to realize that organized labour was merely the visual, institutional symbol of distinct class differences in their society. Moreover, it was unrealistic and utopian to think that these hardening class distinctions could be talked or theorized out of existence. Class conflict was an inherent dimension of the existing socioeconomic system because the means of production were owned and controlled by the upper bourgeoisie which used its powers to exploit and suppress the working people.[14]

Citélibristes maintained that French Canada's political and social leaders had, for a long time, failed to understand the class dimension of modern urban/industrial society. As a result these leaders, relying all too often on a highly conservative and self-serving interpretation of Catholic social thought, remained unalterably opposed to the advancement of the working class and fought the growth of militant unions.[15] According to Gérard Pelletier, many knowledgeable and sincere French Canadians, including a few union leaders, retained a romantic and unrealistic conception of how the workers' struggle should be conducted.

They possessed an idealistic conception of the workers' struggle. They truly believed that the battle was waged exclusively by way of encyclical declarations, intellectual distinctions, and religious manifestations. Certainly they want unionists to pursue the conquest of their rights, but in a war of fancy lace (or choir-boy surplice) surrounded by the sound of organs and gregorian chant. Certainly they want a battle, but a battle between good and evil, a struggle that ends with a sermon. They love unionism, but with a love so sentimental, so fraught with flowery illusions, that this love turns to hate the moment the union faces its first challenge, that is, its first strike.[16]

The asbestos struggle, Citélibristes maintained, had shattered beyond repair this romantic and outmoded conception of how the workers' battles should be conducted. The wildcat strike by 5,000 asbestos miners, they argued, marked a watershed in the political, social, religious, and economic history of Quebec because it was the province's *first* thoroughgoing working-class struggle. In Trudeau's words the strike was "a key episode of social emancipation brought on by pressures emanating solely from the industrial world without confessional or national deviation."[17] What was even more original and exciting was the fact that this new and contemporary force exercising its power over French Canada's collective destiny, breaking the stranglehold of the past and liberating a multitude of creative forces, was none other than the traditionally conservative and nationalist-dominated Catholic labour movement, the CTCC.[18]

Boisvert sought to explain the CTCC's newfound radicalism and militancy in the fact that it had abandoned its thirty-year strategy of approaching all problems "from a Québécois nationalist perspective."[19] He went on to describe *Cité libre*'s conception of the role of organized labour.

What the doctrine of social conservatism, which is the essence of a certain nationalism, had been unable to accomplish, the CTCC accomplished by elaborating a dynamic doctrine fully conscious of the evolution of our milieu and of the economic and social characteristics of a modern industrial society. The CTCC had to become aware of the fact that the capitalist system, because of the inhuman structures that it creates, oppresses, with all the weight of a machine, human beings. The CTCC had to become aware that the true rule of unionism is precisely to liberate these people and to put the machines at their service. Only then, when men regain little by little their humanity, will the society they inhabit truly merit its name. To save society it was imperative to give the person priority over the collectivity. By raising French-Canadian society to the level of an absolute, our nationalism undertook the task of bullying individuals. It had become an unwitting accomplice of the forces which, by oppressing individuals, undermined at the same time the entire society."[20]

The Catholic and nationalist labour movement, Trudeau reminded the Tremblay commissioners, had accomplished little for the working class by expending its energies and time on cultural, religious, or constitutional battles. Only by liberating the worker from the slavery of material needs and the anxiety of insecurity could unions guarantee that each and every one of their members was in a position to participate fully as free, rehabilitated individuals in a society of equals. "Only then will the higher values which society attempts to incarnate become a reality accessible to the general public and this public will have a vested interest in seeing these higher values developed further."[21] Cultural, linguistic, and religious goals were not to be negated but merely placed at the appropriate level in labour's list of priorities.

Both Citélibristes and neo-nationalists exaggerated the importance of the 1949 asbestos strike. Both groups advanced interpretations which were more in line with their respective ideological tenets and aspirations than with the complex realities of the event. The asbestos strike, as is invariably the case with most strikes, meant different things to the various groups involved. For the CTCC leaders, Gérard Picard and Jean Marchand, the strike was an opportunity to undercut the international unions by demonstrating the vigour and militancy of the Catholic labour movement. In effect, it was the CTCC's demand for a degree of industrial democracy through a system of co-management, dealing with certain questions such as promotions, transfers, firings, methods of work, and production levels, which prompted Lewis H. Brown, president of Canadian Johns-Manville, to refuse to negotiate with the Asbestos Federation on the grounds that its leaders were trying to undermine management's rights and prerogatives.[22] For the church the strike was an opportunity to reassert its role of intermediary between the companies, the state, and the unions. Although church leaders were instrumental in settling the dispute, the church, according to one author, lost all credibility in the eyes of the state, that is to say, of

Maurice Duplessis, and was henceforth excluded from any crucial role in subsequent labour disputes.[23] Finally, there is no extant evidence to suggest that the asbestos strikers were conscious of constituting a working class pursuing a class struggle. They were galvanized into action by a desire to share in the prosperity created by the North American postwar economic boom which was contributing to the secularization and liberalization of Quebec society at all levels. The fact that the workers were French Canadian while the company owners and managers were English-speaking and American contributed no doubt to giving the strike nationalist overtones.

LABOUR, THE STATE, AND THE CHURCH

One of the first consequences of organized labour's decision to achieve greater recognition and autonomy, as well as a better deal for its members, was the need to modify the role of the state vis-à-vis unions and labour-management conflicts. The established pattern whereby the state either refrained from intervening or, more often than not, intervened to the benefit of the employers was simply no longer acceptable to the union movement and its most ardent supporters, namely, the neo-nationalists and the Cité-libristes. Given the Duplessis government's overt hostility towards organized labour and its intimate relationship with the financial and industrial élites developing the province's economy, it was almost inevitable that resistance to an attempted redefinition of the role of the state would be forceful and, at time, brutal. There is ample evidence to illustrate that the Duplessis government, via legislation and executive privilege, fought to undermine labour's desire to become the legitimate and autonomous representative of the "fourth estate."[24]

Neither did Duplessis wish to see the state's role redefined as being simply that of a neutral third party responsible for organizing the necessary juridical structures to facilitate harmonious and stable relationships between labour and employers or to intervene, upon occasion, to resolve irreconcilable conflicts and coordinate common objectives. Citélibristes and neo-nationalists gave full support to labour's struggle to break the alliance between government and the financial and industrial élites. The state had a democratic responsibility to govern for all groups and classes in society. Furthermore, the alliance had antinationalist overtones because the working class was predominantly francophone while the financial and industrial élites were predominantly anglophone.

The most odious and visible illustration of this secular alliance between the state and capital was the recurrent use of provincial police to make a mockery of the workers' right to strike by preventing legal picketing and by escorting "scabs" into plants to ensure that companies could maintain production. Neo-nationalists and Citélibristes denounced this intervention of the state on behalf of capital and reinforced their criticism by pointing to strikes – Lachute 1947, Asbestos 1949, Louisville 1952, Murdochville 1957 – where police intervention provoked violence and bloodshed. To recognize unions *de jure* while undermining them *de facto* by undercutting their most influential weapon – the strike – was hypocritical and undemocratic.[25] "The government," wrote Laurendeau in support of labour's perspective, "represents the common good. It must remain above the turmoil so as to be able to arbitrate conflicts. The only partiality it can permit itself must have as its goal the favouring of the weak at the expense of the strong."[26]

An area urgently requiring positive government intervention in support of the workers was that of industrial pollution. In 1948–9, *Le Devoir* shocked the established élites when it carried on a vigorous, hard-hitting campaign against the Duplessis government for not introducing more stringent pollution standards and enforcing them on companies mining clay and asbestos. Investigative reporting revealed hundreds of miners suffering from the deadly silicosis disease and the premature deaths of several dozen miners were linked to the high intake of asbestos and clay fibres.[27] In sum, the state had a responsibility to ensure that all workers enjoyed a healthy working environment by imposing stringent regulations and stiff noncompliance penalties on the companies.

The Duplessis government's most effective method of stifling and controlling the labour movement was through the government-appointed Commission des relations ouvrières (CRO) which possessed broad discretionary powers over unions and existing legislation governing all labour relations in the province. Neo-nationalists and Citélibristes actively supported labour's campaign for a modern labour code and a reformed CRO. Both groups considered the 1944 Loi des relations ouvrières and numerous subsequent amendments to be deficient on several accounts. Existing legislation and the politicized nature of the CRO made it difficult for militant unions to gain and retain certification. All public servants were denied the right to strike or to have recourse to compulsory, binding arbitration. Certified unions in the private sector could only strike after several time-consuming steps – negotiations, conciliation, arbitration. No time limits were imposed by law and arbitration decisions were not binding. The system invariably worked to the benefit of employers, frustrated existing unions, and discouraged other workers from seeking certification. By law, union certificates remained the property of the CRO and could be withdrawn on any number of pretexts.[28] Neo-nationalists were deeply incensed in 1951 when the Duplessis government passed legislation making it impossible to appeal CRO and arbitration committee decisions in the courts. The most immediate result was the certification of an increasing number of company-sponsored or "sweetheart" unions and bitter interunion rivalry which sapped labour's energies and fiscal resources.[29]

A classic example of the turmoil that the politicized CRO could create can be seen in its decision to decertify the Alliance des professeurs de Montréal for having called a strike in 1949 to obtain better salaries, leave without pay for their president, and a grievance committee. A rival teachers' union was formed, resulting in a long and bitter struggle which ended in the courts. The struggle radicalized hundreds of school teachers and was only resolved in 1959 when the Alliance was recertified. Citélibristes and neo-nationalists followed the Alliance's struggle closely and both groups concluded that the incident demonstrated the shortcomings of provincial labour legislation and the CRO.[30]

The Duplessis government rejected all pleas for democratization of the CRO. Instead, it reinforced the discretionary power of the commission by introducing and having passed two legislative measures in January 1954. Bill 19 allowed the minister of labour to decertify, via the CRO, any union which tolerated among its organizers anyone belonging to a Communist party or movement. Bill 20 allowed the CRO to decertify any union in the public sector for calling a strike. Both bills were retroactive to 1944. Both were vindictive and politically motivated, one to undercut the growing radicalization of the new industrial unions affiliated with the CTCC and FUIQ, the other to ensure that the Alliance would not regain union certification through the courts.[31] Union leaders, except for those belonging to the FPTQ, organized a well-attended protest march on the Legislature in Quebec in the cold of winter but to no avail. Neo-nationalists denounced Bills 19 and 20 as arbitrary, undemocratic, unjust, and above all, foolish. Along with the Citélibristes, they supported the protest march and Laurendeau wondered out loud whether Duplessis, driven by his antilabour prejudices, was following in the footsteps of the infamous American anticommunist crusader, Senator Joseph McCarthy, or of the famous marionette and buffoon, Charlie McCarthy![32] This new wave of antilabour legislation ensured the further radicalization of labour leaders, organizers, and militants and, as we shall see, pushed them and their supporters to contemplate direct political action.

The CTCC's relationship with the Quebec Catholic church also called for reformulation in the postwar years. *Cité libre*'s position was clear and categorical. The CTCC had to become fully secularized if it was to accomplish successfully its socioeconomic and political objectives, and thereby become integrated with the mainstream of the Canadian labour movement. While acknowledging the French-Canadian and Catholic labour movement's contribution to the development of a working-class consciousness, the Citélibristes contended that excessive clerical control and participation had stifled the development of the CTCC.[33] Making a claim for what was no longer the dominant situation, Gérard Pelletier argued that

Many priests involved in the labour movement had a tendency to organize fairly innocuous study sessions and many of the chaplains during the early years exercised an awkward and abusive authority. One example only: the unanimity of these clerics prevented the establishment of a strike fund during the founding of the CTCC on the pretext that such a fund "would incite social disorder." Deprived of the necessary tools and rendered overly moderate by a timidity disguised as morality, Christian unionism constituted for a long time an illusion on the level of concrete action.[34]

Cité libre's demands for secularization extended to the teachers' unions in the province. It claimed, with strong supporting evidence, that church leaders were responsible for the Commission des écoles catholiques de Montréal's recalcitrant attitude toward the Alliance as well as the creation of the rival teachers' union in 1951. The church evidently feared for its control over the field of education if the teachers acquired militant, secular unions.[35]

Neo-nationalists adopted a more circumspect approach to the question of secularization of the CTCC. While they made few public statements in favour of church withdrawal from the CTCC, they never once objected to the quiet process of secularization that had been taking place within the movement since 1943.[36] That year it was decided to allow unions and federations to admit non-Catholics as nonvoting members and to drop the adjective Catholic in their titles. Union chaplains also lost their right of veto over resolutions adopted by delegates at annual conventions or union executives at all levels.[37] The influence of the chaplains was further reduced by the creation of the lay-controlled Service d'éducation in 1949 and the Collège ouvrier in 1952. Both bodies played down doctrinal issues and emphasized sociological analysis, economic and political education, and the technical problems of organization, negotiations, and collective agreements.[38] The final steps towards complete secularization began in 1956 when the Fédération de la métallurgie proposed complete deconfessionalization of the CTCC. The executive moved cautiously but with full determination to secularize the movement so that it could become more competitive with the FTQ, especially in the heterogeneous industrial environment of Montreal. Assured of the support of incumbent chaplains and the Catholic hierarchy, thanks to the work of Abbé Gérard Dion, director of Relations industrielles, the CTCC executive proposed deconfessionalization in 1960. The membership adopted a new title – Confédération des syndicats nationaux (CSN). The only real opposition had come from a group of conservative retired chaplains.[39] Convinced that this development was long overdue, the neo-nationalists gave full coverage and complete support to this secularization process.[40] Filion promptly chastised the retired chaplains for their reactionary opposition and declared that deconfessionalization in fact was long overdue.[41] The church, to the surprise of most observers, had proved much less obstinate than either Citélibristes or neo-nationalists had presumed.

NATIONAL ECONOMIC LIBERATION OR CHRISTIAN INDUSTRIAL DEMOCRACY

Neo-nationalists and Citélibristes shared the conviction that organized labour should become an autonomous, dynamic, secular force. Both groups also believed that organized labour could best improve the socioeconomic condition of its members by championing the cause of structural reforms in industrial monopoly capitalism. Yet both groups were motivated by their respective ideological concerns and aspirations. Neo-nationalists supported the movement for greater industrial democracy because not only would it improve the situation of the workers but it would provide French Canadians with a means of overcoming their position of subservience in the Quebec economy. On the other hand, Citélibristes championed the cause of industrial democracy primarily as a way of humanizing an increasingly impersonal and exploitative capitalist system. Democratic unions working to democratize the work-place would contribute greatly to the development of a liberal and social democratic society in Quebec.

After the war, the CTCC turned away from social corporatism as its official objective. In its place it chose to pursue the implementation of industrial democracy through reforms such as co-management, profit-sharing, and co-ownership of industrial enterprises. The impetus for this shift came from a small but highly active and dedicated group of priests involved with the Catholic labour movement as chaplains and industrial relations and social science educators. Brought together after the war under the auspices of the archbishops and bishops of the province of Quebec, these priests organized annual sessions in 1945, 1946, and 1947 on the important question of the professional organization of workers and employers as well as the more innovative issue of the participation of workers in industry. Pleased with the initial activities of these priests involved in social action, the Assembly of Quebec Bishops, during its February 1948 meeting, officially sanctioned the group as the Commission sacerdotale d'études sociales (CSES) under the presidency of Msgr Jean-Charles Leclaire, vicar-general of Saint-Hyacinthe. The CSES's role was to advise the episcopacy on the postwar social and economic problems facing Quebec society. It did this and more, much to the eventual dismay of the conservative members of the hierarchy and the Duplessis government. In fact, the CSES within a year of its formal creation found itself embroiled in the 1949 asbestos strike and its aftermath.[42]

The CSES represented, in effect, the first official attempt to give the social doctrine of the Catholic church a liberal interpretation in its application to Quebec's social and economic problems. The central thrust of the CSES was the elaboration of well-founded socioeconomic and doctrinal arguments for the restructuring and reforming of the existing capitalist system. In the commissioners' view, this objective was to be accomplished by organized labour achieving for its membership gradual participation in the management, profits, and ownership of industry.[43]

The CSES gained public recognition during the asbestos strike when, with the permission of the Quebec episcopacy, it published a press release calling upon all lay and religious organizations as well as individuals to help the church organize a province-wide collection fund to assist the strikers and their families, many of whom were on the verge of starvation and threatened with eviction from their company homes. According to the CTCC, a total sum of nearly $430,000, along with a similar amount of goods, was collected. This large donation of cash and goods was largely responsible for enabling the strikers to prolong their struggle. As subsequent events would show, this action also proved to be the high point of the CSES's involvement in direct social action and contributed to its eventual decline and influence. Many of the more conservative-minded bishops feared this newfound social activism of the church and a backlash set in after the strike was over and the dust had settled. Archbishop Charbonneau of Montreal, chairman of the Commission épiscopale des questions sociales (section française) and an ardent supporter of the work of the CSES, took early retirement on the west coast. Jacques Cousineau, one of the most dynamic and committed members of the CSES, was asked by his superiors to resign his position as moral counsellor of the CTCC's Montreal Central Council in 1950 and he was also removed from the CSES in 1952. For fear of further alienating the Duplessis government and the private sector, the church quietly abandoned its pursuit of industrial democracy.[44]

The historical significance of the CSES resides in two developments. First, CSES members influenced CTCC leaders and delegates to undertake a thorough study of industrial democracy during their 1948 convention and subsequently to commit their movement to the pursuit of this objective. Indeed, it was precisely the CSES's adoption of such a goal that contributed to the length and bitterness of the asbestos strike in 1949. The president of the Johns-Manville corporation, Lewis H. Brown, was convinced that the hidden objective of the asbestos union leaders, encouraged by the CTCC and the CSES, was to participate in the management of his company, thereby undermining the capitalist system. He along with the Duplessis government was fully determined to break the back of this church-inspired and sanctioned movement for industrial democracy. In 1951 the CTCC adopted as part of its revised declaration of principles a statement committing the organization to pursuing the implemention of industrial democracy.[45] Second, the CSES's recommendations on the structural reform of capitalism became the official doctrine of the Quebec Catholic church, when shortly after the asbestos strike the bishops and archbishops published a joint pastoral letter on the problems of the working class in Quebec society.[46]

The pastoral letter's sanctioning of the concept of co-management, profit-sharing, and co-ownership of industry was based, as usual, on the social doctrine outlined in *Rerum Novarum* and *Quadragesimo Anno*, two papal encyclicals devoted to the problems of the working class. What was new and refreshing was that the arguments were also based on a solid description and understanding of the great socioeconomic changes which had taken place, and were continuing to take place, in Quebec society. Industrialization and urbanization had shattered family life and traditional virtues, created serious social tensions and dislocation, a decline in private and public morals, and a general falling-off of the Christian spirit. The greatest sense of alienation had been experienced in the daily lives of the workers who found little personal satisfaction in assembly-line industrial occupations. Transferred to an urban environment, the family and the parish no longer offered the same degree of support and protection for the worker and his family.

But, as the pastoral letter readily admitted, the trend was irreversible, and the new industrial order offered a better standard of living if the benefits were shared more equitably. The family and the parish would have to adapt to the new environment, and other institutions such as cooperatives, *caisses populaires*, and unions were required to reintegrate the worker in society and provide him once again with a sense of control over his life and that of his family.[47] Keenly aware that the workers' growing sense of class consciousness had to be accepted and dealt with constructively, the letter placed its emphasis upon humanizing the work world: "Modern economic life must provide the worker his legitimate portion of responsibility, of culture, and of material goods, in a fully human social order."[48] The first step was to ensure that the worker received a just wage, sufficient to fulfil his and his family's needs, to enable him to acquire private property, and to provide higher education for those working-class children capable of taking advantage of it. Second, to ensure that capital and technology were at the service of the worker and not vice versa, the letter called for a social contract to temper the traditional labour contract which emphasized material remuneration and confrontation. Organized labour and business were enjoined to work voluntarily towards full industrial democracy by instituting a system of co-management, profit-sharing, and co-ownership.[49]

The suggested reforms were not as radical as they seemed on the surface, but neither was the pastoral letter merely a restatement of the long-standing corporatist theories of the Ecole sociale populaire and the traditional nationalists. The voice of labour in the management committees was conceived of as consultative. Co-ownership and profit-sharing, the letter assured the private sector, were to respect the legitimate rights of the owners of the means of production. How this apparently contradictory objective was to be accomplished was not stated. While the letter envisaged an attenuation of class conflict and industrial disputes and the creation of a new sense of confidence and cooperation between capital and labour, its main thrust was not the reestablishment of an ordered hierarchical society but rather the democratization and humanization of the work world of the proletariat. The letter broke new ground in that the bishops demonstrated a sincere desire to view the problems of Quebec society from the workingman's perspective and recommended solutions that went beyond earlier proposals for undermining and shackling the working class. The letter reaffirmed the bishop's desire to assure the masses, now urban rather than rural, that the church was not the instrument of the powerful and wealthy against the powerless and the poor. The "holy alliance" between church and state was weakened considerably as the church gave notice that it no longer accepted the state's partial attitude towards capital and capitalists.

Neo-nationalists followed this evolution within the social thought of the Quebec Catholic church with a great deal of interest and self-satisfaction. Laurendeau and Filion scrutinized closely and approved wholeheartedly the work of the Commission sacerdotale. Reference was made on repeated occasions to concrete examples of co-management and profit-sharing schemes in Europe and the United States, and neo-nationalists were undoubtedly familiar with the 1948 studies of Jean Pierre Després, a Laval social scientist, on the question of worker participation.[50] Neo-nationalists ardently supported the cause of industrial democracy because it would help integrate the working class with the modern world by giving the workers their equitable share of the profits of production and a measure of responsibility in the decision-making process affecting their lives. Reform of the capitalist economy was not merely a demagogic suggestion to appease the masses but a practical recognition of the dignity of man. Sincere, practising Catholics had a moral responsibility to take up the challenge and pursue it to a successful conclusion.[51]

The Catholic labour movement, by taking on the task of creating a more humane socioeconomic structure, was leaving behind the confrontation stage of unionism and entering a new, more creative stage in its development. The Catholic church's decision to give its official support to this radical but necessary endeavour was welcomed as a sign of required solidarity from one of Quebec's most powerful and influential institutions.[52] At no time did the neo-nationalists delude themselves into thinking that the implementation of a new social order was going to be easy. The combined response of Quebec's political élites and big business community to the asbestos strike, where the miners' union had first introduced in a small way the concept of co-management, indicated quite clearly that big business was not going to be very cooperative. Neither were the French-Canadian political and economic élites going to be very compliant. Jules-A. Brillant, a legislative councillor and big businessman, denounced the idea of profit-sharing as revolutionary and heretical. Duplessis began referring to Le Devoir as "bolchevic."[53]

There was, however, another more important motivation for the neo-nationalists' support for industrial democracy. A restructuring of the Quebec economy and of industry along the lines suggested above was perceived as one of the most important methods of achieving a greater control over Quebec's economy by French Canadians. A powerful and active French-Canadian labour movement could, by creating consumer, producer, and housing cooperatives and by achieving full industrial democracy, lead the way to collective economic independence.[54] Fernand Dansereau, *Le Devoir*'s labour reporter, contended that French-Canadian workers were drawn in large measure by their nationalist instincts to demand co-management and profit-sharing. It represented for them not only a means of individual advancement, "but also a means of escaping the total enslavement of an entire people by foreign economic forces."[55] Reflecting, in 1953, on the concerted business-government opposition to the CTCC and FUIQ, Dansereau questioned the church's withdrawal of its publicly stated support for organized labour and the struggle for industrial democracy. Did the church unconsciously oppose the increased secularization and radicalization of the CTCC or did the practical implementation of the social thought of the church threaten in certain areas its own vested interests? Perhaps, he suggested, because the church was becoming heavily dependent upon the Quebec government to finance its educational and social service responsibilities it did not want to bite the hand that fed it. Dansereau was also sceptical of the CTCC's unwillingness to push hard for industrial democracy. He urged the CTCC to channel in a constructive way the unconscious nationalist instincts of the French-Canadian working class. He wondered if the union leaders had lost all hope of achieving on the economic level a certain level of autonomy and self-government for the French-Canadian nation.[56]

The neo-nationalists' scepticism about the direction in which organized labour, especially the CTCC, was moving had, prior to 1958 at least, some basis in reality. Their scepticism applied invariably to Citélibristes who also encouraged and actively supported the CTCC's turning away from nationalist concerns and redefining of its role strictly in terms of socioeconomic objectives. Gérard Picard and Jean Marchand had, with good reason in the late 1940s, decided to break the long-standing association of the CTCC with traditional French-Canadian nationalism because that nationalism had become too intimately identified with the antisocial, antilabour, and big business-oriented Union Nationale government under Maurice Duplessis. Duplessis, warned Picard, was using the rhetoric of provincial autonomy and French-Canadian nationalism to impede the creation of social security programs and in so doing was camouflaging the necessity of regulating the private sector, especially big business.[57] Under these conditions the CTCC felt it was necessary and politically wise to place a strict socioeconomic interpretation upon its demand for co-management, profit-sharing, and co-ownership, as well as all of its other reform proposals. The goal was not the takeover of foreign corporations but the overhauling of the existing capitalist system and the creation of a truly democratic society based on Christian social philosophy. The existing capitalist system recognized only one law, the law of the strongest. This economic and social philosophy had given birth to an economic dictatorship so powerful that even the state, in certain countries, functioned in its interests. It created huge factories and introduced technological innovations which dehumanized and depersonalized the working environment to the point where the worker operated as a less than perfect cog in an increasingly complex and demanding machine. By subordinating everything, including the worker, to the profit motive, modern capitalists had created an economic system incompatible with a truly human civilization. A true democracy required a more equitable sharing of responsibilities and benefits. This could only begin at the plant level and progress from there to entire industries and groups of industries, some nationalized, some private, and some cooperatively owned and operated.[58] The concern of unions under these circumstances had to be restricted to seeking an improvement of the socioeconomic position of the working classes. All other concerns were secondary and in some cases, such as nationalist preoccupations, might even be detrimental to labour's cause.

The Citélibristes agreed entirely with this strategy of "Economie et Humanisme," as it was dubbed by Réginald Boisvert.[59] Trudeau and Pelletier were convinced that only organized labour in Canada had the power and ideological commitment to reform North American capitalism by creating a more humane economic and social system.[60] Yet, to be fair, CTCC leaders and Citélibristes believed sincerely that a reformed Quebec economy would lead not only to a higher standard of living for all working-class French Canadians but would also provide the francophone community with the effective new instruments it required to regain control over its financial and political institutions.[61] The latter development, it was felt, would be a natural by-product of economic reforms. Nationalist objectives should never become the top priority of organized labour. Yet Citélibristes never denied that the CTCC had a special role to play in the survival and expansion of French-Canadian society.

PAN-CANADIAN OR QUEBEC-CENTRED UNIONISM

A subject which revealed the inherent differences between the ideological positions of neo-nationalists and Citélibristes was the very sensitive question of the CTCC's possible affiliation with the newly formed Canadian Labour Congress. The ebb and flow of the labour unity movement between 1955 and 1960 was extremely complicated. The two central reasons for the failure of the unity movement were the opposition of weak union locals and federations within the CTCC and the Fédération du travail du Québec (FTQ), and the gradual association of a revitalized and restructured CTCC with the neo-nationalism taking root in Quebec during the late 1950s.[62] The CTCC leaders, Marchand and Picard, had developed a strong working relationship with the international industrial unions affiliated with the Canadian Congress of Labour and centred in FUIQ. They shared a similar distaste for big business and the Duplessis administration. Consequently, when the CCL and the TLC announced their merger in June 1955, the CTCC executive was attracted by the potential benefits of some form of affiliation with what would become in 1956 the Canadian Labour Congress. Although the 1955 CTCC convention heard its president's report on the question of the impending merger and possible affiliation and voted to set up a unity committee to study the issue, it was already clear that the leadership and a good proportion of the rank and file did not favour the loss of the CTCC's status as a separate national labour organization.[63] Jean Marchand explained the situation in the following terms:

We find ourselves faced by a dilemma: if we maintain the status quo, we are doomed to union inefficiency. The problem exists on the economic and social levels, and at these levels we suffer from a congenital defect, since our present structure does not allow us to cover the economic field we should cover, especially since the advent of large-scale basic industry.

Nevertheless, we must maintain as many of the CCCL's characteristics as we can since they have been at the base of the Confederation's value and dynamism.[64]

The CTCC executive was willing to face the challenge and the unity committee headed by Marchand, after several meetings with the CLC's unity committee, presented the delegates attending the 1957 convention with a fourteen-point program of affiliation. The crucial points were that the CTCC would join as a national union but would lose its city centrals to the CLC within two years; it would cease to function on the federal level; and it would abandon its function as legislative representative in Quebec within two years. Finally, the CTCC would drop its affiliation with the International Federation of Christian Trade Unions and adopt a nonconfessional name.[65] Pandemonium ensued as a large number of delegates, a slight majority as events showed, representing nationalist-minded locals and federations, rejected the program and forced the adoption of a substantially amended set of affiliation conditions. The new version called for the CTCC to continue to operate as a national movement in Quebec alongside the newly formed Fédération des travailleurs du Québec (FTQ), retain its city centrals, remain unbound by CLC decisions in cases of jurisdictional conflicts, and "reexamine" the question of affiliation with the IFCTU.[66]

The prospect of achieving a satisfactory agreement with the CLC was virtually ended. The CTCC's negotiating unity committee had been handed a set of conditions, may of which were *a priori* unacceptable to the CLC, which denied on principle special status for any of its affiliates. Gérard Picard, the retiring president, pleaded with the delegates at the 1958 convention to give the unity committee a more flexible mandate, but to no avail. The nationalist forces in the CTCC were simply too strong.[67] Jean Marchand, who had played his hand very carefully, blamed the failure to achieve some sort of decentralized affiliation on the fact that the CLC did not really want the CTCC to continue to operate as a national union because it wanted its affiliated unions to have the right to negotiate for merger with the CTCC locals and federations. This condition, argued Marchand with a great deal of justification, meant the inevitable demise of the CTCC as a Québécois national organization. That eventuality neither he nor the members could or would accept.[68]

Both neo-nationalists and Citélibristes took a keen interest in the question of affiliation and the CTCC's future direction. *Le Devoir*'s position was from the start unequivocal. The CTCC was perceived as one of the most important institutions of the French-Canadian nation and, as such, had responsibilities towards the cultural milieu which had created it and within which it functioned. Class objectives of the workers must not be sought to the detriment of national objectives of the French-Canadian community. Both must be pursued simultaneously. Moreover, union pluralism despite its inconveniences was considered more humane than a monolithic centralized structure.[69] Filion was highly critical of the unity committee's fourteen-point program of affiliation and indicated *Le Devoir*'s support for the continuation of the CTCC as an independent national labour central with only a limited affiliation with the CLC. If the CTCC, rather than the FTQ, was recognized as the provincial central, then perhaps a closer affiliation might be envisaged. Until that time, the CTCC, suggested Filion in the strongest terms possible, would be better off pursuing its own development, serving both French-Canadian workers and the French-Canadian community.[70]

Citélibristes for the most part welcomed wholeheartedly the initiative taken by the CTCC executive towards achieving affiliation with the CLC, that is, as a provincial labour organization retaining control over its internal structures and its ideological orientation. The Quebec economy was deeply integrated with the Canadian and North American economies and therefore organized labour, to be effective, had no choice but to cooperate and confront the common enemy, corporate and industrial capitalism. Citélibristes, along with the CTCC leadership, felt that closer ties with the CLC would enable the CTCC to take part in and influence the socioeconomic and political policies of the Canadian Labour Congress.[71] On the possibility of nationalism once again gaining the upper hand in the CTCC, Boisvert proffered this warning: "If a conservative wing, nationalist and confessional at all costs, were to succeed in influencing in its direction an important fraction of the CTCC; if this wing were to denounce all open-mindedness as an act of resignation or were to succeed in discrediting any movement of opinion aimed at coordinating in one way or another the action of the CTCC with the general activities of the Canadian labour movement – then the efficacy of the CTCC would be finished for a long time to come."[72]

Undoubtedly, Citélibristes were disappointed at the CTCC's failure to achieve some sort of affiliation with the Canadian Labour Congress. However, they probably also agreed with Marchand that the CLC had not been very accommodating. Certainly Citélibristes did not want to see the demise of the CTCC, an important element in their overall strategy to achieve a more democratic and egalitarian society in Quebec. The democratization of Quebec society, many Citélibristes felt in the early and mid-fifties, could be advanced more quickly if the various progressive labour centrals cooperated in a coordinated program of militant indirect and direct political action.

LABOUR AND POLITICAL ACTION

Citélibristes, to a greater degree than most neo-nationalists, perceived indirect and direct political action as a natural extension of militant and effective unionism. For these liberal and social democrats, the new sociopolitical order had to have the consent of the voting masses and therefore could be achieved responsibly only through the existing political process and political institutions. From its inception in 1950, *Cité libre* had written off the existing traditional parties as anachronistic and reactionary institutions. Nevertheless, the demise of the Bloc had left a residue of defeatism and apoliticism among the younger generation. Pelletier categorically rejected the nationalists' strategy of political education and felt that the apoliticism of Quebec's young men and women in their twenties was leading to a one-party state. He blamed this attitude on a Catholic Action movement "too much oriented toward investigation rather than action," and a renewed postwar affluence. Many of the depression generation of working-class students, like himself, had come to distrust and even lose their faith in the capitalist system, whereas the postwar generation, easily finding summer employment and well-paid positions upon graduation, expressed less concern about the shortcomings and injustices of the capitalist system.[73] Many Citélibristes – Charles Lussier, Gérard Pelletier, Réginald Boisvert, Jean-Paul Lefebvre, and Pierre Vadeboncoeur – took their political responsibilities seriously. They worked long hours trying to recruit new members and create local organizations for the Quebec wing of the CCF. The seeds of their labour bore little fruit while their identification with left-wing politics created problems for them in dealing with members of the judiciary, the church, and, of course, the government. Maurice Duplessis, for example, steadfastly refused to meet delegations from the CTCC or FUIQ if he recognized CCF party supporters in their ranks.[74]

Yet the support of organized labour, the Citélibristes argued, was essential if a successful left-of-centre political party was to take root in Quebec. In the late forties and early fifties the Citélibristes placed their hopes in the CCF, but this party seemed destined to remain in the political wilderness unless an important electoral base could be found. Citélibristes and some union leaders and organizers, encouraged by the development of the CCF in Ontario, felt that organized labour with its ever-expanding membership was the appropriate place to start. After all, was it not the fourth estate that stood to benefit from greater social and economic democracy? By 1950 over one-quarter of Quebec's labour force of nearly one million was unionized and the working class constituted the majority of the electorate. Prior to the creation of the FTQ in 1957, the CTCC, with its nearly 100,000 members, constituted the single largest voting bloc available to serve as a base for a social democratic party. If, as one Canadian Press reporter suggested, white-collar workers in the public and private sectors could be organized by the CTCC then the potential base could be further enlarged.[75] Little wonder that the Citélibristes looked upon the CTCC's newfound militancy and secularization with favour and high hopes.

Indeed, events in the early fifties encouraged and fed these high hopes only to have them dashed by late 1952. The initiative for increased political action within the CTCC came from certain federations and unions, namely the Fédération de la métallurgie and certain regional locals like Shawinigan, Arvida, and Asbestos. Recalling the struggle for the withdrawal of the regressive labour code, Bill 5, and the lengthy and costly asbestos strike, militant unionists were able to get the majority support of CTCC delegates at the September 1949 annual convention for the creation of a "Comité d'action civique," renamed the following year "Comité d'orientation politique." In its *Report* to the 1952 congress, the committee justified political action on the ground that effective unionism demanded participation in the political decision-making process, which since the turn of the century had become increasingly dominated by a plutocracy. "The workers, in their daily activities, collide continuously with this alliance of business and state forces. This is why they must struggle on the political level to regain for the state its full and entire freedom."[76]

According to the committee's terms of reference, the CTCC defined its political action primarily in terms of political lobbying in Quebec City and Ottawa to obtain legislative reform and a program of political education for its members via its paper *Le Travail* and public meetings in its various regional centres.[77] In fact, encouraged by its militant federations and locals and supported by a compliant leadership, the committee campaigned for the CTCC on behalf of four Liberal candidates in the 1952 provincial elections and encouraged workers to vote for other Liberal candidates. Three of the four were elected and one observer felt that half of the Liberal contingent of twenty-three members owed their elections to worker support.[78]

The Comité d'orientation politique acknowledged the importance of the workingman's vote by noting that fourteen Liberal members won in urban ridings while another five came from mixed urban-rural ridings which had important industrial centres. However, it did not acknowledge the success of the campaigns in favour of specific Liberal candidates because the CTCC executive had decided to come out firmly against supporting any political party or any specific candidates.[79] The committee's activities had aroused, undoubtedly, the opposition of conservative elements within the CTCC and the community at large. Rumours, aided and abetted by Duplessis and the Union Nationale, were circulating to the effect that the CTCC was on the verge of creating a labour party to contest the next provincial elections in 1956. The president, Gérard Picard, and the secretary-general, Jean Marchand, were dead-set against such a development. Neither were they willing to have the CTCC identified in any official capacity whatsoever with the provincial Liberal party. Successfully heading off the political activists in the organization, the president announced at the September 1952 convention a policy of political action that was endorsed by the majority of the delegates. Reiterating his arguments of 1949, Gérard Picard declared that the CTCC "had not founded and was not planning to found a political party. The CTCC was not affiliated with nor was it even planning to affiliate with any political party." He did acknowledge, however, that indirect political action on behalf of the CTCC and its local had resulted in the defeat of candidates of one political party (Union Nationale), while helping in the election of candidates of another party (the Liberal party). He went on to argue that political action by organized labour would diminish considerably once the climate of labour relations in Quebec improved and if labour legislation "is prepared and implemented following a tripartite formula which requires the collaboration of the state, business associations, and unions.[80] In sum, he favoured restricting labour's efforts to indirect political action on governments and political education of its members. So did the delegates. They approved an amendment to the constitution prohibiting the confederation and its locals from affiliating with or supporting any political party.[81]

Citélibristes were not at all pleased with the CTCC's decision to refrain from direct political action. While it was understandable that the organization lacked resources to form its own labour party, it could easily have thrown its official support behind the existing social democratic party, the CCF. It is difficult to say to what extent Pelletier's views were constrained by the fact that he was editor of Le Travail. In 1951, he expressly stated that direct political action would destroy organized labour, while well-managed and coordinated indirect political action was necessary and invigorating for progressive-minded unions. Yet, in 1954, Pelletier wondered out loud how Canadians could consider themselves a sovereign people when they continually denounced any talk of direct political action sponsored by organized labour.[82]

Other Citélibristes could speak more forcefully. In December 1952 Trudeau expressed the group's discontent at the CTCC's decision. Trudeau's radicalism, as Charles Lussier recalls, was not tempered by the need to earn his living. This outspokenness and independence irked his colleagues, yet they respected him for it because they knew all too well that few people from the upper class were willing to jeopardize their social status to champion the cause of reform.[83] Trudeau believed somewhat naïvely that "Quebec's workers constituted a powerful cleansing force for the society's democratic laws and customs." The workers' growing sense of class consciousness and antinationalism, their education in the principles and practices of democracy, and their strength in numbers would lead them inevitably as a class to demand that "universal suffrage become a reality rather than a sham."[84] The workers and their leaders had come to understand that the modern state could and did intervene in positive ways on behalf of given sectors of the population, and that, given a conflict of interest, the government normally chose to govern for the benefit of those sectors that brought it to power. Yet most union leaders and labour movements had not, in Trudeau's view, adjusted their conception of political action accordingly. While he approved of the work of the Comité d'orientation politique, he was obviously displeased with the CTCC's leaders for opposing partisan political action and for channelling what little direct action was encouraged within the traditional party structures.[85] He denounced the politicians, the press, petty bourgeois professionals, and union leaders for constantly preaching to the workers "that politics will be dangerous for them." It was fundamentally undemocratic to discourage continually the largest class of citizens from exercising in a spirit of independence their civic functions. "No doubt," wrote Trudeau,

we do not push our impertinence to the point of completely dissuading workers from going to vote. Nor do we despise a number of influential labour leaders for participating in the electoral campaign. Yet we insist that it is absolutely necessary that the worker's vote and the labour leaders' participation must be exercised within the traditional ideological framework of the old parties, that is, to the advantage of established interests. Of effective political action, not too much! Clearly, it is absolutely forbidden to dream of labour candidates, new parties, or independent political action. In short, we accommodate ourselves to the reality of the labour vote very poorly indeed. In fact, we do everything in our power to make it ineffective.[86]

Citélibristes, led by Trudeau, placed their hopes on the newly created industrial union central, the FUIQ. Affiliated with the Canadian Congress of Labour and the CIO, the FUIQ was from the outset committed to political action via the Cooperative Commonwealth Federation. Consequently, FUIQ leaders set up a Political Action Committee which, by April 1954, was publishing its own bulletin entitled *En garde*! When the common front struggle with the CTCC against the Duplessis government's antilabour and undemocratic legislation, Bills 19 and 20, failed to get the support of the Liberal majority in Quebec's Legislative Council, the Political Action Committee concluded that the only effective solution to labour's problems lay in the creation of a political party devoted to the interests of working people. At the FUIQ's 1954 convention in Champigny, delegates adopted a resolution authorizing the Political Action Committee to draft a political manifesto. While there was no intention of founding in the near future a political party, Roméo Mathieu, the FUIQ's secretary-general, reminded delegates that their union central was not officially affiliated with the CCF but merely recognized it as the only existing viable social democratic party and therefore the political arm of organized labour in Canada. He then went on to add: "But there is a possibility of establishing in Quebec a political party which will have a program very similar to that of the CCF party but which will have a distinctive québécois character. This is the only effective solution to our problems."[87]

The Political Action Committee produced the "Manifeste au Peuple du Québec," which set out a wide-ranging program for the creation of a social democratic society in Quebec but did not yet include a call for the creation of a new political party.[88] The committee was deeply divided on the issue. Its members submitted to the delegates a majority report in support of a Quebec-based workers' party and a minority report strongly recommending that the FUIQ support the CCF, a party endorsed by the CCL as the political arm of organized labour. The split within the FUIQ originated in a dispute over Quebec autonomy and reflected a growing sense of neo-nationalism on the part of some of its members. The nationalists of the FUIQ, led by the secretary-general, Roméo Mathieu, felt instinctively that French Canadians in Quebec distrusted the CCF for its Anglo-Saxon origins and its emphasis upon the need for a strong central government. The nationalists pointed to the CCF's opposition to increased taxing powers for Quebec in general and to the adoption of a deductibility formula as recommended by the FUIQ in its brief to the Tremblay Commission.[89] The problem for the nationalists arose from the fact that many of the FUIQ's members belonged to locals affiliated with the CCL and considered that they were affiliated with the CCF. Many others were simply opposed to any sort of political action. When the issue of a separate political party came to a vote the rank and file, encouraged by the president, R.J. "Doc" Lamoureux, strongly favoured the

CCF as their political vehicle for social democracy. A majority of members also rejected Mathieu's plea for a greater representation of French Canadians via the CCL on international labour organizations and symposia. This, they argued, smacked of special status for French Canadians. Frustrated, many of the nationalists who favoured a distinctly francophone social democratic party left the FUIQ to create the Ligue d'action socialiste to spread the idea of social democracy.[90] Discouraged and disillusioned, and feeling that the CCF stood little chance of gaining the essential comprehensive support from organized labour in Quebec, Trudeau and the Citélibristes then embarked on an attempt to create a new political movement acceptable to organized labour. This development will be treated in a separate chapter.

In the meantime, the failure of coordinated union action to force Duplessis to withdraw Bills 19 and 20 prompted a resurgence of pressure within the CTCC for more direct political action. With the full support of Picard and Marchand, the Fédération de la métallurgie gave notice at its annual meeting in July 1954 that it would present a resolution establishing a special fund of $20,000 for political education and authorizing the Comité d'orientation politique to help certain locals set up electoral funds for the support of a select number of candidates independent of the two traditional parties and conscious of labour's interests.[91] The committee took the cue and presented its own resolution to this effect at the September 1954 congress. Opposition was located in the Fédérations du textile et du vêtement, among the municipal employees, and in regional locals, namely, Quebec City and Trois Rivières. Picard argued that direct political action was essential and urgent but experience had demonstrated that unions, if they did not want to lose sight of their own internal objectives, had to remain completely independent of any political party they helped to bring to power. Political action was a means and not an end for organized labour.[92] Jean Marchand favoured strongly the strategy calling for endorsement of special candidates. "This will lead," he declared, revealing the motivation of the executive, "invariably to the creation of a party. When we have succeeded, alone or with others, in electing fifteen independents, it is inevitable that these people will form an association. I do not see anything wrong with this as long as the Confederation remains as independent of this party as it is of all others. Above all, we must guarantee our freedom to defend the workers."[93] The delegates accepted the committee's resolution opening the way for the CTCC's participation in the next provincial election.[94] The decision revealed that the executive and a large sector of the membership desired the eventual formation of a francophone-inspired social democratic party. They were realistic enough to understand that this would not happen without an initial catalytic input on the part of organized labour.[95] In the light of developments within the FUIQ and the CTCC, *Cité libre*'s decision to push for the eventual formation of a new political movement satisfactory to all sectors of organized labour is more understandable.

The neo-nationalists, for the most part, did not share these aspirations, or delusions, as Filion preferred to call them. Jean-Marc Léger, the most radical and politically oriented neo-nationalist, was confident that workers, given the choice, would choose a socialist party over a "liberal" party because the former offered socioeconomic as well as political equality. Léger maintained that the CTCC should move towards the formation of a labour party to allow French-Canadian workers to gain control of the political direction of the *Cité*. "The various ways of defending the interests of the nation, such as the improvement of the lot of the masses, cannot be disassociated: all of the objectives of the nation will be accomplished together or not at all."[96] Laurendeau and Filion, however, were staunchly opposed to the idea of a labour party sponsored by the CTCC or any other labour movement. In their view it was fundamentally undemocratic to call upon workers to vote for a specific party, such as the CCF, simply because they belonged to a certain labour union, the CIO. "I see, on the part of labour leaders," wrote Laurendeau, "a kind of moral swindling, an attempt to undermine what remains of the critical spirit of the masses."[97] *Le Devoir* favoured the thrust of the resolution adopted by the CTCC delegates at their 1952 congress. Laurendeau also gave warning to the traditional parties that if they failed to respond to the needs of a dynamic and expanding labour movement a third party, independent of organized labour, would appear on the scene to attract the votes of disgruntled and frustrated workers.[98] While not denying the legitimacy and necessity of affiliation under certain circumstances, the neo-nationalists maintained throughout the fifties that organized labour should not become affiliated with any political party, new or old. Labour should not be a hostage to any new political movement which presumably might achieve power. A political party, on the other hand, restricted to championing the socioeconomic and political interests of the working class, stood little hope of achieving power. What greater reason was there for maintaining a healthy distance from the labour movement, asked Filion.[99] Furthermore, it was clear that the neo-nationalists had no desire to see an indigenous francophone institution like the CTCC becoming subservient to a pan-Canadian, anglophone-dominated political movement like the CCF. As could be expected, nationalist concerns always underlay the neo-nationalists' perception of the role of organized labour in Quebec, especially when the francophone CTCC was involved.

CONCLUSION

All in all, the labour movement played an important and influential role in helping to shape and reinforce the ideas and strategies of neo-nationalists and Citélibristes. In many areas the labour movement's commitment to certain reforms predated that of both groups, especially in the area of greater provincial control and development of provincial resources. In other areas, such as the relationship between labour and the state, labour and the church, labour's role in overcoming French Canada's economic inferiority, the support and commitment of groups like the neo-nationalists and Cité-libristes gave the labour centrals confidence and helped to prepare the public for the necessary changes. Both groups were intimately aware of the enormous challenges and obstacles confronting the creation of an indigenous and autonomous labour movement capable of representing the interests of the working class against the powerful and influential financial and industrial élites. The state had to assume its appropriate role as neutral third party and the monied classes had to come to accept the participation of the working class in the *Cité libre* as a natural and democratic right.

In the early fifties, the Citélibristes sincerely believed that organized labour was the centre around which all forces for socioeconomic and political reform must coalesce if the alliance between state and business was to be broken and the traditional political élites were to be replaced by élites sensitive to the needs and aspirations of all sectors and classes of society. Given their liberal and social democratic assumptions, it was only natural that the Citélibristes were ardent and active supporters of some form of affiliation of the CTCC with the CLC. It was also consistent with their ideological perspective that the entire labour movement should give its official sanction and support to an existing social democratic party like the CCF or, when that was not feasible, to some new indigenous social democratic movement. Labour's paramount commitment was to the socioeconomic advancement of its members as individuals rather than to the collective survival and expansion of the francophone collectivity in Quebec.

It was on this point that the neo-nationalists broke with the Citélibristes. Working-class francophone institutions, like middle- and upper-class ones, had a responsibility to fulfil the collective as well as the individual aspirations of their members. They, too, considered the labour movement as an indispensable tool for greater equality of social conditions and political rights for the individual working man and woman. They were also adamant in their belief that these objectives could be pursued, indeed must be pursued, simultaneously with the struggle for socioeconomic equality and political autonomy for the French-Canadian nation. Liberal and nationalist "revolutions" had to coincide. One could not be achieved at the expense of the other. This is why the neo-nationalists perceived nationalist concerns and aspirations in the asbestos strike, coloured the struggle for industrial democracy with nationalist goals, and refused to support the movement for francophone-dominated CTCC affiliation with the CLC or to support a pan-Canadian, anglophone-dominated, social democratic party like the CCF. One thing was clear: neither group could be charged with ideological inconsistency. The furrows which they hoed may have been narrow, but they were true.

CHAPTER EIGHT

Reforming Education: Key to National Survival or Prerequisite for Democracy?

The education battle has become, to use the most rigorous of terms, the battle for life. Those who see farther than our collective nose are all saying this in their own manner. Let us hope that their conviction will soon animate the entire population and help to orient Quebec politics toward undertaking rejuvenative reforms.[1]

No subject was more apt to spark a heated and controversial debate in the 1950s than the politically sensitive issue of educational reform. Both Cité-libristes and neo-nationalists proclaimed with force and well-founded conviction that their respective societal models were unattainable without some measure of educational reform at every level of the system. Indeed, their unanimity in this respect gave the chorus of demands for educational reform a degree of zeal and urgency not associated with other reform proposals.

Throughout the debate on education, Citélibristes emphasized time and time again the direct links between a modern, secular, public educational system and the attainment of a greater measure of equality and of political autonomy for individuals and more particularly for the working class. Full and effective actualization of an individual's potential was considered impossible without access to modern educational institutions. Participatory democracy at all levels and in all its forms was inconceivable without universal access to the complete range of modern educational programs funded, directed, and coordinated by the state. Only rational, enlightened citizens could carry on the struggle for socioeconomic equality and enforce meaningful responsible government within the existing system of parliamentary democracy. Only a well-educated and politically conscious society could prevent the emergence of autocratic and tyrannical governments functioning not in the common interest but for the benefit of powerful vested-interest groups.

Such high-minded liberal and social democratic convictions also inspired and motivated the neo-nationalists' demands for educational reform. They, too, desired to see every Quebec citizen achieve as complete self-fulfilment as was possible. Yet the collectivity's well-being and advancement was not merely the sum of each individual's well-being and development pursued independently. Educational reform had, for neo-nationalists, a concomitant goal, the survival and *épanouissement* of a modern francophone nation. Appropriate measures and policies had to be implemented by the Quebec government to ensure that educational reform should not become the Trojan horse leading to the collective suicide of the French-Canadian nationality. Neo-nationalists desired a democratic society of enlightened, educated citizens, the majority of whom would remain francophone in spirit, action, and language. Consequently, their reform suggestions were elaborated with this goal kept clearly in view. They felt confident that individual needs and aspirations could be coordinated with and reinforced by collective needs and aspirations. The challenge was enormous, but an impelling sense of commitment helped overcome a normal human reluctance to adopt the high-risk alternative. French-Canadian society was at a crossroads. It could choose to perpetuate an inefficient, anachronistic educational system and continue to survive merely as a quaint, folkloric pre-industrial community. Or the society could provide itself with a modern educational system and, in the process, become a francophone-inspired and directed modern industrial society.

It would be inaccurate to leave the impression that Citélibristes and neo-nationalists were alone in their concern for educational reform. One hundred and forty briefs presented to the Tremblay Commission dealt with various aspects of education. Teachers' associations, school boards, municipalities, voluntary associations like the chambres de commerce and the Sociétés Saint-Jean Baptiste, classical colleges, professors' organizations, universities, and many more offered educational reform proposals throughout the fifties. In response to these pleas for change, the Conseil de l'instruction publique's Catholic Committee and the Département de l'instruction publique made a number of minor adjustments based on their own investigations. Ironically, it was these inquiries and the briefs presented by the associations mentioned above which provided Citélibristes and neo-nationalists with convincing evidence to substantiate their respective demands for major reforms. This chapter will analyse the *Cité libre* and neo-nationalist critiques of, and reform proposals for, all three levels of education: primary, secondary, and university.

PRIMARY EDUCATION

Despite a century of socioeconomic change, the structure and administration of Quebec's only complete public system, the primary sector, remained virtually intact until the late 1950s.[2] Even the highly conservative members of the Tremblay Commission concurred in their 1956 *Report* that Quebec was at least twenty-five years behind the leading provinces in the field of educational policy and administration.[3] Quebec faced a dilemma. Did the existing educational system correspond to the needs of an era in which science and technology had become dominant? If not, did the proposed reforms not risk distorting "the fundamental principles of an integral education?"[4] Both Citélibristes and neo-nationalists came to the conclusion that the existing primary sector was not fulfilling the educational needs of a secular, urban, industrial society. Both groups agreed that the prevailing system had three serious and potentially damaging flaws: the drop-out rate of young French-Canadian boys and girls in elementary school was abnormally high; the administration of the system was unduly unrepresentative and unresponsive and the influence of the church was too pervasive; finally, the modes of financing primary education were inefficient and self-defeating.

Citélibristes promoted the cause of free and compulsory school attendance to the age of sixteen. They actively encouraged the union centrals to push for this reform. In time, the Montreal Catholic Teachers' Association, the Alliance, and all three provincial union controls supported this proposal.[5] Primary education, it was clearly shown, was élitist in practice if not in principle. Moreover, Quebec's primary school attendance record was the worst in Canada. Research on this sensitive issue was carried out by a leading neo-nationalist educational reformer, Arthur Tremblay, associate director of Laval's Ecole de pédagogie et d'orientation. The Fédération des commissions scolaires catholiques du Québec, provoked into action by the large and progressive Commission des écoles catholiques de Montréal, retained Arthur Tremblay to prepare its brief to the Tremblay Commission. The brief pointed out in a vivid manner that of 1,000 French-Canadian Catholic boys entering grade one only 560 remained by the time grade seven was reached. This was, in the Fédération's view, an appalling state of affairs, considering that primary education was designed, in theory at least, "to give all children a minimum level of education indispensable to all citizens."[6] Following acceptable psychological and pedagogical norms, the Fédération posited that 85 per cent of any given generation of students should reach grade seven and 72 per cent should complete it successfully. It was then shown conclusively that with the school-leaving age set at fourteen only 74 per cent of primary students could theoretically reach or pass grade seven. To achieve the magic number of 85 per cent it was imperative that the present and subsequent generations be kept in school at least until the age of sixteen.[7]

The Fédération's brief so impressed the Tremblay commissioners that they hired Arthur Tremblay to synthesize the 140 briefs dealing in whole or in part with education. Grasping a golden opportunity, Tremblay pushed the analysis further by drawing comparisons between Quebec's English-speaking Protestant system and the French-speaking Catholic system. He demonstrated with great impact the wide and growing disparity in educational achievements between Quebec's Catholic majority and the Protestant minority. Of a generation of French Canadians starting school in 1942–3 only 15.4 per cent reached grade eleven, as compared with 35.9 per cent of an identical generation of English Protestant children. He demonstrated that the attendance rate of French Catholics matched that of English Protestants only to grade six – the minimum education required to receive solemn communion. After grade six the drop-off rate was drastic, less than 20 per cent of French-Canadian boys reaching grade eleven compared with over 50 per cent of English Protestant children. French-Canadian society and its leaders were simply not fulfilling their responsibilities towards the young. The only immediate solution, contended Tremblay, was to follow the recommendation of the Fédération, the Alliance, and the unions and impose compulsory attendance to the age of sixteen.[8]

Citélibristes supported organized labour's argument that a strong link existed between unemployment and inadequate education. In fact, workers who had eight years or less of formal education experienced an unemployment level 50 per cent greater than workers who had attended school for a longer period.[9] Citélibristes, supported by Arthur Tremblay, contended that it was socially and democratically unjust for the state to allow its public elementary sector to systematically eliminate large numbers of working-class children before they had achieved the level of education commensurate with their abilities and their capacity to earn a decent and productive living.[10] They fully supported Father Georges-Henri Lévesque's claim that free and compulsory education to the age of sixteen was a natural, universal, and inviolate right of all children. The state had the responsibility to work towards the elimination of all social, economic, and cultural impediments to this right.[11] Neither was it democratic, claimed a French historian and educational reformer, Irénée Marrou, with the full concurrence of *Cité libre*, to extract "from the working class its best minds in order to incorporate them into the dominant or ruling class," in short, coopting them. This process merely contributed to the impoverishment of the working class by depriving it of its natural élite. An élite drawn from all classes was important and necessary but that élite must not cut itself off from its social and class origins. To ensure that this would not happen, modern technological and industrial societies must reinforce the general elementary education received by the working class with a continually renewed program of "popular education" to allow it to participate "more fully, more consciously, more effectively in our culture and our civilization (professional, union, and civic development but also artistic and cultural)."[12] Quebec society would remain undemocratic as long as its children were denied the essentials of free and compulsory primary education to the age of sixteen.

The neo-nationalists were more circumspect and slower to react. Initially they feared what might be excessive state intervention if compulsory attendance was legislated past the age of fourteen. Filion and Laurendeau steered clear of making public statements on this touchy subject, but gave full play in *Le Devoir* to the arguments of the Fédération, the unions, and Arthur Tremblay's work for the Tremblay Commission. On no occasion did the neo-nationalists oppose the recommendation for compulsory attendance despite the fact that Montreal's schools were already, by 1949, terribly overcrowded and the student population at the elementary level was growing at the rate of 25 per cent annually.[13] Implementation of the measure would most certainly have aggravated the crisis. Neither did the neo-nationalists support or attempt to give credence to the traditional nationalists' arguments against raising the compulsory attendance age from fourteen to sixteen. The Tremblay commissioners feared that such a move would precipitate further state intervention because the state alone could raise the necessary revenues through various forms of provincial taxes. Traditional nationalists maintained that general education for the masses was not required beyond the elementary level. Furthermore, this education must focus on the formation of well-rounded Christian individuals rather than providing young men and women with specialized training for the work-place.[14] In effect, while finding it very difficult to refute Arthur Tremblay's empirically based arguments, the Tremblay commissioners considered him and his reform proposals too radical.[15] They refused to recommend raising the compulsory attendance age to sixteen.[16] Undaunted, Arthur Tremblay, with the support of Cité-libristes and neo-nationalists, kept the issue before the general public. Traditional nationalists, he claimed, were using the Catholic church's alleged opposition to compulsory and free education to retain an élitist, anachronistic, and undemocratic system. He reminded them to reread Cardinal Villeneuve's 17 December 1942 address to the Catholic Committee which rescinded the church's long-standing opposition to state-imposed compulsory education. French Canada would only survive if its young men and women were educated to meet the challenges and imperatives of the modern world.[17]

Neo-nationalists and Citélibristes shared the conviction that Quebec's Catholic school boards and the Catholic Committee of the Conseil de l'instruction publique (CIP) were excessively conservative and unresponsive to the new needs and aspirations of students, parents, and teachers. They were fundamentally undemocratic in their composition. The bitter struggle between the Alliance and the Commission des écoles catholiques de Montréal for union recognition, a grievance committee, and compulsory arbitration led both reform groups to question the widsom of appointed school boards in Montreal and Quebec City. The seven-man appointed CECM – four by the Duplessis government and three by the church authorities – was accountable to no one except Duplessis. The parents as taxpayers, provincial and municipal, had no direct political influence on decisions concerning educational matters. The Duplessis government, charged *Le Devoir*, used the school board appointments as patronage positions and the school board members in turn used their power to grant supply and construction contracts to friends and faithful supporters of the Union Nationale.[18] The neo-nationalists demanded that the Montreal and Quebec City school boards become fully secularized. There was simply no need to call upon clerics for advice in such matters as school repairs, construction, fuel supplies, or salary discussions.[19] The board members should be elected by all the voters in every major urban school board constituency.[20] The various union centrals and the Fédération des commissions scolaires fully supported this proposal to secularize and democratize the boards and thereby reintroduce the voice of parents in educational matters.[21]

By 1960 the neo-nationalists were convinced that the Conseil de l'instruction publique and its denominational committees should be viewed as a pedagogical council and its members chosen, not for their religious affiliation, but rather on the basis of their administrative and pedogogical competence.[22] Most Citélibristes felt that this was not enough. None the less, Quebec's union centrals, the CTCC and the FTQ, by 1958 supported the thrust of the neo-nationalists' recommendation for secularization. They maintained that although respect for religious values was crucial, the Catholic Committee, influenced strongly by the *ex officio* presence of all the province's bishops, had stressed for too long the religious objectives of education at the expense of secular ones. "But the public school," suggested the unions, "is equally at the service of social and cultural values, and must satisfy a certain category of needs in our society, needs which are formally distinct from religious values or the requirements of a religious training. These values and 'temporal' needs cannot in any way be deduced from religious values and needs as such. And, as important as they are, the safeguarding of the latter does not guarantee absolutely the safeguarding of 'temporal' needs which must be pursued for themselves."[23] To guarantee the development of an education policy adapted to all the needs and demands of a rapidly changing and increasingly secularized society, the unions suggested that two-thirds of the Catholic Committee's lay members be selected by the Fédération des commissions scolaires, the teachers' associations, the Fédération des collèges classiques, and the universities. This reform, argued the neo-nationalists, should apply to the entire membership of the committee so as to prevent the general public from directing its wrath against the bishops for the committee's shortcomings and problems.[24]

Prior to 1960, the neo-nationalists refused to support the growing demand for a ministry of education. They feared that the backlash from the church would undermine other urgently required reforms. They also had well-founded doubts about how such a ministry would be operated under the

Union Nationale.[25] Laurendeau and Filion, nevertheless, were not satisfied with the way the existing system was working. In fact, Laurendeau was strongly reprimanded by Cardinal Paul-Emile Léger for having agreed to publish in *Le Devoir* a Marist teaching brother's scathing indictment of Quebec's Catholic education system and the negative role played by the church in that system. Despite Cardinal Léger's warning that the church might be forced to censure *Le Devoir*, Laurendeau encouraged Jean-Paul Desbiens, the Marist teaching brother, to publish his articles in book form.[26] *Les insolences du Frère Untel* became an instant runaway best-seller. Desbiens had gone so far as to suggest, tongue-in-cheek, that the incompetent Département de l'instruction publique be closed permanently and its members put out to pasture decorated with numerous honorary medals, including the one for agricultural merit and a newly created medal for the occasion, "the Medal for Solemn Mediocrity."[27] The state-of-siege mentality of the church hierarchy was confirmed when Frère Untel shortly thereafter was whisked off to Europe, ostensibly to further his education![28]

Despite the growing pressures, fueled in part by the furore over Desbiens' charges, for a ministry of education, the neo-nationalists urged caution. Hoping to head off a looming backlash from the church and conservative nationalists, Laurendeau proposed a formal inquiry to guide the newly elected Liberal government of Jean Lesage. A royal commission on education would assess the validity of various reform proposals and would then make appropriate recommendations to the government.[29] The government agreed and created a Royal Commission of Enquiry on Education, known as the Parent Commission after its neo-nationalist chairman, Msgr Alphonse-Marie Parent, former rector of Laval University. Both Gérard Filion and Arthur Tremblay became members of the commission. The neo-nationalists were thus in an excellent position to influence the direction of education reform in Quebec.[30]

Citélibristes, on the whole, were ardent proponents of a ministry of education which would administer a modern, secularized CIP. They believed that democratic politics had to be reintroduced into the field of educational policy-making and administration. Operating under the guise of apoliticism, the CIP, in fact, had been a highly politicized organization since its inception in the mid-nineteenth century. A ministry of education, wrote Louis Baudouin, "conscious of promoting the development of education must proceed without political motives; it must practice pure educational politics rather than party politics."[31] Addressing the 1956 ICAP symposium on education, Jean-Charles Falardeau hypothesized that the growing trend toward school centralization and increased government financing would necessitate, if democratic rights were to prevail, the creation of a ministry of education.[32]

Yet an indication of the cautious approach of both neo-nationalists and Citélibristes to the question of educational reform was their refusal to support a radical proposal to have Quebec's public education system structured along linguistic rather than confessional lines. Trudeau and Pelletier refused to endorse the idea because linguistic segregation reinforced nationalist tensions within Quebec society. Other *Cité libre* members, Maurice Blain, Marcel Rioux, and Jean Le Moyne, supported Léger's proposal and went on to found Le Mouvement laïque de langue française in April 1961 to campaign for such a reform.[33] Filion strongly opposed the restructuring of Quebec's educational system along linguistic and cultural lines. He called upon the Protestant School Board of greater Montreal to create a system of French-language schools for all non-Catholic groups. While the neo-nationalists pressed hard for increased numbers of secular teaching personnel in the primary system, they remained opposed to any scheme for wholesale secularization. Catholicism remained, for them, an important dimension of the French-Canadian identity.[34]

The ideological campaign for the secularization, democratization, and reorientation of primary education would come to naught unless sufficient fiscal resources were available to the school boards. Citélibristes and the union centrals demanded, without qualms or qualifications, full state financing of primary education. The responsibility could not be left to the municipalities because they lacked constitutional powers to impose democratic forms of taxation. Even if municipalities did acquire new taxing powers, provincial government intervention would be required to regulate the growing disparity between rich and poor municipalities. In sum, primary education was a provincial responsibility and the province had to finance the system on the basis of need and equity for all children, regardless of language, creed, colour, or class.[35]

In the late 1940s and early 1950s the neo-nationalists remained opposed to wholesale provincial financing of primary education because they believed in the autonomy of the local boards. They could also see the manner in which the Union Nationale, through its 1946 Loi pour assurer le progrès de l'éducation, had established its political control over the boards for patronage purposes. One section of the law allowed the school boards to draw upon the *fonds d'éducation* to pay off their deficits. The catch was that, in return, the participating boards had to relinquish their right to raise property tax levels or to borrow for capital expansion without the authorization of the Commission des affaires municipales. The school commissioners, to quote Filion's cryptic phrase, had become "simple furnace stokers." The law was, in Filion's view, fundamentally undemocratic and constituted part of the Union Nationale's concerted attempt "to have the state take over in stages the entire provincial system of primary education."[36]

The neo-nationalists were not totally opposed to some increase in the level of provincial funding for school boards. They approved of the Education Fund but they proposed amendments to make it more effective and democratic for those school boards needing to draw upon the fund. The boards should not have to declare bankruptcy and be placed under the tutelage of the government in order to become eligible for provincial government assistance.[37] Furthermore, the distribution of funds should be automatic once the need was proved. Filion denounced the fact that many school board requests for new school construction were continually turned down while the provincial treasurer transferred nearly $12 million from the Education Fund to the provincial consolidated revenue fund to cover a serious overspending by the minister of highways.

Realizing the impending financial disaster in primary education, Filion and Laurendeau, always leery of the budgetary tactics of the Duplessis government, suggested strongly that the Education Fund remain apart from general revenue and its revenues be substantially increased. All funds should be distributed annually on a per capita student basis to all provincial school boards to prevent the need for deficit financing and introduce a degree of equalization between the various regions of the province. In fact, provincial expenditures on education had risen by only 1.2 per cent, from 12.8 per cent of the 1944–5 budget to 14.0 per cent of the 1952–3 budget. Clearly, education under the Union Nationale was not a priority concern.[38]

Nevertheless, Filion remained convinced that, while government subsidies in the form of statutory uniform grants were necessary, especially for construction, the school boards should do everything in their power to retain sufficient financial autonomy to carry the vast proportion of their operating costs.[39] Undoubtedly, Filion's experience as a school commissioner played an important role in his position on this question.[40] Who, he might have added, would run for school board positions if board commissioners became "simple furnace stokers"? Certainly not Gérard Filion! In short, the school boards had to remain accountable to local taxpayers to guarantee a responsive and democratic educational system. Only then would parents play an active role in the education of their children, so crucial at the primary level.

Neo-nationalists, for fear of arousing church officials and wary taxpayers, shunned ringing declarations favouring complete state control over, and financing of, primary education. They preferred the strategy adopted by Arthur Tremblay, which was to document carefully the financial crisis facing the school boards and persuade institutions and organizations directly involved with primary education to lobby for reforms.[41] Thanks to the work of the Fédération des commissions scolaires and Arthur Tremblay, the *Tremblay Report* acknowledged the magnitude of the financial crisis of the Catholic school boards. Over 50 per cent of the boards were in arrears in 1952 despite the fact that the Union Nationale had taken over the debts of most of them since 1947.[42]

The majority of the debts stemmed from huge loans for school construction and equipment necessitated by the postwar baby-boom.[43] In 1952–3, Catholic public school teachers received hideously low salaries, $1,100 annually for women, lay and religious, and $2,600 annually for male teachers. In contrast, women and men teaching in the Protestant system earned $1,900 and $2,900 annually. Little wonder that Catholic normal schools had difficulty attracting students or that Catholic school boards experienced a 15 per cent annual turnover of teachers and found themselves forced to hire increased numbers of untrained teachers.[44] Citélibristes and neo-nationalists contended that all of these shortcomings could be resolved by substantial salary increases, improved fringe benefits and working conditions, better job security, and social recognition of the importance of education and educators in society.[45] Maurice Lamontagne struck at the heart of the problem when he wrote: "Our society believed that by glorifying the educator it could defy with impunity the economic laws of the market place. It thought that having defined the role of professor as one of the noblest of vocations, it could then, without inconvenience, devalue his services and leave him in economic insecurity."[46] In a modern urban-industrial society social status had become intimately related to economic status. It was high time the Quebec government understood this reality.

Unfortunately for Quebec's French-Canadian children, agreement in the past had normally ended with the recognition of the crisis. Ideological differences and vested interests had prevented the elaboration of a common and coherent solution or set of solutions to the financial crisis confronting Catholic primary education in the province. Yet, by the late 1950s, most neo-nationalists, Citélibristes, and educational reformers supported the compromise solution offered by the Fédération and Arthur Tremblay. It was urgent and imperative that substantially increased revenues be put at the disposal of the school boards. In 1958, Arthur Tremblay estimated that increasing the compulsory attendance to the age of sixteen, abolishing the monthly premiums, improving salaries, pensions, and other benefits would cost the school boards an extra ten or eleven million dollars at the elementary level alone.[47] Add to this the FCS's demonstration that $50 million was required annually to consolidate outstanding debts and to construct modern multi-classroom schools to replace the outmoded one- and two-room schoolhouses, 6,000 in all, scattered throughout rural Quebec and one begins to realize the magnitude of the improvements needed.[48]

The FCS, reformers like Arthur Tremblay and Abel Gauthier, and the union centrals were convinced that only the provincial government had the fiscal resources necessary to finance the modernization of public elementary education. They suggested increased government subsidies for both operating and capital costs be made to the school boards through the Département de l'instruction publique. In 1951, grants from the DIP accounted for 26 per cent of school board revenues – 4 per cent for cities, 31 per cent for towns, and 47 per cent for rural areas.[49] Since the majority of the Département's revenue came from a special Education Fund established in 1946, the Fédération, Tremblay, and the union centrals made several pertinent suggestions to improve the status of that fund. Education must take priority over highway and bridge construction and increased revenues must be channelled into the Education Fund. A significant amount of revenue from the newly created provincial income tax, an increase in the contribution from hydro-electric companies, a province-wide 1 per cent sales tax, and significantly increased royalties on all the province's natural resources, especially the vast deposits of iron ore in Ungava, were some of the proposals put forward to enable the DIP to increase its annual revenues by over 50 per cent.[50]

The basic reason why these recommendations found favour with neo-nationalists was that the Fédération and Tremblay, while favouring increased provincial financial support for primary education, supported the concept of autonomy for school boards. The Fédération's brief to the Tremblay Commission vigorously opposed a suggestion by the Commission des écoles catholiques de Montréal to the effect that all financial responsibilities be taken out of the hands of the school commissions and be given to the province and the municipalities. On the contrary, the FCS recommended very strongly that representatives of the school boards should be called upon to participate in the administration of the provincial education fund to ensure as democratic a distribution of funds as was possible.[51]

Neo-nationalists were all too aware that the bogey of government intervention, especially in primary education, had scuttled numerous well-intentioned reform proposals since the early twentieth century. It could well happen again if a practical solution to the financial crisis of primary education could not be agreed upon. The Fédération's recommendations appeared to be both democratic and sensible. French Canadians had to accept increased intervention of the state but also recognize the need to keep it within the boundaries required by a healthy democracy.[52] Undoubtedly, the neo-nationalists were disappointed with the Tremblay commissioners for rejecting the Fédération's proposal for increased provincial financial support for primary education. Primary education, their *Report* argued somewhat naïvely, should be financed entirely from local tax sources. Provincial government funding of primary education would only serve the socialist objectives of state intervention and undermine an institution and values peculiar to the French-Canadian culture.[53] In sum, the *Report* based its opposition to state intervention on traditional nationalist rather than democratic arguments as it was assumed that the state was a homogenizing, antinationalist force. Neo-nationalists, on the contrary, considered state intervention necessary if nationalist and democratic goals were to be achieved. Motivating both the Citélibristes' and the neo-nationalists' proposals for a reformed primary sector was the desire to ensure that all capable French Canadians became eligible for secondary education – the sector of Quebec's education system which in its existing condition was considered to be the major stumbling block preventing modernization of the entire society. A demographic explosion in the secondary sector would shatter an outmoded system and precipitate its reform.

SECONDARY EDUCATION

At the centre of the ideological battle over education reform in Quebec during the 1950s was the vigorous discussion, at times highly emotional and irrational, about the future of French Canada's oldest cultural and educational institution – the *collège classique*. These church-controlled and operated classical colleges derived their importance and prestige from the fact that they constituted the only educational system which allowed bright and ambitious French Canadians to qualify for the priesthood and university faculties leading to careers in the liberal professions.[54] As long as French-Canadian society remained predominantly agricultural in its economic pursuits and imbued with cultural and spiritual objectives, the classical college system, with its small but continued output of graduates intended for the priesthood and the liberal professions, remained relatively immune from any serious criticism. Only when that society became unalterably industrial in its economic endeavours and secular in its norms and behaviour after World War I did concerned French Canadians realize the full significance of the lack of a dynamic secular élite in the fields of science and technology, commerce, and industry.

The debate on the future of classical education was not entirely an outgrowth of the postwar era. A vigorous campaign had been waged in the 1930s by Adrien Pouliot, chanoine Emile Chartier, Brother Marie-Victorin, and Edouard Montpetit for the introduction of the natural sciences into the classical college curriculum. The traditionalists, who reflected the majority opinion of educators and the concerned public at the time, continued to stress that there existed a fundamental incompatibility between the sciences and the humanities and equated general culture with a literary, moral, and philosophic education.[55]

What distinguished the debate of the 1950s from that of the interwar years was its all-encompassing and potentially devastating outcome. Cité-libristes, very influential in educational circles, questioned seriously both the substance and structure of the classical college system. Their critique was comprehensive and devastating. They found the classical colleges deficient in almost every respect imaginable and called for their abolition and the creation of a state-supported public secondary system. Neo-nationalists also presented an incisive critique of the structure and substance of the system. Rather than proposing its abolition, they concluded, for nationalist reasons, that classical education must be modernized and made available to all capable French Canadians. Traditional nationalists and clerical educators, after a short period of shock and dismay, reorganized their forces in the hope of preserving intact the essence of the classical curriculum by championing a series of minor but well-intentioned structural and financial reforms.

It was a group of dedicated French-Canadian scientists, namely Léon Lortie, Cyrias Ouellet, and Adrien Pouliot, who in the late forties brought to light the lack of French-Canadian scientists and technicians and linked this phenomenon with the socioeconomic and cultural inferiority of French Canadians and their society. Between 1947 and 1949, the Association cana-dienne-française pour l'avancement des sciences held three symposia on the subject of the teaching of science in Quebec and the situation of French Canadians in regard to scientific careers.[56] Statistics for 1945 revealed to Ouellet and Lortie that fewer than 5 per cent of all registered Canadian scientists were French Canadians and only a handful of those had ever done serious research leading to publication. How had this sad state of affairs come about? Ouellet stressed the difficulty of doing graduate work and finding employment in French-Canadian universities, the total lack of preparation and orientation at the secondary level, and the psychological barriers arising from the fear of cultural assimilation. Most jobs in the industrial sector or federal research agencies entailed working in an anglophone environment. Lortie, on the other hand, laid most of the responsibility at the doorstep of the classical colleges which had only reluctantly accepted the sciences and had restricted their teaching to the last two years of the eight-year program. By then, he argued, it was much too late to inculcate a love for the scientific disciplines. Those who did choose to pursue a career in the sciences after receiving the BA degree soon realized the tremendous disadvantage imposed by their limited background. Consequently, few French Canadians persisted long enough to obtain postgraduate degrees.[57]

Neo-nationalists accepted the thrust of the remarks made by these French-Canadian scientists and supported their demand for modernization of the structure and curriculum of classical education. Encouraged by his editor-in-chief, Laurendeau,[58] and motivated by his growing concern about the continued lack of a strong French-Canadian commercial and industrial bourgeoisie, Filion came down hard on the classical colleges. As he viewed the situation in the mid-1950s, Quebec had a 100 per cent greater need for scientists than lawyers. Yet the classical colleges obstinately continued to produce graduates of whom the vast majority chose careers in the low-risk, high-prestige, and well-paid liberal professions.[59] He noted that not one of the handful of French-Canadian entrepreneurs – the Simard brothers, the

Beauchemin brothers, Jules Brillant, or Alphonse Raymond – had received a classical college degree. Coupled with the fact that the social milieu emphasized status and security, the classical college was, according to Filion, the last place to develop "an appetite for risk and adventure. It is not by slogging over Greek and Latin for six years and rationalizing for two more years that one acquires the desire to roll up one's sleeves and dirty one's hands." French Canadians would regain control over their economic life only when the society began to socialize and educate a class of men resigned to sixteen-hour work-days and willing to risk "everything every day, to endure the humiliation of one, of two, of three failures, yet remain ready to begin from scratch in order to succeed."[60] French Canada's classical colleges reinforced the social prestige of the clerical class and the liberal professions at the expense of business and science careers. This situation accounted in large measure for the economic inferiority of French Canadians.

The conservative, tradition-bound colleges had to be modernized if French Canadians hoped to overcome their long-standing position of economic inferiority. French Canadians, Arthur Tremblay admitted, had not succeeded in retaining ownership of the province's major natural resources. Yet, in his view, all was not lost because in large-scale commerce, finance, and industry it was the managerial and technical personnel and not the proprietors who made the crucial policy decisions. "That is why, even if access to the control of large corporations through the acquisition of a majority of the shares has become almost impossible for French Canadians, there remains another method of gaining control of their behaviour and attitudes, of everything, in short, that is most important from a 'cultural' perspective, if French Canadians provide these corporations with technicians at the levels which will determine and direct their concrete policies."[61] French Canadians could guarantee their collective economic, social, and cultural future by revamping their secondary educational system to produce these required technical, managerial, and industrial élites.

Citélibristes and neo-nationalists focused attention on what they considered were three basic structural flaws in the classical college system. The *collèges classiques* were too élitist, constituted a monopoly in the hands of the church, and were extremely ineffectual in preparing sufficient numbers of students for the full range of university faculties and professional schools. Classical education was the prerogative and privilege of the sons of wealthy bourgeois families rather than the right of an intellectual élite drawn from all classes of society. By 1954 the cost of tuition, room and board at one of these colleges averaged $700 a year. A family income of well over $3,000 was required to finance such an endeavour and only 22 per cent of Quebec's French-Canadian families qualified under these financial requirements. Clearly then, most families had to write off secondary education, classical education, that is, for their otherwise eligible children.[62]

Furthermore, both neo-nationalists and Citélibristes pointed to available statistics to illustrate that the classical colleges perpetuated an outmoded social and class structure, thereby preventing the modernization of Quebec society. While the working class constituted the largest social class in French Canada, less than one-third of classical college students came from working-class families.[63] The FTQ and the CTCC denounced the social injustice created by this underrepresentation. The CTCC was quick to point out that the prestigious Collège Jean-de-Brébeuf could not list a single working-class student among its more than 600 students enrolled in 1953–4.[64] The "development of élites" associated with the classical colleges had accentuated class and caste divisions – the clergy versus the laymen, professionals versus workers, and industrialists versus intellectuals – and had stifled the vertical mobility expected in a society undergoing rapid economic expansion. Other alternatives, argued Dansereau, were necessary if French-Canadian culture was to be modernized.[65]

Neo-nationalists and Citélibristes supported, in varying degrees, the secularization of secondary education. They rejected, in principle, continued church monopoly of classical education and focused attention upon some of the nefarious consequences of clerical control in a society undergoing secularization. The prime concern of the church was, and had always been, the renewal and expansion of its personnel or, in other words, the continual reinforcement of its social and class position in Quebec society. "In many classical colleges," wrote Maurice Tremblay, "right up until the end of the eight-year program, the student is considered virtually as a priest and treated accordingly . . . This education, incorporated in a quasi-monastic life style, is completely oriented towards supernatural values: the glory of God and the salvation of the soul through the practice of Christian virtues and the avoidance of sin."[66] Neo-nationalists maintained that the church had acquired its monopoly over classical education by default. Perhaps this was so, but the Citélibristes reminded French Canadians that the church has in fact used its extensive powers as an influential clerical class to prevent any significant encroachment of the state or a secular élite in the field of classical education.[67]

In practical terms, clerical monopolization of teaching positions in classical secondary education prevented the emergence of a strong secular teaching profession.[68] College rectors disliked having to hire lay teaching personnel. When they were forced to do so, lay personnel was restricted from participating fully in making decisions affecting the government of their colleges. Lay teachers were denied all important administrative responsibilities and were not an integral part of the cultural milieu of the college because, for the most part, they lived off campus. Rectors wanted to preserve clerical control and the religious environment of the institutions and too great a number of lay professors would easily jeopardize both of these objectives. Moreover, the salaries paid to lay teachers were between $3,100 and $3,500, some $300 below their counterparts in the Ecole primaire supérieure and nearly $2,000 less than teachers in normal schools. Most taught thirty-five hours of classes a week and held second jobs to support their families.[69] An ugly situation indeed, marked by the absence of the kind of salaries and working conditions that would attract bright and ambitious young French Canadians to the profession of teaching.

The long-term consequence was the virtual emasculation of the faculties of Lettres and philosophy in Quebec's francophone universities. Most of the graduate students were clerics and those few French-Canadian lay students receiving graduate degrees in the humanities, the social sciences, and the pure sciences discovered it was exceedingly difficult, if not impossible, to find employment in the teaching field at the secondary level. Most worked at other occupations or left Quebec in search of employment opportunities in their various areas of specialization. This was Quebec's version of the Canadian "brain drain" during the 1950s. Ironically, a society that flaunted its intimate association with the humanities lacked a vigorous and expanding humanities graduate program to support such a claim![70]

This sad state of affairs was, for Laurendeau, totally unacceptable for several reasons. While it was normal, desirable, and necessary that clerics continue to teach at the secondary level, it was unacceptable that laymen be excluded. This was the case both on the individual level, because young French Canadians could and did have "the desire to teach without wanting to embrace a religious vocation," and on the social level, because French Canadians lived in an increasingly secular world where a specific social class – the clerical class – should not exercise a monopoly. The resulting bitterness, warned Laurendeau, would be directed eventually against the church. The situation was also unacceptable for cultural reasons. The creation of strong secular élites was perceived as crucial to the survival of the French-Canadian nation. The teaching profession was the most obvious place to begin. Secularization at the secondary level would, in time, lead to a greater acceptance of careers in science and business. The graduate faculties of humanities and social sciences would benefit greatly by the creation of job opportunities, and research on all aspects of the French-Canadian society would be encouraged and forthcoming.[71] Rapid secularization of classical college teaching personnel was urgent and imperative.

This brings us to the third structural flaw. The church-controlled classical system was simply not graduating sufficient numbers of qualified candidates for all areas of post-secondary education, thereby retarding the development of French-Canadian social scientists, scientists, and technical and administrative personnel. Clerical control of the important sector of secondary education was anachronistic and destructive because it prevented the emergence of francophone secular élites in nontraditional professions. Combining classical college graduates and some two thousand students enrolled in the last year of the public EPS, Lortie estimated that in 1952 Laval and Montreal could count on a potential group of 3,500 candidates, whereas Ontario's universities could draw upon more than 13,000 students enrolled in grade thirteen of the Ontario public high school system.[72] Even when 64 per cent of classical college graduates and 40 per cent of EPS matriculants successfully entered university, this constituted less than 4 per cent of the eligible French-speaking population. Theoretically, a minimum of 12 per cent of French Canadians were intellectually capable of attending university. To make this feasible, Arthur Tremblay argued very persuasively that 30 per cent rather than 15 per cent of eligible French Canadians should be enrolled in grade eleven.[73]

If French Canadians were to experience the same degree of equality of opportunity as English Canadians, then it was necessary to develop a French-Canadian public high school system equivalent to the system provided for the children of English Canadians. The English Protestant minority in Quebec had tax-supported high schools while the French Catholic majority had to send their children to private secondary schools in order that the intellectually capable ones be eligible for all university faculties and professional schools.[74] The system not only denied French Canadians equality of opportunity as individuals but threatened collective survival as well. It drove hundreds of concerned French parents to enrol their children in English Protestant high schools so they could qualify for entrance to McGill, Loyola, Bishop's, or Sir George Williams, the four anglophone universities. The persistence of inequality of opportunity was forcing French-Canadian parents to deny their children an education in their mother tongue. If this trend continued and took on epidemic proportions, then the future of the French-Canadian collectivity would be seriously and perhaps irrevocably jeopardized.[75]

At the heart of these structural flaws, contended the Citélibristes, was an outmoded conception of education, represented by the rigid classical curriculum and the authoritarian environment which prevailed in most colleges. Citélibristes deplored the excessive clerical atmosphere of the colleges. The petty bourgeois élite emerging from these colleges was thoroughly imbued with an authoritarian, hierarchical spiritual world view and possessed a truncated conception of its responsibilities and role in a democratic society.[76] Roger Rolland, inspired by his own rather bitter college experience, denounced the detrimental psychological and intellectual impact that resulted from an overly Jansenist environment and a curriculum that rewarded unthinking repetition and punished creative and individual expression of emotions and ideas. He recalled an incident when he and five other students were soundly strapped and placed in solitary confinement for wearing their scout shorts to mass and to the study hall. An obsessive fear and negation of the flesh was drilled daily into the hearts and minds of all students. In Rolland's view, the Jansenist environment had a detrimental effect on the teaching of most subjects. He recalled "never having had a warm and prolonged contact with the work of an author. A manual of grammar, of style, of literary history or philosophy always intervened between an author's work (which is the flesh of thought and life) and the virgin open-mindedness of the student. No, life was not admitted at the centre of our schools. The heart was not allowed to function. We were absentees, face to face with other absentees."[77]

Latin, Greek, and French grammar, rather than being a preparation for the reading of the "great authors," had become an end in itself, totally devoid of life, of creative inspiration, or human dimensions. As far as the great authors were concerned, they were all rigidly censored and interpreted for the students by boring textbooks and professors who dictated their judgments on Rousseau and Chateaubriand without having read them. Students wrote, Rolland declared somewhat facetiously, "brilliant" exams on the history of French literature without ever having read a single line of the original Montaigne, Racine, Voltaire, Balzac, or Baudelaire. A similar methodology was used in the teaching of philosophy. None of the original philosophical works were read, not even those of the master of Catholic philosophy, Thomas Aquinas. "Everything was summarized, reduced to syllogisms, in a manual, with a line or two at the bottom of the page for adversaries: Plato, Descartes, Kant, Bergson, etc ... This is how we were trained to think."[78] Rather than illustrating to the students how nature, life, and man were perceived by the great authors, the professors emphasized where these authors had erred and how Catholicism had corrected them. A critical search for truth and beauty was never instilled in the minds of students because French-Canadian Catholicism claimed to have answers to all questions and ready-made solutions to all problems.[79]

Citélibristes criticized the classical college rectors for their persistent and successful defence of the traditional curriculum based on the greco-latin humanities and philosophy. French-Canadian society had to assimilate and use science and technology if it desired to survive in the modern world.[80] The rectors' refusal to pay anything more than moderate attention to science and mathematics revealed their inherent opposition to the new urban/ industrial social order. Classical college educators equated industrialization with materialism and Americanism and these had to be offset by the teaching of a traditional humanism and a Catholic spiritualism.[81] In 1954, the Fédération des collèges classiques spoke out vigorously against the attempt by Montréal and Laval universities to impose a new Latin-science curriculum on their affiliated colleges on the ground that the preservation of the "traditional Latin and Greek curriculum" was essential to the survival and progress of the French-Canadian nationality. A great many Jesuit college rectors simply refused to offer the new curriculum when it was introduced in 1952.[82]

Both the curriculum and environment of the classical colleges left the emerging clerical and petty bourgeois élites ill-prepared to confront and deal with the problems and challenges of the modern world. Despite their highly touted classical education, most graduates, when given a choice of intellectual nourishment, opted for American popular culture and doted on American film stars. The gap between what young French Canadians were taught and what they experienced in the real world quickly undermined the false sense of superiority acquired during eight years of what was termed a "hot house" cultural environment. Most graduates, after an initial stage of personal crisis, merely set aside any pretence to humanistic values and turned their attention to material security and professional recognition.[83] Citélibristes considered the crisis confronting classical education as a microcosm of the broader crisis confronting French-Canadian culture. "Let us examine our bachelor at the end of his secondary program," suggested Marcel Rioux.

Who is he? A man possessed with the ability to shock and astonish? An artist, a poet? It is rare that those who are come to us from the secondary system. Is he a man gifted with a critical spirit, who has a desire to surpass himself? Does he even have an understanding of the problem? Does he want to know truth? Can he even express himself in French? Is he a man of God? Will he be the salt of the earth? Will his religion serve as a lever to shake the world? Look at him when he has become a lawyer, a priest, a doctor, or an engineer. Do you recognize in him everything that the secondary program should have brought him? What has he become? Do we have the right to ignore the global culture of French Canada on the pretext that we will reap an élite at the end of the secondary system and that we will make men out of these graduates. The problems of formal education are directly related to the total environment. What good does it do us to create and borrow the most beautiful programs if we restructure them in our image as soon as we put them into practice.[84]

Only an overall renewal of the French-Canadian society would ensure that educational reforms would be effective. Only a fully democratic society would produce a democratic educational structure and liberal philosophy of education which in turn would serve to reinforce and renew democratic values and behaviour within the society at large.

Agreement on the structural and pedagogical weaknesses of the classical colleges had come relatively easily. Agreement upon a common set of reform proposals proved much more elusive. Citélibristes desired to see the classical colleges go the way of the dinosaurs and be replaced by state-supported public secondary schools. Consequently, they made no positive recommendations for the reform of classical education. On the other hand, the neo-nationalists stressed the importance of retaining classical education, in both its traditional and modern forms, provided it be made universally accessible to French Canadians from all walks of life. Classics for the proletariat might well have served as the neo-nationalist slogan. What arguments did they employ to substantiate their demand for a classical stream in the existing public secondary system?

Quebec had a public secondary sector but it was uncoordinated and truncated. The Ecole primaire supérieur system, since its inception in 1929, had provided technical and business programs for young French Canadians seeking blue- and white-collar occupations in industry and commerce. Pressured by the business and science faculties at Laval and Montréal, the EPS system also developed a curriculum emphasizing science and mathematics, hoping to qualify some of its students for university entrance in these fields.[85] By the late 1940s it became quite clear that the rapidly expanding EPS system simply could not accomplish the complex tasks demanded of it. It was a dead-end tunnel for the vast majority of students.

To qualify for university entrance in only a few faculties, namely science, business, and education, EPS graduates had to pass stringent entrance exams and complete one or two years of preparatory course work.[86] The EPS system did not fill the void even in these university faculties. Arthur Tremblay estimated that less than 15 per cent of the EPS students enrolled in grade eight completed grade twelve, if there was a grade twelve available. Of this small number less than one-third entered university. Even if all of them qualified, which was highly unlikely given the weak nature of the curriculum, the universities would still not have a sufficiently large pool of candidates to draw upon. The first problem confronting French-Canadian educators was not to ensure that more secondary school graduates qualified for university entrance but rather to expand greatly the secondary system by making it accessible to all qualified French-Canadian boys and girls.[87]

Another important factor influencing the neo-nationalists to favour an expanded public secondary system was the fact that the classical colleges accommodated in 1952 only 4 per cent of the French-speaking population of secondary school-age (thirteen- to twenty-year-olds). To maintain even this low level the classical colleges would have to double their facilities and personnel by 1962. The church might well fulfil that challenge but only an expanded public secondary system could accommodate successfully the remaining 8 per cent of capable and eager thirteen- to twenty-year-old French Canadians.[88] In large measure, the demographic crisis had forced the neo-nationalists to comprehend the need for a francophone public secondary system.

Determined that this was the direction in which secondary education should be reformed, the neo-nationalists began a concerted campaign in the early 1950s to convince the Catholic Committee of the CIP of the necessity and urgency for adding a modern Latin-science classical curriculum to the existing EPS system. In 1951, the Département de l'instruction publique, responding to pressures from several quarters, created a subcommittee to study the ways and means of coordinating the various educational streams operating in the province. Arthur Tremblay was the Quebec City representative on this body. In its report, released in 1953, the subcommittee argued strongly for the implementation of a Latin-science stream in the EPS with graduates receiving at the end of grade eleven "a general immatriculation diploma." This diploma would enable students to proceed directly to certain university faculties or schools or to complete a BA in one of the numerous classical colleges. In short, if it was impossible to take the students to the private classical colleges then a modern Latin-science stream should be made available to them. Making the first four years of the classical program tuition-free and close to home, argued the report's authors, would ensure that more students at university would come equipped with a BA.[89]

Neo-nationalists were mildly ecstatic about what Laurendeau termed "a 74-page report with a series of precise recommendations, many of which go to the heart of the issue." They approved wholeheartedly of the recommendation to institute a modern Latin-science curriculum in the EPS. Laurendeau expressed cautious optimism about the prospect of the report gaining the approval of the Catholic Committee, but he felt the provincial government and the school boards would balk at having to find the required financial resources.[90] A concerted campaign against these "radical" reform proposals was launched by the classical colleges. The rectors, sensing that both their monopoly position and their conception of classical education were being threatened, created in June 1953 the Fédération des collèges classiques to lobby for their vested interests. The Fédération, in its brief to the Tremblay Commission, while reluctantly acknowledging the need for a Latin-science curriculum, stated that the private colleges wished to remain faithful to the traditional Latin-Greek curriculum, the only remaining bulwark against "the decline of the religious values of our people and a weakening of French-Canadian cultural values."[91]

The neo-nationalists counter-attacked. A concerted campaign was begun to make the subcommittee report's recommendations public. Hoping to whip up support for the "classicalization" of the public sector and, perhaps, to influence the decision of the Catholic Committee, Arthur Tremblay wrote a monograph outlining in considerable detail the urgent necessity for a full-fledged public secondary system. He envisaged the first four years of the classical curriculum being eventually provided entirely by the public sector while the classical colleges would specialize in providing the last four years or the post-secondary level. If the French-Canadian people did not want to become "a society of impoverished and arbitrary 'classes'," it had to guarantee the renewal of its élites by drawing upon the large pool of talented individuals from the masses. This could only be achieved efficiently and democratically with a fully integrated public secondary system.[92]

Laurendeau's premonitions proved to be fairly accurate. Cardinal Léger and the Catholic Committee approved the recommendation. A pilot project of two classes teaching the Latin-science curriculum was introduced in the fall of 1954 into Ecole Saint-Pierre Claver in Montreal. Laurendeau, awaiting the outcome of this experiment, decried the fact that the Duplessis government was willing to spend large sums of provincial revenue on technical education for the working classes while continually refusing to use the taxpayers' money to make classical education more accessible for working-class children.[93] The implication was, of course, that the Duplessis administration rejected the concept of social and class mobility and preferred the continuation of the unjust and undemocratic status quo. Despite the lack of funds, the Catholic Committee and several school boards proceeded in May 1955 to authorize the continuation or the creation of nineteen classical sections throughout the province from Arvida to Montreal, and by 1961 there were fifty-eight public secondary schools offering the classical or academic stream.[94] Neo-nationalists and educational reformers were undoubtedly reassured and happy when the *Tremblay Report* strongly recommended that the school boards eventually take over the responsibility of providing the full range of secondary programs – general, commercial, scientific, and classical. The private classical colleges would still continue to offer the first four years, for a considerable period of time, but would eventually specialize in the last four years referred to henceforth as college-level rather than secondary-level education.[95]

Neo-nationalists welcomed what they considered to be the most authoritative support for public secondary education in Quebec. Its full implementation would, undoubtedly, create serious financial and personnel recruitment problems. But the school boards, the neo-nationalists maintained, were much better equipped than the classical colleges to direct and assume the costs of expansion over the next ten years. The boards had access to property taxes and were in a position to demand full and equitable distribution of revenues in the provincial education fund.[96] Secularization of the society and substantially increased enrolments had brought an end to the church's *de facto* monopoly in the field of secondary education. Neo-nationalists acknowledged the important role the church had played in the development of secondary education in Quebec but were pleased to see its monopoly coming to an end.

Yet the acceptance in principle of public secondary education meant little if sufficient revenue could not be found to finance such a system. What role should the state play in the funding of secondary education? Should the private classical colleges be integrated, financially that is, with the public system to ensure their continued survival and to prevent them from becoming enclaves for the wealthy while the public system served the needs of the working class? It was these two questions which confronted reformers and worried the Fédération des collèges classiques. The *Cité libre* position on the role of the state in education was well defined by Trudeau. Education in the modern secular state was primarily a function of society. Society through its government had to see that its members received "the minimum requirements for fulfilment." Education at all levels must be accessible by right to everyone and funded by the state. The secular state, Trudeau argued, must view educational expenditures as an investment reimbursable through an equitable system of graduated taxation on students' incomes once they were employed in well-paid jobs. The Quebec state had not only a democratic and social obligation but also a national obligation to implement a comprehensive policy of free education. "For a long time," commented Trudeau, in reference to French-Canadian leaders and social thinkers,

we prided ourselves on having monopolized the domain of ideas, the upper levels of the mind, abandoning – as with the fox and the grapes – to the anglophones the realm of business, of economics, the source of material wealth. Now, we must admit that even in the intellectual domain and the larger area of culture, we are in the process of losing not only our so-called advantage, which was never very real, but also the normal place that we should be occupying. Consequently we are losing ground in both areas: the one which we deliberately neglected for so long and the one in which we flattered ourselves that we were "dominating."[97]

Trudeau could not envisage this comprehensive policy of state-supported public education succeeding without "a grand Quebec policy and the men determined to implement such a policy." Quebec's union centrals and the Alliance shared the Citélibristes' desire for a fully integrated, provincially funded public secondary system. The boost to democratic ideals and socio-economic equality would be immeasurable as would be the benefits accruing to French-Canadian society as a whole.[98]

Neo-nationalists quickly realized that a modern public secondary system was not feasible without direct financial support from the provincial government. The *collèges classiques* were starved for revenues and the local school boards had their hands full trying to find adequate resources for primary education. Neo-nationalists feared that prolonged provincial government inactivity and reluctance to finance adequately a modernized and expanded public secondary system would encourage the college and university rectors to favour the existing program of federal subsidies on the ground that they offered an equivalent of the anglophone undergraduate degree. To undermine the threat of federal intervention in the field of education, the neo-nationalists deemed it urgent for the Quebec state to fulfil its constitutional responsibilities by adequately financing education, especially at the secondary and university levels. Increased state participation would bring certain risks – patronage, interference in internal administration, and potential threats to academic freedom – but Quebec's socioeconomic and cultural crisis warranted taking those risks. Moreover, given the estimated huge sums of revenue required, only a provincial government willing to exercise fully its taxing powers could undertake to finance successfully a comprehensive public secondary system.[99] Only an active and democratic provincial government could guarantee an equality of educational services by imposing special taxes and distributing the revenue to centralized secondary school boards using an equitable equalization formula.[100]

Being convinced of the need for statutory funding and convincing the Duplessis administration of the same were two different matters entirely. A conservative government hell-bent on political longevity was not about to abandon balanced budgets or surpluses and the patronage accruing from discretionary grants in order to adopt an integrated system of large statutory grants to regional school boards. Such an abrupt change in policy and practice would entail increased taxes and/or deficit financing, neither of which Duplessis would undertake unless there was some form of guaranteed political pay-off. Indeed, when it was clear by 1957 that school boards were in serious financial trouble Duplessis chastised them for extending their mandate to include classical education. Filion was livid. The school boards, he responded in a sharp editorial, were merely reacting democratically to pressure from French-Canadian parents who desired better education and greater equality of opportunity for their children.[101]

Neo-nationalists were fond of repeating that the Quebec government had been granted complete sovereignty in the field of education in 1867. What had it done with that authority? Not very much indeed, was Filion's rehearsed response. What was preventing the Quebec government, Filion asked Le Devoir's faithful readers, from taking the necessary measures to end a monopoly the church was only too willing to give up? "Certainly nothing but a stupid routine and a ridiculous faith in bogey-man stories which found credence at the beginning of the century but which only a few retarded minds, the last rejects of a superseded obscurantism, still appear to believe in. All that was required was the death of the prince and the arrival in power of a man of normal intelligence and awareness to make us admit that we were walking on our heads."[102] The prince, of course, was none other than Duplessis and the enlightened individual his future successor, Paul Sauvé, who would initiate a new deal for education in Quebec. In fact, the speed with which Sauvé moved on education seemed to substantiate Laurendeau's thesis that Duplessis and not the church was the major political obstacle to educational reform in Quebec.[103]

Unlike the Citélibristes, the neo-nationalists had no desire to see the church-owned classical college system destroyed or become the preserve of the well-to-do classes while the public sector served the working-class. They considered the private classical colleges to be an important national institution serving the needs of both the Catholic church and, to some extent, French-Canadian society at large. Modern French Canada required a public secondary system to serve its enormous secular objectives, and, consequently, the church's monopoly had to be ended because it could not be expected to accomplish the task. Nevertheless, the neo-nationalists believed that it was politically astute not to alienate unduly the Catholic church. They understood, perhaps better than the Citélibristes, that to do so could very well set the cause of urgent reforms back another generation. French Canada simply could not afford that risk.

It was in the light of these nationalist and political considerations that the neo-nationalists gave their support to the recommendation by the Fédération des collèges classiques that financial parity between the first four years of the classical program and the new public secondary program be ensured by government financial subsidies. The FCC in its brief to the Tremblay Commission favoured a system of government grants to parents of all students attending any accredited secondary institution – $100 for tuition plus another $100 for board if required. The brief also requested special grants to cover the cost of hiring lay teachers at $3,000 a year, construction of new facilities, low-cost loans, and a $75 per capita grant to cover operating costs. Estimated total cost for 1954–5 was $8.8 million, a figure that was nearly double the regular and special subsidies received by colleges in 1953–4.[104] The college administrators, faced with their first serious competition, had moved from an obsessive fear of the state to an almost embarrassing realization of the potential financial benefits to be gained from an arrangement providing access to the public purse. The *Tremblay Report* endorsed the concept of parity proposed by the FCC but rejected their mode of financing. Direct government grants to parents, contended the *Report*, would undermine, like family allowances, an individual's sense of responsibility and open the door to excessive state intervention in education! The *Tremblay Report* proposed instead that a system of new secondary regional school boards be responsible for funding public and private secondary education throughout the province.[105]

Neo-nationalists did not share the Tremblay commissioners' excessive fear of the state, but they endorsed the concept of regional secondary boards heartily. In the interim, they approved increased government statutory grants to the private classical colleges in 1960.[106] Citélibristes were not at all amused at this compromise. Vianney Décarie reminded the Union Nationale government that it had a strict duty to see that public revenue – approximately $7 million – was properly spent. He also called upon the college rectors to upgrade their standards, modernize their curriculum, and improve the quality of their teaching personnel. Only then, perhaps, argued Décarie, could state subsidies to private institutions be justified.[107] It was evident that the only acceptable solution for the Citélibristes was the complete withdrawal of the church from secondary education and the development of a state-controlled public high school system equivalent to, or better than, the one enjoyed by English Canadians in Quebec and the rest of Canada. As long as the church remained involved, the needs of a democratic, secular society would not be served adequately. Neo-nationalists accepted and championed the same objectives but were unwilling for nationalist and political reasons, prior to 1960 at least, to see the church-owned classical colleges forced out of secondary education. They felt a royal commission of inquiry on education was necessary to study the complex ramifications of complete secularization of secondary education. Was such a "radical" move feasible or desirable as long as the church controlled post-secondary education?

THE ROLE OF UNIVERSITIES

The key to national salvation resides in the achievement of excellence in all fields, beginning at the university level.[108]

As was quite natural, Quebec's francophone universities, Laval, Montréal, and Sherbrooke (founded in 1954), held a special place in the hearts and minds of the francophone intelligentsia. This concern and attachment was perhaps most strong for Citélibristes and neo-nationalists. Members of both groups believed that a modernized, secularized, and well-funded system of higher education was indispensable to the renewal and modernization of other educational sectors and Quebec society at large. A closer scrutiny of their respective ideological perspectives reveals, none the less, that their shared commitment to higher education was motivated by views of the university, its role in society, and its relationship with the state which, in some instances, were poles apart.

What marked the neo-nationalists off from their predecessors and the Citélibristes was their increasingly secular conception of universities. Traditional nationalists, like Cardinal Villeneuve and Abbé Groulx, considered the prime function of Catholic universities to be the elaboration and application of the spiritual and social doctrines of the Catholic church to every sector of society, profane and religious. The university's role as a disseminator of secular knowledge was always secondary to its primordial role as a source of moral and spiritual influence.[109]

The introduction of the physical and social sciences helped undermine this conception of the university and the neo-nationalists participated in the resulting elaboration of a secular conception. They contended that the francophone universities should become leading institutions in the prolonged and seemingly eternal struggle for the preservation and renewal of the

French-Canadian nation. "In certain respects, the university is the brain of the nation," wrote Jean Désy in 1952.[110] His neo-nationalist friends at *Le Devoir* concurred wholeheartedly. The French-Canadian people's innumerable sacrifices and its all too many painful setbacks in the struggle for linguistic and cultural survival could only be justified, according to the neo-nationalists, if they led eventually to "a francophone-inspired civilization." Neo-nationalists believed that French Canadians could gain the respect and cooperation of their English-Canadian neighbours if their culture were to offer positive contributions to the national and international dimensions of Canada. A *sine qua non* of a strong and expansive French-Canadian society was the continued nurturing of universities that were primarily centres for the renewal and *épanouissement* of French-Canadian culture. Referring to the bitter struggle of Franco-Ontarians to obtain courses taught in French in the faculties of medicine, science, and social sciences at the University of Ottawa, Filion questioned the justification for the difficult battle to retain the French language at primary level when the culture was being betrayed at the university level. "How can we ask our people to make sacrifices for their schools if our universities deform our leaders?"[111] French Canadians had the right to demand that their universities, including Ottawa, should be totally devoted to the French-Canadian culture in the same way that English-Canadian universities were devoted to the interests of English-Canadian society.

As the neo-nationalists turned their attention to the global renewal of Quebec society, the call to modernize French-Canadian universities became a leading element in their growing list of reforms. Laurendeau ventured the hypothesis that future historians, in assessing the Duplessis regime, would consider its failure to renew and regenerate higher education as one of its most serious shortcomings. Only modernized and well-financed universities could provide the impetus and personnel required for a renewal of the society at large. More specifically, Laurendeau argued persuasively that successful modernization of primary and secondary education was dependent upon the modernization of French Canada's institutions of higher learning, namely, the universities of Sherbrooke, Laval, and Montréal and all their affiliated schools and colleges.[112] Bishop Parent, a committed neo-nationalist and future rector of Laval, had forecast in 1946 that only modernized French-Canadian universities could play a leading role in the emancipation of the French-Canadian people.

This is an important aspect of the role of the university. It is a role of emancipation, destined to free us from a dependence which has no reason to prevail among mature peoples. Here lies, I believe, the central problem of our autonomy. We seem to systematically forget this reality. It is less important to defend one's rights than to learn to exercise those rights. The best, indeed, the only way to become masters in our own country, is to arrange our affairs in such a manner that there will not be an occupation for which a sufficient number of highly qualified French Canadians cannot be found. This is called becoming masters of our own destiny. It involves more than mere suvival, it entails growth and development, and only university education can guarantee both of these factors.[113]

A revitalized Société Saint-Jean-Baptiste de Montréal made precisely the same remarks a decade later in its neo-nationalists-inspired brief to the Tremblay Commission.[114] By the mid-fifties the neo-nationalists possessed a secular conception of higher education which far surpassed the preparation of suitable candidates for the priesthood or the liberal professions. Moral integrity may have been a necessary condition but was no longer considered a sufficient condition for the cultural and economic development of French-Canadian society.

Citélibristes, on the other hand, preached a liberal conception of the university and its role in modern society. Universities and their faculties, they staunchly maintained, should not be the servants of any creed, nationality, or social class. They must devote themselves to the search for knowledge and truth in as democratic a fashion was was possible. Citélibristes readily agreed with Maurice Blain that Quebec's French-Canadian universities were "increasingly powerless to attract and incorporate in the education they provided the grand currents of artistic, scientific, and philosophic thought, to raise themselves by means of rigorous and open-minded dynamism to meet the challenge of intellectual research and aspirations."[115] All agreed that French Canada's universities must be purged of the spectre of clericalism. Furthermore, they and their faculties must not become the vehicles for any narrow doctrine of nationalism.

Both neo-nationalists and Citélibristes underlined certain basic weaknesses which were preventing francophone universities from accomplishing fully their "specified" role within the Quebec and Canadian societies. Because of their opposing conceptions of the university the two groups emphasized similar problems for different reasons and also stressed different concerns. Both groups, for example, struck repeated blows at the élitist composition of the student body enrolled at Laval and Montréal. While both groups made it amply clear that democratization of the university must not signify a lowering of standards as a quick way of increasing enrolment from the working class, they were just as determined that French-Canadian universities should no longer remain class institutions, that is, institutions serving in large measure the sons of the various levels of the bourgeoisie.[116] The class distribution of nearly 3,000 students enrolled at the Université de Montréal in 1952–3 was as follows: 47.7 per cent of the students were sons of professionals or businessmen, whereas these groups represented only 10.4 per cent of the male work-force. On the other hand,

21.3 per cent of the students were sons of skilled and unskilled workers (13.9) and farmers (7.4). These groups constituted 59.7 per cent of the male labour force in the province.[117] The upper classes were clearly overrepresented in the universities while the labouring classes were greatly underrepresented. Neo-nationalists and Citélibristes maintained that as a means of ending this class bias an expanded government program of scholarships and grants was urgently needed. Yet it was also realized that financial incentives were not in themselves sufficient to democratize the student population. Working-class parents had to be educated to believe that university education for their bright children was at least as potent a symbol of social status as a new automobile or television.[118]

Democratization of the university community was for Citélibristes an end in itself. Making university careers more accessible to working-class students would not result in a levelling of classes or the disappearance of all social hierarchy. "Like Maritain we believe that we must attempt continually to reduce the inevitable and accidental inequalities which tend to make us forget the essential equality of men before God. There are those who work to end these inequalities as much as this is possible and there are those who accentuate these inequalities so as to better profit by them. We are of the first group," wrote a youthful Pelletier in 1948.[119] For neo-nationalists, democratization was perceived as one of the most effective means of modernizing French Canada's all-important national institutions of higher learning. The universities were intimately related to the destiny of the nation, and to all classes of the nation. "There are not 'élites' but one élite, that of intelligence, generosity, and hard work," commented Laurendeau to Jean-Marc Léger in 1959.[120] This "national" élite, or meritocracy, had to be recruited from all classes of the nation by removing the financial and cultural barriers to the universities. Modern and well-financed secular universities were essential if French-Canadian society ever hoped to produce sufficient numbers of highly qualified technicians, scientists, administrators, managers, and industrialists. Only then perhaps could French Canadians capture their rightful role in the development of the province's vast natural resources and thereby overcome their long-standing position of economic inferiority.[121]

Citélibristes often appeared to want universities that were not national. This simply was not the case. While continuing to stress that universities should not under any circumstances become the vehicles of any specific ideology, especially nationalism, Citélibristes felt quite sincerely that Laval and Montréal had a significant role to play in the redefinition of French-Canadian culture, as well as in the decision as to which institutions needed renewing, consolidation, or outright replacement. This controversial task could be accomplished only through intensive scientific analysis of all aspects – social, economic, cultural, and political – of French-Canadian society. Sensitive to the oft-repeated charge that Laval was not nationalistic enough because its faculty had failed to formulate a specific doctrine of cultural survival, Falardeau attempted to explain his understanding of how institutions of higher learning should relate to their cultural environment: "I stated that many of my generation sought to be 'realists.' But this realism, far from rejecting a sensual and spiritual allegiance to French Canada, sought to discern the living fibres of the nation beyond the myths, the psychoses, and the exasperating ideologies. While respecting those who considered and still consider themselves 'nationalists,' we believed that seeking to understand our country rather than merely talking in clichés and anachronistic allergies [sic] was being profoundly patriotic."[122] Francophone universities had a responsibility to serve the cultural community in which they functioned but must not become the hostages of an ideology of nationalism.[123]

Neo-nationalists also repudiated the view that the universities must become hostages to the ideology of nationalism. Yet research in francophone universities should, in their view, be directed to solving for the most part the socioeconomic and cultural problems of French-Canadian society. Finding valued support in the *Tremblay Report* and the Laval Faculty Association's brief to that commission, the neo-nationalists called upon the provincial government to create and fund a provincial research institute capable of coordinating university research in all fields and of initiating research programs in areas the institute deemed urgent and important. In short, what French Canada required was a National Research Institute equivalent to the English-dominated National Research Council in Ottawa.[124] Laurendeau had long been firmly convinced that the development of graduate faculties of research and teaching in the sciences, humanities, and social sciences was the key to long-term reform and renewal of secondary and primary education. Only through indigenous original research could the humanities take on a new life, a new meaning for twentieth-century French Canadians, and the universities succeed in producing "men and works reflecting the vitality of the French-Canadian fact and giving the people, especially our youth, an indispensable thrust and encouragement."[125] Clearly, nationalist objectives of research were paramount for the neo-nationalists.

Two other causes taken up by Citélibristes, one for the entrenchment of academic freedom and a second for the expansion of continuing education programs, demonstrated their commitment to both the democratization and professionalization of higher education. Citélibristes supported Maurice Lamontagne's contention that unless the universities could guarantee a decent degree of economic security and unadulterated academic freedom they would never attract enough bright and ambitious French Canadians into the teaching profession. Academic freedom was not only the basis of a strong and viable community of scholars but "the most precious of democratic freedoms because, if it disappears, the other freedoms will not be able to survive in their entirety for very long."[126] The search for knowledge and truth was considered by Citélibristes to be intimately linked with the struggle for freedom. One was virtually impossible without the other. University educators and administrators had a special responsibility to ensure, *de facto* as well as *de jure*, full academic freedom in the pursuit and transmission of knowledge. "It is therefore necessary that knowledge be continually rethought by those who transmit it as well as those who receive it. To teach or to study is to demonstrate or to learn how to think freely," was Cyrias Ouellet's solid advice to a Rassemblement symposium on freedom and the citizen in Quebec City on 30 November 1957.[127]

Academic freedom was fine and necessary. But Jean-Paul Lefebvre, Citélibriste and labour organizer, believed sincerely that the cornerstone of a true "*cité libre*" was "certainly the awareness of freedom among the majority of citizens." Making the universities more accessible to bright and ambitious working-class students certainly helped to perpetuate the bourgeois myth of social mobility but accomplished little for the hundreds of thousands of workers destined to pass their lives on an assembly line or during their leisure hours in front of a television set. What had French-Canadian universities done to raise the general cultural level of the ever-expanding urban working class? A cursory review of the adult education programs at Laval and Montréal led Lefebvre to conclude that little of enduring value had been done to develop and disseminate a popular culture "which allowed an individual to understand his role in the universe and thereby give meaning to his life." Laval and Montréal had failed miserably to take advantage of the electronic media to help working-class families understand and adapt to their new environment or, if the situation warranted it, organize to bring about improvements in the institutions created to serve the needs of all citizens. "Popular education," wrote Lefebvre, "conceived in the right perspective is an eminently revolutionary undertaking." Until the universities fulfilled their responsibilities towards the working class, militants in the numerous cooperative, national, and cultural movements and the unions would have to lead the struggle for popular education. The achievement of full social and political democracy was for Citélibristes heavily dependent upon the ability of a society's educational institutions to improve the cultural level of the masses.[128]

As was the case with secondary education, meaningful improvements in higher education would be costly. The democratization of the student body, the implementation of research projects, the broadening of academic freedom, and the pursuit of academic excellence would all remain in the realm of rhetoric unless the universities were placed on a much firmer financial footing. Under the pressure of increased enrolments, the addition of new schools, and galloping inflation, both Laval and Montréal were in a state of acute financial crisis by the end of the 1952–3 academic year. Montréal, working on an operating budget of $2.95 million for nearly 3,000 students, had a modest deficit of $79,000. The administrators estimated that the university's annual subsidy needed to be raised to $1.5 million and then to $2.0 million from $0.9 million over the next three years to improve salaries and help establish a pension fund. Capital expenditures would require a minimum of $1.0 million annually for six years![129] Laval's financial crisis was much more desperate. In effect, the university was on the verge of bankruptcy with a whopping deficit of $395,000 for the academic year 1952–3. Indeed, the effective Laval deficit for 1952–3 was $737,000 when interest on outstanding debt to the Séminaire de Québec and capital expenditures were taken into consideration. Bishop Alphonse-Marie Parent, vice-rector of Laval, predicted further deficits of $400 to $600 thousand annually for the rest of the 1950s. Those deficits would be substantially higher if Laval continued its much-needed construction program that had been halted in 1953 when the funds ran dry. Laval needed new medical, law, and science facilities and unlike most Canadian universities did not have a single residence to house any of its students for the 1954–5 academic term. Laval's administrators pleaded that government subsidies be raised to $1.3 and then to $1.5 million over the next five years to help the university defray the deficit, pay better salaries, and improve research facilities. The renewal of the construction program at the Sainte-Foy campus would require $1.5 million annually until 1960–1.[130]

Neo-nationalists and Citélibristes agreed that the situation was desperate indeed. The only viable long-term solution lay in substantially increased government funding of the universities through improved student grant/loan schemes and statutory subsidies to cover operating and capital expenditures. Controversy arose over the issue of how this increased government funding should be administered and whether it necessitated a change in the status of Quebec's universities from private to public institutions. The outspoken neo-nationalist historians from the Université de Montréal, Michel Brunet and Maurice Séguin, expressed the view in 1957 that their institution should be nationalized because it was already receiving over 50 per cent of its revenues from the provincial government.[131] "The university," argued Brunet, "has always been a public institution because its *raison d'être*, its aims and its function have always created close relations between itself and society. Since the nineteenth century, however, these relations have been growing closer with each generation. In our democratic, urbanized and industrial civilization, the University is even more than a public institution. It has become, in the Welfare State era, part of a government financial system of education. University training is now a public service."[132] He called upon church leaders not to fight this trend but rather to join forces with the secular leaders of French Canada "to promote the common good of the French-Canadian collectivity."[133]

Citélibristes also believed that Laval, Montréal, and Sherbrooke should become secularized public institutions financed by the state but had some reservations about moving too quickly in that direction. Quebec society had first to rid itself of outmoded procedures of government funding, procedures riddled with patronage, paternalism, and a sense of personal allegiance, and the government had to adopt a system of professional statutory grants voted and scrutinized by the legislature.[134] Dion believed that it would be at least twenty or thirty years before Quebec's universities possessed a sufficiently strong tradition of independence and academic freedom to function properly as state universities. To move in that direction too quickly would spell disaster for them. Dion claimed that "a university, deprived of the prestige and the power of the church, would become merely an instrument of partisan politics and the professors would fall under the 'protection' of nationalistic pontiffs who desired nothing more than the creation of a ministry of propaganda with the task of imposing their truth on all levels of education."[135] Quebec politics was still overwhelmingly dominated by traditional nationalists – "lay moralists and theologians," as Dion preferred to call them   too eager to make the universities tools of their vested class and ethnic interests.

Neo-nationalists at *Le Devoir*, supported by educational reformers like Arthur Tremblay, considered that vastly increased provincial grants to Laval and Montréal were urgent and imperative. The grants should be statutory with no strings attached, no patronage involved, and no favours expected in return.[136] Yet Filion objected strongly to the argument that Montréal, and perhaps Laval, should become in the short term, or even in the long term, state institutions. He agreed wholeheartedly with Bishop Irénée Lussier, rector of Montréal, that in a pluralistic society like that of Quebec universities could not be state universities and remain officially or even informally Catholic institutions. In such a society it was only fair and democratic that all institutions largely funded by the state should serve the needs and interests of all ethnic, social, and religious groups.[137] He warned French Canadians that the Catholic church could not expect to retain control of the universities if the Quebec government became their major source of revenue.

If French-Canadian Catholics wished to retain Laval, Montréal, and Sherbrooke as Catholic universities, it was therefore incumbent upon them to finance directly at least a third of their operating and capital costs.[138] These universities could not remain denominational institutions and receive the bulk of their revenues from the state. In effect, the same argument applied to the denominational elementary and secondary sectors but neo-nationalists were not consistent. This was so, perhaps, because Filion and Laurendeau felt that Quebec's francophone universities should and would remain Catholic. The question was how realistic was their faith in Catholics being either willing or able to contribute the enormous sums required. Given the advanced state of secularization of Quebec society by the late 1950s, one might well question the feasibility of the neo-nationalists' perception of the future of the church-controlled universities.

This somewhat paradoxical position of rejecting state universities while repeatedly calling for increased government funds led the neo-nationalists to come out strongly in favour of a solution proposed by the Faculty Association and the administrators of Laval University.[139] In their separate but equally excellent briefs to the Tremblay Commission both groups suggested the creation of an independent Commission for Aid to Universities and a Provincial Fund for Universities. The former would enable the universities to present their case to the government and, by serving as an advisory body to the minister of finance on the allocation of annual grants to universities, safeguard the independence of those institutions. The latter body would give the universities some assurance of an ongoing and flexible source of revenue so that long-range planning could become a reality.[140]

These proposals were not as antistatist as they might seem on the surface. Unlike the Catholic and Protestant committees of the CIP, the Commission for Aid to Universities was directly responsible to the legislature through the minister of finance. Its function as an advisory body on higher education would undoubtedly be transferred to the future Ministry of Education envisaged by many reformers, including Filion and Laurendeau by the late months of 1960. The recommendations found favour from all quarters for different reasons. To neo-nationalists, the commission represented a barrier against political intervention in higher education and undermined the need to nationalize fully the universities. To Citélibristes, the CTCC, and the FTQ, the commission was viewed as a necessary organization to oversee a smooth transition by the universities from an élitist, clerical, and provincial stage of development to their new status as democratic, secular, and independent institutions of higher learning and research serving the local, national, and international needs of all Canadians but foremost those of the French-Canadian society, because that is where they were located and received the great preponderance of their financial support.[141]

CONCLUSION

Neo-nationalists approached the issue of educational reform with a growing sense of determination that certain reforms were imperative if the French-Canadian nation was to survive and prosper in an urban-industrial environment. It was becoming increasingly clear that the anachronistic nature of francophone and Catholic educational institutions was forcing increasing numbers of working-class and middle-class French-Canadian parents to enrol their children in English-speaking Protestant schools. It was also painfully apparent that the francophone and Catholic system had failed to prepare adequate numbers of French-Canadians for careers in business, science, and related fields, thereby enhancing the anglophone minority's domination of Quebec's expanding economy. Gaining control of Quebec's economy, with the concomitant desire to make French the working language of that economy, was the driving motive behind the neo-nationalists' reform program for education.

To achieve their middle-class and nationalist objectives, the neo-nationalists advocated the secularization, democratization, and state financing of primary, secondary, and under certain circumstances university education. By the late 1950s they were even ready to concede the need for a ministry of education, but wanted a full-scale public inquiry before any precipitate government action was taken. On the surface, their proposals for change appear quite conservative. They were so in a very real sense because at no time did the neo-nationalists question the traditional function of education. They perceived the schools as institutions of socialization and reinforcement of the class system. Yet, considering the social and economic inferiority of Quebec's francophone majority, much of which can be attributed to its outmoded educational institutions, a comprehensive secularization and democratization of those institutions would inevitably create a challenge to the existing relationship between Quebec's two linguistic communities. Not only would a new bureaucratic and technocratic francophone middle class challenge the traditional role of the church. This new class, with the full support of the state, would seek to carve out a predominant role for itself in the heretofore anglophone-dominated private sector. Only when it became evident that modernization and statutory public funding of francophone universities were reforms urgently needed if these institutions were to serve the predominantly secular needs and aspirations of the new middle class did the neo-nationalists become eager proponents of such reforms. Nationalist and class preoccupations, which had long served to prevent educational reform, now became the prime motivating force behind neo-nationalist pleas for modernization of educational institutions and curricula at all levels.

As might well be expected, the Citélibristes' demand for educational reform were propelled by a different set of ideological assumptions. The primary function of education was not the perpetuation of a national collectivity but the creation of a democratic *Cité libre* in which each and every individual could achieve as complete self-fulfilment as was humanly possible. Dynamic political democracy and the achievement of greater equality of condition were virtually impossible without a comprehensive, secular, state-funded system of education. The state had a duty and a responsibility to prepare each and every individual for his self-chosen occupation in society. In a modern urban-industrial society, where the range of occupations far surpasses the traditional professions and the clerical élite, education could no longer be restricted to an élite based on wealth and class considerations. Primary education was urgent and necessary for every individual if Quebec society was to attain a high level of democracy. Consequently, primary education had to be mandatory, tax-supported, and democratically administered. Citélibristes believed that the same principles should apply to secondary education. The classical college system needed to be replaced by a universally accessible public secondary system which would prepare students for the entire range of secular career opportunities and would enable the appropriate percentage of academically qualified candidates to pursue their chosen field of post-secondary education. Francophone universities had to be secularized, in terms both of their internal administrative procedures and of their role within society. Their prime function was the pursuit of secular knowledge and its application to problems confronting society at large. But only when university administrators and faculties had developed a professional conception of their own and their institution's respective roles, and only when the political culture and funding procedures were democratized, would francophone universities, according to some Citélibristes, be ready for complete secularization. The new wave of nationalism sweeping Quebec by the late 1950s raised fears among certain Citélibristes that Quebec's francophone universities would become tools of the nationalist state envisaged by the rising generation of secular nationalists.

NINE

Quebec Confronts the New Federalism

We must fully recognize that the large majority of citizens judge a particular political situation according to its concrete results and not in abstract terms, that is, on the basis of the promises of a new ideology. What people really desire is a satisfactory standard of living and it is only when they are convinced that their economic and political institutions are not accomplishing this fundamental objective that they become attracted by new ideologies.[1]

The prime concern of neo-nationalists and Citélibristes was the comprehensive modernization of Quebec society, in particular, the renewal of the attitudes and mental outlook of the francophone community and the reform of various sociocultural, economic, and political institutions governing its survival and growth. Yet both groups were keenly sensitive to the political context of the situation. Quebec operated within the Canadian federal system and its economy was becoming increasingly integrated into the Canadian and North American economies. It was inevitable that sooner or later both neo-nationalists and Citélibristes would assess the impact of their respective ideologies and reform proposals on Quebec's role within the Canadian nation-state. This was all the more imperative given the evolving nature of Canadian federalism during and after the war. Indeed, this "new federalism" was responsible, in part, for the re-emergence of liberalism and the rise of neo-nationalism in Quebec. Undoubtedly, both ideologies had their origins in the indigenous socioeconomic, cultural, and political forces at work within the province. It became increasingly clear, however, that Ottawa's decision to forge ahead with Keynesian-inspired fiscal and monetary policies and the creation of a highly centralized social welfare state had altered in crucial ways the prevalent conception of federal-provincial relations.

Citélibristes supported in principle, and to some degree in practice, the new federalism, but campaigned to ensure that it remained federal in nature and democratic in spirit and operation. Neo-nationalists rejected in principle and in practice the new doctrine. Their initial response, shared and vigorously supported by traditional nationalists, was conservative in nature. They pleaded for a return to classic federalism. That is, they wanted a faithful adherence to the division of powers outlined in the Constitution of 1867, a division which guaranteed the provinces complete sovereignty within areas of their own jurisdiction as well as the taxing powers to finance those responsibilities. A crucial shift in ideological perspective and strategy occurred in the mid-fifties. Neo-nationalists and traditional nationalists concurred that the best defence was an aggressive offence, although for quite distinct reasons. Neo-nationalists contended that some form of radical constitutional revision was essential to preserve and entrench provincial autonomy and accommodate the "new" Quebec. The advent of a powerful, secular, interventionist state in Quebec would necessitate altering the traditional balance of powers between it and the central government.

Two classic feuds between Ottawa and Quebec served to galvanize neo-nationalist thinking and action on this issue of constitutional change. The first involved Duplessis' struggle for the retention of provincial taxing powers, that is, Quebec's right to collect revenues by any or all forms of direct taxation rather than submit to the tax-rental scheme imposed on the provinces by Ottawa during the war and renewed in 1947 and 1952. The second episode which radicalized the nationalists was Ottawa's decision, implemented at the request of all Canadian universities and in response to the *Massey Report*, to grant federal subsidies to post-secondary educational institutions. Ironically, *Cité libre* supported neo-nationalists in both of these important issues for democratic reasons. Yet the Citélibristes did not derive from these struggles a similar desire for radical constitutional revision, because their democratic and liberal assumptions were not imbued with nationalist values and aspirations. Neo-nationalists felt strongly that the new federalism was a serious threat to provincial autonomy and therefore to the French-Canadian nation. It jeopardized the ability of a modern Quebec state to ensure francophone control and development of a dynamic French-Canadian society. This state would, of course, be governed by the new francophone bureaucratic middle class which, it was thought, would make possible the emergence of a francophone industrial, financial, and commercial bourgeoisie. Citélibristes drew different conclusions from their assessment of French-Canadian society. What was essential, in their view, was not constitutional revision, but rather a "revolution of mentalities." Once French-Canadian socioeconomic and political élites had abandoned their reliance upon an outmoded ideology of nationalism and turned their attention to the development of a modern, secular "*Cité libre*," then majority control of all sectors of Quebec society would, in time, become a reality. The real political obstacle to change and modernization, Citélibristes persuasively argued, was the antidemocratic, socially conservative, nationalistic, Duplessis regime, not the well-intentioned but, at times, misguided federal government.

THE SOCIAL WELFARE STATE: FEDERAL OR PROVINCIAL?

The neo-nationalist counter-offensive against the new federalism was vigorous, unrelenting, and comprehensive. They adopted a dual strategy of attack. First, they laboured to undermine the ideological arguments put forward by the proponents of the new federalism. Second, they encouraged and supported the Duplessis government's political stonewalling of the tax-rental agreements while continually urging that the Quebec government practise a concept of "positive autonomy," the first step being the creation of a provincial income tax system. Neo-nationalists could rely upon the support of traditional nationalists in the church, the liberal professions, and, most importantly, in the small business community. This combined pressure, coupled with the direct influence of the traditional nationalist Tremblay commissioners, eventually prompted a reluctant Duplessis government to create a provincial income tax scheme in 1954. The ensuing bitter political clash with the St Laurent Liberal regime in Ottawa led effectively to the demise of the existing tax-rental arrangements and the adoption of a tax-sharing system open to all provinces.

The new federalism, which aroused such concerted opposition from the nationalist intelligentsia and the Duplessis regime, had its origins in the rapid industrialization and urbanization of the 1920s and the ensuing collapse of the Canadian economy in the depression decade. Nationalist-inspired academics, politicians, and civil servants contended that the federal government required a "new national policy" to recoup its leadership role lost to the provinces in the 1920s. This new policy, as elaborated in the Rowell-Sirois Commission's *Report* of 1940 and the Ottawa Green Book proposals on reconstruction presented to the provincial premiers in 1945, entailed two new roles for the federal government.[2] Through the adoption of Keynesian-inspired monetary and fiscal policies it would regulate the economy to ensure the maintenance of high and stable employment and income. It would also undertake to attenuate some of the worst social effects of industrial capitalism by instituting a comprehensive system of social security. In short, following the thrust of the 1943 *Marsh Report on Social Security*, the federal government intended to lead the way in establishing a social welfare state.[3]

Ottawa proposed to begin by taking over full responsibility for unemployment and paying 20 per cent of public works projects undertaken by provinces and municipalities, providing pensions for all Canadians over seventy and defraying half the cost for needy pensioners between sixty-five and seventy, initiating a provincially administered health insurance scheme and assuming 60 per cent of the cost, and finally, providing special grants-in-aid for public health programs and hospital construction. To finance these social security responsibilities and implement Keynesian fiscal and monetary policies, Ottawa claimed that it required exclusive control over all direct taxation, including personal, corporate, and estate taxes. It would compensate the provinces for their loss in revenue from direct taxation by granting them unconditional annual subsidies on a basis of $12 per capita, adjusted to the growth of the Gross National Product. When the provinces unanimously rejected the Green Book proposals, the federal government proceeded to negotiate separately with them for the renewal of the tax-rental agreements in 1947. All provinces except Ontario and Quebec acceded, thereby relinquishing their constitutional right to levy direct taxes. On the social security front Ottawa adopted a piecemeal strategy. It offered the provinces a wide range of conditional shared-cost programs in the fields of housing, technical education, hospital, and highway construction.[4] By the early fifties, the new federalism seemed well entrenched and Ottawa had regained its leadership role in the Canadian federal system. When Ontario signed the tax-rental arrangements in 1952 most Ottawa politicians and senior civil servants were undoubtedly elated. Surely, most of them thought, Quebec's need for revenue would force the intransigent Duplessis to accept the new federalism shortly. No one, not even the most optimistic neo-nationalist, could have predicted victory for Quebec within three years.

In the initial stage of the struggle against the new federalism, the neo-nationalists shared and reiterated the traditional nationalists' conception of the constitution. The provincial and cultural compact theses of Confederation were trotted out and embellished with the thesis of provincial constitutional "priority" in the field of direct taxation.[5] Late in 1949, a young nationalistic Jesuit, Father Richard Arès, wrote a pamphlet entitled *La Confédération: Pacte ou loi?* in which he defended the dual compact theses of Confederation. He showed how Quebec Liberals under Ernest Lapointe had been convinced of the validity of the provincial and cultural compact theses and then under St Laurent had followed their leader in denouncing those same convictions. Neo-nationalists applauded Arès' lucid defence of the compact theses and warned Ottawa that francophones in Quebec would not subscribe to their own downfall. "Let it be understood in Ottawa: the undertaking which we consented to in 1867 will not be withdrawn as long as we have not given our consent to a new contract." Quebec's defence of its fundamental rights, concluded Laurendeau, was not motivated by a blind attachment to the past but by its perception of those rights as the best political guarantee of French Canada's national survival. The compact theory did not constitute a program of action but was the *sine qua non* of a "positive" provincial autonomy.[6]

Neo-nationalists took strong exception to Prime Minister St Laurent's claim that the federal government had been granted unlimited taxing powers by the constitution.[7] The logical outcome of these unlimited powers, they pointed out, was that the tax-rental agreements were constitutional and any one objecting to them was a separatist. Furthermore, if Ottawa obtained such comprehensive taxing powers then the provinces, constitutionally speaking, could be rendered vassals of the central government. To counter the federalist offensive, the neo-nationalists supported the Duplessis government's contention that the provinces had priority in the field of direct taxation. The "priority" rights thesis, they noted, had been sanctioned by a decision of the Judicial Committee of the Privy Council in 1887. St Laurent's "unlimited" rights thesis was, according to Laurendeau, the cornerstone of the "doctrine of revolutionary centralism which strips the provinces little by little of their powers and brings them increasingly to the position that the men of 1867 wanted to avoid, that is, the unitary state!"[8] The essence of the compact of 1867, the neo-nationalists argued, was a division of fields of jurisdiction between Ottawa and the provinces. Ottawa had been granted control of the major sources of revenue, customs, and excise taxes, because the major expenses resided within areas of federal jurisdiction. In the modern era the major expenditures were in the areas of provincial jurisdiction – education, roads, and social services. Paralleling this development was the fact that the most lucrative source of revenue resided in direct taxes, taxing powers which the constitution had reserved "principally and specifically" to the provinces. Even had direct taxation rights been granted exclusively to Ottawa, respect for the compact of 1867 – the true spirit of Confederation – would have demanded a new distribution of taxing powers to enable the provinces to finance adequately the new services being demanded of them in their areas of jurisdiction.[9]

Neo-nationalists soon realized that it was futile to rely too heavily on constitutional legalities to weaken the arguments of those propounding the benefits of the new federalism. Ironically, the most comprehensive defence of the theory and practice of the new policy was offered by Maurice Lamontagne in *Le fédéralisme canadien: Evolutions et problèmes*, which was published in the summer of 1954 just as its author began an illustrious career as federal civil servant and, later, politician and senator.[10] Lamontagne detailed the external and domestic forces which had precipitated the need for a strong central government in Canada. These forces made it imperative to have a central government capable of implementing Keynesian fiscal and monetary policies and a social welfare state which would attenuate the economic instability and social insecurity resulting from the second industrial revolution initiated and dominated by the private sector. Constitutional revisions were unnecessary given the flexible nature of the Canadian federal system.[11] Functionalism became the operative term for proponents of the new federalism. Reflecting his liberal and technocratic bias, Lamontagne argued that within federalism "there are no absolute *principles* but only different *methods* that must be used or discarded depending on their characteristics and the demands of the functions to be performed. In other words, federalism must be *functional* ... In sum, the central law of federalism can be summarized by a currently popular formula: *as much decentralism as possible, but as much centralism as necessary*."[12]

Quebec's insistence upon the preservation of an outmoded conception of provincial autonomy and its continued rejection of a justified and necessary new federalism were, in Lamontagne's estimation, forcing the province out of the mainstream of Canadian socioeconomic and political development into a separatist backwater. Because separatism was neither desirable nor feasible, even on a limited cultural basis, the only alternative open to Quebec was its *"lucid integration into a new Canadian federalism."* This strategy would provide Quebec with urgently required financial resources to ensure the survival and modernization of the French-Canadian society.[13]

This new federalism required that Ottawa and the provinces move increasingly toward a formula of joint but specialized jurisdictions, especially in the new areas like social security and economic stabilization. Accordingly, the provinces would have the prime but not exclusive responsibility for industrial development and structural unemployment while Ottawa would have the major but not exclusive responsibility for maintaining economic stability through the application of Keynesian fiscal and monetary policies. Ironically, when Lamontagne approached the question of the division of taxing powers he was less enthusiastic about a joint sharing of jurisdiction. With the advent of Keynesian economics the federal government could no longer view taxation strictly as a source of revenue. Taxation became an indispensable instrument of economic control. The federal government, in order to apply effectively Keynesian doctrine, needed access to all forms of taxation, indirect and direct, and to all major categories of public expenditure. Thus he strongly supported the tax-rental agreements because they gave the federal government exclusive control over the major direct taxes – corporate, personal, and estate – which were the most effective in combating both recessionary and inflationary trends in the economy. Furthermore, unconditional grants gave the provinces economic stability without destroying their autonomy. On the other hand, indirect taxes, especially sales taxes at the manufacturing level, were, in Lamontagne's estimation, much better suited to provincial needs. Sales taxes were more amenable to regional variations, were relatively stable despite fluctuations in the overall economy, did not hinder industrial development, and were quite easy to administer.

Effective provincial autonomy in direct taxes was limited because corporate and personal income taxes favoured the industrialized provinces and were highly dependent upon the economic situation or the competitive rates established in other provinces, and because the federal government needed full access to them in order to achieve deficit or surplus budgets.[14]

Neo-nationalists countered Lamontagne's points with a range of theoretical and practical arguments. To begin with, the new federalism was inherently undemocratic because it would lead to the subjugation and eventual demise of the provinces. They rejected the claim that increased centralization would result in progressive and efficient socioeconomic planning. On the contrary, the Ottawa-inspired social welfare state would result in a technocratic and bureaucratic nightmare of statistics, reports, and programs, all unsuitable to the complex and ever-changing socioeconomic realities at the regional and local levels. Ottawa's social welfare state would lead to the regimentation of everyone, making them dependent upon a distant bureaucracy, "not eager to come to life, grow, study, work, suffer, age and die." If this was what Canadians wanted, then the new federalism would provide it. The neo-nationalists were convinced that it was not what the majority wanted. Canadians perceived social life as an affair of private interest and not public right; they considered that economic and social reforms should be initiated and administered at the local and regional levels. They feared ending up like animals in the zoo, contented with everything but lacking their freedom. Quebec's resistance to the new federalism was not strictly ethnic but, rather, reflected a natural, universal resistance to centralist aggression that destroyed, by its very nature, human intelligence, will, and freedom of action. Australia's provincial states, which did not represent the religious or ethnic rights of any minority, were as strongly opposed to excessive centralization as was Quebec in the Canadian federal system.[15]

Drawing upon statistics provided by the Canadian Federation of Mayors and Municipalities, the neo-nationalists demonstrated how Ottawa's abuse of its taxing powers was destroying the democratic essence of Canadian federalism. The amount of taxes collected by all levels of government had grown sevenfold from $780 million (or $76 per capita) in 1930 to $5,346 million ($381 per capita) in 1951. Of the $780 million collected in 1930 approximately $318 million went to Ottawa, $307 million to the municipalities, and $158 million to the provincial governments. In 1951 the revenue collected by Ottawa had reached the astronomical sum of $3,791 million while the provinces received $918 million and the municipalities $636 million. In percentage terms, the federal, provincial, and municipal governments raised 41, 20, and 39 per cent respectively of the taxes in 1930 while in 1951 those percentages were 71, 17, and 12 per cent respectively. The municipalities, which relied heavily on property taxes, had suffered the greatest setback because of their inability to move into the lucrative direct tax field. The tenfold increase in Ottawa's revenues had been precipitated by an enormous expansion in defence spending (8 per cent of the 1930 budget to 42 per cent of the 1951 budget) and a considerable increase in social security and welfare expenditures from $6 million or 1.6 per cent of the 1931 budget to $477 million or 13.4 per cent of the 1951 budget. Numerous municipalities and school boards were declaring bankruptcy while Ottawa boasted about its several budgetary surpluses since 1945.[16]

Neo-nationalists also ridiculed the emergency powers and equalization arguments used to justify Ottawa's monopoly of direct taxation. Experience in both world wars had shown that Ottawa could, when necessary, recuperate full taxing powers under the Canadian constitution. Furthermore, any agreement on a new division of taxing powers, the neo-nationalists suggested, could easily include an appropriate constitutional amendment ensuring the federal government adequate emergency powers. The real crime against the Canadian nation was not to be found in the provinces' struggle for financial autonomy but in the central government's continued practice of equating itself with the totality of the Canadian state. Provincial access to direct taxation need not aggravate regional disparities if a constitutional and democratic equalization formula was implemented. Furthermore, the existing tax-rental scheme had not solved the complex problem of regional disparities because Saskatchewan, which was termed a have-not province, had a per capita income nearly $425 higher than that of Quebec, and although Quebec boasted the lowest provincial per capita debt, its citizens paid higher taxes and received fewer services than residents of New Brunswick, Manitoba, Ontario, and British Columbia. Ottawa's naïve and terribly misguided reliance upon abstract and perhaps soon to be outmoded Keynesian economic theory to resolve the complex question of regional disparities could not justify the destruction of an inherently democratic federal system.[17]

At the heart of the neo-nationalist rejection of the new federalism was the firm belief that the survival and development of the French-Canadian nationality was dependent upon the implementation of a pragmatic and meaningful provincial autonomy. Ottawa's intrusion into areas of provincial jurisdiction was a direct violation of the BNA Act. Federal monopolization of direct taxation made it virtually impossible for Quebec to finance and administer areas of provincial jurisdiction in a manner that best reflected French Canada's distinct social, cultural, and religious values. For example, a vast federal health insurance scheme would impose upon Quebec's francophone majority medical practices such as birth control, abortion, sterilization, and euthanasia, practices which were against its religious and cultural traditions. In the early stages, the neo-nationalists claimed that Quebec would prefer a limited health insurance scheme for lower income groups.[18] Once they had come to realize the potential of an interventionist state they pressed their claim for provincial autonomy on the ground that Quebec City and not Ottawa could best administer comprehensive and universal social welfare programs.

The neo-nationalists' most effective critique of the new federalism was the contention that its protagonists had failed to take into account the ethnic pluralism and regional diversity of the country. In neglecting what were in reality the quintessential features of Canadian federalism the federal Liberal party was destroying rather than enhancing national unity.[19] The St Laurent government, equating progress with material growth, had come to identify national unity with concrete programs like the tax-rental scheme, federal grants to universities, and the trans-Canada highway. Neo-nationalists considered this conception of national unity to be excessively materialistic and bureaucratic. It lacked an important organic component which integrated the geographic, ethnic, linguistic, and religious diversity of modern Canada. The majority of federal technocrats and social planners, wrote Filion, "have a natural tendency to seek people's happiness without regard to how they feel. They impose on politics their own conception of life. If they believe that the symbols of human happiness are the bathtub and the electric fridge, then they want all Canadians, including the Eskimos, to have bathtubs and electric fridges."[20] Most Canadians, the neo-nationalists believed, did not want this naïve and simplistic form of national unity imposed on the country. The fact that Canada remained separate from the United States was the on-going confirmation that the majority of Canadians placed cultural and social values ahead of material development and individual prosperity. If this scale of priorities was to prevail, the provinces had to be guaranteed real and effective autonomy by the defeat of the centralizing, un-Canadian new federalism.[21]

Neo-nationalists vigorously denounced Maurice Lamontagne's contention that Quebec was faced with the dilemma of choosing between separatism and integration in terms of the new federalism. They denied Lamontagne's claim that Quebec was already well along the path of separatism and was impeding the progress of the rest of Canada. The vast majority of French-Canadian nationalists, Filion reminded Lamontagne, had, under the influence of Henri Bourassa, discovered that Canada belonged to all Canadians regardless of their language, culture, and religion. Not a single Québécois, "with a head on his shoulders and his heart in the right place," was disposed to build a Chinese wall on Quebec's borders, cutting French Canada off from a million compatriots serving as the nation's outposts throughout Canada. While readily admitting that the days of open persecution were over, Filion stressed that Quebec remained the bastion and operations base for the French-Canadian nation in North America. Quebec provided a political state endowed with all the prerogatives necessary for the survival and expansion of the French-Canadian culture. The major flaw in

Lamontagne's analysis was its total lack of political reality. Lamontagne was calling upon French Canadians to relinquish to Ottawa many of the prerogatives of the state of Quebec without demanding significant political compensation in return. Asking a minority to negotiate with a majority on such weak terms was tantamount to asking it to commit political suicide.[22] Quebec and not the central government was the political reality to which French Canadians must attach their future as a nation and whose powers they must fight to enhance if circumstances warranted such action.

THE BATTLE OVER TAXING POWERS

Neo-nationalists were more than well-intentioned but ineffective ideologues. They were far too realistic in their commitment to be content with propounding abstract counter-arguments against the new federalism. The Bloc Populaire experience had drawn them to a concept of "positive autonomy." They firmly believed that the Quebec state had to exercise its full range of taxing prerogatives if it desired to counter successfully Ottawa's aggressive policies and practices. Neo-nationalists realized from the outset, as Filion later wrote, that only a strategy of concerted political pressure "could in the long run stump the plunderers from Ottawa."[23] This strategy accounts for the neo-nationalists' decision to support the Union Nationale's continued stonewalling of the tax-rental agreements. In effect, they had no alternative. The provincial Liberal party, weak and divided, simply refused to denounce the new federalism perpetrated by its federal counterpart.[24] Political pragmatism also accounts for the neo-nationalists' decision to support a strategy of political pressure intended to push Premier Duplessis into implementing a provincial income tax system. This act of positive autonomy, the neo-nationalists hoped, would precipitate a political confrontation with Ottawa and open the way for an alternative solution to the tax-rental agreements.

The neo-nationalist campaign for a provincial income tax was initiated in 1948 when André Laurendeau, in one of his last speeches in the Legislative Assembly, called upon the Union Nationale government to exercise the province's taxing powers by legislating a 5 per cent provincial income tax. This was legal under the existing provisions of the Income Tax Act for provinces not signing the tax-rental agreements. Ottawa would then hand the province up to 5 per cent of the federal income tax collected in Quebec and its taxpayers would not have to pay a penny more. Neo-nationalists shortly began to recommend that Quebec collect the tax itself and have its taxpayers deduct their provincial income tax from taxes owed the federal government.[25] By 1950, neo-nationalists had become increasingly impatient with, and critical of, Duplessis' legalistic and essentially negative approach to the preservation of provincial autonomy.[26] They reminded the Union

Nationale that provincial autonomy was not going to be preserved or enhanced by simply pleading with Ottawa to respect the constitution. The only effective strategy against the new federalism was Quebec's aggressive exercise of provincial taxing powers and social prerogatives. If Duplessis was to be worthy of the mantle of Honoré Mercier, it was imperative, suggested Pierre Laporte, that he follow the example of this "positive autonomist" and convene an interprovincial conference. Only then could Quebec hope to convince the other provinces of the nefarious consequences of the new federalism and come to terms with them on a series of plausible counter-proposals, thereby enabling the provinces to confront Ottawa united and strong.[27]

Neo-nationalists were not alone in their attempt to convince Duplessis of the need for a more aggressive positive autonomy stance. Indeed, without the active, well-organized, well-orchestrated support of the traditional nationalists in the Chambre de Commerce de Montréal and the personal intervention of the Tremblay commissioners, it is highly doubtful that the overly cautious, conservative, and obstinate premier would have abandoned his opposition to a provincial income tax scheme. The Chambre de Commerce de Montréal, headed by an energetic administrator who was a graduate of the Ecole des hautes études commerciales, Gilbert La Tour, entered the battle over taxing powers with the publication of a position paper in April 1947.[28] This normally staid, cautious, and business-oriented body had been goaded into action by a young, ambitious economist and traditional nationalist, François-Albert Angers. A close friend of Laurendeau's, Angers was called upon to express the nationalist perspective on federal-provincial relations on numerous occasions in the pages of *L'Action nationale* and *Le Devoir*. He did so with a flair and a polemical style unsurpassed by anyone, except perhaps Trudeau. In 1946-7, Angers demanded that a comprehensive socioeconomic, political, and constitutional counter-offensive be undertaken by the provincial government against the new federalism.[29]

As might be expected of the Chambre de Commerce, its *Mémoire* on federal-provincial taxing matters was well researched, effectively organized, and presented in a style quite different from the customary nationalist manifestoes. The chamber opposed the new federalism for all the prevalent traditional nationalist reasons, but its overriding preoccupation was the preservation of the capitalist economic system. After all, the chamber represented the vested interests of French-Canadian businessmen and professionals who feared that increased centralized control and direction of the Canadian economy would lead to socialism. The implementation of Keynesian fiscal and monetary policies and the creation of a social welfare state necessitated higher levels of taxation and inevitably weakened the private sector, especially family business concerns and professional groups. French-Canadian middle and upper-middle classes were constituted almost entirely of these two occupations. The chamber proposed a compromise solution. Ottawa would have exclusive powers in the field of indirect taxes while the provinces gained exclusive jurisdiction over estate taxes. Ottawa and the provinces would share corporate and personal taxes on the basis of five-year agreements. Provincial priority would be guaranteed by allowing provincial corporate and personal income taxes to be deducted from federal corporate and personal income taxes. Quebec, contended the brief, required the flexibility inherent in access to both direct taxes to ensure the survival of the free enterprise system and stem the onslaught of socialism, which was making significant gains in some provinces and had invaded Quebec with the nationalization of the Montreal Light, Heat & Power Company in 1944. The Chambre de Commerce de Montréal became a vigorous pressure group for the preservation and extension of Quebec's autonomy because autonomy would benefit both the nationalist and class objectives of the petty bourgeois, French-Canadian professional and business groups – old and new. Quebec's control of corporate and personal income taxes would provide the essential flexibility needed to fight creeping socialism, since the government would be capable of shifting the tax burden from small French-Canadian manufacturing, retail, wholesale, and financial businesses to large and wealthy financial, commercial, and industrial corporations owned predominantly by Anglo-Canadian and American interests. The province could also supplement its revenues by implementing a personal income tax and thus not be forced to raise corporate taxes.[30]

Neo-nationalists welcomed this powerful ally – the chamber had 4,300 members and its executive consisted of individuals from all political parties – and for a short while even shared its anti–social welfare philosophy.[31] They were particularly elated when the chamber came out in September 1951 in support of an immediate provincial income tax of 5 per cent.[32] They renewed their efforts but the circumstances were not propitious.[33] While refusing to say so publicly, Duplessis rejected the provincial income tax proposal as "5 per cent autonomy!" He feared, according to Rumilly, that to implement a provincial tax of 5 per cent would constitute a precedent limiting the rights of the province in the field of personal income taxes. Ottawa would, in effect, retain control over the province's tax rates. Furthermore, St Laurent had indicated to Duplessis that the federal government would not turn over to the Quebec government 5 per cent of the federal income tax paid by the province's taxpayers but would allow those individual taxpayers to deduct provincial income tax up to a total of 5 per cent of their federal tax. Duplessis, facing the prospect of a provincial election in 1952, rejected as political suicide any scheme calling for the creation of a provincially administered personal income tax no matter how small.[34]

The neo-nationalists and the Chambre de Commerce de Montréal were perturbed and indignant. The former denounced Duplessis' vaunted verbal and legalistic defence of provincial autonomy, which had not prevented him from granting Ottawa complete control over old-age pensions, accepting many shared-cost programs, and allowing federal grants to universities. The premier, by his shortsighted rejection of a positive approach, was aiding and abetting the constitutional imperialism of Canada's leading public enemy – Ottawa! In effect, all of Duplessis' rationalizations were nothing more than defeats – "strategic retreats."[35] Neo-nationalists argued that if Quebec and Ontario had equitable personal income tax schemes with efficient agencies they could make a strong case for, and eventually win, an increase in the federal deduction from 5 to 10, 15, or even 20 per cent. In the interim, autonomy at 5 per cent was considerably better than autonomy at zero per cent. The Chambre de Commerce concurred entirely, while adding that a 5 per cent tax did not constitute admission of provincial limitation. Nor was it necessary, as Duplessis was continually suggesting, that the province have access to individual tax records from the federal Ministry of Revenue.[36] Nevertheless, Duplessis and the Union Nationale refused to budge on the issue in response to pressure from the nationalists, new and old. The Union Nationale lost fifteen seats to the Liberals in the July 1952 election but Filion remained convinced that Duplessis, "despite the warning that he has just received, will consider himself, like the captain of a ship, Master after God."[37]

It appeared that Duplessis had once again outfoxed the nationalists and could govern for another term without having to consider their politically volatile strategy of positive autonomy. Such was not to be the case. Ontario's Premier Frost announced during Labour Day weekend, 1952, that his government had decided to sign a lucrative tax-rental agreement with Ottawa. Quebec nationalists were shocked and dismayed, to say the least. Ontario's fateful decision to succumb to the new federalism had destroyed that important Quebec-Ontario common front which had on more than one occasion since 1867 defeated the centralist policies and practices of the federal government. Ontario had apparently become a new satellite of the federal government. The tax-rental agreement ensured that the province would receive approximately $25 million more than if it had collected its own corporate and personal income taxes. Canadian federalism, according to the neo-nationalists, had suffered its worst defeat since 1867 and Ontario's Premier Frost "will take his place in history as one of the worst saboteurs of autonomy."[38] The destruction of the common front called for a serious reconsideration of neo-nationalist strategy and tactics. The era of discussion and negotiations with Ottawa was over, and henceforth the issue of provincial taxing rights would have to be decided at the political level.[39] Politics and political pressure tactics became the order of the day for Quebec's increasingly aggressive and frustrated neo-nationalists and traditional nationalists.

It was decided that Duplessis might be moved to abandon his conservative and negative approach to provincial autonomy if he was convinced that there existed a broad base of political support throughout the province for a more activist government. The best way to achieve this objective was to get Duplessis to institute a royal commission on constitutional problems. Institutions, groups, and individuals from all sectors and regions of the province could then be encouraged to make their views known on a wide range of issues and problems. Prompted by the executive of the Chambre de Commerce de Montréal, the Chambre de Commerce de la province de Québec adopted as discussion topic for its 1952 congress the question of taxing matters in federal-provincial relations. Delegates from the province's numerous chambres de commerce approved the Chambre de Commerce de Montréal's 1947 *Mémoire* as the basis for an alternative solution to the tax-rental agreements and the new federalism in general. Delegates also endorsed a resolution calling upon the provincial government to create a royal commission of inquiry to investigate and make recommendations on constitutional and financial problems confronting all levels of the government.[40]

Laurent Paradis, president of the Chambre de Commerce de la province de Québec, a journalist from Trois-Rivières and close friend of Duplessis, persuaded the premier to receive a delegation from the various chambres de commerce. Five hundred delegates from all regions of the province descended on the Legislative Assembly on 26 November 1952 to impress on Duplessis the need for a royal commission.[41] When the organizers met the premier in his office they were led to believe that he would refuse their request. Yet when Duplessis addressed the delegates at large, he referred to the proposed royal commission of inquiry on federal-provincial relations as the most constructive suggestion he had ever heard. This sudden change of heart, according to F.-A. Angers, J.-C. Bonenfant, and Paul Gérin-Lajoie, was brought about when Duplessis realized that the delegation included many Union Nationale sympathizers and regional organizers. Moreover, Bernard Courrette, the unsuccessful Union Nationale candidate in Outremont in the 1952 election, had been chosen to read the brief to the premier.[42]

This was the first important victory Quebec nationalists had tasted in a long time. Neo-nationalists had welcomed the Chambres de Commerce's new initiative. They were confident that a royal commission would discover widespread support for a more positive concept of autonomy to offset Ottawa's demand for increased centralization. Indeed, they predicted that a new era in provincial autonomy had been initiated with Duplessis' sound decision to launch an inquiry into constitutional problems.[43]

The Tremblay Commission, as it came to be called after its president, Judge Thomas Tremblay, gathered momentum quickly after its formation in February 1953. Neo-nationalists and the Chambre de Commerce de Montréal encouraged the commissioners to interpret their mandate very broadly and called upon as many organizations and institutions as possible to submit briefs to the commission.[44] Neo-nationalists stressed the economic benefits to the provincial treasury of a modest 5 per cent personal income tax. With a comprehensive system of provincial direct taxes Quebec could raise $92 million in revenue, a sum only $12 million less than the province would have received for the fiscal year 1952–3 had it consented to the tax-rental scheme.[45]

The strategy and tactics of the nationalists succeeded, much to the surprise of Quebec's citizens and federal bureaucrats and politicians. The Duplessis government introduced Bill 43 on 14 January 1954, outlining the creation of a provincial income tax equal to 15 per cent of the federal income tax applicable for the year 1954. The bill became law in March of that year.[46] A combination of economic and political forces had finally prompted Duplessis to act. His intransigent attitude had cost the province over $76 million in lost revenue between 1947 and 1952 and $34 million in 1952–3 alone.[47] The province was having an increasingly difficult time finding enough revenue to finance all of the highways, bridges, schools, and hospitals that were required. The provincial budget introduced on 12 February 1954 showed a deficit of $23 million when capital expenditures were taken into consideration and provincial revenue had dropped from $280 million in 1952–3 to $225 million in 1953–4. Politically, the campaign of the Chambre de Commerce de Montréal and *Le Devoir* was paying off. Many of the briefs presented to the Tremblay Commission, including one from the town of Port-Alfred, urged the provincial government to exercise fully the taxing rights granted to it by the constitution.[48] Finally, Judge Thomas Tremblay was instrumental in convincing Duplessis that a provincial income tax, instead of destroying his government, would receive overwhelming public support in the province, especially if Duplessis fought to make the tax deductible from the federal income tax. Any blame for double taxation of Quebec's citizens could then be placed on Ottawa's shoulders.[49] Apparently Duplessis was sufficiently impressed to overcome his traditional animosity towards a provincial personal income tax. The province, in effect, urgently required increased revenue and the most important untapped source was personal income.

Nationalists, old and new, were elated with their victory. It symbolized an end to Quebec's rearguard action and a turning point in federal-provincial relations. Quebec's decision was also a gain for democracy because it made the province responsible for collecting the taxes it spent.[50] Yet the victory was only partial and could in fact lead to double taxation. There remained the difficult task of pressuring the St Laurent government and the federal bureaucrats into allowing Quebec taxpayers to deduct their provincial income tax from their federal tax. Nationalists congratulated Duplessis but called upon him to begin negotiations immediately with Ottawa for a "deductibility" agreement. After all, they argued, Quebec would receive less total revenue by collecting its own direct taxes than if it had signed a tax-rental agreement.[51] Neo-nationalists contended that Quebec's particular situation warranted a full deductibility clause for its citizens. Prime Minister St Laurent, in refusing to recognize Quebec's particular status, was running the risk of seriously weakening the Liberal party's solid electoral base in the province while at the same time serving the political interests of the Union Nationale. Duplessis would exploit the issue of deductibility to cover up his government's failure to initiate urgent social and economic reforms. Neo-nationalists pleaded with Ottawa to consider carefully the political ramifications of its continued intransigence. St Laurent could reinforce national unity by placing justice above technocratic efficiency and centralization. All he had to do was override the senior bureaucrats in the Treasury Board and the Bank of Canada and agree to a deductibility scheme for Quebec. If need be, Quebec could press its point home via a plebiscite or by defeating the federal Liberal candidates in the next election.[52]

Neo-nationalist aggressiveness and confidence can be accounted for, in part, by organized labour's decision to support the struggle for provincial autonomy in general and, specifically, the campaign for full deductibility. Organized labour, especially the CTCC and the FUIQ, was highly critical of Duplessis' use of French-Canadian nationalism and provincial autonomy to hide his government's manifest shortcomings. Yet the solution was not to throw the baby out with the bath water. The CTCC favoured full respect for the BNA Act. There was, in its president's well-chosen words,

even something heroic in the perseverance of the CTCC in supporting in such an absolute manner the concept of provincial autonomy. For a good many workers, provincial autonomy evokes the thought of oppression. What good will it do to call them to rally around the flag since the workers cannot forget that the flag already is stained with the blood of many of their comrades? Does this mean that in order to remedy the situation we must seek help from Ottawa and thereby support the destruction of the Canadian constitution? This would be acting in a light-headed manner and relating the solution of important problems to fits of anger. It would be a painful demonstration of our inability to see the situation in its true perspective. It would be forgetting that the powers conceded to Ottawa could never be recovered by renewed temper tantrums.[53]

Reflecting this philosophy, the CTCC gave its full support to the creation of the Tremblay Commission.[54] Led by its radical centrals in Montreal and Shawinigan,[55] the organization also came out in support of the new provincial income tax but contended that it should have been limited to 5 per cent until a deductibility agreement had been reached with the federal government. The union central also suggested that the tax burden should be shifted to corporations and the government should draw substantially increased revenues from the exploitation of Quebec's natural resources. CTCC leaders called upon the federal government to grant full deductibility of the provincial tax or to conclude as quickly as possible an agreement which would guarantee all provinces sufficient taxing powers to finance all their responsibilities.[56] The CTCC was not eager to support "particular" or "special" status for Quebec. To the great surprise of most nationalists, the FPTQ adopted a position identical with that of the CTCC in its March 1954 brief to the Tremblay Commission.[57]

The Fédération des unions industrielles du Québec also came out in favour of provincial autonomy, but its position was both more complex and more comprehensive. Pierre Elliott Trudeau, the FUIQ's legal and technical adviser, was the author of its highly informative and constructive brief to the Tremblay Commission. In the brief, Trudeau outlined what came to be perceived as the Citélibriste conception of Canadian federalism. This conception was both democratic and functionalist. In a federal system the centripetal tendencies of the federal government had to be offset by the centrifugal thrust of the provincial governments. The equilibrium was dynamic and only a functionalist conception of politics and public administration could reconcile federal responsibility for economic stability and regional disparities with the need for provincial autonomy. Furthermore, to avoid the development of special or particular status for any region or ethnic community the solution had to be available to all the provinces.

Underlying Trudeau's and the FUIQ's conception of federalism was an acceptance of Keynesian economics. Only the federal government, because of its control over fiscal and monetary policy, could adopt counter-cyclical budgets to ensure economic stability and fight unemployment. But because provincial economic policies could very well negate federal policies it was necessary to practise fiscal cooperation in a federal state. Any solution that hoped to safeguard workers against excessive unemployment without engendering an undemocratic and inflexible centralism had to be inspired by three principles – proportional fiscal resources, financial equalization, and economic stability. The first principle ensured that the taxing capacity of a province served both levels of government, federal and provincial, in proportion to their respective responsibilities assigned to them by the constitution. This concept of fiscal sharing had to take into account that it was incumbent upon the central government, in conjunction with the provinces, to ensure a vital minimum to all of its members regardless of their geographic location. But since Ottawa alone could be held democratically responsible for a program of financial equalization for the have-not regions, any policy of revenue sharing must grant Ottawa sufficient resources to implement an effective system. For similar reasons, and because the existing constitution provided the federal government with all the necessary powers, no provincial government should be able to hinder the effective implementation of counter-cyclical financial policies needed to ensure a high degree of economic stability.[58]

The FUIQ's brief rejected Maurice Lamontagne's proposal for replacing the existing tax-rental agreements with subsidies determined by the federal government. The incompetence of the Quebec government did not, as Trudeau later expressed it, "justify our putting the future of Canadian federalism entirely into the hands of federal economists."[59] Following the three established criteria, the FUIQ brief recommended that the existing tax-rental agreements be altered to grant the provinces a greater degree of fiscal autonomy. The amount offered to the provinces for evacuating the direct tax field should not be based on taxing capacity but on fiscal need, thereby incorporating the principle of financial equalization. The amount offered had to be high enough to interest all provinces in signing an agreement. Nevertheless, if one or more provinces chose not to sign, the federal government must allow such provinces to collect corporation, income, and estate taxes up to the amount offered in the proposed agreements. The corporations, individuals, and estates paying those provincial taxes would be allowed to deduct them from their federal taxes. In this way, the non-participating provinces would not aggravate inflation by raising their direct taxes and the federal government's taxing powers would be in no way limited, therefore allowing it to confront any emergency situation. It would be easy to verify if Ottawa had set the subsidies too low simply by checking if it funded programs outside its constitutional jurisdiction or if the provinces were forced to resort to double taxation to finance their own responsibilities.[60] The brief stressed the need for an open and courageous federalism with increased avenues of federal-provincial cooperation "for the excellent reason that there is not in the Constitution, nor can there be in administrative practice, an *adequate and exclusive* separation between the executive, legislative, and judicial functions."[61] Democracy and functionalism had to be the ruling principles in a federal system if a true *cité libre* was to emerge.

Neo-nationalists welcomed organized labour's support for provincial autonomy in general and the deductibility formula in particular.[62] Despite the growing opposition from several quarters in Quebec and the prospect of double taxation for Quebec citizens, the federal government remained stubbornly attached to the tax-rental agreements. In fact, the confrontation with Ottawa lasted nearly a year. The proponents of provincial autonomy won a victory of sorts but not before the public witnessed an outburst of rhetoric from frustrated federal politicians, including Prime Minister Louis St Laurent. The finance minister, Douglas Abbott, rejected Quebec's demand for deductibility on the grounds that it implied provincial priority in the field of direct taxation. Such a thesis was unacceptable because it would mean the demise of the tax-rental agreements and eventually the decline of the federal state through the erosion of its economic power.[63] The prime minister joined the fracas in September 1954 when, in a speech aboard the Cunard liner *Saxonia* moored in the port of Montreal, he reprimanded Quebec for opposing Canada's economic development for fear of increasing federal influence and power. He recalled how a hundred years earlier the autonomy claims of the Southern states had precipitated a brutal civil war leading to their subjugation.[64] A week later St Laurent implied that the confrontation had been brought on by Quebec's nationalists, at heart a group inspired by the separatist theories of Abbé Groulx. He rejected the province's demands for "deductibility" of its 15 per cent income tax on dual grounds. Quebec was a province like the others and had no right to "special" status. Moreover, no province had a priority right in the field of direct taxation.[65]

The federal counter-attack was ill-conceived. It backfired and gave the neo-nationalists and the Duplessis government new ammunition. Neo-nationalists advanced a conspiratorial and cynical hypothesis to the effect that the Anglo-Canadian civil service establishment in Ottawa, fearing that St Laurent would perhaps resign in the near future to be replaced by an Anglo-Canadian, had called upon him to break the back of the Québécois nationalist and separatist resistance to the new federalism. If there was any man capable of doing the job it was a prestigious French-Canadian prime minister. This "*Saxonia*" strategy, as Laurendeau termed it, would have disastrous consequences. It would serve to prolong the battle, compromise Canadian unity, and persuade many French Canadians that Ottawa's policies and politics were motivated exclusively by English-Canadian interests and aspirations. It forced the socially conscious French-Canadian nationalists to support a socially regressive regime in Quebec, thereby delaying urgently required socioeconomic reforms in that province. Everyone lost, except Maurice Duplessis and the Union Nationale.[66]

While claiming that most Québécois no longer considered separatism a desirable alternative, the neo-nationalists affirmed loudly that Quebec was not a province like the others.[67] Laurendeau best expressed the neo-nationalist perception of Quebec as the national state of the French-Canadian nation when he wrote that a majority "expresses itself in Ottawa, this majority is English-Canadian. A majority expresses itself in Quebec City, this majority is French-Canadian. There is in our political and social realities a sort of identification between Ottawa and English-Canadian life on the one hand, between Quebec City and French-Canadian life on the other hand."[68] It was important for English Canadians to realize that Quebec was, and wanted to be, different because the majority of French Canadians perceived a strong Quebec state as the only feasible springboard leading to a full and effective participation in Canadian social, economic, and political affairs.

Quebec's nationalists had assessed the situation correctly. Maurice

Duplessis was not one to back off when the going got tough. In a speech given at Valleyfield on 26 September Duplessis declared: "Never has an English-Canadian politician had the nerve to declare that Quebec was not different from the rest of Canada. It required a compatriot to say this! The words of M. St Laurent are an invitation to assimilation."[69] Revealing his skill as a veteran politician, he reiterated his government's willingness to negotiate a solution which respected provincial rights but also reaffirmed that the province would never sign a tax-rental agreement.[70] St Laurent, realizing belatedly the dangers of continued direct confrontation, allowed "his instinct for moderation and compromise" to take over. He notified Duplessis on 28 September 1954 of his willingness to meet and discuss the situation with him privately. Duplessis agreed and they met in the Windsor Hotel in Montreal on 5 October 1954.[71]

The outcome of the meeting and subsequent correspondence was that Duplessis agreed to amend the section of the provincial Income Tax Act which claimed that the province had a constitutional priority in the field of direct taxation. St Laurent accepted the view that the provinces required increased revenue to finance necessary services and building projects, but stressed that any change in the tax-rental agreements must be open to all Canadian provinces. Duplessis opened the door for a "temporary" solution when he indicated to the prime minister that the province's 15 per cent tax, because of the act's higher exemptions, was equivalent to 10 per cent of the federal income tax collected in Quebec. St Laurent grasped at the opportunity to avoid a formula which was dependent on the principle of deductibility. In a letter to Duplessis on 15 January 1955, and in a brief statement to the House of Commons on the 17th, the prime minister announced that the federal government would reduce its income tax by 10 per cent in all provinces not signing a tax-rental agreement. All provinces were free to withdraw immediately from the 1952 agreements and the reduction would be retroactive to 1954 for the province of Quebec.[72] St Laurent had neatly side-stepped the political dangers inherent in double taxation and the constitutional implications of a particular agreement for the province of Quebec.

Having been led to believe by a *Financial Post* report that Ottawa was on the verge of accepting the deductibility formula, it was with bitter disappointment that the neo-nationalists greeted the prime minister's unilateral decision to reduce federal personal income taxes by 10 per cent. They considered Ottawa's imposed solution to be purely provisional. The struggle for a more satisfactory solution based upon a rational division of responsibilities with a corresponding equitable sharing of taxing powers had to continue.[73] Quebec was reconquering slowly its financial autonomy but Canadians would soon realize that "québécois irredentism had saved once again the federal nature of the country."[74] Trudeau was as perturbed as the neo-nationalists by St Laurent's unilaterally imposed reduction formula. It would hinder the application of counter-cyclical economic measures and was unjust because Quebec would receive less revenue than would have been provided by a tax-rental agreement. Finally, the 10 per cent reduction, because of Quebec's higher exemptions, placed the small Quebec wage-earner in a better financial position than his compatriots in the rest of Canada enjoyed. This *de facto* special status was detrimental to national unity. "It is abundantly clear," concluded Trudeau, "that the fiscal imbroglio is not resolved by the federal government's 'solution'." He hoped that federal-provincial discussions in preparation for the 1957 agreements would result in a more acceptable formula.[75]

Realizing that the temporary solution did indeed place Quebec in a *de facto* special status position, Ottawa presented the broad outlines of a permanent alternative solution to the tax-rental agreements at the October 1955 federal-provincial conference. When it became clear that other provinces, namely Ontario and British Columbia, seemed prepared to follow the path chosen by Quebec and reenter the field of direct taxation, Ottawa moved quickly.[76] St Laurent made the federal government's offer public on 12 January 1956. The terms of that offer, as summarized by Filion, were as follows: Ottawa accepted for all the provinces the principle of deductibility for provincial taxes up to a limit of 10 per cent for personal income taxes, 9 per cent for corporation taxes, and 50 per cent for succession duties. Equalization payments would be based on the average of the per capita revenue of the two wealthiest provinces, Ontario and British Columbia. The provinces would be guaranteed a five-year minimum based on figures for the 1956–7 fiscal year. And finally, any province wishing to impose corporation taxes beyond 9 per cent would have its equalization grant reduced accordingly.[77]

Neo-nationalists were undoubtedly elated. Yet they did not gloat over their important victory for provincial autonomy. They were pleased that Ottawa had finally come around to a formula remarkably similar to the one proposed by the Chambre de Commerce de Montréal several years earlier. Ottawa had not capitulated to the nationalists but had merely abandoned tax territory it had unjustly occupied. The central government was simply acknowledging the desire of all Canadians for a reasonable and balanced conception of federalism.[78] In reality, Quebec's push, now supported by other provinces, for a greater share of direct tax revenue was only just beginning.[79] Neo-nationalists encouraged the Duplessis government to document its financial needs for educational reform measures, social security programs, highway construction, and resource conservation. In this way Quebec could justify its claim to 15 or 20 per cent of personal and corporate taxes.[80]

A new era in Canadian federalism was beginning. The combination of the Duplessis government's stubborn but passive resistance to the new federalism and the neo-nationalists' strategy of aggression based on their concept of an interventionist Quebec state had succeeded in breaking the centralizing momentum of the Keynesian-inspired, social welfare – oriented federal government. The Liberal party's new national policy was indeed going to leave its mark upon the country but not to the degree and in the manner first envisaged by its authors. The new federalim would have to be adapted to the diverse cultural and regional realities of the country, realities which were being fostered and channelled by increasingly prosperous and aggressive provincial governments by the mid-fifties. Quebec's neo-nationalists understood from the outset that provincial control over higher education was imperative for the building of a francophone-inspired and directed Quebec society. It was this belief which motivated them to contest most vigorously federal grants to Canadian universities.

FEDERAL GRANTS TO UNIVERSITIES: A CLASH OF NATIONALISMS

The 1950s witnessed a second major confrontation between Ottawa and the Quebec government. The battle erupted over the federal government's decision, announced by Prime Minister St Laurent in July 1951, to provide a sum of $7.1 million for federal grants to be paid directly to Canada's universities on the basis of 50 cents per capita of the provincial populations.[81] The decision to forge ahead with this audacious and unprecedented scheme of statutory nonconditional grants to Canadian universities had been prompted by a strong recommendation in the Massey Commission's *Report* and concerted lobbying by the National Conference of Canadian Universities (NCCU).[82] The Massey Commission's terms of reference did not include the question of federal support for higher education but two of its members, Norman Mackenzie, president of the University of British Columbia, and Father Georges-Henri Lévesque, dean of Laval's Faculty of Social Sciences, convinced the other members that there were solid grounds for a scheme of federal grants to universities.[83]

Quebec's francophone universities, realizing that they would be ill-advised to accept the grants without some form of provincial approval, pressured the federal government via the NCCU to negotiate an arrangement with the Duplessis government.[84] Ottawa obliged and negotiated an arrangement with Quebec whereby federal funds available to Quebec universities for 1951–2 were administered by a Quebec-Ottawa committee and the cheques were countersigned by the provincial representative on the committee.[85] Sensitive to the loud outcry from nationalist circles and hoping perhaps to keep Quebec universities under his government's political control, Duplessis refused to renew the arrangement after 1952.[86]

At the heart of this confrontation over federal grants to universities was the politically sensitive question of which level of government, federal or provincial, could best guarantee the survival and well-being of the French-Canadian and English-Canadian cultures and languages in Canada. Given the expanding influence of the "American way of life" in Canada, English-Canadian nationalists were convinced that only an activist and supportive federal government would ensure the development of the two founding cultures. A country fragmented by regionalism, numerous ethnic groups, and two main languages was simply too vulnerable to the powerful American menace.[87] A small proportion of French Canadians, for whom Father Lévesque became the spokesman, argued that the federal government had an important role to play in the survival and expansion of the French culture and language throughout Canada. French Canada was not Quebec, and the French language and culture were not the monopoly of the francophone majority of that province. Canada was perceived by these liberal-minded nationalists to be a bilingual and bicultural nation-state. The central government, if it was going to support actively cultural development, had the democratic responsibility to support both official languages and cultures. To support one while neglecting the other was tantamount to building a nationalist state that would, in time, suffocate the other culture and language.[88]

Any concept or program that drove a wedge between the neo-nationalists' concerted attempt to forge a growing identification between an activist Quebec state and the French-Canadian nationality was bound to be attacked vigorously and ruthlessly. French-Canadian protagonists of an active federal government in the field of language and culture in general, and education in particular, were denounced as naïve and optimistic idealists by those who wished to be charitable and as cynical and unscrupulous "vendus" by others.[89] Neo-nationalists agreed that the "American way of life" was having a profound impact on modern Canada, but for them that was not reason enough to destroy the constitution and preach federal intrusion into the field of education, an area of exclusive provincial jurisdiction.[90] They rejected the *Massey Report*'s contention that the federal government had a right and a responsibility to provide grants to universities because these institutions contributed to the development of general nonacademic culture and provided numerous benefits to Canadian society as a whole. To accept such a rationale would open the door wide to eventual federal participation in primary and secondary education because both levels provided, to a lesser degree, the same benefits to Canadian society.[91] Laurendeau reminded Father Lévesque that in his 1935 pamphlet entitled *La mission des intellectuels Canadiens-français* Lévesque had singled out centralization as the greatest danger to the survival of the French-Canadian nationality. He had written that this survival "rests on principles superior to the common good of Confederation itself; it rests on natural law." In 1951 Father Lévesque was invoking those same natural rights to justify federal participation in an area of provincial jurisdiction. The only consistency that Laurendau could perceive in Father Lévesque's thought was his opposition to federalism.[92]

Underlying the neo-nationalist rejection of federal grants to universities and support for cultural and linguistic development in general was the firm conviction that a national minority could not relegate, even in the smallest measure, responsibility for its future to federal institutions controlled by another majority culture. Quebec was the homeland – la patrie – of the French-Canadian nationality. A dynamic interventionist Quebec state, not federal services and the bureaucratic paternalism of English-dominated Ottawa, was the single most important guarantee of francophone cultural and linguistic survival. While a small minority of English Canadians had become more sympathetic toward and tolerant of the French fact, the French-Canadian nationality was simply not mature and influential enough to forsake its reliance on provincial autonomy in return for greater participation in Canadian life.[93] French Canadians were certainly not going to relinquish constitutional guarantees without some quid pro quo from English Canada.[94] Neo-nationalists, firmly convinced that Ottawa was well along the road to becoming the capital of English Canada, emphasized stongly that French Canadians had no choice but to confide the maintenance, defence, and expansion of their culture to their national government in Quebec. Quebec City, not Ottawa, was the capital of la nation canadienne.[95]

The question remained dormant as Duplessis rejected the federal grants for 1954–5 and 1955–6 and the nationalists waited impatiently for the release of the Tremblay Commission's Report. As in 1951, it was a unilateral decision by the federal government that initiated a second round of heated ideological rhetoric and political manoeuvring. While receiving an honorary doctorate from the Université de Sherbrooke on 7 October 1956, St Laurent announced that Ottawa was thinking of raising the per capita grant to universities and having the funds distributed by the NCCU. A couple of weeks later, in response to a categorical rejection of his proposal by Duplessis, St Laurent made it clear that the terms of the appropriation would be changed. The grants were going to be offered directly to the universities through the NCCU. Since the provincial government could not veto acceptance of funds from institutions like the Carnegie Foundation, neither could it veto grants from the NCCU. The prime minister expressed the hope that Quebec's universities would preserve their autonomy and use it to fulfil their educational functions without worrying about political considerations. The proposal was made official when the prime minister addressed a special conference of the NCCU on "Canada's Crisis in Higher Education," held in Ottawa, 12–14 November 1956. The grants would be doubled and, if one or more institutions refused them, the agreement would allow the NCCU to hold the funds in trust until they were requested.[96]

Fearful that Ottawa's latest lucrative offer would entice Quebec's universities to accept the grants from the NCCU, the neo-nationalists restated their arguments against them and called upon all concerned French Canadians to express their views in *Le Devoir*.[97] The response was lively and, once again, revealed the bitterness and animosity surrounding the issue. In fact, the Citélibristes were divided on the issue. Prominent faculty members like Jean-Charles Falardeau and Léon Dion supported the new scheme as did Marcel Lambert, Jean-Claude Corbeil, and Jacques Perrault. Maurice Blain denounced all those who formulated nationalist myths to justify Quebec's rejection of the grants. If French-Canadian culture was not sufficiently strong and lively to confront the risks involved, then it was condemned to a slow disappearance. He personally would opt for the risk involved with an aggressive and confident attitude toward the future. Furthermore, if the universities were to retain their academic freedom while satisfying their financial needs, it was essential to balance provincial support with federal support.[98]

Falardeau took a different tack. He denounced Duplessis and his regime for the lack of a coherent and positive education policy and characterized the premier as "a thundering Jupiter, gatherer of clouds," whose strength stemmed from the pusillanimity of those who tolerated him and his regime. The university administrators along with their faculties, he claimed, had the authority and wisdom to decide what was best for their institutions. Laval's faculty association had indicated its support for federal grants in its briefs to the Massey and Tremblay commissions and now supported Ottawa's new proposal.[99] These Citélibriste academics welcomed labour's partial support. Gérard Picard, president of the CTCC, called upon his compatriots to cease considering Ottawa as a foreign government and to set realistic limits to cooperation while energetically defending the province's particular spiritual and cultural values. He accepted St Laurent's recent proposal because it did not involve federal legislative activity in education and the funds would make it possible for a greater number of young working-class men and women to pursue university careers.[100]

Neo-nationalists received the expected support from traditional nationalists,[101] while Michel Brunet, the outspoken neo-nationalist historian, denounced Falardeau for his incomplete concept of democracy. Duplessis, noted Brunet, had been elected in four consecutive elections by the people of Quebec and had the necessary political mandate to force the universities to reject the federal grants if he felt they endangered the province's cultural autonomy. The spectacle that the Québécois had witnessed since 1944 was fundamentally undemocratic. Federal authorities persistently asked the Quebec people to dissociate themselves from the only government responsible for speaking in the name of the Québécois collectivity. The Québécois, while maintaining a critical eye on the provincial regime, had a democratic responsibility to denounce the continuation of this federal policy. Only the

Quebec state, provided it had the cooperation of qualified university personnel, could implement a dynamic education policy ensuring the full development and expansion of the province's educational system at all levels.[102]

Neo-nationalists got welcome support for their opposition to federal grants to universities from an unexpected source, a prominent Citélibriste. Pierre Elliott Trudeau opposed the grants not for nationalistic reasons, but rather on the grounds that they thwarted the smooth functioning of federalism because they were undemocratic and unconstitutional. In a brilliant article in the January 1957 issue of *Cité libre*, Trudeau countered successfully each and every argument advanced by his friends favouring the grants. The grants could not be considered a form of equalization because they were offered to all provinces. They were contrary to Keynesian macroeconomics since they increased expenditure at a time of inflation. The federal government had no constitutional competence in an area of provincial jurisdiction. To the argument of urgent need, Trudeau replied that an educational and cultural crisis could not be equated with individual deprivation and starvation and did not warrant setting aside the provisions of the constitution. The solution to the crisis had to come through the normal democratic process within the province. But most importantly, Trudeau, in agreement with the nationalists, was adamant in his belief that the federal authorities should not use their taxing powers to circumvent the constitution. The federal system would soon be destroyed if the central government justified grants to any group or institution provided the revenue came from the Consolidated Revenue Fund. Constitutional decisions had clearly shown that Ottawa could not dispose "of these funds through legislation that encroaches upon provincial jurisdiction." As Trudeau had argued in the FUIQ brief, the central government violated "the principle of proportional division of fiscal resources" by taxing to the extent that it acquired "a surplus large enough to give grants to all the universities."[103] While he did not let the nationalists off scot-free, they were undoubtedly happy to have such a brilliant critic on their side for a change.

Neo-nationalists sympathized with the universities and their faculties. They were well aware of the economic plight of Quebec's francophone universities. Despite the socioeconomic upheaval brought on by industrial expansion and urban growth, the francophone universities, essential to the evolution of the society's value system, had not been given the financial and political support they warranted. If Duplessis' rejection of the grants was to be meaningful and acceptable in terms of provincial autonomy, the province must provide equivalent statutory grants to compensate for their loss. To those who argued that the federal grants did not constitute legislative intervention, the neo-nationalists retorted that experience with personal income taxes since 1917 had illustrated that for English Canadians it was social and political realities that created rights and not vice-versa. The precedent of the grants, they were convinced, would lead the majority of English-Canadians favouring federal rights to legislate in the field of education. The decision to accept or reject the grants had to be made with this cold and conclusive experience in mind. Not to do so would be self-deluding and irresponsible.[104]

Prior to *Le Devoir*'s open forum, Filion had proposed a solution which he felt Quebec's particular status warranted. Ottawa could grant the Quebec government a larger slice of the direct taxing sources or it could add $2 million to the province's equalization payment. Public opinion could then be used to persuade the premier to direct the extra $2 million to higher education.[105] It was Filion's first alternative which a neo-nationalist member of the Tremblay Commission, Richard Arès, supported. He wanted Ottawa to reduce its personal income tax by one or two percentage points so Quebec could raise its personal income tax by an equal amount. The problem of double taxation would be avoided and the province would acquire the extra revenue required for the universities.[106] A clear sign that the neo-nationalist campaign was having some impact was Duplessis' announcement, on 14 November 1956, that his government would introduce legislation during the fall session increasing provincial assistance to education at all levels. In fact, university grants were raised substantially. Laval's grant went from $1.8 million in 1956 to $3.1 million, while that of Montréal rose from $4.0 million to $6.3 million in the same year.[107]

The issue of federal grants remained unresolved as long as Duplessis retained power. The NCCU continued to hold increasingly large sums of money intended for Quebec's universities but never accepted.[108] Encouraged by the neo-nationalists, Duplessis' successor, Paul Sauvé, raised the issue at his first federal-provincial conference. To everyone's surprise, Sauvé managed to convince Prime Minister Diefenbaker to recommend to Parliament an alternative method of allowing Quebec to raise more revenue for its universities.[109] After two years of further negotiations, the Lesage government finally got the Diefenbaker government to grant Quebec more corporate tax points.[110] Quebec's neo-nationalists had won another round in the pursuit of their goal, the creation of an activist Quebec state whose particular status would be acknowledged by an "opting-out" formula for federal programs, starting with federal grants to universities. The Quebec state was becoming identified increasingly with the needs and aspirations of the province's francophone majority, a majority led by the new secular middle class.

CONSTITUTIONAL REFORM

The emergence of the new federalism, symbolized by social security measures, federal monopolization of direct taxation, and federal grants to universities, focused attention by the mid-fifties on the nature of the BNA Act.

Nevertheless, the Citélibristes were not driven by nationalist preoccupations to campaign for constitutional revision. They considered that Quebec had sufficient constitutional prerogatives and taxing powers to serve the modern needs and aspirations of its citizens. Ottawa merely had to respect provincial prerogatives and refrain from thwarting the spirit and letter of the constitution by abusing its taxing powers. In the early fifties, nationalists, old and new, shared this perspective. Neo-nationalists were convinced that Ottawa's new economic and fiscal policies and social security schemes marked a serious departure from the federal system defined in the BNA Act. This new federalism was the thin edge of the wedge, the first stage in the evolution toward a unitary English-Canadian nationalist state.

Neo-nationalists demanded a return to the federalism outlined in the constitution, whereby legislative and taxing powers were shared between the central and provincial governments so that neither could interfere in the other's prerogatives and responsibilities. The provinces were sovereign powers, albeit to a limited degree, within their fields of jurisdiction and constitutional revision was impossible without their consent.[111] While federalism was primarily a politico-juridical system accommodating the political aspirations of national groups and distinct regions, it was also more democratic. It corresponded best to a Christian conception of man and society because, like Christianity, federalism gave priority to the values of humanism, pluralism, and personalism.[112]

By the mid-1950s most neo-nationalists were dissatisfied with this conservative plea for return to the "classical" form of federalism, as they saw it, inherent in the BNA Act. Two factors combined to radicalize their outlook on the constitution. Ottawa's recalcitrant attitude in forging ahead with as many facets of the new federalism as were politically and economically feasible forced the neo-nationalists to reconsider their defensive strategy. But more important was their growing awareness of the enormous potential inherent in a secular, interventionist Quebec state fully devoted to the interests of the province's francophone majority. The neo-nationalists' commitment to implementation of a modern social welfare state run by the new francophone middle class precipitated a campaign for radical constitutional revision. To the astonishment of Duplessis and his cabinet, the conservative and traditional nationalist Tremblay commissioners were swayed by neo-nationalist pressures and gave the campaign an aura of official sanction. The premier was so enraged that he simply refused to release the *Tremblay Report* until nationalist pressures forced him to do so.

The first clear and comprehensive expression of the neo-nationalists' desire for radical constitutional change came in February 1954 when the Ligue d'action nationale presented its brief to the Tremblay Commission. The brief, authored by the radical neo-nationalist Jean-Marc Léger, described what the Ligue's members believed were the necessary constitutional changes to ensure the survival and growth of an autonomous French-Canadian province – or state as the brief preferred to call it – within Canada. The single most powerful force necessitating change was the demand for state participation in and control of areas traditionally left to the private sector. Given the federal nature of the Canadian nation-state and the presence of two distinct societies, it was inevitable that a power struggle would ensue between the provinces and the central government over the new fields of government activity and the taxing resources to finance those new endeavours.[113]

Starting from the nationalist premise, "that to govern any people, *a hierarchy* of powers based on a maximum of decentralization constituted the most productive formula because it was the most humane," the Ligue d'action nationale called for the urgent creation of a new constitution in which the rights and powers of the provinces were clearly paramount. Canada required a full-fledged confederal system in which the provincial states retained all the residual powers and granted the central government only limited economic and political responsibilities. Maximum decentralization was essential so the francophone-dominated province of Quebec could have exclusive jurisdiction over all sociocultural institutions, associations, and programs, moulding them to reflect the particular values and aspirations of the French-Canadian people. A true confederal system also required that the provinces would make all of the judicial appointments within the provinces and would have direct representation on the Supreme Court, a new constitutional court, and a permanent intergovernmental council (Conseil des états). The Senate would be transformed into a diet and all of its members would be appointed, not by Ottawa, but by the provincial states. All taxing powers and sources of revenue, including those from the exploitation of natural resources, would reside in the hands of the provinces unless specifically delegated to Ottawa. All of these measures, explained the Ligue's brief, were needed to confirm the confederal character of the proposed new constitutional system. To allay charges of separatism or "special status," the Ligue called upon all provinces to support the creation of a true confederal system.[114]

Whereas the Ligue d'action nationale had rejected the "special status" route for Quebec, the Société Saint-Jean-Baptiste de Montréal, in its brief to the Tremblay Commission, maintained that special status was the only politically feasible constitutional alternative to the new federalism. The Société's brief, written by the neo-nationalist historian Michel Brunet, contended that the federal government, controlled by the Anglo-Canadian majority, had become its national government and Ottawa its national capital. It was inconceivable that such a government could serve the needs of

Canada's French-Canadian minority. Since provincial autonomy was not a nationalist imperative for English Canadians, French-Canadian nationalists could not realistically expect English-Canadian provinces to support a highly decentralized confederal system.[115]

The new federalism was not compatible with the continued survival of the French-Canadian nation. The English-Canadian majority would never allow Quebec to separate. Consequently, argued the Société's brief, there remained only one viable alternative. French Canadians could overcome the worst disadvantages of the Conquest of 1760 by creating a vigorous and autonomous francophone nationalist state in the province of Quebec. It was necessary for French Canadians, concluded the *Mémoire*, "to become aware that they constituted a nation-state. Like English Canadians who looked upon the central government as their natural political focus, French Canadians had to learn to consider their provincial government of Quebec as the legitimate guardian of the common good of their nationality. They will then strive to make it a great modern government fully conscious of its heavy responsibilities and having the firm determination and the means to fulfil those responsibilities."[116] This could be accomplished if Quebec demanded and received the full degree of special status that the constitution of 1867 had granted the province.[117] In precise terms, this meant that Quebec, unlike the other provinces, would need taxing powers to allow it to finance and administer the full range of social security, health, education, and cultural services required by an urban-industrial society.

Neo-nationalists anxiously awaited the Tremblay Commission's *Report* to see how its predominantly traditional nationalist commissioners viewed the question of constitutional reform.[118] They were not disappointed, only miffed at the fact that, as we have seen, Duplessis refused for a couple of months to make the *Report* public, and only then on a highly restricted basis.[119]

In effect, the *Tremblay Report* recommended extensive decentralization, either in the confederal form proposed by the Ligue d'action nationale or, if the English-Canadian provinces refused that approach, then in the special status form for the province of Quebec as proposed by the Montreal SSJB. Under the guise of what the commissioners termed "a return to the Constitution," and the "spirit of federalism," radical changes were recommended in the existing distribution of taxing powers and the shared federal-provincial responsibility for social security and health programs. Reiterating traditional nationalist arguments for federalism, the *Tremblay Report* proposed that the federal and provincial governments agree upon a maximum national tax burden. Having agreed upon a national tax level, the federal and provincial governments would then share the field of direct taxation, the only one negotiable since the constitution had given Ottawa exclusive jurisdiction over indirect taxes. The direct taxes, because they had "a qualitative relationship with the functions of collective life," would be shared according to the "functions which sociological reality respectively assigns to them today, just as it did in 1867."[120] This criterion prompted the following reallocation of direct taxes. All sales taxes on consumer goods, services, and financial and commercial transactions, because of their potential "to raise barriers within the country," were assigned to the federal government. The three major direct taxes, corporate, personal, and succession duties, along with real estate and natural resource exploitation revenues, would become the exclusive prerogative of the provincial governments. The *Tremblay Report* justified this drastic reversal in the allocation of financial resources to the central and provincial governments by recommending a simultaneous return to "the spirit of the Constitution" in social matters. The provinces, with their fattened treasuries, were called upon to resume their exclusive constitutional responsibilities in the field of social security. Ottawa would alleviate its financial responsibilities by $403 million in withdrawing its two major national social security measures, unemployment insurance and old age pensions, which would then be assumed exclusively by the provinces.[121]

A degree of political realism prompted the commissioners to advance two less radical solutions, one termed intermediate, the other temporary. Taking into account the tremendous difficulty in transferring immediately to the provinces certain institutionalized federal programs, the *Report*'s intermediate settlement called for the continuation of the federal veterans' aid, unemployment insurance, and old age assistance programs. To finance these programs Ottawa would have access to 50 per cent of corporation taxes. The temporary step towards this intermediate plan was none other than the proposal initially outlined by the Chambre de Commerce de Montréal in 1947. According to this plan the federal and provincial levels would agree on a maximum tax burden, perhaps 30 per cent of national production, of which 60 per cent would be available to Ottawa and 40 per cent to the provinces and municipalities. The provinces would have exclusive access to succession duties. The two remaining major direct taxes – corporate and personal – would be levied concurrently with the provincial taxes deductible from federal taxable income. This solution was the least satisfactory because it failed to attack the constitutional basis of the fiscal problem and it took for granted that existing social security programs should be left in Ottawa's hands.

In response to the two major arguments that underlay the new federalism – equalization and counter-cyclical financing – all three of the *Tremblay Report*'s proposals included a scheme of interprovincial financial equalization based on the fiscal and social needs of the provinces running deficits. All three proposals also called for concurrent provincial participation, because of increased provincial economic stability and access to the credit of the Bank of Canada, in the implementation of appropriate counter-cyclical measures such as public works projects. Furthermore, the decentralization inherent in all three alternatives necessitated the institutionalization of inter-governmental relations. The *Report* therefore recommended the establishment of a Federal-Provincial Relations Secretariat and a permanent Council of the Provinces.[122] Thus what comes out loud and clear from a comprehensive reading of the full *Report* is the sincere conviction that the minimum requirement for the continued survival and expansion of an autonomous francophone nation in North America was a high degree of special status for the province of Quebec, while the maximum requirement was the reshaping of the Canadian federal system into a highly decentralized confederal system in which Ottawa would become little more than a mediator between strong provincial states. Were the commissioners merely stating the most extreme alternative, hoping to attract support for the special status option?

Neo-nationalists praised the *Tremblay Report* as "a work distinguished by the vitality and originality of its thought," while denouncing Duplessis for putting 3,000 copies under lock and key at provincial police headquarters. They were determined to make the *Report*'s contents public and spark a debate on its proposals for constitutional revision. Making use of a contraband copy of the four-volume *Report*, *Le Devoir*, during late April and nearly all of May 1956, devoted a series of nineteen in-depth articles to describing and analysing its contents.[123] Neo-nationalists strongly supported efforts by the Chambre de Commerce de la province de Québec to keep the *Report* alive by devoting its November 1957 annual convention to a wide-ranging debate on the *Report*'s recommendations. The Duplessis regime's undemocratic policies and practices, the neo-nationalists argued, would persist as long as Quebec's citizens failed to understand their democratic responsibilities. Public debate on such an important subject as constitutional revision was imperative. *Le Devoir* gave full coverage to the Chicoutimi convention and the neo-nationalists maintained that wide dissemination of the *Tremblay Report* would reestablish in Quebec the viability of a positive and dynamic provincial autonomy. Indeed, the *Report* was perceived by neo-nationalists as only the beginning of a general offensive against Ottawa. They would do their utmost to guarantee that it did not become lost "in the mists of parliamentary hill in Quebec City."[124]

Of the two constitutional options put forward by the *Tremblay Report* – comprehensive decentralization and special status for Quebec – the neo-nationalists favoured the latter. "Québec," Laurendeau had written in the fall of 1953, "is a particular case. We will recognize this in our legislation, or else we will prolong indefinitely federal-provincial squabbling."[125] The *Report*'s two recommendations, that Quebec regain its full authority in social matters along with exclusive access to direct taxes, might seem revolutionary, noted Filion, but they merely underlined the degree to which Canadian society had evolved since 1867. It was only logical that the Canadian constitution be revised to reflect the new socioeconomic realities. Neo-nationalists conceded that a small élite of influential, liberal-minded English Canadians was willing to restructure Canada on a bilingual and bicultural basis, so that the two national communities would be "equals in everything and everywhere and capable of developing freely via their respective institutions in all parts of the country." Yet the vast majority of English Canadians, spurred on by old prejudices, unconscious antipathies, the fear of the new and unknown, were simply not ready to accept a policy of legal and constitutional equality. Consequently, French Canadians had no alternative but to turn to the only state and only government over which they exercised an undisputed authority. The experiences of the Turkish minority in Cyprus and the European minority in Algeria were illustrative of the fears engendered when a minority was called upon to deliver the direction of its collective life into the hands of the majority. It was never accomplished voluntarily and peacefully, noted Filion, without significant constitutional guarantees. Since those were not forthcoming in the near future, French Canadians had to go it alone in an autonomous Quebec state.[126]

If the *Tremblay Report* had reinforced the neo-nationalists' decision to push for special status, then Prime Minister Diefenbaker's totally inept neglect of Quebec after his landslide victory of 1958 confirmed and solidified their impulse for constitutional change. In many respects, the Diefenbaker Conservative regime was the embodiment of the "two nation" thesis. Ottawa attended to the sociocultural, economic, and political needs of English-speaking Canada as defined by Diefenbaker, while the centre of the French-Canadian nation, Quebec, remained dormant and unprogressive.[127] Neo-nationalists, supported by traditional nationalists, adopted a dual strategy. Pressure was applied to the Duplessis government to push for a greater share of direct taxation, 15 per cent of corporation taxes, 15 per cent of personal income taxes, and 100 per cent of succession duties. The reconquest of the province's autonomy was a long and arduous task and would not be accomplished in one round. "The essential thing," wrote Filion, "was never to back up and now and then to move forward."[128] Second, *Le Devoir* kept the question of constitutional revision alive by providing an open forum on the question. Most contributors reinforced the neo-nationalist position by outlining what they perceived as the only feasible route open to Quebec, the achievement of special status to ensure the survival and modernization of the French-Canadian nation.[129]

CONCLUSION

The respective responses of neo-nationalists and Citélibristes to the new federalism illustrate clearly and dramatically their basic ideological differences regarding the nature of the ills confronting Quebec society and the solutions to those problems. While the neo-nationalists used the rhetoric of liberalism and democracy to oppose the centralist tendencies of the new federalism, their main preoccupation was the retention and, finally, the enhancement of provincial autonomy to guarantee that the new francophone middle class would have sufficient political power to create a francophone-inspired and controlled, interventionist, social welfare state. Only by winning control of a powerful Quebec state, contended the neo-nationalists, could the new francophone middle class undermine the ascendancy of the traditional political and clerical élites and the anglophone financial, commercial, and industrial élites. An interventionist Quebec state would foster the development of a strong francophone presence in the private sector and provide the francophone urban masses with modern educational and sociocultural institutions. In short, the emerging neo-nationalist middle class shrewdly equated its own class interests with the aspirations and interests of the French-Canadian nation. Its members sincerely believed they could ensure the survival and development of the latter by advocating and advancing the interests of the former. The rapidly expanding strength of this new middle class was not readily apparent to most observers in the 1950s. The nationalist-minded sector of Quebec's traditional clerical and professional élites, confident that they could retain their long-standing predominance over the francophone community, decided to support the neo-nationalists' vigorous attack against the new federalism and eventually their innovative campaign for dramatic constitutional revision. Nationalist preoccupations served to conceal an emerging class struggle and few traditional clerical or professional class spokesmen realized how effective a powerful interventionist Quebec state would be in the hands of a new, militant, secularized francophone middle class.

Citélibristes were not moved by nationalist preoccupations to propose constitutional revision. An interventionist Quebec state had sufficient existing constitutional power, in their view, to build a liberal, democratic society which would serve the needs and aspirations of all its citizens, regardless of race, colour, creed, or class. Ottawa merely had to be brought to its senses and persuaded to discontinue its antifederalist and antidemocratic practice of using its taxing, declaratory, and residual powers to circumvent the spirit and letter of the constitution. Yet few Citélibristes understood the urgent and imperative need for the federal government to support the linguistic and cultural aspirations of both founding societies. Father Georges-Henri Lévesque found little active support outside the universities for a bilingual and bicultural Canada in general and for federal grants to post-secondary education and the development of the fine arts and popular culture of both cultural communities in particular. Neo-nationalists opposed, on principle, any direct federal intervention in the field of culture, while most Citélibristes had not, by the late fifties, come to perceive the need for active and direct federal participation in the preservation and development of the French-Canadian culture and language. The attention of both groups was centred on terminating the undemocratic, antisocial, antilabour regime of Maurice Duplessis and the Union Nationale.

CHAPTER TEN

"Purity in Politics": Democratizing a Political Culture

In our relations with the state, we are fairly immoral: we corrupt our civil servants, we blackmail our MPs, we pressure our tribunals, we defraud the public treasury, we obligingly blink our eye "to benefit our work." In electoral matters, our immorality becomes truly scabby. Such and such a habitant, who would be ashamed to enter a brothel, sells his conscience at every election for a bottle of *whisky blanc*. Such and such a lawyer, who demands the maximum sentence for robbers of church poor-boxes, thinks nothing of adding two thousand fictitious names to the voters' lists. In short, stories of electoral dishonesty scandalize hardly anyone any longer since they have occupied for so long the early years of our collective memory.[1]

Pierre Trudeau was not the first, nor would he be the last, to charge his compatriots with condoning and participating in a generalized system of immoral administrative and electoral practices. For a wide variety of very complex reasons, urban, middle-class French Canadians became very concerned about the ethics of politics and administration in the 1950s. Witness Pax Plante's and Jean Drapeau's Ligue d'action civique's successful ten-year morality campaign against Montreal's civic administrators.

Two developments distinguished the 1950s "purity in politics" campaign from previous ones in Quebec. To begin with, the campaign was motivated by the new ideological perspectives. The growing demand for the professionalization of administrative structures and procedures and for the democratization of the political process reflected the secular "liberal" values and middle-class interests of both neo-nationalists and Citélibristes. While both groups sincerely believed that modernizing Quebec's political culture would benefit society at large, these middle-class reformers, by virtue of their education in the social and administrative sciences and their liberal cultural values, were well positioned to benefit personally from this development. Nevertheless, their class interest was reinforced by the fact that it could be made to coincide with the general interests of a Quebec society desperately in need of a more democratic political culture. The comprehensive moderni-

zation process would only take root and flourish if the citizens sanctioned
the necessary reforms by way of the vote and if corrupt patronage practices
were eliminated or curtailed.

The "purity in politics" campaign was further motivated to a great
extent by a pragmatic and urgent political objective. Neo-nationalists and
Citélibristes considered the Duplessis regime to be the greatest obstacle to
the democratization and modernization of Quebec society and were convinced that it had to be replaced as soon as possible by a modern, secular,
and democratic government. A well-orchestrated, substantive campaign
illustrating widespread and deep-seated corruption would most certainly
contribute to the eventual defeat of the Union Nationale.

Citélibristes, because of their ideological commitment to democratic
principles and practices, were the first to draw close attention to a wide
range of corrupt electoral practices prevalent in "la belle province." Few
Citélibristes were interested in a "purity in politics" campaign. Rather, they
concentrated their attention on identifying what they considered were the
root causes of the widespread acceptance of undemocratic electoral and
administrative practices and the persistence of authoritarian norms and
values at all levels of Quebec society. French Canadians, the Citélibristes
hypothesized, had never accepted democratic principles and practices as
values to be defended and fought for in their own right. The villains responsible for this sad state of affairs were the church, which preached an anti-
secularist, theological, and clericalist ethos, and French-Canadian nationalists, who continually placed priority on collectivist rights at the expense of
individual rights and self-fulfilment.

The neo-nationalists, as we shall soon see, strongly rejected the *Cité libre*
interpretation. As committed secularists they also favoured more democratic
electoral and administrative practices in their province, not strictly as a
means to an end, but as developments good in themselves. Unlike their
precursors, the neo-nationalists believed that their society could become
progressively democratic while remaining French-Canadian. They were
confident that rational and sensible people could mediate the clash of individual and collective rights. Little thought was given to the irrational forces
at work within any society, traditional or modern. Yet it was the neo-nationalists, determined to rid the province of the conservative, undemocratic
Duplessis regime, who after the 1956 provincial election spearheaded a
concerted and widespread "purity in politics" campaign. This campaign
would prove to be very popular, and indeed very effective in undermining
the Union Nationale during the 1960 provincial election.

OBSTACLES TO DEMOCRACY

The constant imposition of lay and clerical censorship, the frequent appeals
to authority – political and religious – the abrogation and, on several occa-

sions, complete disregard of civil liberties, the avowed acceptance of corrupt electoral and administrative practices alerted both Citélibristes and neo-nationalists to the fragile state of democracy in Quebec society.[2] The most blatant distortion of parliamentary democracy was the Union Nationale's refusal to implement a more equitable degree of representation by population. Although rural Quebec accounted for only approximately one-third of the population, two-thirds of the Legislative Assembly's members represented rural constituencies.[3] The vast majority of Union Nationale legislators – 90 per cent in 1952 and 85 per cent in 1956 – represented ridings outside the metropolitan regions of Montreal and Quebec City.[4] The electoral dice were heavily loaded in favour of the Union Nationale which, ever since the institution of rural credit in the late 1930s and the extensive program of rural electrification in the years following the war, had gained the unquestioned allegiance of the habitants and the agricultural communities that served them. The Union Nationale, in 1948, won nearly 90 per cent of the 92 seats in the Assembly with only 52 per cent of the popular vote. The results prompted Jean-Marc Léger to remark that liberal parliamentary democracy sprinkled with a heavy dose of social security measures did not constitute a "popular" democracy.[5] One Citélibriste argued that the failure of successive Quebec governments to implement redistribution had ingrained in French Canadians a deep scepticism toward the political process. "We taught the Québécois voter," wrote Charles Lussier,

by way of a static and unchanging distribution for decades, that his suffrage right no longer corresponded to the mandate granted. There is no longer a correlation between the right and the exercise of the right since the results are so far removed from the stated verdict. The citizen has learned, via the cynicism of numbers, that his vote no longer constitutes a single entity. From an individual with the right to express himself as a distinct entity we have made a partial person, so reduced that he or she no longer possesses in practice an effective voice in the political system.[6]

Little wonder that absenteeism was high and the political conscience of most Québécois underdeveloped. If one of the basic tenets of democracy, representation by population, was continually disregarded by the political élite, how could respect for the political system be expected of the masses?

Despite a gain of fourteen seats by the Liberal party in 1952, Filion feared that no effective parliamentary opposition existed. Duplessis, continuing to consider himself "Master after God," dismissed any and all suggestions for electoral redistribution.[7] Citélibristes and neo-nationalists were caught in a dilemma. The more they emphasized liberal social and economic reforms as an effective opposition party platform, the more conservative-minded rural voters would turn to Duplessis' Union Nationale. The base of any reform party would obviously have to reside in urban-industrial centres. Duplessis instinctively understood this and consequently considered it political suicide to proceed with redistribution.

At the root of Quebec's undemocratic political system and the *raison d'être* for the political longevity of traditional parties like the Union Nationale was the mode of party financing. Quebec's political parties depended almost entirely upon large contributions from wealthy individuals and companies to finance extravagant campaigns. The incumbent party under the system had, of course, tremendous built-in advantages. The major advantage was that the Union Nationale, through its control of the administration, could practise both small and large patronage on a wide scale. In return for past, present, and future supply and service contracts with numerous government departments, party bagmen put pressure – termed *le chantage* – on small and medium-sized companies to make generous contributions to the "election fund." When supply and service contracts were large or when construction projects – roads, bridges, buildings – were involved, the Union Nationale developed and refined a system of very lucrative "kickbacks." The Salvas Commission, instituted under the Lesage administration in October 1960, received testimony to the effect that the companies learned very quickly to include the kickback costs in their original bids. In short, the burden fell on the taxpayers not the companies.[8]

Pressure was exerted on both individuals and companies applying for and receiving on an annual basis liquor licences from the Quebec Liquor Commission to make appropriate contributions to the party. The government's control of mineral, forest, and water resources also provided it with an excellent source of party funds. Neo-nationalists and Citélibristes contended, without being able to supply proof, that the large mining, forestry, and hydro-electric companies made generous contributions to the "election fund" in return for low royalties and tax concessions. The fact that royalties were substantially lower and tax concessions generally more numerous in Quebec than in Ontario gave the charges some credence. It was also common knowledge that Duplessis enjoyed close friendships with the corporate barons, and his trips to Ungava at the company's expense were well-publicized events.[9]

The Union Nationale's "election fund" was legendary. It was estimated that the party spent between $2 and $3 million on the 1952 election and nearly $15 million on the 1956 election, if supplemental government contracts for services and construction were taken into account. In 1956, the Union Nationale spent at least $2 million on publicity in newspapers and on radio and television while the Liberal party barely managed to afford $275,000 for this most crucial facet of modern politics.[10] The end result of this undemocratic mode of party financing was, according to Citélibriste and neo-nationalist spokesmen, the destruction of political party independence and the subversion of the common interest in favour of the vested interests of the monied classes.[11] Quebec's politicians, including the premier, were not deciding the political destiny of the province's inhabitants. Like the log-drivers in the forest industry who used their skills to remain afloat while in no way altering the direction of the current, Quebec's politicians were using "reigning passions and energies to retain power for themselves." The real dominant forces in provincial politics, contended Trudeau, were international capitalism and clericalism: "They do not make decisions with the state which could represent the temporal common good; they make decisions among themselves and there remains nothing for the state to do but to sanction their modus vivendi."[12]

Neo-nationalists and Citélibristes called for public disclosure of all electoral expenses, including source of funds, especially the large contributions. It was also contended that democracy would best be served if limits were set on campaign expenditures and public funds were made available to all recognized parties and candidates.[13] These reforms would have at least the effect of freeing the parties from the special interests of the private sector and would end the blackmail tactics of the bagmen directed at individuals and companies.

What was more difficult to remedy by means of structural changes was the government's ability to pass electoral legislation which, under the guise of efficiency and cost-saving, served the political interest of the incumbent party. The most blatant example of this sort of activity was demonstrated by Bill 34, pushed through the Assembly in January 1953 despite the outcry of parliamentary and extraparliamentary opposition forces. Basically, Bill 34 did two things. It allowed the returning officer in urban ridings – a cabinet appointee and usually a friend of the government – to appoint only one enumerator to prepare the voting list. Normally, a deputy returning officer was appointed from a list provided by the government party organization while the poll clerk was named from a list provided by the opposition and both were charged with preparing the voting list. Henceforth, only the government appointee was going to have that responsibility. While the old system militated against third parties, the new system was designed to undermine the opposition party. In addition, Bill 34 provided all election officials acting in that capacity with immunity from the courts. The neo-nationalists were furious. Speaking from experience, Laurendeau illustrated how the use of a single enumerator in rural areas, a practice initiated by Duplessis in 1945, had served the Union Nationale's interests admirably. He called upon the Legislative Council, that supposedly august council of sober second thought, to reject "this filth, . . . this legislation of confusion and corruption."[14] Georges-Emile Lapalme, the Liberal leader, was preparing to gain a seat in the Legislature in a by-election in Outremont. Laurendeau charged that Bill 34 was introduced at a convenient time to prevent Lapalme from acquiring a position where he could attack Duplessis head on.[15]

While the bill did not prevent Lapalme from being elected, it did lay the groundwork for some of the most blatant electoral scandals in the 1956 election. Enumerators sympathetic to the Union Nationale cause left hundreds of suspected Liberal voters off the lists, while adding hundreds of fictitious names, including those of children and deceased voters, to enable Union Nationale organizers to practise impersonation and "telegraphing" on a wide scale. Ballot boxes were stuffed and election officials, in the Montreal region especially, could hardly be distinguished from Union Nationale party organizers, the lines between the civil service and party having been so badly blurred.[16] To top it all off, Union Nationale goon squads, with revolvers in hand, raided polling stations in Montreal-Laurier, intimidating voters, stuffing, smashing, or stealing ballot boxes.[17] All in all, it was an election few Montrealers would soon forget. It was as if Trudeau had received a resounding reply to his 1952 query: "In our country, must heaven continue to delegate indefinitely its authority via boxers, master blackmailers, professional gangsters, all resorting to the use of firearms, robberies, lies, and intimidation?"[18] Unfortunately for the reformers the reply had been – Yes!

Neo-nationalists and Citélibristes deplored the fact that the cancer of "electoralism" permeated every branch of the Duplessis administration and extended frequently into the deliberations of the Assembly and the actions of the judiciary. Duplessis intimidated the Assembly through his control of the speaker and his autocratic paternalistic treatment of his caucus and cabinet members. He made a mockery of the Quebec Civil Service Commission by appointing the party faithful to important and lucrative administrative positions, and then conscripting many of them for service with the Union Nationale during election campaigns.[19] A loyal and partisan bureaucracy made the entrenchment of patronage in all its forms and practices possible and very difficult to discover and eradicate. Neo-nationalists called repeatedly for the modernization of Quebec's civil service. Improved salaries, appointments based on competitive examinations under a merit system, and the establishment of criteria of promotion were some of their recommendations. Not only would the problem of patronage be attenuated, but the bureaucracy would be professionalized, a development considered a *sine qua non* for an efficient and effective modern interventionist state.[20]

At the root of this extensive patronage network, as the neo-nationalists correctly perceived, was the irresponsible manner in which the Duplessis regime allotted and spent public revenues. In the jargon of the day, Duplessis' ministers were not authorized to spend, but rather to "consecrate" public revenue to certain projects and services which would reap the greatest political payoff. A large degree of discretionary power rested in the hands of the various ministers in two ways. First, most ministers with the support of Duplessis received their funds on a nonstatutory basis. This allowed them to retain a fair degree of administrative and political control over the institutions and organizations receiving government revenues, whether they were school boards, municipalities, hospitals, or local voluntary associations. Second, most ministers were allowed to spend far in excess of the amounts stipulated in the annual budgets without seeking the approval of the Assembly. The discrepancy in election years was phenomenal. In 1948-9, $225 million was spent rather than the $142 million projected in the budget, while in 1952-3, expenditures surpassed the $261 million budgetary estimates by $61 million![21]

Obviously, a lot of what is traditionally termed "bribery" was perpetrated during the campaigns, necessitating the use of funds far beyond the normal needs of the administration. Numerous road-paving and bridge-building contracts were suddenly approved and granted to "faithful" contractors on a regional basis. Countless temporary appointments were made in every department, but especially the Roads Department, while Department of Health officials paid the hospital bills of hundreds of potential and known party supporters. Laporte referred to this sort of patronage as "the 'gratitude' imposed on the voters by Union Nationale candidates."[22] The only way to undercut the largesse of the various departments was to make them accountable – i.e., responsible – to the Assembly for all of their expenditures. Responsible government in the fullest sense of the term had to become the order of the day in Quebec.[23] The neo-nationalists failed to mention the fact that nineteenth-century reformers in Upper and Lower Canada had fought for responsible government because it would remove patronage from the hands of the governors and place it in the hands of the incumbent and duly elected party in the Assembly!

Surpassing by far in its political effectiveness the "bribing" and "blackmailing" of individuals was the Union Nationale's reliance upon discretionary grants and subsidies to public institutions such as hospitals, school boards, urban and rural municipalities, colleges and universities, private associations like the chambres de commerce, parish organizations, and agricultural organizations.[24] Most of these institutions and associations were desperately in need of funds. Consequently, thousands of people employed in their service refused to criticize the Duplessis government either out of a false sense of gratitude, or, more often than not, out of simple fear. What the government could grant on a basis of favouritism it could just as easily withdraw.[25] One Citélibriste, Marcel Rioux, provided this fitting description of the "ancien régime" mentality and practices of the Duplessis "clique."

Bernanos compared the black market which flourished in Europe after the last great war to the cathedrals of the Middle Ages: a vast system in which the hands played a dominant role, hands which carried the stones, hands which exchanged merchandise for cash. Duplessis had perfected this system and made hand to hand exchanges the strength and the symbol of his régime. Nothing was granted in a rational or impersonal manner; no one even trusted the postal service; everything passed from hand to hand, the chain of hands grew indefinitely; the more numerous were the hands the greater the number of individuals tied into the régime. Nothing resisted the hand which gave. The hand which received became in turn the hand which gave. An infernal cycle of hands was built, beginning with the great hand of the chief and extending right down to the gangster who gave him a helping hand during elections. A good illustration of his system was the fact that Duplessis even bragged that the bishops ate out of his hand. And when this vast undertaking of hands had finally built a bridge, another hand rose to bless the fruits of all these hands. The vicious cycle was completed.[26]

In the name of democracy and the efficient administration both of government business and of the recipient organizations and institutions, the latter, contended Citélibristes and neo-nationalists, should receive the bulk of their government funding in the form of statutory grants appropriated by the Assembly. In this manner, the grants would lose their stigma of charity or special privileges and the incumbent government would not lay itself open to the charge of practising favouritism and blackmail.[27] Both groups believed that appropriate structural changes in the political process and government administration, combined with a scrupulous respect for full "responsible" government, could eliminate a great amount of patronage and allow a more democratic and efficient governing process to flourish. In sum, politics and human nature being what they were – certainly not roads to sainthood – patronage had to be circumscribed and placed out of reach by an appropriate institutional framework and procedures. Democracy and the modern state for these reformers were synonymous with a rationalized and democratized political process and an efficient, well-educated, well-paid, professional bureaucracy.

It was one thing to recommend structural changes. It was another and much more difficult challenge to undermine a prevalent political culture which allowed the Duplessis government to destroy the reputation and viability of its political opponents. The tactic or "brush" generally used by Duplessis was guilt by association or innuendo, while the "tar" consisted of socialism and/or communism. What doctrinaire liberalism and freemasonry had been to the ultramontane-castor element in the nineteenth century, socialism and communism became for right-wing forces in the twentieth century. Laurendeau dubbed this practice "Operation Panic." Each time, Duplessis' allegation concerned a serious "error" but it was an "error" which involved only a handful of individuals. Yet, precisely because the majority lacked confidence in its own values and ideological outlook, the defenders of the faith felt obliged to root out all heresy no matter how insignificant. Consequently, the flock of conformists, in a state of communal, patriotic, and religious panic and overreaction, applied the charge of communism "to men who did not merit it, imagined plots, conspiracies, and infiltrations, and multiplied their denunciations, condemnations, and maledictions, finally launching a crusade against the infamous person – often an individual who was a good family man and church warden. It was in this fashion that we procured momentary peace of soul, with a minimum of social and intellectual activity, and the death of the imagined culprit. *Operation panic* became *operation scapegoat*."[28] In accordance with this well-established tradition, both Trudeau and Filion were labelled by clerics as communist sympathizers merely on the grounds that the former had attended a conference on economics in Moscow and given his critical yet balanced impressions of the Soviet system in *Le Devoir*, while Filion had done the same for the Communist regime while on a tour of China.[29]

In 1952 Duplessis and his cronies spread rumours to the effect that a Communist, Harry Binder, had plotted the destruction of Montreal's Hôtel de ville while other Communists were secretly plotting to make off with the Polish treasures held for the ousted Catholic Polish regime by the Quebec government, and that the Liberal party, encouraged by its leader, Georges-Emile Lapalme, was openly wooing the votes of Communists in Quebec.[30] The anticommunism theme played as important a role in the Union Nationale's 1956 election propaganda as it had in 1948 in the aftermath of the Gouzenko affair.[31] Indeed, the anticommunist campaign was so effective that, according to abbés Dion and O'Neill, it influenced hundreds of clerics and nuns throughout the province to vote for the Union Nationale. The rumour was spread that Lapalme had admitted in secret to being a Communist.[32] The abbés denounced the election propaganda circulating in Quebec as "lies erected into a system," charging that "Lies are used to foster the inferiority complexes and the fears of the general public, to distort the ideas of the opposition, to destroy the reputation of people ... For example, we are told that to advocate social security measures is to flirt with communism, to promote health insurance is to undermine our religious communities, that to feed hungry men and women of Third World countries impoverishes us and encourages communism, etc."[33]

Had "Operation Panic" been restricted to the realm of election propaganda it might have been written off as the work of a few right-wing extremists. Such was not the case in Quebec. In 1937, under pressure from the Catholic hierarchy, namely, Cardinal Villeneuve, Maurice Duplessis institutionalized "Operation Panic" by using the powers of the state to seek out and destroy nascent Communist organizations in the province. The 1937 legislation – Loi protégeant la province contre la propagande communiste, generally known as the infamous "Padlock Law" – empowered the attorney general, Maurice Duplessis, to close and lock any building used for the dissemination of communism or bolshevism. The legislation conveniently provided no definition of these terms.[34] The act was used extensively by the government, especially after 1944, to harass and curtail with some success the activities of the Quebec Communist party, the Parti Ouvrier Progressiste.[35]

Le Devoir, while it had initially supported the Padlock Law under Georges Pelletier, came to oppose it as undemocratic and arbitrary because it was an unwarranted intrusion of the executive branch of government into the realm of the judiciary.[36] Neo-nationalists and Citélibristes actively supported the Canadian Civil Liberties Association and the Parti Social Démocratique in their concerted attempts to have the Padlock Law rescinded in the courts on the grounds that it was a serious violation of the civil liberties of all Québécois, specifically, of the freedom to print and read what they wanted as long as it was not defamatory of individuals or groups or threatened the survival of the state.[37] The Padlock Law was eventually overthrown by the Canadian Supreme Court, much to the dismay of Duplessis and the Catholic hierarchy and to the joy of all civil libertarians in Quebec. The reformers were undoubtedly pleased that the state was no longer performing the work of the church. If the Catholic church opposed socialism and communism on spiritual grounds then it must say so in the pulpit but not call upon the long arm of the state to enforce its dogma.

In the meantime, the Duplessis government pursued its anticommunist campaign for its own political purposes. In January 1954, it introduced and passed another questionable piece of legislation entitled Bill 19, which allowed the minister of labour to decertify, via his Commission des relations ouvrier, any union which tolerated among its organizers or officials anyone belonging to a Communist party or movement. To add insult to injury, Bill 19, like its twin Bill 20, which allowed the government to decertify any union in the public service sector for calling a strike, was retroactive to 1944. It was evident that Bill 19 was vindictive and politically motivated to undercut the growing radicalization of organized labour in Quebec, especially the new industrial unions affiliated with the CTCC and FUIQ.[38] Union leaders, except for those belonging to the TLC, organized a well-attended protest march on the Legislature in Quebec City in the cold of winter, but to no avail. *Le Devoir* denounced both Bills 19 and 20 as arbitrary, undemocratic, unjust, and above all foolish. Neo-nationalists supported the protest march and as noted earlier, Laurendeau speculated whether Duplessis was following in the footsteps of Senator Joseph McCarthy or Charlie McCarthy.[39]

While the reformers could illustrate and denounce the arbitrariness, the patronage, and the "Operation Panic" tactics and behaviour of the Duplessis government, it proved more difficult to eradicate from the general psyche a widespread and deeply ingrained sense of fear that had become, over a prolonged period, one of the most insidious consequences of a conservative, monolithic, and enclosed society. The theme of fear ran through all the letters to the editor after the 1956 election, with the majority of the authors requesting, and in some cases pleading, for anonymity so that their jobs would not be jeopardized and their families harassed. What Laurendeau found refreshing was that most of the letters also expressed a profound disgust and indignation at the revelation of the political and administrative corruption in the province. "Will shame be the beginning of wisdom?" he asked wistfully. One published letter suggested, in the strongest terms possible, that the church itself had been affected by the climate of fear and intimidation. Had most clerics, its author wondered, refused to denounce the immoral political culture taking root in the province for fear of losing increasingly important government support for a wide range of secular services provided by the church?[40] In sum, French Canadians from the first to the fourth estates had nothing to fear but fear itself. Neo-nationalists hoped that disgust and indignation at the revelations would have the effect of "psychological shock" and thereby serve as "a foundation on which we could build something more substantial – a true democracy."[41]

It was with a well-timed intention to shock that Le Devoir reprinted in August 1956 a scathing denunciation by two Laval clerics, Fathers Gérard Dion and Louis O'Neill, of the widespread corrupt administrative and electoral practices prevalent in Quebec. French Canadians, charged Dion and O'Neill, had become "a venal people."[42] Neo-nationalists and Cité-libristes gave full coverage to outspoken clerics like Dion and Lévesque when they addressed various groups in and out of the province on the question of democracy and civil education.[43] Both groups denounced the old guard in the church hierarchy for attempting to muzzle these clerics on the pretext that church personnel should not get involved in political matters. It was implied that church officials had their hands too full with the politics of government subsidies to speak out forcefully against the subversion of democratic norms and values. One Citélibriste noted that the church's role in the denunciation of political immorality in Quebec, starting with the declaration of the abbés Dion and O'Neill, was proper, because Christian honour was at stake, and necessary, because a strictly lay campaign would have been quickly painted by the right-wing forces as a Communist plot to subvert the legitimate authority of the government![44]

FRENCH CANADIANS AND DEMOCRACY

Citélibristes were not satisfied with merely documenting and publicizing the authoritarian and undemocratic nature of Quebec's political culture. Led by Charles Lussier and Pierre Trudeau,[45] Cité libre hypothesized that French-Canadian society had remained impervious to democratic norms and values for two basic reasons. One was that French Canadians had been taught by their church an undemocratic conception of authority, of the nature and origin of power, and of the role of secular government and the state. Second, the long-standing dominance of the ideology of nationalism in Quebec had led to a very unhealthy emphasis on collective rights and the neglect of individual rights.[46]

It was quite natural that the church should teach that spiritual authority emanated from God. What was less natural, and in the end subversive of democracy, was the doctrine that secular authority also emanated from God. The church persisted in teaching, even in the 1950s, that sovereignty of the people was an error based on the "false principle that man has no other master than his own reason, . . . [and] if it is admitted, it will have as a consequence the weakening of authority, making it a myth, giving it an unstable and changeable basis, stimulating popular passions, and encouraging sedition."[47] Misguided by naïve but well-intentioned church leaders, French Canadians had lost, in their understanding and exercise of authority, "a sense of priorities. Confusion then becomes so generalized that we end up protecting authority at the expense of freedom. The proper order of things has been reversed and men keep quiet because they have slowly lost the ability to understand the situation."[48] This authoritarian philosophy and frame of mind permeated all but a few of French Canada's social, political, and cultural institutions and was responsible, in part, for that society's continued acceptance of undemocratic norms and values.[49]

On the whole, though, the Citélibristes regarded the ideology of French-Canadian nationalism as largely responsible for the undemocratic nature of Quebec's political culture. The central thrust of Cité libre's thesis was that French Canadians had not adopted parliamentary democracy out of a deep understanding of its intrinsic worth but rather for nationalist reasons. Responsible government, universal suffrage, and "purity in politics" were perceived and effectively used as tools among many others, like language, religion, and the parish, to guarantee the collective survival of the French Canadians. Unlike provincial autonomy, something French Canadians had gained through numerous battles, democracy had been handed to them by the British as a benevolent but all too premature gift in the decades following the Conquest. New France was portrayed by Trudeau as an authoritarian, quasi-feudal, oppressive colonial society whose subjects were ruled by an autocratic monarch on the basis of the divine right of kingship. In sum, New France was certainly not a hotbed of democracy, and when representative government was instituted by Westminster in 1791 against the wishes of three-quarters of the Canadiens, they were neither "psychologically nor politically prepared for it." The French-Canadian petty bourgeois political élite, led by Papineau, later attempted to gain control of the nonelective bodies – the legislative and executive councils – and establish a separate Laurentian republic on the banks of the St Lawrence. Papineau's inept leadership, combined with superior British forces, spelled disaster for that strategy. A second, more moderate, generation of French-Canadian political leaders, namely Lafontaine and Parent, chose an alternative strategy of cooperation. But again, in Trudeau's view, that cooperation was based on an "outward acceptance of the parliamentary game, but without any inward allegiance to its underlying moral principles."[50]

The crucial century of political history following the Conquest set the stage for the development of French-Canadian political thought in general and that society's perception of democracy in particular. "Fundamentally, all French-Canadian political thinking," wrote Trudeau,

stems from these historical beginnings. In the opinion of the French in Canada, government of the people by the people could not be *for* the people, but mainly for the English-speaking part of that people; such were the spoils of conquest. Whether such a belief was well founded is entirely irrelevant to the present argument. So the *Canadiens* believed; and so they could only make-believe in democracy. They adhered to the "social contract" with mental reservations; they refused to be inwardly bound by a "general will"which overlooked the racial problem. Feeling unable to share as equals in the Canadian common weal, they secretly resolved to pursue only the French-Canadian weal, and to safeguard the latter they cheated against the former.

In all important aspects of national politics, guile, compromise, and a subtle kind of blackmail decided their course and determined their alliances. They appeared to discount all political or social ideologies, save nationalism.[51]

Out of historical necessity and a devotion to cultural survival French Canadians had learned quickly to use democracy rather than adhere to it as a political creed to be fought for and cherished in its own right. This political opportunism on the federal level, whereby priority was always placed on ethnic survival at the expense of the common good, when transposed to the provincial level, argued Trudeau, resulted in widespread political immorality, that is, an almost total concern for individual advancement to the detriment of the national interests of French Canadians. French Canadians, not having experienced the combative struggle against democracy's ideological and institutional opponents, were unable or unwilling to combat internal obstacles confronting an established democracy. Neither were French Canadians eager to seek out new modes of representative and participatory democracy, modes which would not only free each and every individual from state oppression but ensure that the state was a true servant of its citizens.[52]

On the surface, the *Cité libre* hypothesis seemed attractive, plausible, even convincing. It gained approval, much to Trudeau's dismay and that of some of his sympathetic critics, from conservative-minded French and English Canadians who claimed it substantiated the long-standing and widely held notion that democracy was an innate part of the English way of life but alien to the French. Perhaps, as one of his critics noted, Trudeau had left his interpretation open to this sort of distortion by implicitly assimilating undemocratic behaviour to an aberration of the spirit. In reality, argued this critic, the political behaviour of the French-Canadian people merely reflected the fact that the democratic model was not sufficiently developed to be persuasive enough to impose certain norms of political behaviour on the society at large.[53]

In an article published in 1958, Léon Dion made several pertinent and enlightening remarks about the state of democracy in Quebec. As a political scientist Dion perceived three conditions essential to a practical and viable democracy. First, the democratic spirit was not a natural disposition of mankind and could only be applied in its fullest form at the level of political collective organization. Second, while democracy could be taught through books and conferences, democratic education, to be effective and durable, needed to be reinforced by attitudes and conduct experienced on a daily basis. Finally, for democratic norms and values to be fully integrated they had to find, sooner or later, expression at the level of political action.[54] Dion rejected the rather pessimistic monolithic historical picture painted by Trudeau. French Canada had a liberal and democratic tradition in its past, namely the *patriote* movement of the period 1810–40: a "movement which expressed the petty bourgeoisie's fervent assimilation of the ideals of the era and the objectives of representative and responsible government." To distort the past merely because the more predominant and widely accepted conservative religious tradition of the petty bourgeois lay and clerical élites had come to permeate French Canada's social and political insitutions for a variety of complex historical reasons was misleading and self-defeating.[55]

Dion's analysis might have been strengthened by making the point that there is more than one species of democracy, that all species do not conform or need to conform to the Anglo-Saxon model forged in the crucible of the industrial revolution and the rise of modern capitalism. He might also have added that a highly personalized political and administrative process was the norm in most traditional societies. Marcel Rioux and Guy Rocher, two sociologists, mentioned both these pertinent points and indicated that French-Canadian democracy, because of the deterministic and fatalistic tendencies which characterized its culture, was closer to the Franco-Prussian form of democracy than the Anglo-Saxon variety. They also warned against the widely held assumption, among reformers and traditionalists alike, that the increased industrialization of Quebec would mean the automatic adoption of the Anglo-Saxon model of democracy.[56]

None the less, Dion did help to draw the debate back to the situation at hand when he suggested that a closer scrutiny of contemporary Quebec revealed that liberal and democratic attitudes and behaviour were beginning to manifest themselves throughout a wide range of groups, including unions, farm organizations, and student and teacher movements – thanks to the development of new social functions and classes initiated by renewed industrial expansion. What a contrast! Such a widespread discussion concerning the best means of spreading the practice of democratic norms and values would have been virtually impossible twenty years earlier, Dion reminded his audience. Stop assuming a cultural determinism, recognize the democratic thrust at work among numerous groups within Quebec society, and organize the required strategy of action accordingly was his plea. The situation would not be improved "by striking one's chest in despair or by anxiously awaiting the arrival of a new saviour," Dion warned caustically.[57]

Naturally, the neo-nationalists rejected the *Cité libre* explanation for Quebec's undemocratic political culture. Much of the public apathy toward corruption in the Duplessis government was attributed by Laurendeau to postwar prosperity. French Canadians, still haunted by the painful memory of poverty on quasi self-sufficient farms, made few demands of their politicians, nor were they always aware of the politicians' manifest deficiencies.[58] Neo-nationalists were elated at Léon Dion's attempt to set the historical record straight and at his optimistic analysis of the contemporary situation.[59] In fact, Pierre Laporte, after being attacked for publishing Trudeau's essay in *L'Action nationale*, made criticisms similar to those presented later by Dion. In brief, Trudeau had oversimplified and distorted the historical record and had failed to mention the contemporary resurgence of democratic activity, thereby hoping to reinforce the *Cité libre* critique and condemnation of French-Canadian nationalism.[60] Laurendeau stressed that French Canada did possess a deeply rooted tradition of freedom and liberation. But because that society's past was that of a conquered and colonized minority the idea of freedom and liberation had become intimately related to the concept of nation. In advocating the freedom of the nation to which they belonged, young French Canadians, he pointed out, sincerely felt that they were also pursuing their individual freedom. While agreeing that this perspective was too simplistic, Laurendeau argued that the existing love of collective freedom could with time be extended and diversified to encompass an effective and realistic appreciation of individual freedom. "The love of freedom has not suffered unduly because a number of individuals have started to seek freedom in collectivities. Freedom is not more dogmatic because of this approach: in fact it is perhaps better rooted and especially more easily rooted in such collectivities."[61] Neo-nationalists were determined to destroy the belief that the French-Canadian culture and its people were inherently undemocratic.[62] They hoped also to ensure that nationalism did not become the scapegoat for French Canada's sociopolitical ills.

One effective way of accomplishing this objective was to focus attention on the political culture of Quebec's English-speaking minority. Trudeau characterized the political behaviour and mentality of the anglophone community as schizophrenic. He wondered how wealthy, upper-middle class, anglophone Quebecers could as voters elect Liberal opposition members to Parliament while as directors and managers of wealthy corporations they financed the retention of power by a regressive, undemocratic Union Nationale government.[63] The explanation Laurendeau found in his "Negro King" (*Roi nègre*) thesis, according to which the wealthy anglophone community, especially its press, behaved in Quebec as if it was a British community in an African colony. In return for continued economic control, Quebec anglophones were apparently quite willing to allow the Negro King, Duplessis, control over the political institutions and to run his tribe as he pleased. To demand and impose the higher political and moral standards anglophones normally expected in public life in Ottawa and in other Canadian provinces would jeopardize their privileged economic position in Quebec. How else could one explain the continued silence of the anglophone press regarding Duplessis' arbitrary decision to have *Le Devoir*'s parliamentary correspondent, Guy Lamarche, evicted from his press conference? Furthermore, the *Gazette* and the Montreal *Star* seldom did investigative reporting on the extensive patronage and corrupt electoral practices of the Duplessis government.[64] "Let sleeping dogs lie" appeared to be their motto. The anti-Duplessis forces seldom received support and encouragement from the anglophone press in Quebec. Consequently, democracy and parliamentary rule regressed and arbitrary rule went uncontested. Laurendeau agreed that the major responsibility lay with the francophone community. But support from liberty-loving anglophones would go a long way in helping to dispel the Negro King mentality and lay the basis for political cooperation between the two communities.[65]

Their diagnosis of Quebec society as being gravely stricken with the cancer of authoritarianism and political corruption did not lead to despair among the Citélibristes and neo-nationalists. The cancer was benign and a rehabilitative cure, if applied immediately and with conviction, could be successful.[66] The cure, prescribed by the Citélibristes and supported by the neo-nationalists, was a massive program of political education. "We all know," declared Pelletier to his ICAP audience in 1954, "that democracy will only have meaning on the day the majority of citizens have faith in it, when a new political hope will have replaced the present indifference and scepticism, and when we will have stopped being democrats only in self-defence."[67] Groups of enlightened French Canadians needed to rediscover the audacity of their early missionaries, explorers, and "coureurs de bois" and, like them, be willing to sacrifice everything for a purpose, in this case in order to convince the ruling élites and the masses that the future of their nation was linked to the rapid emergence of a regime of personal freedom and popular sovereignty.[68]

Many Citélibristes, assuming the role of political educators, worked through existing institutions such as the unions and sought new institutions and new vehicles to carry their message of democracy to the people of Quebec. With the cooperation of academics from Laval and Montréal, some Citélibristes helped found in 1954 Quebec's equivalent to Ontario's annual Couchiching conference. Recalling the Rouge movement's nineteenth-century struggle for democracy, the Quebec conference was appropriately named Institut canadien des affaires publiques. The annual symposia, dealing with themes from popular sovereignty to the Third World, were broadcast over Radio-Canada. Judging by the vigorous response, both negative and positive, in Quebec's major dailies, the programs were followed by a large audience and helped generate public debate on issues previously considered taboo. Through this program of democratic education, *Cité libre* members gained wide public recognition as well as the confidence which propelled some of them on to higher aspirations, namely the creation in Quebec of a truly democratic political party.

CONCLUSION

At first glance the "purity in politics" campaign conducted by neo-nationalists and Citélibristes appears superificial and no more than secular moralizing. In fact, it was an integral part of the ideological development of both groups. The campaign was prompted, to a great extent, by the realization that their reform proposals for education, social services, economic development, and intergovernmental relations would come to naught or be impossible to implement if the Quebec government lacked an efficient and highly skilled bureaucracy and continued to practise small and large patronage on a wide scale. In effect, what these reformers were attempting to break was a well-entrenched political culture. Politics for most Québécois, as was the case for anglophones in other Canadian regions, was synonymous with patronage and this had produced an electorate, especially among the intellectual élite, that was both cynical about and fearful of politics and the political process. To some extent, the traditional nationalists' continued rejection of an increased role for the state in education and social services resulted from their belief that the malady of patronage would be extended very quickly to heretofore healthy areas or to other classes. Both groups felt that if the practice of patronage was curtailed and circumscribed by institutional and legislative changes and the bureaucracy modernized, a majority of Québécois would feel less reluctant about supporting increased government intervention in, and perhaps control of, crucial sectors of Quebec society. A modern political culture would serve the needs and aspirations, somewhat different, one might add, of both neo-nationalists and Citélibristes.

In addition to ideological motivations, both groups were undoubtedly driven by the desire to achieve a practical political objective, the defeat of the Union Nationale. This gave the "purity in politics" campaign a sense of urgency, because many of the reforms were deemed long overdue and only the overthrow of the government would destroy the power base of the traditional, rural-oriented political élites which had a vested interest in the preservation of the status quo, especially the widespread practice of patronage. To a degree, the debate reflected the aspirations of a new middle class taking root in Quebec's urban centres. Yet neither group mentioned that the existing pattern of political and adminstrative corruption was being reinforced continually by the economic inferiority of the French Canadians. There were few secular careers open to educated middle-class French Canadians apart from law, medicine, and positions in small business concerns. The doors to high finance, commerce, and industry, especially above the level of foreman and clerk, were virtually closed to francophones educated in classical colleges or the commercial schools. Only in the public sector or in the newly developing para-public sector of unions, cooperatives, and *caisses populaires* did French Canadians have complete occupational mobility and the opportunity of working in their own language and culture. Given the historical paucity of good administrative positions in the public sector, the recourse to patronage was almost inevitable. With the expansion and evolution of the educated middle classes in the postwar years, the problem of career opportunities was further aggravated. The traditional patronage system, combined as it was with Duplessis' restricted view of the scope of government activities, no longer served the interests of the francophone middle classes, especially the new urban sector. The role of the state had to be expanded and the competition for the new career opportunities had to be established on a more democratic and professional basis. While patronage would resurface in new and more sophisticated forms, both groups firmly believed that it could be attenuated and controlled by means of appropriate limits which would allow democratic norms and values to take root.

Neo-nationalists felt intuitively that Quebec voters, especially the urban voters, were ready after the 1956 election for a general clean-up of the political and administrative practices of their government. In June 1958, shortly after the election of Jean Lesage to the leadership of the Liberal party, *Le Devoir* revealed the natural gas scandal, bringing to light the hand-to-hand, under-the-table style of the Duplessis regime. Filion and Laurendeau, drawing upon pretty solid evidence, charged that several ministers in the Duplessis cabinet had obtained shares in a newly formed private corporation set up to supply natural gas to Hydro-Québec. Two principles were involved. Cabinet ministers had used the information available to them as ministers to make profitable investments in the private sector, and Hydro-Québec, a crown corporation, had divested itself of a profitable sector of its operations, the supply of its own natural gas. Both the democratic and nationalist sensibilities of the neo-nationalists were stung and they hit back with a vengeance and a fury expected by few Québécois.[69] While Filion later admitted that few ministers made extensive financial gains, and most had got involved through sheer ignorance of the implications of their actions, the revelation of the scandal did come, as the neo-nationalists hoped it would, to symbolize the "ancien régime" mentality of the Duplessis administration. In that respect, the scandal helped to discredit the Union Nationale in the eyes of an increasing sector of Quebec's electorate which was coming to expect that its government should reflect modern values and behaviour.[70] In the long run, the neo-nationalists' pragmatic approach to this question of patronage and democracy was probably more effective in destroying the Duplessis regime than the hypothetical views of the Cité-libristes concerning French Canadians and democracy. Nevertheless, the Citélibristes had a strong and valid self-interest in perpetuating the thesis that French Canadians had never accepted democracy for itself and that nationalism was the prime cause of the political immorality of French Canadians. It reinforced their primary objective, the creation of a pluralistic and democratic society, the true *cité libre*, based on the pursuit of social and economic objectives for all classes and individuals rather than collective cultural and linguistic objectives. But as Laurendeau so often stressed, the pursuit of the former need not and should not preclude the pursuit of the latter. To argue the contrary was to succumb, as Léon Dion would say, to the pessimistic sense of historical determinism – *notre maître, le passé* – which had been so long preached by the traditional nationalists but which did not reflect historical reality. In sum, the "purity in politics" campaign was crucial because it forced reformers to scrutinize more carefully their past in an attempt to perceive the potential alternatives of the future.

ELEVEN

Ideologues in Search of a Political Party

Therefore, if it is illusory to think that the democratic model cannot inspire political institutions and procedures in a society whose structure does not allow the expression of attitudes and behaviour conforming to the norms and values of democracy, it is equally important to understand that every effort must be made to formulate and support these norms and values when they are beginning to manifest themselves on the social level in certain attitudes and conduct. Furthermore, serious frustrations will surface if these efforts do not acquire, at the same time, a political character or if, for one reason or another, they are prevented from emerging on the political scene.[1]

It became painfully evident by the mid-1950s that all reform aspirations expressed by neo-nationalists and Citélibristes would be subverted indefinitely unless a political movement strong enough to defeat the Union Nationale could be created. Both groups assessed the reasons why past attempts at building a viable and influential third party dedicated to reform had failed. Because the groups differed as to what these reasons were it was difficult for them to come to terms on the appropriate strategy and tactics required to create a new political party. Moreover, their conflicting ideologies prevented in the end any meaningful and fruitful cooperation. Consequently, one of the traditional parties, the Liberal party of Jean Lesage, was able to step into the political vacuum created by the deaths of Maurice Duplessis and Paul Sauvé.

Several alternatives were available to these ideologues. They considered seriously the possibility of strengthening the Quebec wing of the CCF, known as the Parti Social Démocratique (PSD). Both groups concluded, after the dismal showing of the PSD in the 1956 provincial election, that the party had no future in Quebec for the main reason that it had been identified since its inception with Canada's English-speaking majority. The second option, proposed by militants in the labour movement, was the creation of a francophone social democratic party closely affiliated with organized labour. Citélibristes, working on Trudeau's assumption that neither social democracy nor democratic socialism could be achieved before liberal democracy had taken root in Quebec, rejected this option. So did neo-nationalists, for a class-based party violated the democratic rights of working people.

The third alternative entailed what Pierre Elliott Trudeau conceived as and entitled a strategy of *"démocratie d'abord."* That is, the creation of a political movement devoted first and foremost to the reestablishment of parliamentary democracy in Quebec. There were two inauspicious and unsuccessful attempts to create such a political movement. First there was Le Rassemblement, formed in the summer and fall of 1956 after the disastrous provincial election in which the Union Nationale steamrollered its Liberal opposition. Then there was the Union des forces démocratiques, which emerged still-born in 1958. For a wide variety of reasons, which will be dealt with below, both of these attempts to create a third party committed strictly to *démocratie d'abord* failed miserably. A few neo-nationalists like André Laurendeau supported this option momentarily but soon turned their full attention to reforming the Quebec Liberal party. Neo-nationalists, sensing intuitively the desire and need for cultural and ideological continuity, maintained that a comprehensive modernization of Quebec society could best be achieved by appealing to the francophone community's desire for more cultural, socioeconomic, and political autonomy. In sum, because comprehensive modernization threatened the collective integrity of the French-Canadian nation, any political party committed to the secularization and liberalization of Quebec society had to be devoted simultaneously to achieving cultural, socioeconomic, and political equality for the francophone nation.

An auspicious conjuncture of circumstances resulted, by the late 1950s, in the emergence of a rejuvenated Liberal party under the leadership of Jean Lesage, a former cabinet minister in the St/Laurent government. The provincial Liberal party became an effective political alternative to the incumbent Union Nationale because it chose to combine its commitment to political and social welfare state liberalism with nationalist-oriented reform proposals so ardently and persuasively articulated by the neo-nationalists. This fortuitous choice, readily supported by the aspiring new middle class and reinforced by the nationalist awakening of the francophone urban working class, brought the Liberal party to power and set the pattern of Quebec politics for the 1960s and beyond.

OBSTACLES TO MODERNIZATION

Why had a viable reform party committed to political modernization not emerged in postwar Quebec? Citélibristes like Trudeau and Vadeboncoeur maintained that the political platforms of traditional nationalists were overly idealistic, antistatist, and deeply imbued with an ingrained strain of apoliticism. Political power, Citélibristes argued quite logically, was the key to the achievement of social and economic autonomy. Unfortunately, nationalists, by practising a policy of apoliticism, were responsible, in Trudeau's words, "for the fact that we find ourselves today, regardless of the direction we look, facing a destiny tragically devoid of grandeur."[2]

Few neo-nationalists were willing to go this far. Laurendeau acknowledged that traditional nationalists, upon occasion, had lacked a sense of political realism and had gotten caught up in unimportant squabbles over details and personality clashes. Yet he also stressed that their severe critique of political parties and the political process was often quite justified and should not be mistaken for a desire to withdraw from the political process. The several attempts of traditional nationalists since the 1870s to create a party based on the principles of Catholicism and nationalism bore witness to their perseverance and audacity in the face of continuing defeat. In effect, traditional nationalists, Laurendeau reminded Trudeau, were highly politicized individuals struggling to put into place a political system and political institutions more in tune with their conservative social and economic values. Contrary to conventional wisdom, corporatism as envisaged by these traditional nationalists was certainly not an apolitical system.[3]

By the mid-1950s, neo-nationalists and Citélibristes alike realized that the most powerful impediment to the political modernization of Quebec was the continued domination of the state by the highly conservative rural petty bourgeoisie. It became painfully obvious that Maurice Duplessis and the successive cabinet members of the Union Nationale simply did not comprehend the nature and extent of the socioeconomic changes that were transforming irrevocably Quebec society. Pierre Laporte best described the quintessential conservative nature of Maurice Duplessis, the Trois-Rivières lawyer who epitomized the rural and small-town professional petty bourgeoisie and the political élite that had come to represent its interests. "Duplessis," wrote Laporte, "was horrified at the thought of change – not only in his immediate circle but in the provincial administration as well. Born in the last quarter of the nineteenth century, he apparently lived through the tremendous industrial changes of the past fifty years without being influenced by them in any way. He did adopt a timid program of social welfare, but his odd manner of striving to make it as ineffectual as possible clearly indicates that he moved forward in this field against his true wishes."[4]

Reflecting its constituency and its own class interests, the traditional francophone political élite, referred to by one political scientist as "la partitocratie" or career politicians, remained firmly wedded to the doctrine of economic liberalism and shunned the invasion of the sacrosanct territory of the private sector by the public sector. This élite's cautious and conservative outlook was reinforced continuously by the fact that the Union Nationale depended in large measure on the financial support of the English-Canadian, British, and American economic élite which controlled the province's economy. With the professionalization of politics, the *partitocratie*, which emerged with the Union Nationale in the thirties, owed its existence and perpetuation not to some source of dominant social or economic power but to the party, its leader, and its organization.[5] The conservative nature of the Union Nationale was reinforced by the increased percentage of cabinet ministers drawn from the ranks of the lower middle-class back-benchers, namely the "small shopkeepers, merchants, and administrators," who because of their local prestige could sway large numbers of voters. Twelve of Duplessis' thirty-four cabinet ministers came from this lower middle-class which made up a third of the members of the legislature.[6] The fact that the vast majority of Union Nationale members – 90 per cent in 1952 and 85 per cent in 1956 – represented constituencies outside the metropolitan regions of Montreal and Quebec City explains why these upper and lower middle-class politicians experienced little pressure from their supporters to modernize the political process and political institutions of Quebec society. In fact, most of the pressure and the requests undoubtedly favoured continuity with the past and the preservation of the status quo. In sum, the political élite in the Union Nationale was made up predominantly of "a group of notables," coming from the traditional liberal professions and the small and medium business sectors. Not surprisingly, this group became decidedly hostile to the emergence of a bureaucratic middle class which challenged directly its control over political institutions and the French-Canadian society.

Neo-nationalists were well aware that the Union Nationale was none other than the traditional Conservative party joined by a few disgruntled Liberals and a handful of greedy, misguided nationalists. *Le Devoir* extended its support to the Union Nationale in the 1948 election on the ground that it was the lesser of two evils. It hoped that concerted pressure from the neo-nationalists would prompt the Duplessis government to introduce socioeconomic reforms.[7] What the neo-nationalists failed to understand was that, given the nature of the political élite in the Union Nationale, the political incentives capable of forcing that élite to support the political modernization of Quebec society were simply nonexistent. While Citélibristes had written off the Union Nationale from the outset, it took the neo-nationalists five years to understand and admit that the Union Nationale was unmovable. As to envisaging an independent nationalist political movement, that was completely out of the question. The dismal Bloc experience was still too fresh in their minds. Most neo-nationalists undoubtedly agreed with Claude Ryan's negative response to the question "Should we undertake political action?" –

although for somewhat different reasons. Nationalist and civic-minded French Canadians should concentrate on the formation of civic education organizations to teach French Canadians the principles and practice of democracy. The coming generation must devote its talents and energies to the "positive expansion of our culture" by creating new institutions to serve the cultural, social, and economic needs of an urbanized and industrialized French-Canadian nation.[8] The neo-nationalists' strategy was theoretically sound but they soon came to realize that full-scale socioeconomic and cultural modernization was impossible without political modernization.

THE CRITIQUE OF THE PARTI
SOCIAL DÉMOCRATIQUE

The Citélibriste and neo-nationalist assessments of direct political action by organized labour were linked inextricably, as we shall see, to their respective views on the potential of the Parti Social Démocratique. Citélibristes were divided by the mid-fifties. Vadeboncoeur and Rioux, committed social democrats, strongly favoured organized labour's support for, and direct affiliation with, the only existing social democratic, anticapitalist party in Quebec, the PSD.[9] Trudeau and Pelletier, on the other hand, felt it was premature to commit organized labour to the PSD, provincially or federally. Plenty of work had to be done before French-Canadian workers would choose to vote outside traditional party lines and even more before such workers would put their confidence in a francophone social democratic party, whether it was the PSD or any alternative. The CCF simply had no cultural or political roots in Quebec and would not develop any unless a French-Canadian radical base was created first. The divisions within the FUIQ, Trudeau felt, could best be resolved by concentrating on the CTCC formula, the election of a small number of social democratic candidates in order to reveal the class bias of the two traditional parties. "And the CCF," he concluded, "will depend on this education to defeat the ignorance of the presumptions which continue to prevent us from using the cadres and the experience of the only truly democratic party in Canada."[10] In sum, the interim strategy would give the PSD an opportunity to overcome some deeply ingrained obstacles and elaborate a program suited to the needs of a modern, urban industrial society that was 80 per cent francophone.

Trudeau's and Pelletier's scepticism about the immediate prospects of the PSD appeared well founded. The traditional hostility of francophone lay and clerical élites toward the CCF was still very prevalent during the 1950s. These élites contended that the Quebec Catholic church's unofficial condemnation of the CCF persisted despite the moderating overtones of the 1956 Winnipeg declaration. The socioeconomic policies promulgated by the CCF were incompatible with Catholic social doctrine. The PSD and its leaders, Thérèse Casgrain and Jacques Perrault, were leading unsuspecting French Canadians down the dangerous path to socialism, a doctrine that was anti-Christian and anti-Catholic, as well as antinationalist. The real objective of the CCF party, contended F.-A. Angers, was the destruction of the Canadian federal system and the assimilation of the French-Canadian people. Socialism by its very nature was destructive of distinct nationalities because it was based on the centralization of power in the unitary state. "To support the CCF party would be to run the risk of collective suicide!" was Angers' all too shrill warning to his compatriots.[11] Angers' lashing out at the CCF was most likely prompted by Father Gérard Dion's attempt to clarify the Catholic church's position vis-à-vis the CCF. Dion had demonstrated skilfully that the Canadian episcopacy's 1943 declaration allowing Catholics the freedom to vote for any Canadian party that adhered to the fundamental principles of Christianity was intended to apply to the CCF. The 1943 declaration had not mentioned the CCF but a press release to that effect was supposed to have accompanied the declaration. The conservative Catholic press, in English as well as French Canada, refused to print it. Many Quebec bishops and the Jesuits at the Ecole sociale populaire obstinately interpreted the declaration in a manner totally contrary to what was intended. Father Dion denounced this behaviour as unjust and dishonest. It created tremendous prejudice against a valid political party, the PSD, and undermined respect for the Catholic Church. Dion reminded clerics that the socialism of the CCF party was in the Fabian tradition of the British Labour party. The CCF did not advocate the abolition of private property and was the most democratic of all Canadian parties.[12]

Clarifications aside, the hostile and exaggerated outbursts from traditional nationalists did little to improve the prospects of the PSD. Yet they were expected and for the most part ignored by the left wing. When, however, political leaders like Georges-Emile Lapalme entered the fray and resorted to tactics similar to "Operation Panic," Citélibristes, labour leaders, and social democrats felt obliged to respond. One such incident occurred during the 1956 election when Lapalme accused the PSD of being the most centralist party in Canada, the party which advocated Ottawa's participation in education in Quebec. Union leaders from all three Quebec centrals, the FTQ, the FUIQ, and the CTCC, plus Jean-Marc Léger, René Lévesque, Pierre Trudeau, and Jacques Perrault, issued a lengthy statement in *Le Devoir* defending the PSD and attempting to set the record straight. Their manifesto denounced the Liberal party's hypocritical strategy of appealing to racial prejudice and nationalism in order to undermine the PSD, while at the same time denouncing the Union Nationale for its appeals to religion, race, and the flag! After all, was it not the PSD which supported an income tax deductibility formula giving justice to Quebec's taxpayers while the Liberals continued to oppose such a scheme? If the PSD was responsible for the centralist tendencies of some members of the national CCF then Quebec Liberals were similarly responsible for the centralist and undemocratic behaviour and programs of their federal counterparts, such as centralized social security, federal grants to universities, naming the CN hotel in Montreal the Queen Elizabeth, using closure to pass the Pipeline Bill ("a measure of economic colonialism more objectionable than the Ungava scandal"). Revealing their disillusionment at the Liberal party's coalition with the *Bérets blancs* of the Ralliement des créditistes, the authors warned reformers that the Liberal party did not essentially differ from the Union Nationale.

We recognize the desire of honest men to get rid of Mr Duplessis. We admit that a Liberal victory would provide for a year or two (time enough to get organized) a delay in our incessant march toward the degradation of democracy. But what we cannot understand is that intelligent people continue to expect democratic and social reforms from a party that, even in opposition, always refused to side with the people against big business (Asbestos, Louiseville, Noranda), and which in the middle of the election campaign demanded a sacred union of all opposition forces, that is, with the clear exception of those forces which are authentically democratic and socially progressive.[13]

The warning was no doubt intended, in part, for the neo-nationalists at *Le Devoir* who had come out in favour of the Liberal party and its coalition with the Créditistes prior to the 1956 provincial election.

Neo-nationalists took a much more conciliatory view of the CCF and its provincial wing, the PSD. They followed closely, and encouraged, the slow but perceptible evolution within the PSD, speaking favourably of its newly acquired francophone leadership and pointing out that Catholics could vote, in good conscience, for CCF and PSD candidates. While sympathetic to the growth of a social democratic party in Quebec, the neo-nationalists none the less doubted that the CCF or the PSD would make appreciable political headway in the province. They offered two reasons to explain their scepticism about the CCF's prospects. The party's brand of socialism was anti-nationalist and excessively centralist. Few CCF leaders, organizers, and members of Parliament realized that French-Canadian workers and their labour leaders were more than members of the proletariat destined to achieve their needs and aspirations in an Anglo-Canadian socialist party. They failed to understand that French-Canadian workers were as much, if not more, creatures of their cultural milieu as they were products of their class. They had no more desire than English-Canadian workers to reject their cultural heritage to pursue socioeconomic objectives. This failure to come to terms with the French-Canadian nationality, argued Laurendeau, stemmed from the fact that the CCF had been conceived and developed by anglophones and therefore, understandably, approached problems and recommended solutions spontaneously from the "English" point of view. French Canadians, accepting a sincere invitation to join the party, were, none the less, rarely made to feel at home. "It is not a question of race," wrote Laurendeau in 1948, "but a question of milieu. Our reflexes are not the same, and we feel like strangers in a house built entirely by others."[14]

Yet the problem was not entirely cultural. French-Canadian politicians had learned to work within the Conservative and Liberal parties. The CCF's conception of federalism was much too centralist to suit the neo-nationalists, whose conception of provincial autonomy far surpassed that of their more traditional precursors. To a great extent, the CCF's strong emphasis on extensive federal initiative in areas of social security and economic development reflected the fact that the party had its origins in the depression years. Politicians of all parties and constitutional "experts," struck by the inability of the provinces to finance and administer programs in their field of jurisdiction, had chosen increased centralization as the solution to the country's socioeconomic woes. CCF policies, as Thérèse Casgrain continually reminded Filion, were only slightly more interventionist than those being put into place by the federal Liberal party.[15] The argument was weak and unconvincing, considering that the neo-nationalists continually denounced the Liberal party for its excessively centralist policies and programs. Furthermore, the neo-nationalists could see nothing in the Winnipeg declaration which indicated that the CCF had attenuated its centralist policies. Consequently, the party remained unacceptable to those québécois for whom increased provincial autonomy was paramount.[16]

The 1956 provincial election results simply confirmed the misgivings expressed by neo-nationalists and some Citélibristes about the prospects of the PSD. All twenty-six candidates lost their deposits and the party received only 0.6 per cent of the vote. "The heavy hand of history," that is, the CCF's English-Canadian image and its centralist policies, accounted in large measure for the PSD's dismal failure.[17] Simply put, the party's liabilities far outweighed its assets. By 1956 the neo-nationalists had written off the PSD as the viable alternative for French Canadians disillusioned with the two traditional parties. "A left wing," wrote Laurendeau, "is being formed in French Canada. Still very fragile, it is aware of its existence and seeks out its meeting place. Some believe they have found this place in the CCF, which had the sensitivity to change its Quebec name to *Parti Social Démocratique*. I feel a great deal of respect for those expressing their sincere support for the CCF but I do not believe that the solution lies in this direction."[18] Echoing Laurendeau's assessment, one Citélibriste, Trudeau, declared that the PSD could not serve, at least in the foreseeable future, as a successful rallying point of left-wing forces in the province. Trudeau acknowledged the divisive role of nationalism but laid the responsibility for the PSD's failure on the fact that the party was excessively doctrinaire in its political strategy and political thought. This extremism and rigidity were due in great measure to the fact that successive teams of burnt-out provincial leaders and organizers were replaced by political neophytes, destroying any nascent continuity and maturation in strategy and policies.[19]

Revealing the growing tensions between the liberal and social democrats in *Cité libre*, Pierre Charbonneau rejected outright the PSD as a viable political vehicle for social change in Quebec. Socialism in any of its various forms, declared Charbonneau, was not the solution to Quebec's economic problems. Echoing the ideas of French Christian democrats such as Raymond Aron and Bertrand de Jouvenel, Charbonneau argued that socialism was not the antithesis of capitalism but merely an alternative mode of political and socioeconomic organization intended to overcome the central problem common to both, that is, coming to terms with urban-industrial society. The task confronting left-wing forces in Quebec was not to demand collective ownership of the instruments of production but rather the modernization of Québécois-owned industry and commerce to enable francophones to benefit from a closer integration of the Canadian and North American capitalist economies. Furthermore, the worst features of the capitalist economy had been attenuated by the social welfare state and Charbonneau urged left-wing French Canadians to work towards the creation of a Quebec variant of the welfare state being constructed in Ottawa.[20] While Citélibristes disagreed among themselves about the long-term necessity of social democracy, by 1956 most had reached a consensus, shared by neo-nationalists, that the PSD was not the party capable of serving as the David to defeat the Goliath, the Union Nationale.

DÉMOCRATIE D'ABORD!

By 1956, neo-nationalists and Citélibristes had agreed momentarily to set aside their ideological differences and work towards the creation of a political movement that would unite all left-of-centre forces in the province. The objective was the defeat of the Union Nationale at the next provincial election expected in four years' time. The decision by the neo-nationalists to join this venture had not been precipitous. As early as 1954, they had conceded that only a third party was capable of harnessing rapid socioeconomic developments to ensure a greater equality of condition and the survival of the French-Canadian nation. Pressure within the unions for direct political action and the creation of a francophone social democratic party was, in Laurendeau's view, symptomatic of the fact that the traditional political élites of French Canada had lost touch with a large sector of working-class voters. Initially sceptical about the chances of any new third party taking root in Quebec, both Laurendeau and Filion were willing to concede by the summer of 1955 that such a development was necessary, feasible, and would be welcomed as long as it was not a direct creation of organized labour.[21] A new third party not having emerged prior to the 1956 provincial election, the neo-nationalists decided to throw their support behind a seemingly reinvigorated provincial Liberal party under the leadership of Georges-Emile Lapalme, Jean-Louis Gagnon, Jean-Marie Nadeau, and Paul Gérin-Lajoie.[22] In the event, the party's commitment to a number of major social and economic reforms failed to attract the massive support expected from the urban working class, while alienating the old guard and frightening the party's traditional source of funds, the anglophone economic élite.[23]

This fourth consecutive defeat of the Liberal party was a sobering blow to the neo-nationalists. Dismayed and discouraged, and allowing little time for the dust to settle, Laurendeau undertook an analysis of provincial politics in general and the future of the Liberal party in particular. His verdict on the party was harsh and devastatingly accurate. It had made little progress in urban working-class ridings. The vaunted break with the federal party was belied by the presence of several Liberal cabinet ministers on the hustings. Continued waffling on the issue of provincial autonomy had caused the party heavy losses among nationalists, old and new. Finally, the coalition with the Créditistes, hundreds of *bérets blancs* popping up at Liberal rallies throughout the province including the Montreal Forum, created acute embarrassment for party officials and damaged the left-of-centre image that Lapalme and the reform wing had cultivated so assiduously since 1950. In sum, the Liberal party, despite a minor facelifting, remained basically the same party handed down from Taschereau, controlled by the same urban anglophone and francophone élites and fund-raisers. An authentic and thorough-going renewal of the party had not taken place and Laurendeau doubted that it ever would occur. The Liberal party's reputation was also its Achilles' heel. "The heritage that it carries," concluded Laurendeau, "is made up of morally questionable credits. It is a machine, but the party has no heart."[24]

The neo-nationalists' condemnation of the Liberal party naturally found strong support among Citélibristes and union activists, both groups having written off the party in the late 1940s on the ground that it was the instrument of the urban petty bourgeois élites, anglophone and francophone. Nothing in the interim had occurred to convince them of the contrary.[25] Having duly eliminated all existing traditional political movements, Citélibristes and neo-nationalists had two alternatives open to them. They could continue, like Don Quixote, to tilt at windmills and refine their respective ideologies. Or they could commence to lay the foundation of an authentic left-of-centre political movement. No mean venture indeed. Yet widespread support for such an undertaking appeared to exist among the intelligentsia at least. Three-quarters of the sixty or so letters from *Le Devoir*'s readers after the 1956 election spoke of the need for a party that was left-of-centre on social and economic issues.[26]

In an attempt to explain the neo-nationalists' decision to abandon the traditional parties, Laurendeau outlined what he considered the underlying forces behind the growing desire for a left-of-centre political party.

We are contributing to a realignment of political forces in Quebec. In the past, all parties were socially conservative. They continue to remain so (except the PSD) but this no longer corresponds to reality. Today, many Liberals, on social questions, would feel at home with Mr Duplessis. Because they are powerful, they are preventing their party from renewing itself. On the other hand, many Liberals could get along much better with unionists, with CCFers, with independent nationalists than they do with the financial supporters of their own party. Each of us, in his or her own way, feels torn between old allegiances which retain their material prestige but have lost their significance, and allegiances which still remain confused and imprecise, allegiances which indicate our duty in less clear terms but which perhaps better represent the future.[27]

In sum, neither of the existing traditional parties reflected the vastly altered socioeconomic realities of modern Quebec. Political pluralism had not succeeded, as yet, the socio-ideological pluralism already well entrenched in modern Quebec. The political crisis in Quebec stemmed not from the fact that French Canadians refused to support a social democratic party like the PSD but rather from the long historical absence of any left-of-centre social and political tradition in the province. The dominant clerical and secular right-wing forces had always managed to suppress the development of an indigenous left-wing tradition and political movement in the province by uttering cries of doctrinaire liberalism, freemasonry, and communism. Quebec, politically speaking, was a truncated society. A healthy, democratic society required an established left-of-centre political tradition and party to prevent right-wing ideological and political forces from lapsing into authoritarianism, legalism, and institutional rigidity. The danger facing Quebec was not the "left-wing infiltration" denounced by Robert Rumilly but, on the contrary, the virtual nonexistence of a left-wing mentality and established political tradition.[28]

The Liberal party's crushing and humiliating defeat in the 1956 election, followed by the neo-nationalists' scathing indictment, served as catalyst for the initiation of a new political movement, a movement which had been, in fact, in the process of gestation for several months. The Rassemblement, as it was called, held its founding convention on 8 September 1956. The hundred or so delegates attending the convention elected an executive and a board of directors, most of whom had been involved initially in the preliminary meetings on 14 April and 23 June. Pierre Dansereau, dean of science at the Université de Montréal, became president, Trudeau, vice-president, and Jean-Paul Lefebvre, director of the Service d'Education at the CTCC, was chosen secretary-treasurer. The eight directors were: Arthur Tremblay, Amédée Daigle, and Guy Hamel of Quebec City; Maurice Mercier of Victoriaville; André Laurendeau, Jacques V. Morin, Jacques Hébert, and Gérard Pelletier of Montreal.[29]

What sort of individuals were attracted to the Rassemblement, an organization which chose to define itself ambiguously as a movement of education and democratic action rather than a new political movement? Gérard Bergeron provided a reasonably accurate description of the Rassemblement's membership.

The Rassemblement-type is a man in his thirties who experienced, as an infant, the depression and the war as an adolescent. As he entered maturity some ten years ago, this person engaged in social action, usually in the labour movement. There he developed an acute social conscience which has brought him to revolt on numerous occasions against the unbelievable political mediocrity of his milieu. Duplessism disgusts him and the Liberals, who deceived him, tell him nothing that is worthwhile. He would not be French Canadian if he had not inherited a solid mistrust of politics ("politicaillerie") from previous generations. Today, this person is becoming politically aware: in the years following the war, he believed in a policy of "social action first" and adjusted his conduct accordingly. But in the heat of the battle, this person came to realize progressively that all social problems are initially posed and finally resolved in "politics." But how could one get involved in politics? Two large parties existed, were viable, but he rejected both indiscriminately without any further due process. Other parties only have a marginal or symbolic existence, such as the PSD. Politically speaking, the Rassemblement-type is disoriented, anxious, and sometimes bitter. The social force he represents lacks political expression. It functions in a vacuum.[30]

Rassemblement supporters were people from organized labour, the cooperative and agricultural movements, journalists, teachers, and academics. No members, apart from those belonging to the PSD, brought any direct political experience with them.

The Rassemblement's founding convention went smoothly. In fact, it raised expectations beyond reasonable limits and, in large measure, this accounted for the disillusionment that set in eighteen months later. A constitution and a statement of principles, drawn up in draft form at the June preliminary meeting, received quick and full endorsement by the delegates. The Rassemblement set as its objective the organizing of all citizens wishing to create a truly democratic society in Quebec, a society capable of dealing with its social, economic, and political problems in accordance with the declaration of principles of the movement. Despite pressures from union activists and a small group favouring the creation of a francophone social democratic party, the majority of the delegates chose not to define the Rassemblement as a political party or to seek affiliation with any existing party. It was also stated on several occasions that in no way did the delegates want the movement to be portrayed simply as "a political morality league." The constitution described, in an ambiguous fashion, the movement's primary objective as one of education.

The Rassemblement is a movement of democratic education, whose primary intention is to provide the setting and instruments necessary for the people of Quebec to acquire a solid political formation.

In the pursuit of these objectives the Rassemblement proposes: (a) to respect the rights of all classes of society; (b) to see primarily the support of the working classes; (c) to establish a mode of financing (primarily through the individual contributions of its members) that will ensure its independence and thereby allow it to seek continually the common good in all things.[31]

The ambiguity resided in the term "the necessary instruments," which could, when the circumstances were appropriate, be interpreted to mean a political party.

As a matter of fact, the Rassemblement's statement of principles had many of the ingredients of a political platform. Arranged under five separate themes, "the political system, the economic system, the social system, the cultural and educational system, the national and international system," the declaration of principles outlined, in a highly theoretical and abstract manner, the central features of a fully democratized society, the true *cité libre*. The chosen political system was parliamentary democracy. It alone allowed the creation and development of a society enabling the individual to actualize his or her full potential. The liberal democratic state emphasized and guaranteed the civil liberties of its citizens while the periodic necessity to solicit the explicit consent of the citizens ensured an orderly renewal of the institutions and laws governing the society. Parliamentary democracy made possible the creation of a secular state capable of protecting the individual against the increasingly complex network of social, economic, and administrative institutions, while guiding the various interest groups and classes towards a set of common goals. In sum, the democratic state made possible the participation, in varying degrees, of all of its citizens in the governing process.

The Rassemblement's approach to the problems of economic organization and development was strictly functionalist. The objective was the abolition of the exploitation of man by man and an equitable distribution to all citizens of the fruits of the growth in production and expansion of leisure. A mixed economy of private, cooperative, and public concerns, including nationalization of key sectors, was considered most likely to fulfil the desired human and economic objectives. The primary objective of social legislation and institutions was to guarantee the right to work at just and equitable remuneration. Co-management, profit-sharing, and, eventually, co-owner-ship would prevent the dehumanization of work through technological change. A full slate of social security programs would ensure all citizens, deprived by nature or by accident of the capacity to work and fulfil their own needs, a reasonable standard of living. A truly democratic society was dependent upon a free flow of information and knowledge. "The citizen has the primordial right to gain access to all levels of education and all cultural instruments, according to his skills and talents, regardless of his wealth or civil status." Following the imperatives of its democratic principles the Rassemblement stressed its support for the multiracial federalist state. The ultimate allegiance of man was to his fellow man regardless of race, colour, or religion. Consequently, a fully responsible democratic state had to come to the support of less fortunate individuals and groups wherever they might be found.[32]

There was no massive rush to join the ranks of the Rassemblement. Nevertheless, by April 1957, the movement had 511 members from thirty-eight centres and had set up sections in Montreal, Quebec, Ottawa, Magog, and Val d'Or. Within weeks of its formation, the Rassemblement was racked with internal dissension on the question of membership qualifications and party affiliation. The executive was forced to call a special conference in May 1957 to sort out the problems. One group, centred in Ottawa, favoured an open membership policy. Anyone should be allowed to join the Rassemblement as long as he or she adhered to its principles, objectives, and constitution. An open policy was rejected by the delegates on the ground that it would enable any of the existing political parties, namely, the Liberals, to infiltrate and take over the movement. A Montreal group wanted a highly restrictive membership policy which would refuse admission to anyone who was a member or an official in any capacity of an existing political party, including the PSD. Again the delegates rejected a closed-door policy, arguing that as long as the Rassemblement refused to become a political movement its members should not be prohibited from involving themselves in direct political action. Who, then, would be eligible? After considerable wrangling the delegates, in frustration, accepted the following compromise. All indi-viduals were free to join the Rassemblement as long as they did not belong to an association whose goals and means were incompatible with those of the Rassemblement. Included among excluded associations were all political parties whose programs, choice of candidates, and modes of financing were not submitted to the democratic control of party members whose rights and privileges were prescribed in a written constitution.[33]

The compromise satisfied no one and, to a great extent, marked the beginning of the end for the Rassemblement. The only parties whose members were qualified to join the movement were the PSD and the CCF. No matter what the delegates might say to the contrary, the Rassemblement quickly became identified publicly as the educational wing of the PSD. This was precisely what the movement's founders, Trudeau, Marchand, Laurendeau, Pelletier, and Dansereau, had been determined to avoid.[34] The compromise eliminated the potential support of left-wing Liberals and went against the Rassemblement's stated objectives, the coalition of all left-wing forces and the entrenchment of democratic norms and practices in Quebec. Union leaders like Jean Marchand and neo-nationalists like Laurendeau and Arthur Tremblay quickly became frustrated and disillusioned with the Rassemblement's lack of political realism, that is, its unwillingness and/or inability to become the required political force capable of producing a political realignment in Quebec and defeating the Union Nationale.

Neo-nationalists, in effect, had conceded by the spring of 1957 that the Rassemblement lacked the political clout to forge a coalition of indigenous left-wing forces into a dynamic political movement. To make their point in the most diplomatic way possible, Laurendeau invited Gérard Bergeron, a political scientist at Laval, to assess the Rassemblement's prospects. Bergeron had attended some of its early meetings as a member and he was in a good position to analyse the movement's prospects. In a hard-hitting series of articles published in Le Devoir under the pseudonym Isocrate, he severely criticized the Rassemblement's leaders for their lack of political realism.[35] When Trudeau and Jean-Paul Lefebvre discovered Isocrate's identity they were furious and questioned his allegiance to democratic values and principles.[36] On the whole, though, Bergeron was correct. The Rassemblement's program was highly abstract and theoretical and its leaders extremely idealistic in thinking they could base a political movement on the slogan démocratie d'abord. The movement's inability to evolve into a dynamic political party was confirmed in November 1957 when René Tremblay announced that the Rassemblement, having failed to get the required political support, would concentrate on political research and education.[37]

Laurendeau, along with other neo-nationalists and unionists, quietly withdrew from the Rassemblement in December 1957. In doing so, he offered, in as diplomatic a fashion as possible, three reasons for its failure to take hold as a serious political movement. The first was that nowhere in its principles of public discussions did the Rassemblement reflect the new nationalism taking root in Quebec. Second, it was not truly a Rassemblement because it had failed to take the necessary measures to attract reformers from all quarters without calling upon them to deny their origins. The reference here, of course, was not only to the left-wing element of the Liberal party but also to the left-wing nationalists. Finally, the Rassemblement's discussion of politics had been too intellectual, too disinterested, rather than being "solidly grounded in the environment and geared for action."[38] Furthermore, argued Bergeron, there was a huge credibility gap between the Rassemblement's claim that "Duplessisme" was rapidly destroying the last vestiges of democracy in Quebec and its decision to concentrate on a long-term strategy of political education. If the Rassemblement's members fully realized the dimensions of the crisis and the magnitude of the challenge confronting democrats in Quebec, they would begin to think of political action in more realistic terms. "The man of action," concluded Bergeron caustically, "does not emerge once the process of self-justification is complete but when, having grasped the rules of the game of action, he draws the practical consequences for his own action. *The rules of the game are a given*: except for the revolutionary scenario, which the Rassemblement moreover rejects. We do not choose these rules."[39]

It was painfully obvious by the summer of 1958 that the Rassemblement formula had failed to generate any political momentum. Yet Citélibristes, namely, Trudeau and Pelletier, and labour organizers from the CTCC and the newly created Fédération du travail du Québec, remained unconvinced that the Liberal party, even under the new leadership of Jean Lesage, could become a major instrument of reform and democratization of Quebec society. Sensitized by the criticisms made of the Rassemblement, Trudeau published a manifesto in October 1958 calling for the formation of a new political movement, the Union des forces démocratiques. Unlike its predecessor, its objective was specific and its role short-term, the defeat of the Union Nationale and the reestablishment of political democracy in Quebec. Accordingly, the criterion of admissibility was changed to an open-door policy. All that would be asked of members and groups was that they adhere to the constitution and principles of the movement. Pressure would be brought to bear on existing parties which claimed to be democratic by asking a large number of prominent political personalities, from within and outside existing parties, to sign a public manifesto promising to do everything in their power to rally all democratic forces in a new political coalition. As a measure of good faith, the signatories would also promise not to adhere to a party which refused to join the Union des forces démocratiques![40]

The procedural strategy had a bad taste of boy scout amateurism and a large dose of political naïveté. When a public manifesto was signed finally by twenty-one "eminent" political personalities in April 1959, only one Liberal, Marc Brière, endorsed the document and he had not been mandated by the party. Other signatories included Pelletier (CTCC), Jacques Hébert (LAC), Jean-Robert Ouellet, Roger Craig (PSD), and Pierre Trudeau as third president of the Rassemblement. Few prominent and inspiring new faces! Furthermore, the immediate objective was no longer the formation of a new political movement but rather a discussion concerning which of the following was the most appropriate formula for direct political action: the fusion of various opposition groups into a new political movement; the creation of an alliance around a basic program, each party retaining its own identity; or the arrangement of an electoral deal to guarantee only one opposition candidate in each county.[41] Obviously, Trudeau and his fellow political neophytes were learning their political lessons the hard way. Demonstrating the characteristics of an overly weighted balloon, the Union des forces démocratiques was barely airborne when it came crashing to the ground, dragging the Rassemblement with it.[42]

The reasons for the failure of the Union des forces démocratiques were numerous and varied. René Tremblay argued that the Rassemblement had never managed to become a political movement because of the tremendous difficulty of elaborating a concrete program, a difficulty due in large measure to the wide diversity of viewpoints and ideological perspectives of its members. Furthermore, he added, many of its members feared political action while others were not in a position to get involved to that extent.[43] Trudeau's rationalization for the Rassemblement's failure involved laying the responsibility on "the partisans of liberalism, socialism and nationalism who are less concerned with seeing democracy triumph then reinforcing their respective groups."[44] Neither Tremblay nor Trudeau referred to the criticisms of neo-nationalists; nor were they willing to admit publicly that they lacked the political organizational skills, the determination, and the energy to create a new political party.[45] The movement was sorely in need of veteran organizers like the Liberal Jean-Marie Nadeau but, unfortunately, it never was able to attract them for lack of credibility and financial resources.

All of these criticisms can be applied in varying degrees to the Union des forces démocratiques. Owing to the difficulty of elaborating a concrete program reflecting the socioeconomic, cultural, and political needs of Quebec society, Trudeau offered reformers the next best alternative, a crusade for political democracy. What sincere reformer dare refuse to answer the call! Had most of them not agreed with Trudeau's thesis that political democracy was not firmly rooted in Quebec, that it was still in its initial stage, the struggle against ideological and institutional obstacles, and that French Canadians continued to behave as if they did not believe in political democracy? Political democracy, Trudeau reminded his labour and socialist friends, was the *sine qua non* of all other forms of democracy. Social democracy, and perhaps some day, democratic socialism, would require crusades of their own. But to introduce them into a society lacking an entrenched tradition of political democracy was, in Trudeau's view, suicidal. The outcome was either a fascism of the right or a totalitarianism of the left.[46] Trudeau called upon the depression generation of French Canadians, whether they were political democrats, social democrats, democratically minded nationalists, or democratic socialists, to destroy authoritarianism in the political sector as they had done in many of their professions. His manifesto clamoured for "*Democracy first*, this should be the rallying cry of all the reformist forces in the province. That some are active in the Chambers of Commerce and others in the labour movement, that certain activists believe in the glory of free enterprise while others teach socialist theories, there is nothing wrong in this – providing that they all agree to achieve democracy first: it will then be up to the sovereign people to choose freely the form of social and political organization it prefers."[47]

There were essentially two things wrong with Trudeau's analysis. Quebec society, as Léon Dion continually pointed out, had developed a series of democratic institutions since the 1930s and, furthermore, had a long-standing tradition of political democracy and social egalitarianism. Rid the society of its excessive clericalism and replace the existing conservative-minded political élite with a new generation of better educated, urban-oriented political leaders, and these traditions would reassert themselves, he argued. Moreover, contrary to what Trudeau believed, the ideology of democracy was no less ambiguous or prone to varying interpretations than the ideology of nationalism. Neither was it politically realistic to argue that a political party could be based strictly on a program for democracy. Had Citélibristes and neo-nationalists not agreed that no party could be founded on the ideology of nationalism alone? Failing to hammer out a wide-ranging political program, the Union des forces démocratiques blossomed only to wilt shortly thereafter. It came under sharp criticism from committed democratic socialists like Pierre Vadeboncoeur who denounced l'Union as "Mr Trudeau's private club" and an antechamber of the Liberal party.[48] Neo-nationalists supported, in principle, the concept of a coalition of opposition forces to defeat Duplessis but basically used the threat of such a coalition to keep the heat on the Liberal party, enabling its reform wing to put its stamp on the party platform for the next election.[49] The rapid demise of the Union des forces démocratiques was precipitated in large measure by rapidly changing events, primarily the regeneration of the Quebec Liberal party. It is to this important phenomenon that we now turn.

REJUVENATION OF QUEBEC'S LIBERAL PARTY

The respective attitudes and perceptions of Citélibristes and neo-nationalists toward the Quebec Liberal party helped determine, in part, the direction charted for it by its small but dynamic reform wing. The attitude maintained by Citélibristes toward the Liberal party, including its reformist elements, was one of contempt and rejection. The party was considered to be the spokesman and instrument of Quebec's primarily anglophone economic élites. No amount of persuasion employed by the reformist wing could make Citélibristes and militant unionists believe that the internal functioning and financing of the Liberal party could be democratized. A reform-oriented party platform was considered merely window-dressing. Citélibristes saw little hope for the Liberal party as long as party structures remained in the hands of a small group easily controlled by party financiers.

Neo-nationalists, understanding intuitively that politics was the art of the possible and determined to defeat the Union Nationale, adopted, by the spring of 1958, a more conciliatory attitude toward the Liberal party. Aided and abetted by a timely conjuncture of circumstances both within and outside the party, they alternately cajoled and pressured its reform wing to adopt an increasingly neo-nationalist election platform.

Influenced by the assessments of Gérard Bergeron, the neo-nationalists became convinced that the coalition of opposition forces, attempted in 1956 and talked about in the Rassemblement, could, if certain conditions prevailed, be formed around the Liberal party. Bergeron demonstrated that "mathematically, Duplessism is precarious. It rules by a narrow margin." All that was needed for a Liberal victory, he contended, was a 5 to 6 per cent shift in the popular vote in specific regions. This small increase would translate easily into a significant shift in the number of seats. An electoral system that had worked to the advantage of the Union Nationale, because of the overrepresentation of rural areas, could be made to work to the advantage of the Liberal party, predicted Bergeron, if the party brought together an appropriate leader with a timely program of reform measures in areas that included a wide spectrum of voters.[50] Three problems were of concern to the neo-nationalists, once they had decided that the Liberal party offered the only hope of defeating the Union Nationale in 1960. First, an appropriate successor had to be found for Georges-Emile Lapalme who had led the party through two successive defeats in 1952 and 1956; second, the internal administration and financing of the party had to be democratized, enabling it to attract organizers and candidates from all social classes and regions in Quebec; third, the party had to hammer out a political program which reflected the needs and aspirations of the "new" Quebec.

The question of leadership was potentially the most volatile issue. If the choice of a successor resulted in bitter internecine squabbles which bubbled over into the public arena, then the game was over. There was a strong possibility that this might occur. A young, ambitious, nationalist-oriented Liberal organizer and constitutional adviser, Paul Gérin-Lajoie, began campaigning shortly after the 1956 election and influenced the Young Liberals to call for a leadership convention. When Gérard Bergeron, writing as Isocrate in Le Devoir in the spring of 1958, questioned the leadership abilities of Lapalme, it was interpreted by the latter as a conspiracy on the part of Bergeron and the neo-nationalists of Le Devoir to have him replaced by Gérin-Lajoie.[51] There is simply no evidence to support this charge.

Bergeron, convinced that Paul Sauvé would succeed Duplessis, felt that Gérin-Lajoie, while highly talented, was a political lightweight by comparison and would never stand a chance of defeating the Union Nationale. While he refused to say so directly, it was clear to those reading closely his assessments of the various candidates that he felt Jean Lesage was best suited to lead a team of reform-minded Liberals against the Union Nationale.[52] It was in fact two ex-members of the Faculty of Social Sciences at Laval, Maurice Lamontagne and Father Lévesque, who first convinced Lapalme that he should step down and then persuaded Jean Lesage to enter the race for the leadership. Gérin-Lajoie had two strikes against him. He was considered too much of a nationalist as he had made a reputation as one of the strongest proponents of the Tremblay Commission. Moreover he was regarded as too much of an egotist and lacking in the necessary leadership qualities of compromise and cooperation. Lapalme, assured of a strong role in the party, acquiesced to the pressure and Lesage was easily elected at the 31 May 1958 leadership convention. He garnered 630 votes on the first ballot compared with 145 for a humiliated Gérin-Lajoie, his closest rival.[53] Traditional party organizers considered that they had a safe candidate in Lesage. He was perceived as fairly conservative on socioeconomic issues and a strong federalist.

Neo-nationalists kept a close watch on developments in the Liberal party and were, to a considerable extent, swayed by Bergeron's perceptive analysis of the situation. Undoubtedly, their natural sympathies and instincts drew them toward the candidacy of Gérin-Lajoie. But the evident reluctance of the party to support him, his inexperience, and his abrasive personality traits led them to believe that he could not win the leadership. To support him strongly would merely divide the party. Furthermore, the fact that Jean Lesage was a former Liberal federal cabinet minister under the St Laurent government no longer carried the stigma suffered by Godbout or Lapalme. The federal Liberal party had been replaced in Ottawa by the Conservative party. The provincial Liberal party could adopt, henceforth, an aggressive stance on the question of provincial autonomy without embarrassing its federal counterpart.[54] As always, neo-nationalist support for Lesage was conditional. Party delegates, as the neo-nationalists had expected, opted for the candidate with prestige and political experience – *le grand chef* – while paying only scant attention to his views on important questions such as provincial autonomy, political reform, and social progress. Laporte even suggested that Lesage would have trouble healing the wounds caused by the leadership race and that it was possible Gérin-Lajoie would bolt the party to form a coalition with Jean Drapeau and the Ligue d'action civique.[55] Perhaps the challenge facing Jean Lesage was best expressed by Gérard Filion in an editorial following the convention.

Mr Lesage, even if he was superhuman, could not constitute by himself a magic formula of success. There exists at present in Quebec a strong desire for political reform and social progress. This desire seeks to express itself in some manner. Mr Lesage can channel or thwart this determination for change. It is not because he is a former federal cabinet minister, because he has an attractive personality, or because he expresses himself in a warm and friendly manner that he will become indispensable. These are only secondary attributes. What Quebecers want to know is quite simply: will he accomplish what Mr Duplessis refused to do and will he reject what Mr Duplessis did? Will he succeed in imposing his will on the party? If yes, his chances are good; if not, he must resign himself immediately to calling a third convention to select yet another, a third, bogey-man.[56]

What was it, exactly, that the neo-nationalists wanted? What guarantees were required to gain their support? The first condition that the Liberal party had to fulfil was to rid itself of its deadwood, politicians like Sarto Fournier who claimed to be Liberals but served the interests of the Union Nationale. Second, the party should seek actively the support of progressive elements in the province, those groups striving to reestablish a minimum of democracy in Quebec, such as the unions, cooperatives, associations for educational reform, agricultural organizations, university faculties, nationalist groups, and the PSD. The commitment to the democratization of the party's structures and financing must also be accompanied by a serious commitment to the modernization and democratization of the political process and the administration of public affairs in the province. It was also imperative that the Fédération libérale provinciale, formed in 1955, be accepted fully by the local organizers of the party and that it create a provincial organization completely independent of the federal Liberal party. The Liberal party was no longer representative of the full range of social classes in Quebec society. Only a serious commitment to socioeconomic and political reforms would attract ambitious young leaders from the new middle class and organized labour. It was, in effect, a vicious circle. The Liberal party needed to attract a new generation of organizers and candidates but this would not occur unless it undertook a regeneration of itself and its program.[57] This was a seemingly impossible task to all but a small dedicated group of reformers and neo-nationalists.

The reformist wing of the Liberal party found it much easier to impose a new program on the party than to democratize the party's internal structures and financing procedures. Local organizers and candidates, argues one political scientist, learned quickly to circumvent the Fédération libérale provinciale by refusing to cooperate with it or by taking its functions over and continuing to operate in the traditional manner.[58] How did the Liberal party propose to differentiate itself, ideologically speaking, from the Union Nationale? Was it going to stress its liberalism by moving farther to the left on socioeconomic issues and concentrating on the renewal of democratic traditions in Quebec, as Trudeau and his Citélibriste colleagues were urging? Or was the Liberal party going to put increasing emphasis on the nationalist aspirations most clearly and vividly expressed during the 1950s by the neo-nationalists? As events were to show, reformist Liberals came to perceive that, as the neo-nationalists had claimed for some time, a combination of these two ideological currents could produce a very potent political force. It would be a force which could regenerate the dormant but, none the less, very real desire of all French Canadians for cultural and linguistic equality and fuse it with the urgent need expressed by increasing numbers of French Canadians, working-class and new middle-class alike, for the modernization of the political, social, and economic institutions of their society.[59]

This combination of class and national aspirations, while seldom acknowledged, provided the differentiating factor underlying the formulation of the Liberal party's program. Jean-Louis Gagnon, director of the Liberal organ *La Reforme*, agreed with Laurendeau that a political party could not be created around nationalist doctrines alone. To be effective, nationalism had to be related to concrete socioeconomic and political realities expressed by the ideology of either conservatism, liberalism, social democracy, or socialism. Quebec, in Gagnon's view, was not ready for either of the two latter options. The Union Nationale expressed the conservative-nationalist option. That left the liberal-nationalist option as the only feasible alternative. "It appears to me," suggested Gagnon, "that the survival and expansion of French Canada are essentially a question of culture. That education at all levels is accessible to everyone is necessary but not sufficient. We must start with a renewal of all institutions and, keeping in mind the requirements inherent in the North American environment, we must learn how to foster a sufficiently genuine humanism if we wish to be something other than a *mirror image of the French*. Because we are a minority we do not have the right to be mediocre."[60] Gérard Bergeron, drawing upon Trudeau's political lexicon, referred to this combination of nationalism and liberalism as "a 'functional' nationalism," that is, an operational nationalism which was geared to the achievement of political power to implement concrete socioeconomic and political reforms. "Nationalism must lead to political action. If not, it remains academic or romantic: events confuse or use it. This is what is happening at the moment," Bergeron warned in 1959.[61] In effect, what Bergeron was preaching was the neo-marxist belief that nationalism could, under the appropriate conditions, be used by the ruling bourgeoisie to channel the support of the masses for radical socioeconomic and political reforms.

The Liberal party was worried about the skilful use of nationalism by Jean Drapeau, the defeated mayor of Montreal, to build a third party in Quebec. Regional branches of the Montreal-based Ligue d'action civique were cropping up throughout the province in the summer and fall of 1959 and Drapeau was considered the most serious threat to the successful regeneration of the Liberal party.[62] *Le Devoir*, to a degree, played up the threat of a nationalist-inspired third party to keep the heat on the Liberals but realized, nevertheless, that the formation of any third party would divide the opposition forces and seriously threaten the chances of defeating the Union Nationale. Trudeau denounced the attempt by Drapeau to divide reformist forces and his friend, Jacques Hébert, resigned as director of the LAC organ, *Vrai*, on the grounds that the LAC had no business entering provincial politics championing nationalist aspirations.[63]

By the summer and fall of 1959, it was clearly evident that nationalist and separatist ideas and doctrines were once again becoming important debating subjects among the politicized college and university students. Right-wing nationalist and separatist spokesmen expressed their views in *Chantiers*, *La Nouvelle France*, and *Laurentie*, while socialist-minded French Canadians found a forum in Raoul Roy's *La Revue socialiste*.[64] To perceptive journalists and political activists, one thing was becoming increasingly clear. The industrialization and urbanization of French Canadians had not destroyed, but rather reinforced, their will to survive as a distinct national group. Coupled with the new liberal values associated with modern urban living, as expressed by the liberal and social democrats in *Cité libre*, ICAP, and organized labour, the impact of this national reawakening could be sufficiently powerful to sweep the Union Nationale out of office.

It is in the context of these developments and assumptions that one must analyse the Liberal party's 1960 program. Relieved of his leadership duties, Lapalme prepared, during the spring and summer of 1959, a series of draft proposals dealing with everything from educational to municipal and administrative reform, always with a strong emphasis on the role of the state in the renewal of every aspect of French-Canadian culture. Party leaders and organizers debated the proposals at the summer retreat of Bona Arsenault at Bonaventure on the Baie des Chaleurs. A consensus was reached and Lapalme expressed the reform proposals during the budget debate in December 1959. All seemed for nought. Duplessis had died suddenly in early September to be replaced by the youthful and aggressive Paul Sauvé proclaiming his famous *désormais!*, with its message that henceforth things would change. The Liberal party went into a tailspin when a survey poll indicated in November that Sauvé would sweep the province at the next provincial election. Rumours circulated, and were confirmed at a later date, that leading Liberals, at the instigation of Father Lévesque, had tried to talk Lapalme into leading a coup to regain the leadership from Lesage. Realizing that if the attempt failed he would destroy his political career, Lapalme rejected the proposal and argued that Liberals had to sweat it out and try to counter Sauvé with solid criticism, as *Le Devoir* was doing.[65] Laurendeau pointed out that if Sauvé moved too quickly on crucial socioeconomic issues he would split his party. Furthermore, argued Laurendeau, Sauvé's *désormais* did not extend into the area of political reform. The new premier categorically refused to institute an inquiry into the natural gas scandal or other extensive forms of corruption and patronage in the administration.[66]

Fortunately for the Liberal party, Paul Sauvé died suddenly on 2 January 1960 after little more than three short months in office. Even *Le Devoir* regretted the loss of Sauvé, observing that his successor, Antonio Barrette, did not have the leadership qualities to renew the Union Nationale even in opposition.[67] Liberal hopes were revived and Lesage's spirits were lifted as he prepared to lead his party into the coming provincial election. Party officials quickly agreed that the Liberal program would consist of a condensed version of the lengthy draft proposals prepared by Lapalme in the summer of 1959. Lapalme was quick to oblige and prepared a fifty-four point outline that was much more progressive and nationalistic than anything the traditional wing of the party wanted or would have proposed.[68] In contrast to 1956, the prime emphasis of the Liberal platform in 1960 was on wide-ranging reforms which would ensure the survival and expansion of the French-Canadian nationality. The commitment to greater equality of opportunity and minor steps in the direction of equality of condition remained, but the whole was cloaked in the broader concern for the fulfilment of the national aspirations of French Canadians or, as they were increasingly wont to refer to themselves, Québécois. Under the theme *"La vie nationale"* the Liberal party urged the creation of a Ministère des affaires culturelles, free education at all levels including university, and, following the recommendations of the Tremblay Report, the creation of a Commission provinciale des universités and a royal commission of inquiry on education. "In the Quebec context," explained Lapalme, "the French Canadians constitute a clear majority, a nationality that must be fully developed ... It is through our language and culture that we can affirm our French presence on the North American continent."[69] The impact of neo-nationalism on the proposed economic reforms was quite remarkable. Lesage was quoted to the effect that a general increase in the standard of living expected from an expansionary economy could not satisfy French-Canadian national aspirations unless it was accompanied by greater French-Canadian control and management of the Quebec economy. To overcome the problem of economic inferiority, the Liberal party proposed the formation of a Conseil d'orientation économique, "the top planning agency of our industrial and economic life," and a Ministère des richesses naturelles to promote the formation of francophone industrial concerns, guarantee the employment of francophone technical and administrative personnel by foreign corporations, restrict all future hydro-electric development to Hydro-Quebec, increase all royalties where possible, and, finally, abolish company towns. The Liberal party promised to assume greater provincial responsibility for unemployment and to do its utmost to modernize the agricultural economy to help stem what had become, by 1960, a veritable process of rural depopulation.[70] There were numerous ridings in which farming was combined with employment in extractive and forest industries and the Liberal leaders felt that the right mixture of national and socioeconomic concerns would gain the party many of these seats.

The area where national and socioeconomic objectives could be easily moulded into concrete vote-getting projects was, of course, social security. Reflecting the age-old nationalist concern with the family – the nucleus of the French-Canadian society – it was proposed that the Ministère de la jeunesse become le Ministère de la famille et de la jeunesse. Old age and other pensions would be supplemented by provincial allocations, while parents with children from sixteen to eighteen years old in school would receive provincial family allowances. The province would join the federal hospital insurance scheme, "taking into full consideration the constitutional rights of the province of Quebec and the unique characteristics of its population, especially the institutions directly involved in this scheme."[71] In sum, the Liberal party perceived the need for an active and interventionist state, especially in the areas of education, social services, and resource development. How interventionist was never clearly spelt out. Any projected comprehensive secularization of education or social services would have laid the Liberal party wide open to the charges of socialism and anticlericalism, something its leaders wanted to avoid at all costs.[72]

The neo-nationalist imprint on the Liberal party was most prominent in the areas of provincial autonomy and federal-provincial relations. Here again the influence of Lapalme was paramount, as was the increased militancy of Liberal delegates attending party conventions. Lapalme, influenced by his party's bitter tongue-lashing from the neo-nationalists for its refusal to sanction the provincial income-tax scheme, was determined that the Liberals would never again be embarrassed on the issue of provincial autonomy. Throughout 1958 and 1959 he played up the significance of the *Tremblay Report*, a comprehensive document from which the Quebec government should proceed at once to prepare "an overall plan that would become our national policy, because we do constitute a nation in the province of Quebec."[73] Lesage, in his barn-storming tour of the province, called the *Tremblay Report* Quebec's charter of constitutional and fiscal autonomy and urged Duplessis to convene immediately an interprovincial conference to plan the provincial counter-offensive on Ottawa.[74] "Must I remind you," declared Lesage in language familiar to all Quebec nationalists, "that autonomy, for us Liberals, constitutes the primary foundation of our development as a distinct ethnic group. The province of Quebec, because of its faith, its ethnic composition, and its traditions, is not in the same situation as the other provinces. The British North America Act recognizes this situation. Our policies in the area of federal-provincial relations must be audacious, progressive, dynamic, and above all positive."[75] What could be clearer? The Liberal party, in what would prove to be a watershed decision, had become an ardent proponent of a "positive autonomy" for Quebec, an autonomy which signified a "special status" position for the province.

The Liberal party's 1960 platform expressed this constitutional commitment in a number of concrete proposals. Through a flurry of new bureaucratic structures – Ministère des affaires fédérales-provinciales, Conseil permanent des provinces, Secrétariat permanent fédéral-provincial – Quebec would seek to replace the existing tax-sharing arrangements and conditional grants with a new, constitutionally entrenched system of tax-and revenue-sharing more favourable to the provinces. The basis for discussion with Ottawa would be none other than the multivolumed *Report* of the Tremblay Commission. If Quebec could convince other provinces to support its call for a new division of powers, then fine. If not, Quebec would go it alone. To be accurate, reform proposals were not absent from the program. Labour legislation was going to receive a thorough overhaul, the legal status of women was to be improved, electoral reform introduced, and the civil service modernized.[76] Somehow in the heat of the election, the tenor of which became increasingly nationalistic, these proposals received less attention from the politicians and the editorialists than did the Liberal party's newfound commitment to the rising neo-nationalistic expectations developing throughout the province.

Neo-nationalists were elated, even ecstatic. On the question of Quebec's constitutional future, Laurendeau had only one caveat concerning the Liberal party's seven proposals. In calling for patriation of the constitution (Article 44), no mention had been made of an appropriate amending formula. It was nevertheless "a balanced, very precise, and quite innovative party platform," commented an impressed Laurendeau. The important question to ask was whether the Liberal party's conversion to a positive, concrete, and dynamic provincial autonomy was authentic or simply election propaganda. While rejecting the *Globe and Mail*'s claim that Jean Lesage had become more of an autonomist and nationalist than the late Maurice Duplessis had been, Laurendeau did admit that Lesage had become an excellent spokesman for a neo-nationalist program which, in his view, echoed the wishes of the grassroots of the Liberal party. The fact that the Conservative party ruled in Ottawa was sufficient to ensure that Lesage would soon become a partisan supporter of provincial autonomy.[77] What is more, the Liberal party's commitment to cultural renewal was novel and impressive. The Liberals, indeed, had struck a sensitive nerve in the national psyche of French Canada.[78] A full range of socioeconomic reforms revealed a party devoted to the renewal and modernization of the French-Canadian culture.

Québécois, remarked Filion with an evident sense of expectation, at long last had "a clear and free choice." As far as the neo-nationalists at *Le Devoir* were concerned, after sixteen years of uninterrupted Union Nationale government, "It was time that things changed."[79]

Citélibristes and union activists had remained virtually silent on the resurgence of the Liberal party. When Trudeau, Pelletier, Marchand, and René Lévesque were approached by Maurice Sauvé and asked to run as Liberal candidates, only René Lévesque accepted.[80] Ironically, Lévesque, like Trudeau, had been a vociferous critic of Bergeron's thesis to the effect that "l'union des forces démocratiques" could only take place around the Liberal party. Jean Marchand, on the other hand, agreed with Bergeron but could not persuade his colleagues to go with him. The group, especially Trudeau, could not stomach Lapalme's paternalistic attitude toward the younger reformers. Moreover, Citélibristes were leary of the Liberal party's commitment to the neo-nationalist doctrines of *Le Devoir* and the *Tremblay Report*.[81] Trudeau also questioned the democratic credentials of reformist-minded Liberals, who, shortly before the election, accepted government appointments to the Conseil supérieur du travail, the Commission d'étude du système administratif de Montréal, and the Commission d'enquête sur l'assurance-hospitalisation![82]

René Lévesque, however, had not been influenced by the antinationalist stance of *Cité libre* members. Lévesque had been attracted to the neo-nationalist ideas of *Le Devoir* and had come to know Laurendeau through the latter's television work. The bitter strike at Radio-Canada during the winter of 1958–9 confirmed his intuitive support for neo-nationalist solutions to Quebec's problems. Having lost his Radio-Canada position as "animateur" of *Point de Mire*, Lévesque was also in search of a new career. He revealed to Bergeron in February 1960 that he had come to understand and accept Bergeron's plea for urgency. Lévesque also indicated that he was relatively pleased with the electoral program of the Liberal party and had decided to run as a Liberal candidate in the fast-approaching provincial election.[84] Few, if anyone, could have foreseen that Lévesque would become one of the major political forces behind the Quiet Revolution of the 1960s.

Trudeau's reticence toward the Liberal party remained. But his disappointment with the Ligue d'action civique and the PSD for having refused to accept his formula of a union of political forces outside of all existing parties was made quite apparent. "It is obvious to everyone that both the PSD and the Action civique have chosen these past few years to become doctrinaire in their political thought, intolerant toward democratic action, and dreamers when it comes to general strategy. As a result, the Liberal party has been able to obtain at very little cost a monopoly over the votes of oppositionists. And the corollary is that a René Lévesque – desiring suddenly to pursue a political career – finds it practically impossible to act elsewhere than in the Liberal party."[84] Reformers voting Liberal would do so because it was the lesser of two evils. In fact, Trudeau desired a Liberal defeat so those understanding the urgency of démocratie d'abord could once again attempt to bring about a union of authentic reformist forces in the province.[85]

The Liberal party slogan, "It is time for a change," placed in the context of the party's neo-nationalist program, symbolized the "quiet revolution" in action. Yet few political pundits or political party organizers were willing to predict the outcome of the June 1960 provincial election. The Liberal *équipe de tonnerre*, comprising René Lévesque, Paul Gérin-Lajoie, Georges-Emile Lapalme, René Hamel, and Jean Lesage, led the party to a victory in which it garnered 52 per cent of the popular vote for fifty-one seats. The Union Nationale, under the hotly contested leadership of Antonio Barrette, the ex-minister of labour in the Duplessis cabinet, managed to hold forty-three seats with 48 per cent of the popular vote. A shift of 7 per cent in the popular vote had given the Liberal party thirty-one seats more than in 1956. The Union Nationale's grip on the province had proved tough to crack. Considering the natural gas scandal of 1958, the death of two prominent leaders, and the revelation of patronage – *l'affaire* Pelletier – only days before the election, it was surprising that the Union Nationale lost the election by only eight seats. Obviously, the party machinery had a life of its own and operated, over the short term at least, without strong political leadership at the top. The Liberals were aided by serious divisions within the Union Nationale resulting in a poorly planned electoral strategy and increasingly defensive posturing by Antonio Barrette. The sad state of the Quebec economy, suffering a recession and high unemployment like most regions of Canada, did little to bolster the sagging fortunes of a party already perceived by most urban French Canadians as too conservative on socioeconomic and cultural issues and heavily ridden with the cancer of patronage.[86]

The ideology of neo-nationalism, engendered in the pages of *Le Devoir* and *L'Action nationale* and given official sanction in the *Tremblay Report*, had proved to be the successful political formula for the reinvigorated Liberal party. The neo-nationalist thrust of the party program appealed to the increasingly secularized and urbanized electorate in Montreal and in the surrounding region, which comprised nearly half of Quebec's population. In the Eastern Townships, where manufacturing and resource industries were numerous and urban values prevailed, the Liberals won nine seats. In Northern Quebec and the Lower St Lawrence, regions heavily dependent upon extractive industries dominated by foreign corporations, the Liberal party capitalized on the absence of the Union des Electeurs to win seventeen seats. For economic and nationalist reasons, the CTCC had been extremely successful in organizing workers, predominantly French-Canadian, in the extractive and pulp and paper industries in these regions. Undoubtedly, CTCC organizers were influential in persuading many of their members to vote for a party which promised a thorough overhaul of labour-management relations legislation and made a commitment to greater francophone participation in, and control of, the development of the province's resources.[87]

Neo-nationalists were undoubtedly pleased with the Liberal victory on 22 June 1960. The victory was marginal but the Union Nationale had received a severe setback and would need time and reorganization before presenting a serious threat to the Liberals.[88] In the meantime, it was imperative that pressure be kept on the Liberal party and its *équipe de tonnerre* to ensure an early start on the systematic implementation of its program. Five months after the election, *Le Devoir* was relatively pleased with the new government's record except on the crucial issue of educational reform. Sensing that Lesage was being pressured by conservative elements, in and outside the party, the neo-nationalists reminded the premier that they would not allow the Liberals to forget their important election promises, especially the commitment to comprehensive educational reform.[89]

"First of all we must salute those who freed us from the Union Nationale," was Trudeau's initial response to the Liberal victory. None the less, he was quick to point out that the slim margins of many Liberal candidates reinforced the thesis of those who, proposing a union of democratic forces, had warned against the potential divisiveness of right-wing or left-wing doctrinaire parties. Unwilling to suffer defeat lightly, Trudeau even went so far as to suggest that his formula for a union of democratic forces would have ensured a stronger and more reformist government.[90] Assessing the situation critically, he concluded that the extraparliamentary reformist forces must carry out a dual function. The reformist wing of the Liberal party was weak and would encounter serious opposition from vested interests, both within and outside the party, once it began to implement "reforms which are far in advance of general opinion, but which also are not fully understood by its own partisans." Consequently, all reformers, including social democrats, had a responsibility to support and encourage all reform efforts of the Liberal government. Furthermore, because of the weakness of the parliamentary opposition, reformers also had a duty to serve as constructive critics of the government and to propose new reform measures when the time was appropriate. For the intellectuals and political pundits this dual role did not pose insurmountable difficulties. For political activists, like Marcel Rioux and Pierre Vadeboncoeur, who wanted to get on with the business of creating a social democratic party in Quebec, the dilemma was more concrete. Trudeau again disagreed on the question of priorities. Social democracy could not come to Quebec before political democracy. "In conclusion," he wrote, "I believe that men of action must support the Quebec Liberal party in all of its reformist endeavours."[91] Trudeau, the intense rationalist, remained consistent even in defeat. His deep commitment to democratic principles overshadowed his commitment to any specific political movement or party and prevented him from becoming an active participant capable of moulding government policy in the desired direction. His devotion to the survival of a reformed and modernized French-Canadian society was also beyond question. Yet his overly rationalist mistrust of nationalism prevented him from understanding the forces behind the neo-nationalism sweeping the province and from realizing that those national aspirations had to be channelled in the appropriate direction. But that is anticipating the events of the 1960s!

CONCLUSION

Of the two competing ideologies it was neo-nationalism which found expression on the political level. This was so for three main reasons. First, there was *Cité libre*'s inability to come to terms with contemporary French-Canadian neo-nationalism. Nationalism and liberalism, the Citélibristes contended, were mutually exclusive because collective aspirations usually gained the upper hand over individual rights. The historical evolution of French-Canadian nationalism was for them confirmation of this argument. Ever since its inception in the early nineteenth century, nationalism had been an influential element in French-Canadian politics and political culture. Initially associated with political liberalism and republicanism, French-Canadian nationalism, after the Rebellions of 1837–8, became a thoroughly conservative, defensive, and reactionary ideology aimed at guaranteeing the survival of a predominantly rural, Catholic, and preindustrial society while, at the same time, allowing the anglophone majority to pursue unhindered the commercialization and industrialization of the economy. The professional and clerical élites who articulated and disseminated this ultramontane nationalism in its various forms did so, of course, to solidify their control over this society. *Cité libre*'s sincere but misguided attempt to alter dramatically French-Canadian politics by placing an exclusive priority on individual and class aspirations proved to be unacceptable for French Canada's middle-class leaders, old and new. The strategy of *démocratie d'abord*, to be followed in due course by social democracy, threatened to bring about a closer similarity between French and English-speaking Canadians and their respective societies, thereby undermining the separate identity of French Canada and the leadership role of French-Canadian middle and upper middle-class leaders. Moreover, contrary to the belief of many social scientists, including those in *Cité libre*, the dual process of modernization and urbanization did not result in the demise of nationalistic aspirations but rather in their renewal and reorientation. Led by the new, urban middle class, the French-Canadian working and lower-middle classes turned increasingly to neo-nationalism as the ideology best able to resolve the tensions of modernization and fulfil their new secular expectations.

As political organizers the Citélibristes lacked most of the prerequisite skills and resources. They got little help from organized labour – the CTCC, the FUIQ, and later the FTQ – which proved incapable for several reasons of coming to terms on a coordinated policy for some form of direct political action or strong support for the PSD. The Citélibristes' thesis that French Canadians were not born with an understanding of democratic principles and practices led them to abandon the PSD and campaign for *démocratie d'abord*. Hampered by an intense idealism, few resources, and limited political leadership skills, the Rassemblement, and the Union des forces démocratiques barely got off the ground before they came crashing back to reality. French-Canadian voters possessed a healthy mistrust of political movements based on abstract ideological principles and lacking concrete socioeconomic and political reform proposals. It was asking them to buy a pig in a poke. Furthermore, while Trudeau's thesis about French Canadians and democracy had some validity, French Canadians in the majority considered themselves neither bereft of democratic principles nor undemocratic in their behaviour. To attempt to create a political movement on these presumptions was unrealistic and, undoubtedly to many French Canadians, downright insulting.

The neo-nationalists won the day because they understood intuitively and intellectually that nationalism was an integral part of French Canada's political culture and sense of collective security. They also understood that by the 1950s liberalism, socially and culturally speaking, had become prevalent throughout Quebec's urban centres and was even beginning to make serious inroads in the more prosperous rural regions and communities. This fact was demonstrated vividly by the favourable response to the emergence of the social welfare state and the growing interest in prolonged education and the full range of secular careers for young francophones. A shrewd combination of nationalism and liberalism, the neo-nationalists argued, could bring about the defeat of the regressive Union Nationale administration. A government imbued with neo-nationalism could then carry out a comprehensive socioeconomic and political modernization of Quebec under the guidance and control of a secular, urban, well-educated, francophone middle-class élite. Furthermore, the neo-nationalists accurately perceived that French-Canadian leaders in the public and private sectors could use a Quebec interventionist state to wrest control over Quebec's economy from Montreal's English-speaking financial, commercial, and industrial élites.

By the late 1950s political developments proved propitious. The Quebec Liberal party, still largely controlled by the federal-oriented old guard but eager to gain access to the fruits of office after sixteen years in the political wilderness, heeded the demands of its local organizers and Montreal-based reform wing and became the political expression of neo-nationalist aspirations. The combination of liberal and nationalist reforms helped the Liberal party to defeat an unresponsive and anachronistic Union Nationale government in the June 1960 election. Little did the Liberal old guard, including the generally astute Lesage, realize how politically potent and volatile this combination of liberalism and nationalism would be.

Conclusion

At the outbreak of World War II no one could have predicted a serious challenge to the century-old ideology of traditional French-Canadian nationalism. Indeed, the depression decade had witnessed a vigorous resurgence of this type of nationalist rhetoric and activity in Quebec. Yet by the end of the 1940s traditional nationalists found themselves fighting a defensive, rearguard campaign to maintain a sympathetic hearing. Their influence was waning rapidly at every level of Quebec society. The Duplessis era, characterized as "la grande noirceur," had sown the seeds of its own demise. Challenging traditional nationalism for hegemony were two ideological forces, liberalism and neo-nationalism. A direct outgrowth of the rapidly advancing secularization and modernization of Quebec society, liberalism reemerged in the forties and fifties to contest what its spokesmen termed the state-of-seige, *ancien régime* ethos of traditional nationalism. Proponents of liberalism were members of the rising, urban-centred middle class, a class which included liberal-minded members of the traditional professions but found its driving force in the new professions of science, social science, and administration. Moreover, this renewed liberalism also attracted a number of working-class leaders. It was this fact which expanded its social and economic base and, of course, gave the ideology its political potential. Worker attitudes were moulded by an increasingly militant labour movement dominated by members of the new middle class, progress-oriented technocratic liberals, and social democrats.

The second challenge to traditional nationalism came from within its own social and intellectual confines. Spurred into action by the rapid socioeconomic evolution of Quebec and the emergence of a "new federalism," a younger generation of well-educated, urban-oriented French-Canadian nationalists increasingly questioned the basic tenets of the old nationalism, finding them deficient and ineffectual. They then set themselves the challenging task of redefining those tenets, forging in the process a new nationalism which better reflected and, in fact, reinforced the socioeconomic aspirations and needs of a modern, urban-industrial, francophone society. In the short run, they also succeeded in obfuscating the reality that neo-nationalism's main beneficiary would be the new francophone middle class. In doing so, they managed to enlarge considerably their social base, thereby accentuating the political strength and influence of neo-nationalism. By the late fifties, neo-nationalist reforms and socioeconomic aspirations were being expressed by the francophone labour movement, by francophone teachers' federations, by the growing cooperative movements, by social service agencies, by municipal administrations, and, even if to a lesser extent, by the francophone business community led by the aggressive Chambre de Commerce de Montréal.

In their quest for the support and allegiance of Quebec's citizens the respective spokesmen for liberalism and neo-nationalism offered two distinct sociopolitical models. The *Cité libre* envisaged by Citélibristes entailed a sociopsychological revolution of significant proportions which would break the existing traditions and behaviour patterns of French-Canadian society. Their "revolution of mentalities" entailed a complete separation of church and state and the secularization of all temporal functions, including primarily, social services and education. The Catholic church would no longer function as a powerful public institution determining and carrying out policy in the secular realm. The cancer of clericalism would be eradicated from Quebec society as the power and prestige of the clerical leaders subsided and their position was assumed by a new secular middle class better equipped, psychologically and intellectually, to fulfil the needs and aspirations of the québécois. This "revolution of mentalities" also called for the abandonment of nationalist preoccupations and the pursuit of both the liberal objective of full and effective equality of opportunity for each and every individual and the social democratic goal of ever-increasing equality of conditions for all classes. It is in the light of these goals that the Citélibristes became ardent advocates of a secular, interventionist state, a state capable of regulating, and when necessary controlling the development of Quebec's economy to ensure an equitable distribution of its enormous assets. A modern state would also encourage the organization of the fourth estate and enable increased working-class participation in the economy through the implementation of industrial democracy. Instrumental in this "revolution of mentalities" and the cornerstone of a dynamic *cité libre* was the creation of a universally accessible, secular, state-funded educational system at all levels.

The achievement of these liberal and social democratic aspirations and the implementation of a *cité libre* could be successful, contended Citélibristes, only if Quebec's political culture, institutions, and governmental processes were thoroughly democratic in spirit and practice. Only a healthy and vigorous parliamentary democracy would make possible the creation of a powerful interventionist state while, at the same time, protecting the full range of individual "civil liberties," political, economic, legal, and egalitarian. Since the Citélibristes' objectives were liberal and, to a lesser degree, social democratic, they did not consider constitutional reform necessary. On the contrary, what was necessary was Ottawa's respect for the inherently democratic form of federalism embodied in the existing constitution. Quebec and the other provinces had sufficient constitutional powers to accomplish all of the required socioeconomic reforms and programs. It was necessary first, however, to defeat the Union Nationale and put into power a political movement committed to *démocratie d'abord* and the comprehensive reform of French-Canadian attitudes and institutions. The "new" Quebec would be progressive, liberal, democratic, and dedicated, above all, to the development of all individuals and classes. It would not be the political instrument of any specific national collectivity or social class but would serve the common interests and aspirations of all its citizens. Citélibristes were convinced that French Canadians could best retain their culture and language by pursuing, with the help of a modern state, their own individual socioeconomic and cultural interests. The end result would be the emergence of a modern, urban-industrial francophone society – a society progressive and dynamic enough to integrate and assimilate the best features of other cultures as well as contributing in all fields of endeavour to Canadian society as a whole and to the international scene.

It was in the pursuit of their political objective that the Citélibristes failed. Their call for "l'union des forces démocratiques" was ill-conceived and rested on the false assumption that parliamentary democracy was virtually nonfunctioning in Quebec. They should have swallowed the intellectual and personal inhibitions which separated them from Quebec's official Liberal party and should have helped its struggling reform wing modernize the party's policies and internal operations. They chose not to do so, thereby encouraging the conversion of the Liberal party's reform wing to the cause of neo-nationalism. As a result, liberal and social democratic interests and aspirations fell, by default, to the weak and ineffectual Parti Social Démocratique. Citélibristes also failed, in the 1950s, to perceive the need to break the increasingly exclusive identification of the federal government with the needs and aspirations of English-speaking Canadians. An increasingly interventionist federal government had to be perceived by French Canadians as willing and capable of promoting the development of French-Canadian society and the French language. The best place to start was in its own backyard. French Canadians had to be made welcome in all federal institutions and departments and those agencies had to serve francophones in their maternal language. Overly preoccupied with internal Quebec developments, the Citélibristes found little time to devote to the pursuit of liberal objectives at the federal level. Ironically, it would take a neo-nationalist, André Laurendeau, to turn Citélibristes in that direction in the early sixties.

The "new" Quebec championed by the neo-nationalists, while similar in some features to that proposed by the Citélibristes, was fundamentally quite different. They encouraged and supported the increased secularization and democratization demanded of a modern urban-industrial social order. What they then proceeded to elaborate was a set of reform policies which would guarantee increased francophone control over modern Quebec. The secular, interventionist state called for by the neo-nationalists would evolve into a nationalist state devoted to the socioeconomic, cultural, and political aspirations of Quebec's francophone majority. Quebec City, dominated by an aggressive, well-educated, bureaucratic middle class, would become identified increasingly as the capital of the "Québécois" nation.

The largest social class in modern Quebec was the working class. Determined that this class would remain francophone in language and culture, the neo-nationalists became strong advocates of a better deal for the fourth estate. They supported the cause of organized labour and its struggle for industrial democracy as measures good and necessary in themselves. Yet they viewed these measures primarily as a means to overcome the long-standing economic inferiority of French Canadians as individuals and as a collectivity. The modernization and secularization of education at all levels would undoubtedly improve equality of opportunity for working-class francophones but the neo-nationalists' prime concern was the creation of well-educated, secular, francophone élites in the education, administrative, industrial, and scientific fields. To ensure comprehensive political control of Quebec society by this emerging francophone middle class and entrench constitutionally the "special role" of Quebec as the political tool of the French-Canadian nation, the neo-nationalists became ardent advocates of constitutional reform. Quebec, they argued, with the support of the nationalistic Tremblay commissioners, must be granted full control over all three major direct taxes (personal, corporate, and estate) and the full range of social security programs.

Neo-nationalists did not foresee the development of a social democratic society in Quebec. For them, the province's economy should evolve into a mixed economy with an increasingly francophone-dominated private sector working in cooperation with an interventionist state. Moreover, class relationships would continue unaltered except that the new francophone middle class would displace the traditional clerical and professional class as the dominant sociopolitical force, and would challenge the anglophone industrial and financial bourgeoisie for an increasingly larger share of economic power. The quickest and surest way of achieving their concomitant class and nationalist objectives was to defeat the Union Nationale. This could be achieved via a political party devoted to neo-nationalist objectives, a party led by a francophone middle-class élite which stood to gain from this identification of class and nationalist interests. The Quebec Liberal party, eager to regain access to the spoils of office, succumbed to the pressures of its nationalist reform wing and a youthful generation of regional delegates. It became the political expression of neo-nationalist aspirations, the harbinger of the Quiet Revolution. The gamble paid off. Neo-nationalists awoke on the morrow of the 22 June 1960 provincial election more confident and aggressive than ever about implementing their wide-ranging socio-economic and political reforms. The "quiet revolution" of ideologies and mentalities, under way since the war, was about to enter a new phase. The "not-so-quiet revolution" of the sixties and seventies was beginning. The challenge of execution of new ideas and programs lay ahead. No one was willing or able to predict the outcome, although many of the neo-nationalists like Laurendeau, Filion, Laporte, and Tremblay were, or would be, in an excellent position to influence the course of events. As for the Citélibristes, by the mid-1960s they would be ready to seek a countervailing force in the federal government.

Notes

ABBREVIATIONS

AE	*Actualité économique*
AN	*Action nationale*
Bulletin	*Bulletin de la Fédération des colleges classiques*
CHR	*Canadian Historical Review*
CJEPS	*Canadian Journal of Economics and Political Science*
ES	*Enseignement secondaire au Canada*
JCS/REC	*Journal of Canadian Studies/Revue d'études canadienne*
QQ	*Queen's Quarterly*
RHAF	*Revue de l'histoire de l'Amérique française*
RS	*Recherches sociographiques*

CHAPTER ONE

1 Jean-Charles Falardeau, "Le Québec n'est plus un passé mais un avenir," *Revue de l'Institut de sociologie* 1 (1968): 73.

2 Fernand Dumont, "Les années 30: La première révolution tranquille," in F. Dumont et al., *Idéologies au Canada français 1930–1939*, 1–20.

3 Jean Hamelin and Jean-Paul Montminy, "La mutation de la société québécoise, 1939–1976, temps, ruptures, continuités," in F. Dumont et al., *Idéologies au Canada français 1940–1976*, table 1:68.

4 See André Raynauld, *Croissance et structures économiques de la province du Québec.*

5 Gilles Lebel, *Horizon 1980*, table 8-1, 161, 170. Value of production grew at an average annual rate of 4.2 per cent from $68 to $356 million between 1946 and

1966, whereas employment in the primary sector declined at a rate of 3.7 per cent annually from 367,650 to 168,394 jobs during these two decades.

6 Cf. Maurice Saint-Germain, *Une économie à libérer: Le Québec analysé dans ses structures économiques.*

7 See Everett Hughes, *French Canada in Transition,* chap. 7; and Philippe Garigue, "Une enquête sur l'industrialization de la province de Québec: Schefferville," *AE* 33 (octobre-décembre 1957): 419–36.

8 Roland Parenteau, "The Impact of Industrialization in Quebec," in *The Canadian Economy,* ed. J. Deutsch, 511–12; Mario Dumas, "L'evolution économique de Québec, 1940–1965," in *Economie québécoise,* ed. Robert Commeau, 226.

9 Lebel, *Horizon 1980,* 161–85.

10 Albert Faucher and Maurice Lamontagne, "History of Industrial Development," in *Essais sur le Québec contemporain,* ed. Jean-Charles Falardeau, 24–30; P. Harvey, "The Economy of Quebec," *University of Toronto Quarterly* 27 (April 1958): 333, 336–7.

11 Raynauld, *Croissance et structures économiques,* 97; Lebel, *Horizon 1980,* 195, 198; Saint-Germain, *Une économie à libérer,* 88–90.

12 Lebel, *Horizon, 1980,* 161, 199–208. Employment in tertiary activity rose from 507,975 to 1,147,473 and total value of production climbed from $1.1 to $6.5 million between 1946 and 1966.

13 F.P. Dagenais, "Le mythe de la vocation agricole du Québec," in *Mélanges géographiques canadiens offerts à Raoul Blanchard* (Québec: Presses du l'Université Laval 1959).

14 Nathan Keyfitz, "Population Problems," in *Essais sur le Québec contemporain,* ed. Falardeau, 68–72.

15 The number of tractors rose from 5,869 in 1941 to 70,697 in 1961, enabling farm proprietors to carry on with less manual labour while at the same time increasing the acreage under cultivation. Average acreage of farms rose from 117 acres to 148 acres between 1941 and 1961. *Census of Canada 1971,* 4.2, tables 2 and 7.

16 Nathan Keyfitz, "L'exode rural dans la province de Québec, 1951–1961," *RS* 3 (1962): 303–16.

17 Gérard Fortin, "Socio-cultural Changes in an Agricultural Parish," in *French-Canadian Society,* ed. Marcel Rioux and Yves Martin, 86–107.

18 John Irwin Cooper, *Montreal: A Brief History,* 117–78; Norbert Lacoste, "Les traits nouveaux de la population du Grand Montréal," *RS* (septembre-décembre 1964): 270–1. By 1961 the ethnic composition of Montreal Island was 62 per cent French, 18 per cent British, 6 per cent Italian, 4 per cent Jewish, and 10 per cent other.

19 Jacques Brazeau, "Les nouvelles classes moyennes," *RS* 7 (janvier-août 1966): 154.

20 Ibid., 155; Hubert Guindon, "The Social Evolution of Quebec Reconsidered,"

CJEPS 26 (November 1960): 544. He wrote in part: "The bourgeoisie was clerically created and the avenues of social promotion were clerically controlled; the clergy taught not only religion and profane science, but also manners – bourgois manners, a style of life very different from one's family."

21 Jacques Brazeau, "Quebec's Emerging Middle Class," in *French-Canadian Society*, 322.

22 *Report of the Royal Commission on Bilingualism and Biculturalism* (Ottawa 1970), 3b: 447-69. Cf. Jacques Dofny and Marcel Rioux, "Social Class in French Canada," in *French-Canadian Society*, 312-16.

23 Claude Ryan, "Une classe oubliée," *AN* 25 (février 1950): 93-110; "Les classes moyennes au Canada français," *AN* 25 (mars 1950): 207-28; 25 (avril 1950): 266-73. Jean-Charles Falardeau, "The Changing Social Structures," in *Essais sur le Québec contemporain*, 116-18.

24 See Frederick Elkin, *Rebels and Colleagues: Advertising and Social Change in French Canada*.

25 Hubert Guindon, "Social Unrest, Social Class and Quebec's Bureaucratic Revolution," *QQ* 71 (Summer 1964): 153.

26 Dorval Brunelle, "La structure occupationnelle de la main d'oeuvre québécoise 1951-1971," *Sociologie et sociétés* 7 (novembre 1975): 67-88. Applying a functional definition of occupation, Brunelle demonstrates that the vast majority of white-collar occupations created by industrial and post-industrial capitalism have to be classified in the manual labour category. In short, a process of proletarization of middle-class occupations is well advanced in Quebec.

27 Philippe Garigue, "Organisation sociale et valeurs culturelles canadiennes-françaises," *CJEPS* 33 (May 1962): 197-8, 201.

28 Guindon, "The Social Evolution of Quebec Reconsidered," 546-51 (quote 546-7); idem, "Social Unrest, Social Class and Quebec's Bureaucratic Revolution," 150-4.

29 Brazeau, "Quebec's Emerging Middle Class," 323-7.

30 Brazeau, "Les nouvelles classes moyennes," 157.

CHAPTER TWO

1 Jean-Paul Montminy et Jean Hamelin, "La Crise," in Fernand Dumont et al., *Idéologies au Canada français 1930-1939*, 25.

2 Dumont, "Les années 30: La première révolution tranquille," in *Idéologies au Canada français*, 1-20.

3 François Hertel, *Pour un ordre personnaliste*. Several chapters of the book first appeared as articles in *L'Action nationale*, 1937-8; an overview of these developments can be found in André-J. Bélanger, *Ruptures et constantes*, chap. 1, "Les idéologies pionnières: La Relève et la *JES*," 15-61.

4 Michael D. Behiels, "The Bloc Populaire Canadien and the Origins of French-Canadian Neo-nationalism, 1942-8," *CHR* 50 (December 1982): 487-91.

5 Filion, "La démission de M. Laurendeau," *Devoir*, 9 juil. 1947; Behiels, "The Bloc Populaire Canadien and the Origins of French-Canadian Neo-nationalism," 509–12.

6 Ken Johnstone, "Who'll *Le Devoir* Battle Next?" *Maclean's Magazine*, 14 April 1956, 95.

7 Ibid., 94–5; *Biographies canadiennes-françaises* (Montréal: n.p. 1965), 521. Interview with Gérard Filion, 4 Sept. 1976. Filion indicated that he had accepted the position of director on condition that he was able to hire André Laurendeau as his associate editor-in-chief.

8 See his *The True Face of Duplessis*. Laporte was the only staff member of *Le Devoir* to carry his distaste for the Duplessis regime to the point of running as an independent Liberal candidate in 1956 and 1960.

9 "Le moindre mal," *Devoir*, 8 nov. 1947.

10 Filion, "Nous tiendrons de coup," *Devoir*, 30 jan. 1956. In 1952, 1956, and 1959 *Le Devoir* had a registered circulation of 19,053, 25,586 and 31,966 respectively *'52, '56, '59 Ayer Directory of Publications* (Bala Cynwyd, Pa.: Ayer Press 1952, 1956, 1959).

11 Filion, "Positions VIII–Comme journal catholique," *Devoir*, 22 avril 1947. In the 1955 subscription campaign organized by *Les Amis du Devoir*, 1,150 clerics contributed nearly $15,000 of the $63,000 collected. See Louis O'Neill, "Pourquoi le clergé soutient-il *Le Devoir?*" *Ad Usum Sacerdotum* 10 (février 1955): 76–9.

12 "C'est la loi de l'amitié qui explique l'étonnante durée du *Devoir*," *Devoir*, 1 fév. 1960.

13 "Position I," *Devoir*, 12 avril 1947.

14 Ramsay Cook and Michael D. Behiels, *The Essential Laurendeau*, 6–7.

15 Laurendeau, "Le nationalisme s'enracinera-t-il mieux qu'en 1936?" *Le Magazine Maclean*, janvier 1962, 3.

16 "Manifeste des Jeune-Canada," *Devoir*, 17 et 20 déc. 1932, in *The Essential Laurendeau*, 34–6.

17 André-J. Bélanger, *L'apolitisme des idéologies québécoises: Le grand tournant de 1934–36*, 257–304.

18 Robert Rumilly, *Henri Bourassa: La vie publique d'un grand Canadien* (Montréal: Les Editions Chantecler, 1953), 741. Bourassa made these charges during three conferences at the Palestre Nationale in April and May of 1935.

19 André Laurendeau, *Notre nationalisme*, 39–44 (48 quoted).

20 Ibid., 35.

21 Ibid., 43.

22 Bélanger, *Ruptures et constantes*, 15–16.

23 Robert Charbonneau et al., "Préliminaires à un manifeste pour la patrie," *La Relève* 3 (septembre-octobre 1936): 9.

24 Bélanger, *Ruptures et constantes*, 33–5.

25 Laurendeau, "Méditation devant une carte du monde," *La Relève* 3 (septem-

bre-octobre 1936): 4–5; "Explication: A propos de Notre Nationalisme," *AN* 7 (février 1936): 120–2.

26 Laurendeau, *La crise de la conscription: 1942*, 10; "Blocs-Notes," *Devoir*, 30 nov. 1962.

27 Laurendeau, "Vocation créatrice de l'homme," *AN* 8 (septembre 1936): 5–17; "Le chrétien et le monde moderne," *AN* 8 (octobre 1936): 111–17.

28 Laurendeau, "La fécondité de l'argent, mécanisme contre nature," *AN* 9 (janvier 1937): 41.

29 Ibid., note.

30 Laurendeau, "Actualité: A propos d'une récente encyclique," *AN* 10 (novembre 1937): 181–2.

31 Ibid., 191.

32 Laurendeau, "La grève du textile," *AN* 10 (septembre 1937): 5–7. See two other articles in the same issue on the labour question, 7–12.

33 Cf. note 30 and "Introduction à la thèse de Rosenberg," *AN* 10 (septembre 1937): 14–5.

34 "Croisade antifasciste?" *AN* 11 (janvier 1938): 41–51.

35 Editorial, "La Guerre," *AN* 14 (septembre 1939): 3–10.

36 Ligue pour la défense du Canada, "Manifeste au peuple du Canada," *AN* 19 (janvier 1942): 48–50.

37 Laurendeau, "La conscription et le prétendu 'droit de veto' du Québec," *AN* 18 (décembre 1941): 258–65.

38 F.-A. Angers, "Un Vote de Race," *AN* 19 (mai 1942): 299–312.

39 Behiels, "The Bloc and the Origins of French-Canadian Neo-nationalism," 489–91.

40 Michael D. Behiels, "The Bloc Populaire Canadien: The Anatomy of Failure, 1942–48," *JCS/REC* 18 (Hiver 83–84 Winter): 45–63.

41 "The Bloc and the Origins of French-Canadian Neo-nationalism," 492–4.

42 Ibid., 497–500.

43 Ibid., 501–9.

44 "The Bloc: The Anatomy of Failure," 64–74.

45 Interview with Jean-Marc Léger, 11 June 1982; Equipe de recherches sociales, "Pour rétablir le dialogue," *Devoir*, 27 août 1949.

46 Jean-Marc Léger et al., "L'ennemi dans nos murs," *AN* 31 (février 1948): 110–11.

47 Ibid., 112.

48 Interview with Jean-Marc Léger, 11 June 1982. He is at present sous-ministre adjoint in Quebec's Ministère de l'Education.

49 Michael Behiels, "Le père Georges-Henri Lévesque et l'établissement des sciences sociales à Laval, 1938–1955," *Revue de l'Université d'Ottawa* 52 (juil.-sept. 1982): 355–76.

50 Interview with Senator Arthur Tremblay, 25 Sept. 1981.

CHAPTER THREE

1 André Laurendeau, "Y a-t-il une crise du nationalisme? II," *AN* 41 (janvier 1953): 27.

2 Laurendeau, "Y a-t-il une crise du nationalisme? I," *AN* 40 (décembre 1952): 212.

3 Laurendeau, "Y a-t-il une crise? II," 27.

4 Everett C. Hughes, *French Canada in Transition*, chapters 1 and 18; Horace Miner, *St. Denis: A French-Canadian Parish*, chapters 4 and 9.

5 Laurendeau, "Le quatrième état dans la nation," *AN* 30 (octobre 1947): 83.

6 Ibid., 84; Laurendeau, "Les logis de la misère," *AN* 30 (septembre 1947): 34.

7 Filion, "Un avertissement sévère," *Devoir*, 9 jan. 1954.

8 Laurendeau, "Canada Français 1952," *Devoir*, 16 avril 1952.

9 Laurendeau, "Questions au ministre des élections à propos de colonisation," *Devoir*, 17 jan. 1950; "Une oeuvre vitale," ibid., 7 oct. 1950.

10 Laurendeau, "Le quatrième état," 84–8.

11 Laurendeau, "Conclusions très provisoires," *AN* 31 (juin 1948): 414–16. Esdras Minville contended that industrial society was the antithesis of French-Canadian civilization. The latter was "spiritualiste, personnaliste, communautaire et qualitative," whereas the former was materialist, technical, individualistic, and quantitative. See his "Conditions de notre avenir,' in Falardeau, *Essais sur le Québec contemporain*, 232–5; and his "Les conditions de l'autonomie économique des Canadiens français," *AN* 33 (mai 1951): 268–71.

12 Claude Ryan, "L'Eglise Catholique et l'évolution spirituelle du Canada français," *Chronique sociale de France*, 65è année (15 septembre 1957): 444.

13 Laurendeau, "Le quatrième état," 89–90; Jean-Marc Léger et al., "L'ennemi dans nos murs," *AN* 31 (février 1948): 97–9; Laurendeau, "Les conditions d'existence d'une culture nationale," *AN* 37 (juin 1951): 375–8.

14 Léger, "L'ennemi dans nos murs," 100.

15 Laurendeau, "Y a-t-il une crise? I," 215–17; Esdras Minville, "Les faits économiques," *AN* 29 (mars 1947): 204–29.

16 Michel Brunet, "Les crises de conscience et la prise de conscience," *AN* 44 (mars 1955): 598–9.

17 Filion, "Un avertissement sévère," *Devoir*, 9 jan. 1954.

18 Ibid., and Laurendeau, "Y a-t-il une crise du nationalisme? II," 8; Gérard Dion et Joseph Pelchat, "Repenser le nationalisme," *AN* 31 (juin 1948): 408; Filion, "Ouvrir les voiles, mais garder le gouvernail," *Devoir* 2 juin 1954.

19 Ryan, "L'Eglise Catholique et l'évolution spirituelle du Canada français," 450–1.

20 Léger et al., "L'ennemi dans nos murs," 99–105.

21 Ibid., 107.

22 Dion et Pelchat, "Repenser le nationalisme," 408, 410–11.

23 Ryan, "Le sens du national dans les milieux populaires," *AN* 31 (mars 1948): 171–3; Robillard, "Pour un nationalisme social," *AN* 31 (avril 1948): 288.

24 Léger et al., "L'ennemi dans nos murs," 107–9; Dion et Pelchat, "Repenser le nationalisme," 408–9; Laurendeau, "Nationalisme, pas mort!" *Devoir*, 21 juin 1949.

25 Léger, "La Nation aux enchères," *AN* 37 (juin 1951): 445–6.

26 Michael D. Behiels, "L'Association catholique de la Jeunesse canadienne-française and the Quest for a Moral Regeneration, 1903–1914," *JCS/REC* 13 (Summer 1978): 27–41.

27 Gabriel Clément, *Histoire de l'Action catholique au Canada français*.

28 Laurendeau, "Y a-t-il une crise? II," 21.

29 Ibid., 20; and Léger, "Urgence d'une doctrine nationale," *AN* 32 (décembre 1948): 265.

30 Laurendeau, "Y a-t-il une crise? II," 22–5.

31 Ibid., 9.

32 Michel Brunet, "Trois dominantes de la pensée canadienne-française: L'agriculturisme, l'anti-étatisme et le messianisme," in his *La présence anglaise et les Canadiens*, 130–2.

33 Ibid., 113–66. The precise historical validity of Brunet's thesis has been challenged by William F. Ryan, *The Clergy and Economic Growth in Quebec, 1896–1914* (Québec: Les Presses de l'Université Laval 1966), and Yves Roby, *Les Québécois et les investissements américains (1918–1929)* (Québec: Les Presses de l'Université Laval 1979).

34 Ryan, "Le sens du national," 174–7; Dion et Pelchat, "Repenser le nationalisme," 409–10; Léger et al., "L'ennemi dans nos murs," 110–11.

35 Laurendeau, "Conclusions très provisoires," 420.

36 Ibid., 420–4; Laurendeau, "Pour continuer la lutte," *Devoir*, 9 sept. 1947; and "Y a-t-il une crise? II," 12–14. What Laurendeau failed to mention was the fact that the socioeconomic reforms elaborated by the traditional nationalists were always very conservative in intent and were impregnated with a religious rather than a secular view of Quebec society.

37 Laurendeau, "Y a-t-il une crise? II," 7, 10. He gives credit to the four-volume series of studies directed by Esdras Minville, *Etudes sur notre milieu* (Montréal: Fides 1942–5), to the American sociologist E.C. Hughes, *French Canada in Transition*, and to two Quebec novelists, Roger Lemelin, in *Au pied de la pente douce*, and Gabrielle Roy, in *Bonheur d'occasion*, for driving home an awareness of the industrial reality and future of the French-Canadian people.

38 Léger, "Le Canada français à la recherche de son avenir," *Esprit* 20 (septembre 1952): 261.

39 Filion, "Un avertissement sévère," *Devoir*, 9 jan. 1954; and "Ouvrir les voiles," ibid., 2 juin 1954.

40 Laurendeau, "Canada français vue de Londres, 1952," *Devoir*, 16 avril 1952.

41 Fondation Lionel Groulx, Fonds André Laurendeau, "Ce que nous sommes," speech given at Chicoutimi in 1945 to celebrate the Dollard des Ormeaux holiday.

42 Léger, "Mesure de notre nationalisme," *AN* 39 (juin-juillet 1952): 348.

43 *L'Action nationale*'s entire October 1948 issue was devoted to the task of showing that democratically minded French Canadians and English Canadians should work towards the objective of creating a republican form of government in Canada as quickly as possible. See also Laurendeau, "La république c'est l'avenir," *Devoir*, 21 déc. 1948.

44 Léger, "Mesure de notre nationalisme," 348; Léger, "Le nationalisme à l'heure de la révolution, *AN* 42 (septembre 1953): 13.

45 Léger, "Urgence d'une doctrine nationale," 267.

46 Laurendeau, "En guise de préface," *AN* 32 (septembre 1948): 8.

47 Léger, "Etapes de la révolution politique," *AN* 37 (janvier 1951): 61–2; "Le temps de l'impatience," ibid., 38 (septembre 1951): 60–9; "Une révolution silencieuse," ibid., 39 (mai 1952): 300–8; and "Dimensions de la liberté Canada français," *Revue socialiste* 3 (hiver 1959–60): 1–6.

48 Léger, "Urgence d'une doctrine nationale," *AN* 32 (décembre 1948): 268.

49 Ibid., 271; and Léger, "La nation aux enchères," 447–8.

50 Dion et Pelchat, "Repenser le nationalisme," 411–12; Equipe de recherches sociales, "Pour établir le dialogue," *Devoir*, 27 août 1949; Laurendeau, "En guise de préface," 9; Filion, 'Vous avez changé," *Devoir*, 3 sept. 1949; Jacques Perrault, "La révolution sociale devant l'autonomie nationale," ibid., 11 déc. 1948.

51 The most accessible expression of the *Cité libre* viewpoint is Trudeau's lengthy introduction, "La province de Québec au moment de la grève," in P.E. Trudeau, ed., *La grève de l'amiante*, 1–91.

52 Laurendeau, "Québec joue son role de capitale nationale du Canada français," *Le Magazine Maclean*, novembre 1961, 3; "Humanisme et Patrie," *AN* 44 (janvier 1953): 3; Léger, "Le Canada français à la recherche de son avenir," 278.

53 Laurendeau, "Humanisme et Patrie," 3–4; "Nationalisme et progrès social," *AN* 45 (janvier 1955): 433.

54 Laurendeau, "Y a-t-il une crise? I," 305; Léger, "Le Canada français à la recherche de son avenir," 277.

55 Léger, "Mesure de notre nationalisme," 351.

56 For a confirmation of this claim see J.I. Gow, "Les Québécois, la guerre et la paix 1945–1960," in Jean-Yves Gravel, *Le Québec et la guerre*, 133–67.

57 Laurendeau, "Humanisme et Patrie," 4–5. For a similar viewpoint see Pierre de Grandpré, "Le social et le national," *AN* 46 (octobre 1956): 137–8, and his "Cette 'droite' et cette 'gauche', I" ibid. (novembre 1956): 245.

58 Laurendeau, "Blocs-Notes," *Devoir*, 7 avril 1959; Léger, "Mesure de notre nationalisme," 348–52.

59 Léger, "Une trahison à combattre; une imposture à dénoncer," *AN* 45 (juin 1956): 934–5.

60 Grandpré, "Les Canadiens français et la France," 486.

61 Grandpré, "Cette crise de la conscience intellectuelle," *AN* 45 (mars 1956): 639–43.

62 Grandpré, "Les Canadiens français et la France," 486; "Le social et le national," 139–40.

63 Ibid., "Les Canadiens français et la France," 487.

64 Robert Rumilly, *L'infiltration gauchiste au Canada français*, 10–29. For Rumilly's assessment of the Duplessis regime see his *Quinze années de réalisations* (Montréal 1956).

65 *L'infiltration gauchiste*, 146.

66 Jean Marcel Deslauriers, "Nos nouveaux maitres," *Tradition et progrès* 1 (mars 1957): 7–16.

67 See various issues of *Laurentie* and André d'Allemagne, *Le RIN et les débuts du mouvement indépendantiste québécois* (Montréal: Editions Etincelle 1974), 19–22, 137.

68 L'Action nationale, "Repenser vos problèmes," *AN* 45 (mars 1956): 573–7.

69 "Une trahison à combattre; une imposture à dénoncer," 939–40.

70 See Raymond Barbeau, "Gauchisme, une forme de nationalisme?" *Tradition et progrès* 1 (mars 1957): 29–33.

71 Vanier, "Aller à gauche et à droite," *AN* 46 (octobre 1956): 121–5.

72 Rumilly, *L'infiltration gauchiste*, 56–72; for his condemnation of these French periodicals see chap. 1.

73 Ibid., 79–86. See also Barbeau, "Gauchisme, une forme de nationalisme?" 24–5. Of the neo-nationalists he states in part: "Ont-ils des liens intellectuels, moraux ou politiques avec les descendants de Jaurès, de Blum, de Trotsky, de Marc Sangnier, de J. Foliet, suivent-ils aveuglement Mendès-France, le P. Bigo, les Encyclopédistes, Teilhard de Chardin, Loisy, les crypto-de-toutes-couleurs, les démo-tout-ce-qu'on voudra, les Mounier, les Béguin."

74 Léopold Richer, "J'ai repris ma liberté," *Notre Temps*, septembre 1956, quoted in Grandpré, "Le social et le nationale," 139; Rumilly, *L'infiltration gauchiste*, 114–15; and Albert Roy, "Droite vs Gauche," *Tradition et progrès* 1 (mars 1957): 21.

75 Barbeau, "Gauchisme, une forme de nationalisme?" 28.

76 Ibid., 34–5.

77 Jean Deslaurier, "Le Dialogue Nationaliste," *Tradition et progrès* 1 (juin-juillet-août 1957): 7–8.

78 Ibid., 13–14.

79 Ibid., 12–13.

80 Le Comité d'études, "Principes de libération nationale," *Tradition et progrés* 3 (été 1960): 7–10.

CHAPTER FOUR

1 Maurice Blain, "Sur la liberté de l'esprit," *Esprit* 20 (août-septembre 1952): 212.

2 Ibid., 203.

3 John D. Harbron, *This Is Trudeau*, 51. Interview with Charles Lussier, 8 Sept. 1976. He recalls that it proved difficult to sell all the five hundred issues priced at fifty cents each.

4 Edith Iglauer, "Prime Minister Pierre Trudeau," *New Yorker* (5 July 1969): 38; Harbron, *This Is Trudeau*, 10-14; Gérard Pelletier, "Introduction," in *Réponses de Pierre Elliott Trudeau* (Montréal: Editions du Jour 1968): 13-15; for Trudeau's love of the environment see an extract from his "L'Ascetisme en canot," cited in Ramsay Cook, *The Maple Leaf Forver*, 39-40.

5 Iglauer, "Trudeau," 39-40; Richard Gwyn, *The Northern Magus: Pierre Trudeau and Canadians* (Toronto 1980), 32-4, 52.

6 François Hertel, "Lettre à mes amis (15 août 1950, Paris, France)," *Cité libre* 2 (février 1951): 34-5.

7 Harbron, *This Is Trudeau*, 20.

8 Cook, *The Maple Leaf Forever*, 31.

9 Iglauer, "Trudeau," 41; Gérard Pelletier, "Introduction," 17-18. For a colourful account of his 1960 trip to China with Jacques Hébert see their *Deux innocents en Chine* (Montréal: Les Editions de l'Homme 1961).

10 Cited in Iglauer, "Trudeau," 44.

11 *Canadian Parliamentary Guide* (Ottawa: Queen's Printer 1974).

12 "Entretien avec Gérard Pelletier," *Liberté* 7 (mai-juin 1965): 222; and Adéle Lauzon, "Gérard Pelletier: Des ennemis à la douzaine," *Le Magazine Maclean*, novembre 1964, 24.

13 Cf. Gabriel Clément, *Histoire de l'Action catholique au Canada français*, bk. 2, chap. 2, "Une cité étudiante (1942-1949)."

14 Lauzon, "Gérard Pelletier," 24.

15 Pelletier, "Le Manifeste des Jeunes-Québec," *Devoir*, 10 jan. 1948; "Scruples ou inertie," ibid., 31 jan. 1948; "Syndicats et sections de jeunesses," ibid., 21 fév. 1948; "Deux ages deux manières," ibid., 25 sept. 1948; "Notre réponse aux surréalistes," ibid., 13 nov. 1948.

16 Interview with Charles Lussier, 8 sept. 1976. He recalls how Duplessis pressured the president of the union of tramway workers to drop Charles Lussier as its counsel and appoint another lawyer more favourable to the Union Nationale. Duplessis simply refused to see lawyers, in or outside the legislature, who were associated with the CCF.

17 Gérard Pelletier, " '*Cité libre*' confesse ses intentions," *Cité libre* 2 (février 1951): 7-8.

18 M. Charest, "Le pain du jour: Réginald Boisvert décrit le grisaille d'une petite ville ouvrière," *Le Magazine Maclean*, mars 1964, 41.

19 Harbron, *This Is Trudeau*, 50–1. A good selection of Maurice Blain's essays can be found in his *Approximations* (Montréal: HMH, 1967).

20 André Major, "Pierre Vadeboncoeur: Un socialiste de condition bourgeoise," *Le Magazine Maclean*, juin 1972, 20–1.

21 Interview with Charles Lussier, 8 Sept. 1976. Pelletier, "Matines," *Cité libre* 21 (juillet 1958): 3; La rédaction, "Règle du jeu," ibid. 1 (juin 1950): 1–2. Pelletier believed strongly that the depression experience had created two distinct groups within his generation. One group, deeply impressed by the spectacle of poverty and suffering, found careers in the social sciences, labour unions, or journalism and developed a strong consciousness of their social responsibilities. The second group, determined never to go hungry again, sought security in wealth at the cost of becoming heartless exploiters of the rest of society. "Entretien avec Gérard Pelletier," 258.

22 For a thorough discussion of personalism and its influence on French Canada in the 1930s see Michael K. Oliver, "The Social and Political Ideas of French Canadian Nationalists, 1920–1945," (PHD diss., McGill University, Montreal, 1956), chap. 5. See also Bélanger, *Ruptures et constantes*, chap. 1, "Les idéologies pionnières, la Relève et la JEC."

23 Gérard Pelletier, "La responsabilité laique: mythe ou réalité," *Cahiers de l'Action catholique* 44 (avril 1944): 350.

24 Interviews with Charles Lussier, 8 Sept. 1976 and Léon Dion, 1 Sept. 1976. Dion remarked that *Cité libre*'s emphasis on personalism accounted for his lukewarm attitude toward the group.

25 Interview with Jean-Charles Falardeau, 1 Sept. 1976. An attempt in 1957–8 to set up a Quebec editorial team failed for lack of support in the city.

26 Pelletier, " '*Cité libre*' confesse," 5.

27 Trudeau, "Politique fonctionnelle I," *Cité libre* 1 (juin 1950): 21.

28 Réginald Boisvert, "Domiciles de la peur sociale, *Cité libre* 1 (juin 1950): 19.

29 La rédaction, "Règle du jeu," 3; for Pelletier's high estimation of Mounier see "Entretien avec Gérard Pelletier," 250.

30 " '*Cité libre*' confesse," 5.

31 Léon Dion, *Quebec: The Unfinished Revolution*, 127.

32 Interview with Charles Lussier, 8 Sept. 1976, and Jean-Charles Falardeau, 1 Sept. 1976.

33 Roger Rolland, " 'Projections libérantes'," *Cité libre* 2 (février 1951): 33.

34 Cf. Nive Voisine, et al., *Histoire de l'Eglise catholique au Québec, 1608–1970*, chapters 3 and 4; Jacques Grand'Maison, *Nationalisme et religion* (Montréal: Beauchemin 1970), 34–8; and Pierre Maheu, "Le pouvoir clérical," in *Les québécois* (Montréal: Parti Pris 1971), 171–90.

35 Jean Le Moyne, "L'atmosphère religieuse au Canada français," *Cité libre* 12 (mai 1955): 1–2.

36 Maurice Blain, "Sur la liberté de l'esprit," *Esprit* 20 (août-septembre 1952): 210–11.

37 Pelletier, " '*Cité libre*' confesse," 3; and "Histoires de collégiens qui ont

aujourd'hui trente ans," *Cité libre* 1 (juin 1950): 5–6.

38 Ibid.

39 Ibid., 8–9; see also Jean-Guy Blain, "Inquiétude et tradition," *Esprit* (août-septembre 1952): 244.

40 Le Moyne, "L'atmosphère religieuse," 11. Of his early religious experience he wrote: "Mon experience de la vie religieuse ambiante se borne à ce qu'il fallait absolument ou recevoir ou subir. Sans aucune participation à quoi que ce fût de surégatoire, j'ai reçu la foi, j'ai subi le reste, et, sauf à de très rares exceptions, la curiosité des choses de la foi m'est venue d'ailleurs, premièrement d'un père qui interrogeait la Bible avec angoisse et qui m'avait pas, bien entendu, appris à l'interroger ici" (9).

41 Ibid., 11–12.

42 Voisine, *Histoire de l'Eglise catholique*, 75–7. Of this experience Pelletier writes: "Puis entrés dans le movement de rénovation, convainçus qu'il faillait parer aux catastrophes imminentes, ils se sont heurté la tête aux vieilles solives à demi pourrisantes mais dures encore suffisamment pour contusionner bien des fronts." " 'Cité Libre' confesse," 4.

43 Maurice Blain, "Sur la liberté," 213.

44 Le Moyne, "L'atmosphère religieuse," 3; Trudeau, "La province de Québec au moment de la grève," in *La grève de l'amiante*, ed. Trudeau (Montréal, 2nd ed., 1970), 58–9; Maurice Blain, "Sur la liberté," 208–9.

45 Le Moyne, "L'atmosphère religieuse," 3; Cf. Maurice Tremblay, "La pensée sociale au Québec," manuscript, 1950, cited in Marcel Rioux, "Sur l'évolution des idéologies au Québec," *Revue de l'Institut de sociologie* 1 (1968): 114. Tremblay writes: "L'Eglise est sans doute parvenue par cette attitude de défense farouche à l'égard des influences protestantes et à l'égard du modernisme français, à maintenir la culture canadienne-française intégralement catholique; malheureusement, il faut avouer que ça a été, dans une large mesure, au prix d'un dogmatisme étroit et stérilisant et d'un autoritarisme figé dans le conservatisme. Ce catholicisme canadien français nous apparaît en effet, dans l'ensemble, comme un catholicisme de conserve, à l'arrière-garde des transformations radicales que l'évolution du monde exige de la chrétienté."

46 Pelletier, "D'un prolétariat spirituel," *Esprit* 20 (août-septembre 1952): 192–3; Jean-Guy Blain, "Inquiétude et tradition," ibid., 242.

47 Trudeau, "Matériaux pour servir à une enquête sur le cléricalisme," *Cité libre* 7 (mai 1953): 30.

48 Maurice Blain, "Sur la liberté," 208, 211.

49 Pelletier, "Dialogue avec un suicide," *Cité libre* 11 (février 1955): 1–10. Cf. Jean-Guy Blain, "Inquiétude et tradition," 243.

50 Pelletier, "Dialogue," 7.

51 Le Moyne, "L'atmosphère religieuse," 7–11; Robert Elie, "Réflexions sur le dialogue," *Cité libre* 3 (mai 1951): 34; Ernest Gagnon, "Visage de l'intelligence," 236–7.

52 Cf. Voisine, *Histoire de l'Eglise catholique*, 74. In 1955 the province of Quebec had 8,000 Catholic priests (one per 500), 40,000 nuns, 10,000 brothers, and over 10,000 laymen fulfilling various administrative functions in over 2,000 parishes.

53 Pelletier, "Crise d'autorité or crise de liberté," *Cité libre* 5 (juin-juillet 1952): 6–7.

54 Rolland, "Matériaux pour servir à une enquête sur le cléricalisme II," *Cité libre* 7 (mai 1953): 38–9.

55 P.E. Trudeau, "'Je reviens de Moscou'," *Devoir*, 14 and 21 juin 1952. Trudeau got back at Father Braüm when he noted that on 3 March 1955 the Soviet officials had expelled an American Assumptionist priest from the Soviet Union for spying on behalf of the United States consulate in Moscow. "Les deux mesures," *Cité libre* 12 (mai 1955): 44–5.

56 Trudeau, "Matériaux pour servir à une enquête I," 33–4. Of these three figures he wrote: "De la sorte, des gardiens de la lumière au Québec accumulent dénonciations et diffamations, au nom du catholicisme (le leur, évidemment), mais au plus grand profit de l'Union Nationale, du capitalisme international et du tous les intérêts qui s'inscrivent en marge de l'histoire. Ils veulent faire du Québec le dernier bastion du cléricalisme et de la réaction politique, une terre de refuge où puissent échouer toutes les épaves idéologiques que charrie l'histoire" (35–6).

57 Pierre Dansereau, "Lettre à un séminariste sur l'aliénation des intellectuels," *Cité libre* 32 (décembre 1960): 16.

58 Le Moyne, "L'atmosphère religieuse," 4.

59 "Lettre à un séminariste," 15.

60 The Citélibristes acknowledged the strong influence of Emmanuel Mounier, the editor of *Esprit*, and had proposed sending him a copy of the first issue. Unfortunately, to their deepest regret, Mounier passed away before its publication. Cf. "Faites vos jeux," *Cité libre* 1 (juin 1950): 37; and Pelletier, "Trois paroles d'Emmanuel Mounier," ibid., 3 (mai 1951): 45–6.

61 Le Moyne, "Jeunesse de l'homme," *Cité libre* 2 (février 1951): 10, 11–12.

62 Jacques Maritain, *Humanisme intégral* (Paris: Editions Montaigne 1936), 126–41.

63 Pierre Vadeboncoeur, "Réflexions sur la foi," *Cité libre* 12 (mai 1955): 21.

64 Boisvert, "Foi Chrétienne et mission temporelle," *Cité libre* 13 (novembre 1955): 1–8; J.-G. Blain, "Inquiétude et tradition," 245.

65 Pius XII, "Discours du 21 février 1946," cited in Trudeau, "Matériaux pour servir à une enquête I," 31.

66 Rolland, "Matériaux pour servir à une enquête II" *Cité libre* 7 (mai 1953): 41.

67 Pelletier, "Faites vos jeux," *Cité libre* 3 (mai 1951): 44–5.

68 Pelletier, "Crise d'autorité," 1–3; "D'un prolétariat spirituel," 197–8.

69 "Réflexions sur le dialogue,' 31; Louis O'Neill, "La vraie liberté des laïcs dans le domaine intellectuelle," *Ad Usum Sacerdotum* 10 (juillet 1955): 186–97. He contended that the risks of an excessive limitation of freedom of thought and

expression are always more dangerous and menacing to social stability than the risks inherent in open critical debate.

70 Anonymous, "Sur la condition du philosophe," *Cité libre* 7 (mai 1953): 15–19.

71 Maurice Blain, "Faites vos jeux," *Cité libre* 11 (février 1955): 28–31.

72 Cf. Institut canadien des affaires publiques, *Le peuple souverain* (Rapport de la première conférence annuelle, Ste Marguerite, 29 sept. au 2 oct. 1954), 7–8.

73 Pelletier, "Crise d'autorité," 3.

74 "Feu l'unanimité," *Cité libre* 30 (octobre 1960): 8–11. Cf. Pierre Charbonneau, "Lettre ouverte à Gérard Pelletier sur l'unanimité," ibid. 32 (décembre 1960): 23–5.

75 Pelletier, "Crise d'autorité," 3–4; Cormier, "Petite méditation sur l'existence canadienne-français," *Cité libre* 1 (juin 1950): 29–30.

76 Trudeau, "Matériaux pour servir à une enquête I," 31–2.

77 Ibid., 37; Cf. Dansereau, "Lettre à un séminariste," 17.

78 Interview with Charles Lussier, 8 Sept. 1976. He recalls how his brother, André, Trudeau, and Pelletier received a warm reception from Cardinal Léger at a private house in Lachine in the late 1950s. Cardinal Léger assured them that he favoured many of the recommendations of the Citélibristes in the area of church-state relations and he credited *Cité libre* with having helped alter the attitude of many clerics.

CHAPTER FIVE

1 Maurice Blain, "Sur la liberté de l'esprit," *Esprit* 20 (août-septembre 1952): 210.

2 Ibid., 209.

3 Ibid., 210.

4 Pierre Vadeboncoeur, "Notre mission inattendue," *AN* 22 (octobre 1943): 107.

5 "Etat et Nation," *AN* 27 (janvier 1946): 10–18 (10 quoted).

6 Cormier, "Pour un humanisme ouvrier: Notes sur l'autonomie quotidienne," *AN* 30 (novembre 1947): 172–83.

7 Trudeau, "D'abord social, puis républicain," *Devoir*, 6 juil. 1949. Vadeboncoeur supported Trudeau's arguments in his "Portrait–ou caricature?–du 'nationaliste'." ibid., 14 juil. 1949.

8 Cormier, "Petite méditation sur l'existence canadienne-française," *Cité libre* 1 (juin 1950): 26–7, 28, 36.

9 Trudeau, "La province de Québec au moment de la grève," 90.

10 Ibid., 11; Jean-Guy Blain, "Pour une dynamique de notre culture," *Cité libre* 5 (juin-juillet 1952): 21; Vadeboncoeur, "L'irréalisme de notre culture," ibid., 4 (décembre 1951): 20; Rioux, "Idéologie et crise de conscience du Canada français," ibid., 14 (décembre 1955): 3; and Dumont, "De quelques obstacles à la prise de conscience chez les Canadiens français," ibid., 19 (janvier 1958): 24.

11 "La province de Québec au moment de la grève," 13.

12 Ibid., 11–12; Blain, "Pour une dynamique," 21.

13 Vadeboncoeur, "L'irréalisme," 21.

14 Rioux, "Idéologie et crise de conscience," 14. For a similar statement see Trudeau, "La province de Québec au moment de la grève," 12.

15 Cf. Maurice Tremblay, "Orientations de la pensée sociale," in *Essais sur le Québec contemporain*, 194–208. Many of Tremblay's ideas had initially been expressed in a manuscript, "La pensée sociale au Canada français," Québec, June 1950; Blain, "Pour une dynamique," 21.

16 Rioux, "Idéologie et crise de conscience au Canada français," 14; Ernest Gagnon, "Visage de l'intelligence," *Esprit* 20 (août-septembre 1952): 232.

17 "La province de Québec au moment de la grève," 14–37.

18 Ibid., 88. Jean-Charles Falardeau had raised most of these critical point in his conclusion to the 1952 Laval symposium on French Canada and industrialization. "Perspectives" in *Essais sur le Québec contemporain*, 246–9.

19 Vadeboncoeur, "A Break with Tradition," *QQ* 65 (Spring 1958): 92.

20 Vadeboncoeur, "Pour une dynamique," 13.

21 Ibid., 16–17; Rioux, "Idéologie et crise de conscience," 19.

22 Tremblay, "La pensée sociale," 47, cited in Rioux, "Idéologie et crise de conscience," 20.

23 Tremblay, "La pensée sociale," 24. He wrote: "partant du postulat de la transcendance du catholicisme sur le protestantisme, de la vérité sur l'erreur, l'auteur transpose inconsciemment cette transcendance sur le plan culturel, pour accorder à la culture canadienne-française catholique une supériorité absolue par rapport à la culture anglo-protestante." For a published expression of his critique of the nationalist ideology see his "Conflict d'allégeances chez les Canadiens français," *Ad Usum Sacerdotum* 13 (janvier 1958): 19–25; and his "Réflexions sur le nationalisme," in *Ecrits du Canada français* 5 (1959): 11–43.

24 Rioux, "Idéologie et crise de conscience," 21–8; Maurice Blain, "Sur la liberté," 201–4, 209.

25 Vadeboncoeur, "A Break with Tradition," 92–6; "Critique de notre psychologie de l'action," *Cité libre* 8 (novembre 1953): 11–22.

26 Vadeboncoeur, "Critique de notre psychologie," 26–7. For another expression of these views see his "A Break with Tradition," 97–102.

27 Pelletier, "Dissidence," *Cité libre* 8 (novembre 1953): 32.

28 Ibid., 33.

29 Fernand Dumont, "De quelques obstacles à la prise de conscience chez les Canadiens français," *Cité libre* 19 (janvier 1958): 22–8.

30 Trudeau, "Conclusion," in *La grève de l'amiante*, 396; Rioux, "Idéologie et crise de conscience," 28–9.

31 Rioux, "Idéologie et crise de conscience," 29. For a similar response see Jean-Guy Blain, "Pour une dynamique," 26.

32 M.-J. d'Anjou, "Le cas de '*Cité libre*'," *Relations* 11 (mars 1951): 69–70.
33 Interview with Charles Lussier, 8 Sept. 1976.
34 Robert Rumilly, *L'infiltration gauchiste au Canada*, 1–29.
35 Ibid., 77–95.
36 Jacques Cousineau, *Réflexions en marge de "la Grève de l'amiante"* (Montréal: Les cahiers de l'Institut social populaire, no. 4, septembre 1958), 6. Cf. Cousineau, *L'Eglise d'ici et le social 1940–1960* (Montréal 1982), chap. 12, "La grève et l'Eglise d'ici (1949)," 168–84.
37 *Réflexions en marge*, 16–22.
38 Ibid., 39.
39 F.-A. Angers, "Pierre Elliott Trudeau et *La grève de l'amiante* I," 47 (septembre 1957): 10–22 (18 quoted).
40 Angers, "Trudeau et *La grève de l'amiante*–VI," 48 (septembre-octobre 1958): 45–56.
41 Trudeau, "Le père Cousineau, s.j., et *La grève de l'amiante*," *Cité libre* 23 (mai 1959): 34–48.
42 Jean-Guy Blain, "La grève de l'amiante," 46 (octobre 1956): 177.
43 Pierre de Grandpré, "Le social et le national," *AN* 46 (octobre 1956): 135; Cf. his "La province de Québec au tournant du demi-siecle: Evolutions de la pensée sociale," *Devoir*, 9 juin 1956.
44 Laurendeau, "Sur cent pages de P.E. Trudeau, I–II–III," *Devoir*, 6, 10, 11 oct. 1956 (article III quoted).

CHAPTER SIX

1 Filion, "Si Jean Talon revenait," *Devoir*, 6 mai 1959.
2 Cf. Kenneth McRoberts and Dale Posgate, *Quebec: Social Change and Political Crisis*, chap. 5. Gérard Bergeron et al., *L'état du Québec en devenir* (Montréal 1980), 21–36.
3 Richard Arès, SJ, *Notre question nationale* (Montréal: Editions de l'Action nationale 1943), vol. 3; F.-A. Angers, "Le rôle de l'Etat dans la vie économique d'une nation," *AN* 22 (novembre 1943): 196–203; "L'avenir économique des Canadiens français," ibid., 46 (novembre 1956): 402–3; Esdras Minville, "Les conditions de l'autonomie économique des Canadiens français," ibid., 33 (mars 1951): 268–73.
4 Gérard Fortin, "Le nationalisme canadien français et les classes sociales," *RHAF* 22 (mars 1969): 525–34; Hubert Guindon, "The Social Evolution of Quebec Reconsidered," *CJEPS* 26 (November 1960): 548–51. Guindon's thesis was that massive industrialization had not altered the composition of the power structure at the top levels in Quebec. The traditional élites, thanks to the converging interests of the clergy, existing political parties, and foreign capitalists, had managed, up until 1960 at least, to consolidate and even strengthen their position.

5 Quebec, Royal Commission of Inquiry on Constitutional Problems, *Report*, 5 vols. (Quebec: Queen's Printer 1956), 3, bk. 1: 65–133. Cited hereafter as *Tremblay Report*.

6 See for example La Chambre de Commerce du district de Montréal, *Mémoire à la Commission royale d'enquête sur les problèmes constitutionnels*, vol. 4, *La politique économique du Québec* (mimeo in Bibliothéque de la Législature, Québec).

7 René Chaloult, *Mémoires politiques*, 268–70, 281–95. Pierre Laporte, *The True Face of Duplessis*, 118–20.

8 Conrad Black, *Duplessis* (Toronto 1976), 204.

9 Cited in Herbert F. Quinn, *The Union Nationale*, 81.

10 Black, *Duplessis*, 585–7.

11 Robert Boily, "Les hommes politiques du Québec, 1867–1967," in *Le personnel politique québécois*, ed., Richard Desrosiers, 77–82.

12 McRoberts and Posgate, *Quebec: Social Change*, 78–9.

13 Pierre Laporte, "Soyons riche, ou nous périrons," *AN* 46 (septembre 1956): 27.

14 Ibid., 30; Roland Parenteau, "Quelques raisons de la faiblaisse économique de la nation canadienne-française," *AN* 45 (décembre 1955): 330–1.

15 Parenteau, "Richesse et misére du Canada français," *Chronique sociale de France* 65e année (15 septembre 1957): 425–6.

16 Gérard Filion, "Une double tentation," *Devoir*, 12 mai 1954. His remarks were prompted by a conference given by a French economist invited by the secretary of state, Maurice Lamontagne, to speak at a Université de Montréal symposium on "le rôle du patronat." Yves Urbain, "Les Canadiens français ne sont pas maîtres chez eux!" *Devoir*, 11 mai 1954.

17 Filion, "Une double tentation," *Devoir*, 12 mai 1954; "C'est la loi de l'amitié qui explique l'étonnante durée du Devoir," ibid., 1 fév. 1960.

18 Léger, *Notre situation économique: Progrès ou stagnation?*

19 Ibid., 21; Parenteau, "Quelques raisons," 317–18; "Richesse et misère," 427–8; "L'émancipation économique des Canadiens français," *AN* 49 (juin 1960): 797–801; Roger Vezina, "La position des Canadiens français dans l'industrie et le commerce," *Culture* (septembre 1954): 291–2; Michel Brunet, "L'infériorité économique des Canadiens français," in his *La présence anglaise et les Canadiens*, 226–7. The research done for the Royal Commission on Bilingualism and Biculturalism using 1961 census data painted a bleak picture of the economic inferiority of French Canadians in terms of income, education, occuption, and ownership of industry and commerce, thereby confirming many of the purely subjective charges made in the 1950s. See *Report of the Royal Commission on Bilingualism and Biculturalism*, vol. 3, *The Work World*, 11–60.

20 Parenteau, "Richesse et misère," 427.

21 Errol Bouchette, *L'indépendance économique du Canada français*.

22 French Canadians, it was noted by a couple of sociologists, were not advancing very rapidly in the managerial and administrative fields for very clear-cut ethnic reasons. Many turned down promotions in these areas when such promotions entailed having to move to a predominantly Anglo-Canadian environment. On the other hand, English and American businessmen preferred to promote only those individuals to high-ranking positions in whom they had full confidence and could identify with culturally and socially. E.C. Hughes, "Regards sur le Québec," in *Essais sur le Québec contemporain*, 223–8; J.-C. Falardeau, "L'origine et l'ascension des hommes d'affaires dans la société canadienne-française," *RS* 6 (janvier-avril 1963): 33–45. This subject was surveyed haphazardly by Conrad Langlois in 1960, "Cultural reasons for the French-Canadian Lag in Economic Progress," *Culture* 21 (juin 1960): 152–70.

23 Jacques Mélançon, "Retard de croissance de l'entreprise canadienne-française," *AE* 30 (janvier-mars 1956), in Bédard, *L'essor économique du Québec*, 168–71; Mélançon, "L'industrie canadienne-française et ses besoins de capitaux," *AE* (janvier-mars 1949), in ibid., 314; Albert Faucher, "Investissement, épargne et position économique des Canadiens français," *L'enseignement primaire* 15 (avril 1956): 499–605; Parenteau, "Quelques raisons," 320–1.

24 Parenteau, "*Quelques raisons*," 324–5; Mélançon, "Retard de croissance," 160–1; Vezina, "La position des Canadiens français," 291–9; Norman K. Taylor, "French Canadians as Industrial Entrepreneurs," *Journal of Political Economy* 48 (February 1960): 37–52.

25 Filion, "Une double tentation," *Devoir*, 12 mai 1954; "La concentration industrielle," ibid., 13 sept. 1950; L'embourgeoisement," ibid., 15 sept. 1954; Léger, *Notre situation économique*, 23–6; Laporte, "L'enjeu: Notre survivance ou notre disparition," *Devoir*, 23 août 1957.

26 Filion, "Que faire de nos hommes de science?" *Devoir*, 4 juin 1955.

27 Filion, "Une double tentation," *Devoir*, 12 mai 1954; "C'est la loi de l'amitié qui explique l'étonnante durée du *Devoir*," ibid., 1 fév. 1960.

28 Serge Gagnon, "Pour une conscience historique de la révolution québécoise," *Cité libre* 83 (janvier 1966): 9–17; and Léon Dion, "Le nationalisme pessimiste: Sa source, sa signification, sa validité," ibid., 18 (novembre 1957): 6.

29 Brunet, "Introduction," *La présence anglaise*, 14; Séguin, "La conquête et la vie économique des Canadiens," *AN* 28 (décembre 1946), reprinted in *Economie québécoise* (Sillery, Québec 1969), 346; Guy Frégault, "La colonisation du Canada au XVIIe siècle," *Cahiers de l'Académie française* 2 (1957): 81.

30 Maurice Séguin, *La nation "canadienne" et l'agriculture (1760–1850)*.

31 Séguin, "La Conquête et la vie économique," 347–56.

32 Lionel Groulx, *Pour bâtir* (Montréal 1953), 185–6.

33 Guy Frégault, *Canadian Society in the French Regime* (Ottawa 1954), 14–15.

34 Société Saint-Jean-Baptiste de Montréal, *Canada français et union canadienne*, 34.The author was Michel Brunet, neo-nationalist historian at the Université

de Montréal. See also his "La conquête anglaise et la déchéance de la bourgeoisie canadienne (1760–1793)," *La présence anglaise*, 49–54.

35 Séguin, *La nation "canadienne,"* 53–4. "La cause profonde de ce mal," wrote Séguin in 1946, "de cette impossibilité pour les Canadiens d'entreprendre, en maîtres, la mise en valeur complète des ressources de leur patrie, est l'Occupation étrangère, en elle-même, indépendamment de ses modalités, indépendamment de la conduite des organisateurs de cette occupation, de leur politique d'association ou d'assimilation." "La conquête et la vie économique," 356.

36 Frégault, *Canadian Society in the French Regime*, 15; and his *La guerre de la conquête 1754–1760* (Montréal: Fides 1955), concluding chapter.

37 Brunet, "La conquête anglaise," 54–100.

38 Ibid., 111.

39 Ibid., 116–18.

40 Brunet, "Trois dominantes de la pensée canadienne-française: L'agriculturisme, l'anti-étatisme et le messianisme," *La présence anglaise*, 113–66.

41 Filion, "Il faut se salir les mains," *Devoir*, 5 mars 1960.

42 Laporte, "Soyons riches, ou nous périrons," 31–2; Parenteau, "Quelques raisons," 319–24; Léger, *Notre situation économique*, 6–9; Filion, "Progrès ou stagnation?" *Devoir*, 7 sept. 1957; "La phobie de l'étatisme," ibid., 17 sept. 1958; Laurendeau, "Y a-t-il une crise du nationalisme? II," *AN* 41 (janvier 1953): 8–11; "Blocs-Notes," *Devoir*, 23 sept. 1953; "A propos d'une longue illusion," ibid., 19 mars 1960.

43 Filion, "Que faire de nos hommes de science?" *Devoir*, 4 juin 1955; "Libération ou révolution," ibid., 14 mars 1956; "Si Jean Talon revenait," ibid., 6 mai 1959; Léger, "Pour sortir du mensonge," *AN* 42 (mars-avril 1954): 375–6; Parenteau, "L'émancipation économique," 805, 809–10; Brunet, "Organiser un état provincial dynamique," *Devoir*, 29 jan. 1960. By 1959 even Father Richard Arès had come to accept the necessity of a strong and active Quebec state. "Où va le Canada français–IV?" *Devoir*, 7 mai 1959.

44 Paul Sauriol, "Entre la servitude économique et la nationalisation," *Devoir*, 20 oct. 1958; "*Le Devoir* et la libération économique de notre groupe," ibid., 29 jan. 1960.

45 Filion, "La phobie de l'étatisme," *Devoir*, 17 sept. 1958; Laurendeau, "Duplessis et le socialisme," ibid., 24 fév. 1959; Parenteau, "Quelques raisons," 327–8; Brunet, "Trois dominantes," 143–4, 156–7; "Le nationalisme canadien-français et la politique des deux Canadas," *La présence anglaise*, 249–50, 288–9.

46 Filion, "C'est la loi de l'amitié . . ., *Devoir*, 1 fév. 1960.

47 Ibid.

48 Dion, "Le Nationalisme Pessimiste," 9–10, 14.

49 Cf. Maurice Séguin, *L'idée d'indépendance au Québec: Génèse et historique*.

50 See various editorials by Laurendeau, Filion, Laporte, and Sauriol, *Devoir*, 15

sept., 18 oct. 1947; 3 juin, 16 août 1948; 19 fév. 1949; 6 avril 1951; 19 mars, 26 nov., 6 déc. 1952; 18 sept. 1953; 22 juin 1954; 20 jan. and 20 oct. 1955; 12 jan., 1 and 15 juin 1951; 22 fév. 1957.

51 Filion, "La reprise de nos richesses naturelles," *Devoir*, 25 nov. 1953.

52 Filion, "La reprise de nos richesses naturelles," *Devoir*, 25 mai 1949; "Mauvaises fréquentations, mauvaise politique," ibid., 17 juil., 1954; Pierre Vigeant, "Les compagnies qui exploitent nos richesses naturelles," ibid., 30 nov. 1954; "Les Canadiens français et le capital étranger," ibid., août 1952; Laurendeau, "Compagnie américaine, ouvriers canadiens-français," ibid., 26 août 1952.

53 Filion, "Des chantiers sans blasphémateurs," *Devoir*, 16 oct. 1948; "Après nous le désert," ibid., 10 déc. 1955; "Faudra-t-il étatiser les papeteries?" ibid., 29 oct. 1955; "Régie du papier et des forêts"; ibid., 14 jan. 1956. The Duplessis government introduced legislation calling for a two-price system and close government supervision of cutting and conservation programs.

54 Paul Sauriol, "L'étatisation de l'électricité et l'autonomie provinciale," *Devoir*, 4 avril 1957; "Entre la servitude économique et la nationalisation," ibid., 20 oct. 1958.

55 Laurendeau, "Ce que dit la loi au sujet de l'Ungava," *Devoir*, 29 mai 1956; Robert Rumilly, *Maurice Duplessis et son temps* 2: 102–3, 111, 127–8, 234–5; Conrad Black, *Duplessis*, 585–9. Both Rumilly and Black discount or ignore the neo-nationalists' critique.

56 Pierre Laporte, "Après l'Iron Ore sera-ce Krupp-Eaton?" *Devoir*, 8 oct. 1957; "Une province qui se contente des miettes I–V," ibid., 24, 25, 27, 28, 29, jan. 1958; Laurendeau, "Les ressources naturelles du Québec," ibid., 6 déc. 7; "Québec donne aux étrangers," ibid., 4 sept. 1951; "Compagnie américaine, ouvriers canadiens-français," ibid., 26 août 1952; "Les gachis de l'Ungava," ibid., 2 déc. 1954; Filion, "Un peuple de gueux dans un pays riche," ibid., 2 juin 1956; "Une question primordiale," ibid., 13 juin 1956.

57 Laurendeau, "Le Nouveau-Québec ou un nouveau 'Québec'?" *Devoir*, 2 déc. 1947; "A qui servira d'abord le fer de l'ungava?" ibid., 4 mars 1949; "L'Ungava un crime ou une nécessité?" ibid., 29 mai 1956; Laporte, "Une province qui se contente des miettes VI–VIII," ibid., 30 jan., 1 and 3 fév. 1958; Vigeant, "Les gisements de l'Ungava," ibid., 12 août 1955; "Le textile, le pétrole, et le fer," ibid., 12 avril 1957; "Le scandale de l'Ungava I & II," ibid., 7 and 8 juin 1960. See also Mgr Labrie, *La Côte-Nord et l'industrie sidérurgique*, 1–12. The pamphlet includes articles by two Laval scientists, Dr Roger Potvin and Dr Albert Cholette, on the feasibility of processing Quebec iron ore in electric furnaces, 13–32.

58 Filion, "La reprise de nos richesses naturelles," *Devoir*, 25 nov. 1953.

59 Filion, "La famille urbaine est une exilée," *Devoir*, 27 août 1949; "Sous le signe de la sécurité sociale," ibid., 16 sept. 1950; "L'assurance-santé," ibid., 20 jan. 1954; Sauriol, "Vers une réforme de nos démocraties étatistes?" ibid.,

5 oct. 1949; Laporte, "La sécurité sociale," ibid., 26 sept. 1952.

60 Filion, "La bonheur dans l'irresponsabilité," *Devoir*, 7 déc. 1949; "Les limites de la sécurité sociale," ibid., 6 août 1952; "On ne résoudra pas la question par un non," ibid., 26 jan. 1957; Sauriol, "L'assurance-santé et l'autonomie provinciale," ibid., 15 mars 1948.

61 *Tremblay Report* 3, bk. 1: 65–133.

62 CTCC et FTQ, "Les centrales ouvrières du Québec et l'assurance-santé *Relations industrielles* 13 (1958): 175–208.

63 Sauriol, "Nos ressources naturelles au service des nôtres," *Devoir*, 29 sept. 1959; "*Le Devoir* et la libération de notre groupe," ibid., 29 jan. 1960; Filion, "Pour une politique économique," ibid., 24 oct. 1959; Vigeant, "Pour une politique économique rationnelle dans le Québec," ibid., 11 jan. 1960; Parenteau, "Le Canada français n'a pas de politique économique," ibid., 1 fév. 1960; "L'émancipation économique des Canadiens français," 809–10; Léger, *Notre situation économique*, 44–7; SSJB de Montréal, *Canada français et union canadienne*, 108–15.

64 Marcel Trudel, "La Nouvelle-France," *Cahiers de l'Académie canadienne-française* 2 (1957): 23–50.

65 Jean Hamelin, *Economie et société en Nouvelle-France*, Conclusion.

66 Fernand Ouellet, "M. Michel Brunet et le problème de la Conquête," *Bulletin des recherches historiques* 57 (1956): 92–9.

67 Ouellet, "M. Michel Brunet," 99–101; and Fernand Ouellet, "Les Fondements historiques de l'option séparatiste dans le Québec," *CHR* 43 (September 1962): 185–203, and his monumental *Histoire économique et sociale du Québec 1760–1850*, especially the conclusion.

68 Maurice Tremblay, "Orientations de la pensée sociale," in *Essais sur le Québec contemporain*, 193–205, citation 200.

69 Trudeau, "La province de Québec au moment de la grève," in *La grève de l'amiante*, 12.

70 Ibid., 19–37.

71 Trudeau, "*Le Devoir* doit-il préparer ses lecteurs au socialisme?" *Devoir*, 2 fév. 1955; "Les Canadiens français rateront (encore une fois) le tournant ..." ibid., 29 jan. 1960.

72 "Manifeste politique de FUIQ," reprinted in L.-M. Tremblay, *Le syndicalisme québécois*, 263–7; "Déclarations de principes de la Confédération des travailleurs catholiques du Canada," in ibid., 259–62; Jean Marchand et al., "Table Ronde sur l'Etat provincial," *Devoir*, 14 juil. 1959.

73 CTCC, *Mémoire à la Commission Tremblay*, 3–11; Roger Mathieu, "Rapport du Président Général de la CTCC," *Procès-verbal*, 39ième session du Congrès de la CTCC (Montréal 1960), 15–20; FUIQ, *Mémoire à la Commission Tremblay*, 19–21; "Manifeste politique de la FUIQ," 265. See also Gabriel Gagnon, "Pour une planification régionale et démocratique," *Cité libre* 29 (août-sept. 1960): 9–12.

74 Pierre Harvey, "The Economy of Quebec," *University of Toronto Quarterly*, 27 (April 1958): 330–40; André Raynauld, "Les problèmes économiques de la province de Québec," *AE* (octobre-décembre 1959): 414–21.

CHAPTER SEVEN

1 Pierre Vadeboncoeur, *La ligne du risque*, 207.

2 Evelyn Dumas, *Dans le sommeil de nos os*, 9–24, 149–52.

3 Hélène David, "L'état des rapports de classe au Québec de 1945 à 1967," *Sociologie et sociétés* 7 (novembre 1975): 47, table 1, 63.

4 Gérard Dion, "Les groupements syndicaux dans la province de Québec (1955)," *Relations industrielles*, 2 (décembre 1955): 7–14; Louis-Marie Tremblay, *Le syndicalisme québécois: Idéologies de la CSN et de la FTQ 1940–1970*, 126–30.

5 Dion, "Les groupements syndicaux," 14–16, 22; Tremblay, *Le syndicalisme québécois*, 130–4.

6 Jean Marchand, "La CSN a quarante ans," *Relations industrielles* 16 (octobre 1961): 471. For a similar assessment of the CTCC in its formative years see Samuel H. Barnes, "The Evolution of Christian Trade Unions in Quebec," in *Readings in Canadian Labour*, ed. E.A. Kovacs (Toronto 1961), 58–61.

7 Jacques Rouillard, *Les syndicats nationaux au Québec de 1900 à 1930*, 240–50.

8 Dion, "Les groupements syndicaux," 17–24; Tremblay, *Le syndicalisme québécois*, 26–37. For an overview of the internal developments in the CTCC see also Jean-Louis Roy, *La marche des québécois: Le temps des ruptures (1945–1960)*, 87–161.

9 Gilles Beausoleil, "Histoire de la grève à Asbestos," in *La grève de l'amiante*, 165–211; and "Histoire des négociations," in ibid., 212–38. For an excellent synthesis see Hélène David, "La grève et le bon Dieu: La grève de l'amiante au Québec," *Sociologie et sociétés* 1 (novembre 1969): 249–54.

10 Laurendeau, "Le movement ouvrier s'affirme," *Devoir*, 4 jan. 1949. As a warning to the Duplessis government, Laurendeau wrote: "Traiter le syndicalisme, qui sent sa force, comme un mauvais écolier, c'est risquer de l'exaspérer, c'est déformer son caractère et l'empêcher de donner sa nature."

11 Laurendeau, "Blocs-notes," *Devoir*, 20 mai 1949; Filion, "Le Bien peut sortir du mal," ibid., 6 juil. 1949; Dansereau, "Les travailleurs accouchent d'une conscience de classe," ibid., 27 avril 1953.

12 Filion, "Les osus plus fort que les principes," *Devoir*, 30 avril 1949; Laurendeau, "Lettre ouverte à l'Ambassade des Etats-Unis," ibid., 9 mai 1949; "Que veut-on dans l'amiante?" ibid., 2 mai 1949.

13 Dansereau, "Les travailleurs accouchent d'une conscience de classe," *Devoir*, 27 avril 1953.

14 Réginald Boisvert, "Domiciles de la peur sociale," *Cité libre* 1 (juin 1950): 13–14.

15 Pelletier, "Refus de confiance au syndicalisme," *Cité libre* 7 (mai 1953): 1–6.

16 Ibid., 7. This criticism was also applied to the leaders of the Montreal teachers' union, the Alliance. See La rédaction, "La querelle des instituteurs," *Cité libre* 4 (novembre 1951): 4.

17 Trudeau, "Epilogue," *La grève de l'amiante*, 401.

18 Ibid., 392–4.

19 Boisvert, "La grève et le mouvement ouvrier," in ibid., 357.

20 Ibid., 359. See Trudeau, "Réflexions sur la politique au Canada français," *Cité libre* 6 (décembre 1952): 65.

21 "Introduction," *Mémoire de la FUIQ (CCL) à la Commission royale d'enquête sur les problèmes constitutionels*, 8.

22 Alfred Charpentier, *Les mémoires d'Alfred Charpentier* (Québec: PUL 1971), 330–3; Jacques Rouillard, "Mutations de la Confédération des Travailleurs Catholiques du Canada (1940–1960)," *RHAF* 34 (décembre 1980): 382–3.

23 See Hélène David, "La grève et le bon Dieu," 254–68. Although the author does neglect the neo-nationalist interpretation, she considers both the *Cité libre* analysis and Father Jacques Cousineau's rejection of that analysis. She concludes that both views are incomplete and advances the following hypothesis: "bien que la grève de l'amiante ait été un conflit industriel qui à opposé 5,000 mineurs aux sociétés minières ainsi qu'au gouvernement qui soutenait ces dernièrs, *le conflit de l'amiante* recouvre en fait deux affrontements de nature très différente: *le conflit de class dans une situation industrielle se double d'une lutte de pouvoir entre la hiérarchie religieuse et l'Etat*" (256). The article goes on to demonstrate by a highly theoretical analysis that the state emerged the winner in this battle with the church. The labour movement gained a degree of recognition and autonomy but henceforth had to confront a more determined and powerful state without the church's support. "A Asbestos, le mouvement ouvrier dut s'appuyer sur une situation pré-industrielle pour pouvoir affronter son adversaire et aboutir à un systeme de négotiation dans le cadre d'une société industrielle capitaliste" (268).

24 See Léo Roback et al., *The Duplessis Government and Quebec Labour* (Montreal: Research Associates 1952), cited extensively in Hélène David, "L'état des rapports de classe," 38–42.

25 Filion, "La justice sociale à coups de matraque," *Devoir*, 17 mai 1947; "La matraque à Asbestos," ibid., 23 fév. 1949; "La justice sociale à la pointe du revolver," ibid., 13 déc. 1952; "La déchéance de l'Etat québécois," ibid., 28 août 1957; Laurendeau, "Qui fait le jeu des communistes?" ibid., 21 jan. 1953; Pelletier, "Refus de confiance au syndicalisme," *Cité libre* 7 (mai 1953): 1–3; Trudeau, "Epilogue," *La grève de l'amiante*, 388–91.

26 Laurendeau, "La grève," *Devoir*, 16 août 1952.

27 Filion, Sauriol, Laurendeau, *Devoir*, 19 fév., 30 mars, 3 and 17 mai, 7 juillet, 1948, 15 and 25 jan., 4 fév., 1 avril 1949; Pelletier, "La silicose," ibid., 17 avril 1948. He called for a public inquiry.

28 Laurendeau, *Devoir*, 22 déc. 1947, 18 and 30 nov. 1948, 4 jan. 1949, 27 mars 1952; Filion, ibid., 23 sept. 1950, 25 sept. 1957; Dansereau, ibid., 26, 28, 29 fév. 1952, 29 avril 1953, 4 mai 1954. Charles Lussier, "La grève dans nos cadres juridiques," in *La grève de l'amiante*, 263–76. Vadeboncoeur, "Le refus d'améliorer les lois, ou la violance du législateur . . .," *Thémis* 8 (février 1958): 186–91.

29 Laporte, *Devoir*, 31 jan. 1951, 14 déc. 1951; Dansereau, ibid., 26, 27, 29 fév. 1952; 29 avril 1953; 17 avril 1954.

30 La rédaction, "La querelle des instituteurs," *Cité libre* 4 (décembre 1951): 1–15; "Note sur les anomalies juridiques du retrait de certificat," ibid., 16–19; Pelletier, "L'art de la poudre aux yeux," ibid., 28 (juin-juillet 1960): 11, 13. He deplored the so-called "new deal" for labour proposed by Barrette.

31 Pelletier, "Les Bills 19 et 20," *AN* 42 (mars-avril 1954): 351–62; Laurendeau, "M. Duplessis s'arme contre les syndicats," *Devoir*, 20 nov. 1953; Dansereau, "A l'occasion des bills 19 et 20," ibid., 15 janv. 1954.

32 Laurendeau, "Il y a deux McCarthy mais un seul Duplessis," *Devoir*, 15 jan. 1954; Filion, "Pour éviter la lutte des classes," ibid., 15 déc. 1953.

33 Trudeau, "La province de Québec au moment de la grève," in *La grève de l'amiante*, 31–5.

34 Pelletier, "Le syndicalisme canadien-français," in *Canadian Dualism/La dualité canadienne*, ed. Mason Wade, 288.

35 La rédaction, "La querelle des instituteurs," 1–15.

36 Filion, "Le collège du travail," *Devoir*, 10 avril 1948. He argued that it should be controlled by laymen not clerics.

37 See Roger Chartier, "Chronologie de l'évolution confessionnelle de la CTCC (CSN)," *Relations industrielles* 16 (février 1961): 102–12.

38 Roy, *La marche des québécois*, 90–5.

39 Chartier, "Chronologie de l'évolution confessionnelle," 102–12; Gérard Dion, "Invitations à repenser le syndicalisme catholique," *Ad Usum Sacerdotum* 10 (octobre 1954): 1–3; "L'Eglise et les orientations nouvelles de la CTCC," ibid., 12 (novembre 1956): 20–1; "Autour d'une querelle d'étiquette et de principes," ibid., 14 (novembre 1959), 190–9; "Confessionalité syndicale et régime juridique du travail dans le Québec," *Relations industrielles* 15 (avril 1960): 162–80.

40 Laporte, *Devoir*, 12 sept. 1955; Lamarche, ibid., 27, 28, 30 sept. 1960.

41 Filion, "Un débat à ne pas passionner," *Devoir*, 15 août 1959.

42 Jacques Cousineau, SJ, *L'Eglise d'ici et le social 1940–1960*, vol. 1, *La Commission sacerdotale d'études sociales*, 19–33. Founding members included Cousineau himself; Father Paul-Emile Bolté, PSS, professor of "morale sociale" at the Grand Séminaire de Montréal; Father Emile Bouvier, SJ, director of industrial relations at the Université de Montréal; Father Gérard Dion, professor of industrial relations at Laval, and Canon Henri Pichette, general chaplain of the CTCC.

43 See CSES, *L'organisation professionnelle dans le Québec, compte rendu des Journées sacerdotales d'études sociales, 1945 et 1946*, 1–35; CSES, *La participation des travailleurs à la vie de l'entreprise, compte rendu des Journées sacerdotales d'études sociales de 1947*, 1–45; CSES, *Worker's Share in Business Life* (Montréal 1950); Abbé Gérard Dion, "The Social Doctrine of the Church and the Economic Management of Enterprises," *Relations industrielles* 6 (septembre 1951): 98–108.

44 Cousineau, *L'Eglise d'ici et le social*, 1:92–110, 168–84; "Secourons les travailleurs de l'amiante," *L'Action catholique*, 30 avril 1949, cited in Gérard Dion, "L'Eglise et le conflit de l'amiante," in *La grève de l'amiante*, 249–51.

45 CTCC, *Procès-verbal du congrès* (1948), 225; *Procès-verbal du congrès* (1951), 217. Cf. Jacques Rouillard, "Mutations de la Confédération des Travailleurs Catholiques du Canada," 382.

46 Lettre pastorale collective de Leurs Excellences Nosseigneurs les Archevêques et Evêques de la province civile de Québec, *Le problème ouvrier en regard de la doctrine sociale de l'Eglise* (Montréal 1950), 1–79. In fact the CSES was responsible for preparing the drafts of the pastoral letter. See S. Barnes, "Quebec Catholicism and Social Change," *The Review of Politics* 13 (January 1961): 67; Cousineau, *L'Eglise d'ici et le social* 1:111–25, 185–96.

47 *Le problème ouvrier*, 4–12.

48 Ibid., 21.

49 Ibid., 24–30.

50 Laurendeau, "Pour la sécurité syndicale," *Devoir*, 8 mars 1949; Filion, "La participation des travailleurs à la vie de l'entreprise," ibid., 15 oct. 1949; Laurendeau, "Quand une idée est dans l'air," ibid., 4 oct. 1947; Richard Arès, SJ, *Essais de réforme de l'entreprise aux Etats-Unis* (Montréal 1950). Jean-Pierre Després, "La participation ouvrière," *Revue de l'Université Laval* 2 (mars 1948): 599–610 and (avril 1948): 713–20.

51 Laurendeau, "Quand une idée est dans l'air," *Devoir*, 4 oct. 1947.

52 Filion, "La deuxième ère du syndicalisme," *Devoir*, 17 sept. 1949; "Un document qui annonce des grandes choses," ibid., 22 mars 1950.

53 Cited in Laurendeau, "La participation aux bénéfices est-elle une hérésie?" *Devoir*, 12 juin 1951; "Trois attaques en trois jours," ibid., 5 fév. 1954.

54 Filion, "Socialisme ou coopératisme," *Devoir*, 29 mai 1948; "Québec terre d'avenir du coopératisme," ibid., 8 oct. 1955.

55 Dansereau, "La situation ouvrière dans Québec III," *Devoir*, 28 avril 1953.

56 Ibid., "La situation ouvrière dans Québec V," 30 avril 1953.

57 "Rapport du Président Général de la CTCC," *Procès-verbal* (Montréal 1949), 37–40.

58 Ibid., 47–54; "Rapport du Président Général de la CTCC," *Procès-verbal* (Québec 1951), 28–39.

59 Boisvert, "Domiciles de la peur sociale," 14. The expression originated with the worker priests of the Dominican Order in France after the war.

60　Pelletier, "Syndicalisme Canadien et influence américaine," *Esprit* 22 (1954): 1028; Trudeau, "Epilogue," 398.

61　Trudeau, "Epilogue," 402–3.

62　Fraser Isbester, "Quebec Labour in Perspective," in *Canadian Labour in Transition* (Scarborough 1971), ed. R.U. Miller and F. Isbester, 245–53; Stuart Jamieson, "Labour Unity in Quebec," in Wade, *Canadian Dualism*, 290–308; Gérard Dion, "La CTCC et l'unité ouvrière canadienne," *Relations industrielles* 12 (janvier-avril 1957): 32–53.

63　CTCC, *Procès-verbal* (Québec 1955), 22–47, 173–4.

64　*Labour Gazette* 56, no. 11 (November 1956): 1389–90, cited in Isbester, "Quebec Labour in Perspective," 250.

65　"Projet du comité de l'unité syndicale," *Procès-verbal* (Québec 1957), 185–8.

66　Ibid., 189–95. For a good account of the inner conflict and an assessment of the nationalists' victory see Gérard Dion, "La CTCC et l'affiliation au CTC," *Ad Usum Sacerdotum* 13 (mars 1958): 52–7.

67　"Rapport du Président de la CTCC," *Procès-verbal* (Montréal 1958) 39–43.

68　*Labour Gazette* 60, no. 12 (December 1960): 1270, cited in Isbester, "Quebec Labour in Perspective," 251.

69　Filion, "Face à la fusion des unions internationales," *Devoir*, 17 mars 1956; "FAT,–CIO et Cie Ltée," ibid., 25 avril 1956; Laurendeau, "L'avenir de la CTCC," ibid., 31 juil. 1956; "Pourquoi parler de pluralisme?" ibid., 27 oct. 1953.

70　Filion, "Que deviendra la CTCC?" *Devoir*, 28 sept. 1957; "Point n'est besoin de presser les événements," ibid., 20 sept. 1958; "Un débat à ne pas passionner," ibid., 15 août 1959. Gérard Dion agreed that what was required was a CLC which acted merely as a federation of autonomous provincial unions. "Le régionalisme syndical est-il désuet?" *Ad Usum Sacerdotum* 13 (juin-juillet-août 1958): 124–34.

71　Boisvert, "La grève et le mouvement ouvrier," 376–8; Pelletier, "Syndicalisme canadien et influence américaine," 1020–8; Trudeau, "Epilogue," 403–4.

72　Boisvert, "La grève et le mouvement ouvrier," 374.

73　Gérard Pelletier, "Partisans nos frères," *Devoir*, 20 déc. 1947; "Le parti unique par la faute des jeunes?" ibid., 16 oct. 1948; "Scrupules ou inertie?" ibid., 31 jan. 1948; "Différences," ibid., 22 mai 1948. Pelletier welcomed the existence of a young group of socialists who rejected the nationalist interpretation of the rebellions of 1837–8 in favour of a class interpretation. "Le manifeste des Jeunes-Québec," ibid., 10 jan. 1948.

74　Interview with Charles Lussier, 8 sept. 1976.

75　Richard Daignault, "L'histoire de la CTCC," *Devoir*, 16 juin 1953.

76　CTCC, "Rapport du comité d'orientation politique," in *Procès-verbal* (Shawinigan Falls 1952), 93.

77　Gérard Picard, "Rapport du président général de la CTCC," *Procès-verbal* (Montréal 1949), 43–7, Résolution, 75–6; Fernand Jolicoeur, "Role du comité d'action civique de la CTCC,' *Devoir*, 15 sept. 1950.

78 Richard Daignault, "L'influence des syndicats dans notre système politique," *Devoir*, 17 juin 1952.

79 "Rapport du comité d'orientation," 88–92; The 27 March 1952 resolution of the executive is provided on p. 80 with the following note: "le comité s'est appliqué à exécuter, dans la mesure des moyens dont il disposait les recommandations de cette résolution . . ."

80 Picard, "Rapport Moral du président général de la CTCC," *Procès-verbal* (Shawinigan Falls 1952), 25–34 (quotes 26 and 32).

81 Ibid., 168.

82 Pelletier, "Le mouvement ouvrier et la politique," *Devoir*, 15 sept. 1951; "Commentaires," in *Le peuple souverain* (ICAP 1954), 14.

83 Interview with Charles Lussier, 8 Sept. 1976.

84 Trudeau, "Réflexions sur la politique," *Cité libre* 6 (décembre 1952): 66.

85 Ibid., 65.

86 Trudeau, "Une lettre sur la politique," *Devoir*, 18 sept. 1954.

87 Cited in Dansereau, "L'action politique des syndicats ouvrières ne fait que commencer," *Devoir*, 7 juin 1954.

88 FUIQ, "Manifeste au Peuple du Québec," in *Constitution et manifeste politique* (Joliette 14 mai 1955), 11–18.

89 Tremblay, *Le syndicalisme québécois*, 130–6; Fernand Dansereau, "La FUIQ précise ses buts et ses moyens d'action" *Devoir*, 24 mai 1954.

90 Tremblay, *Le syndicalisme québécois*, 137–8. See also Roch Denis, *Luttes de classes et question nationale au Québec, 1948–1968*, 160–9.

91 Dansereau, "Une fédération ouvrière propose une action électorale aux autres mouvements populaires du Québec," *Devoir*, 5 juil. 1954; "Les syndicats s'occuperont de plus en plus de politique," ibid., 2 mars 1954; La CTCC cherche encore la voie de son action politique," ibid., 13 avril 1954; "Un mouvement politique qui prend naissance?" ibid., 4 mars 1954; Jean Marchand, "Nos batailles ne font que commencer," ibid., 5 juillet 1954.

92 "Rapport du président général de la CTCC," *Procès-verbal* (Montréal 1954), 28–9.

93 Cited in Dansereau, "Gérard Picard et Jean Marchand interviennent en faveur d'un action politique plus poussée," *Devoir*, 24 sept. 1954.

94 CTCC, "Rapport du comité d'action politique," *Procès-verbal* (1954), 179–80.

95 Fernand Jolicoeur, director of the Service d'Education of the CTCC, pointed out to his French-Canadian readers that French-Canadian workers were turning away from the traditional capitalist parties but had shown little interest in supporting the CCF or its Quebec wing, the PSD, neither of which had succeeded "à prendre un visage sympathique aux Canadiens français." "Les problèmes ouvriers du Québec," *Chronique sociale de France* 65e année (15 septembre 1957): 438–9.

96 J.-M. Léger, "La CTCC envisage l'action politique," *AN* 38 (décembre 1951):

274; "Etapes de la révolution politique," ibid. 37 (janvier 1951): 58–63.

97 Laurendeau, "Action politique et action syndicale," AN 39 (janvier-février 1952): 66–8.

98 Filion, "Le dynamisme de la CTCC," Devoir, 25 sept. 1952.

99 Filion, "Action politique et syndicats," Relations industrielles 15 (octobre 1960): 496–9.

CHAPTER EIGHT

1 Laurendeau, "A l'heure des réformes," Devoir, 15 mars 1958.

2 Léon Lortie, "Le système scolaire," in Essais sur le Québec contemporain, 169.

3 Tremblay Report, 3 bk. 1: 143.

4 Léon Lortie, "Discours inaugural du président," in L'éducation (Rapport de la troisième conférence annuelle de l'ICAP, 1956), 8. Lortie, a chemistry professor at the Université de Montréal, was a close friend of many Cité-libristes and a founding member of ICAP.

5 Alliance des professeurs catholiques de Montréal, Mémoire à la Commission d'enquête sur les problèmes constitutionnels, 19; Mémoire de la Fédération du travail de Québec à la Commission royale d'enquête sur les problèmes constitution-nels, 9; and Mémoire de la CTCC à la Commission royale d'enquête sur les problèmes constitutionnels, 27.

6 Fédération des commissions scolaires catholiques de Québec, Les problèmes des commissions scolaires: Solution proposées (Mémoire à la Commission royale d'enquête sur les problèmes constitutionnels, 4 juin 1954), 53. This figure of 56 per cent was later revised upwards to 68.5 per cent by Arthur Tremblay.

7 Ibid., 54–5, 216.

8 Contribution à l'étude des problèmes et des besoins de l'enseignement dans la province de Québec (Annexe no. 4 de la Commission d'enquête sur les problèmes constitutionnels, Québec 1955), 20–41. In effect, statistics showed that enrolment in the Catholic schools of five to nineteen-year-olds as a percentage of the Roman Catholic population had remained constant at 60 per cent between 1939 and 1953, whereas it had increased in Protestant schools from 74 to 83 per cent. Tremblay Report 4, table 61: 158–9.

9 FTQ et CTCC, "Mémoire sur l'éducation," Relations industrielles 13 (1958): 209–13.

10 A. Tremblay, "La démocratisation de l'enseignement," in L'éducation, 25; and J.-C. Falardeau, "Conditions et conséquences d'une démocratisation de notre enseignement," ibid., 35.

11 G.-H. Lévesque, "Le droit à l'éducation," Revue Dominicaine (juillet-août 1958): 4.

12 Irénée Marrou, "Le dilemme de l'éducation contemporaine," in L'éducation, 11–12; see also Pierre Dansereau's comments, "Communion et Communica-tion," ibid., 19.

13 Paul Sauriol, "Les données démographiques de notre problème scolaire," *Devoir*, 11 avril 1949; Paul Gérin-Lajoie, "Où va la Canada français? VII," ibid., 12 mai 1959.

14 *Tremblay Report* 3, bk. 1: 156; Paul-Emile Gingras, "L'éducation," *AN* 44, no. 10 (juin 1955): 866–72; and Gingras, "L'éducation," ibid., 45, no. 7 (mars 1956): 615–18.

15 Interview with Arthur Tremblay, September 1981; René Durocher et Michèle Jean, "Duplessis et la Commission royale d'enquête sur les problèmes constitutionnels, 1953–1956," *RHAF* 25 (décembre 1971): 355–6.

16 *Tremblay Report* 3 bk. 1: 155–6.

17 A. Tremblay, "La conjoncture actuelle en éducation," in *L'éducation au Québec face au problèmes contemporains* (Saint-Hyacinthe 1958): 30, 39–40.

18 Laurendeau, "L'Etat, roi et maître?" *Devoir*, 9 sept. 1948.

19 Filion, "Le dirigisme scolaire," *Devoir*, 24 oct. 1951; La rédaction, "La querelle des instituteurs," *Cité libre* 4 (décembre 1951): 2–4.

20 Laurendeau, "M. Duplessis se congratule avec trop de chaleur," *Devoir*, 29 nov. 1951; A. Tremblay, "La démocratisation de l'enseignement," 28–9; Filion, "Crise scolaire," *Devoir*, 26 nov. 1955.

21 FCS, *Les problèmes des commissions scolaires*, 25; FTQ et CTCC, "Mémoire sur l'éducation," 221–2; Alliance, *Mémoire à la Commission Tremblay*, 24.

22 Filion, "Il ne faut pas faire des évêques des boucs émissaires," *Devoir*, 9 nov. 1960. See also Marcel Faribault, "L'éducation au Canada français," 803–4.

23 FTQ et CTCC, "Mémoire sur l'éducation," 225.

24 Filion, "Il ne faut pas faire des évêques des boucs émissaires," *Devoir*, 9 nov. 1960.

25 Filion, "Pas d'école d'Etat ni d'instituteur fonctionnaire," *Devoir*, 29 oct. 1957; "A propos de ministère de l'Education," ibid., 14 oct. 1960.

26 Fondation Lionel-Groulx, Fonds André Laurendeau, dossier Cardinal Paul-Emil Léger, Cardinal Léger à Laurendeau, 30 sept. 1960; Laurendeau à Cardinal Léger, 18 oct. 1960.

27 [Jean-Paul Desbiens], *Les insolences du Frère Untel* (Montréal: Editions de l'Homme 1960), 51–2.

28 Fondation Lionel-Groulx, Fonds Laurendeau, dossier Jean-Paul Desbiens, numerous letters to Laurendeau, 1960–4. Desbiens was very bitter toward his superiors and when he returned to Quebec in the mid-1960s he worked as a journalist for several years.

29 Laurendeau, "Pour une enquête royale sur l'éducation," *Devoir*, 15 nov. 1960. Arthur Tremblay had been less hesitant and as early as 1958 openly advocated the creation of a Ministry of Education. A. Tremblay, "La démocratisation de l'enseignement," 29.

30 The commission eventually recommended the creation of a Ministry of Education after having assured themselves that the church would *not* fight the development. Neo-nationalists strongly supported the recommendation and

the Liberal government's decision to create a ministry in 1964. Léon Dion, *Le Bill 60 et la société québécoise*, 51–80.

31 L. Baudouin, "Rapport générale," in *L'éducation*, 58.

32 Falardeau, "Conditions et conséquences," 38–9.

33 Léger, "Flagrance d'une injustice," *Cité libre* 16 (février 1957): 60–6. A more radical version was proposed in 1954 by the Société Saint-Jean-Baptiste and accepted by the Tremblay commissioners. A Department of National Education consisting of five councils would run all French-language schools to ensure the survival of the French-Canadian culture. See *Tremblay Report* 3 bk. 2: 210–11, and Société Saint-Jean-Baptiste de Montréal, *Canada français et union canadienne*, 80–6. The Association canadienne des éducateurs de langue française also published a manifesto calling for the dissemination within and outside Quebec's education institutions of a vigorous and authentic "éducation nationale." See their manifesto, "L'éducation patriotique," *AN* 45 (avril 1956): 685–703. See also Jacques MacKay et al., *L'école laique* (Montréal 1961).

34 Filion, "La vraie question," *Devoir*, 13 mai 1959; "La foire aux ignorants," ibid., 12 nov. 1960; "L'économie de querelles scolaires," ibid., 16 nov. 1960.

35 L. Baudouin, "Rapport générale," in *L'éducation*, 60–4; FTQ et CTCC, "Mémoire sur l'éducation," 213–16.

36 Filion, "L'école d'Etat, l'instituteur fontionnaire," *Devoir*, 5 juin 1948; Laurendeau, "Les centralisations d'un décentralisateur," ibid., 21 oct. 1948.

37 Filion, "Une proposition démagogique," *Devoir*, 10 jan. 1948.

38 Filion, " 'Pistolets de paille, paroles de neige, vaines cacades'," *Devoir*, 21 sept. 1949; Laurendeau, "Le nouvel impôt sur le revenu," ibid., 12 fév. 1954.

39 Filion, "Sur la gratuité des livres et les octrois scolaires," *Devoir*, 6 fév. 1952; "Un fossile politique," ibid., 7 déc. 1956; "Pas d'école d'Etat ni d'instituteur fonctionnaire," ibid., 29 oct. 1957.

40 Gérard Filion, *Les confidences d'un commissaire d'écoles*.

41 Laurendeau, "Pendant que nous dormons sur nos retards," *Devoir*, 16 déc. 1957.

42 *Tremblay Report* 4, table 65: 166–7. Gross funded debt of school corporations dropped from $83.0 million in 1947 to $24.9 million in 1948 only to climb to $83.9 million again by 1952. The situation in 1952 was somewhat less serious than in 1946–7, since revenues had more than doubled since 1942 from $40.3 to $87.8 million.

43 Ibid., table 61, 158–9. Between 1945 and 1953 the number of Catholic children – aged five to nineteen – enrolled in school rose from 544,500 to 686,500. See also FCS, *Les problèmes des commissions scolaires*, 126–8. The Fédération demonstrated that the urban school boards were most severely affected. In 1950–1 nearly one-third of city school commission revenues went to paying interest on outstanding debts and buying back bonds that came due,

compared with 13 and 22 per cent respectively for rural and town boards. While the property tax rate went from $1.16 to $1.23 per hundred dollars of evaluation between 1945 and 1951 the revenue from this tax source constituted 59 per cent rather than 73 per cent of total board revenue. The loss had been offset by the introduction of a sales tax in some school board districts in 1950, but most merely went deeper into debt.

44 Ibid., 73–4; *Mémoire de la Corporation générale des instituteurs et institutrices catholiques de la province de Québec à la Commission royale d'enquête sur les problèmes constitutionnels*, 6–10; Tremblay, *Contribution à l'étude des problèmes*, 81.

45 Baudouin, "Rapport générale," 61–3. He pointed out that teachers' pensions because of the miserably low salaries in the past averaged $20 a month! André Laurendeau, "Le rôle social du travailleur intellectuel," *Devoir*, 16 avril 1948, made the same point somewhat more forcefully. See also his "Les 'économiquements faibles'," ibid., 5 avril 1951, and A. Tremblay, *Contribution à l'étude des problèmes*, 58–63.

46 M. Lamontagne, "Le professeur," in *L'éducation*, 44.

47 Tremblay, "La conjoncture actuelle en éducation," 36.

48 FCS, *Les problèmes des commissions scolaires*, 200–1.

49 Ibid., 128–30, 199. Questioning the traditional antistatist mentality, the authors of the brief asked: "Les corporations scolaires seront-elles moins libres si l'aide governementale est plus considérable? Les parents seront-ils pour cela privès davantage de leur droit de surveillance de l'enseignement qui est donné à leurs enfants dans les écoles publiques?" Their reply of course was "no." Tremblay, *Contribution à l'étude des problèmes*, 96; Abel Gauthier, "Inventaire des besoins actuels," in *L'éducation au Québec face aux problèmes contemporains*, 27.

50 FCS, *Les problèmes des commissions scolaires*, 203–5; Tremblay, *Contribution à l'étude des problèmes*, 133–5. All of these proposals found favour with the unions. See FTQ et CTCC, "Mémoire sur l'éducation," 213–16.

51 FCS, *Les problèmes des commissions scolaires*, 180, 205–6.

52 Laurendeau, "Pendant que nous dormons sur nos retards," *Devoir*, 16 déc. 1957.

53 *Tremblay Report* 3 bk. 1: 180, 183–4; see also Paul-Emile Gingras, "La gratuité scolaire," *AN* 48 (novembre-décembre 1958): 77–8.

54 Paul Gérin-Lajoie, "Changing Patterns of Classical Education in Quebec," in *NCCU Proceedings* (1956), 74–6. Claude Galarneau, *Les collèges classiques au Canada français* (Montréal 1978).

55 Louis-Philippe Audet, *Histoire de l'enseignement au Québec* 2: 287–9.

56 See *L'enseignement des sciences au Canada français* (Québec: Ecole de pédagogie et d'orientation de l'Université Laval 1948); *La situation des Canadiens français dans les carrières scientifiques* (Québec: Ecole de pedagogie et d'orientation de l'Université Laval 1948); *L'enseignement des sciences à l'Université* (Québec:

Ecole de pédagogie et d'orientation de l'Université Laval 1949).

57 Cyrias Ouellet, "Les Canadiens français dans les carrières scientifiques," *Revue de l'Université Laval* 3 (octobre 1948): 133–7; Léon Lortie, "Perspectives scientifiques," *L'Action universitaire* 1 (octobre 1947): 43–53; all of this rhetoric seems to have accomplished very little by 1952. See two letters addressed to Laurendeau from the dean of the Faculty of Science at Laval, M. Adrien Pouliot, "La crise de l'enseignement dans le Québec," *Devoir*, 5 mars 1952.

58 Fondation Lionel-Groulx, Fonds André Laurendeau, dossier Cardinal Paul-Emile Léger, Laurendeau à Cardinal Léger, 18 oct. 1960.

59 On the average, 72 per cent of graduates of classical colleges opted for the liberal professions as their career choice. The breakdown was as follows: Collèges diocésains-ruraux 84.9 per cent, urbains 72.5; collèges non-diocésains-ruraux 66.6, urbains 64.9. Tremblay, *Les collèges et les écoles publiques*, 60–1.

60 Filion, "Les carrières des bacheliers," *Devoir*, 23 juin 1954; "Il faut des techniciens, on nous donne des plaideurs," ibid., 1 juin 1955. For a highly emotional and defensive rejection of Filion's arguments see Abbé Richard Joly, "Les carrières des bacheliers," *L'enseignement secondaire au Canada* 34 (novembre 1954): 57–63.

61 Tremblay, *Contribution à l'étude des problèmes*, 150.

62 Laurendeau, "Les conditions d'existence d'une culture nationale," *AN* (juin 1951): 381–2; "Québec a-t-il assez de revenus?" *Devoir*, 21 déc. 1954; "Le cours classique et 'le plus grand nombre possible'," ibid., 1 mars 1950.

63 Dansereau, "Communion et communication," in *L'éducation*, 19; Tremblay, *Les collèges et les écoles publiques*, 54–5. Using a sample of colleges affiliated with Laval, it was shown that 60.6 per cent of the students in diocesan colleges came from farming and working-class families, while 37.0 per cent had white collar or professional backgrounds. In urban nondiocesan colleges only 23.0 per cent came from farming and working-class families, while 73.1 per cent had white collar or professional backgrounds (50 per cent were in the latter category).

64 FTQ et CTCC, "Mémoire sur l'éducation," 220; *Mémoire à la Commission Tremblay*, 29; for proof of the CTCC's statement see *Mémoire du Collège Jean de Brébeuf à la Commisssion royale d'enquête sur les problèmes constitutionnels*, table 8, 118.

65 Dansereau, "Communion et communication," 20–1.

66 M. Tremblay, "Orientations de la pensée social," in *Essais sur le Québec contemporain*, 202; for clerical confirmation of this interpretation of the church's view of the role of classical education see Mgr Marie-Antoine Roy, "Le collège classique au service du Christ, de l'Eglise, de la Société," *ES* 26 (octobre 1946): 15–16; "Réponse de son Eminence Le Cardinal Paul-Emile Léger," cited in *Bulletin* 3 (octobre 1957): 8

67 Filion, "Les laics dans l'enseignement secondaire," *Devoir* 4 fév. 1948; "C'est la loi de l'amitié qui explique l'étonnante durée du *Devoir*," ibid., 1 fév. 1960; see articles by Maurice Blain, Marcel Rioux, and Jean Le Moyen, in *L'école laique*, 41–78,

68 In 1951 secular priests accounted for 84.4 per cent of the teaching personnel in the classical colleges. By 1961 this had dropped to 58.2 per cent, while the number of lay teachers rose from 8.8 to 35.1 per cent. Claude Galarneau, "Les collèges classiques au Canada français," *Les Cahiers des dix* 42 (1979): 87.

69 See Pelletier, "Visite aux supérieurs II," *Devoir*, 12 jan. 1949; François Zalloni, "L'enseignement au seuil d'une crise V," ibid., 2 jan. 1953; Gilles-Yvon Moreau, "Les problèmes des laics dans l'enseignement secondaire," ibid., 14 mars 1957.

70 Pelletier, "Visite aux supérieurs I," *Devoir*, 11 jan. 1949; Filion, "Les laics dans l'enseignement secondaire," ibid., 4 fév. 1948, and "Le noeud gordien de l'enseignement," ibid., 9 juin 1954.

71 Laurendeau, "Sur l'avenir de l'enseignement secondaire," *Devoir*, 27 sept. 1951; "Comment sortir de l'impasse?" ibid., 15 fév. 1952; "Les conditions d'existence," 382; Laurendeau, Gingras, Décarie, Henripin, et Trudeau, "Des vices mortels aux réformes urgentes . . .," *Devoir*, 15 mars 1958.

72 Lortie, "Le système scolaire," 180.

73 Tremblay, "Who Goes to University?" in *Canada's Crisis in Higher Education*, ed. C.T. Bissell, 66–8; *Les collèges et les écoles publiques*, 70–1; and *Contribution à l'étude des problèmes*, 39.

74 Laurendeau, "You, Poor Majority!" *Devoir*, 20 déc. 1951; "Pourquoi cette anomalie dure-t-elle?" ibid., 13 mai 1952; Faribault, "L'éducation au Canada français," *AN* 45 (mai 1956): 802; Lortie, "Le système scolaire," 174.

75 Filion, "Le noeud gordien," *Devoir*, 9 juin 1954; Laurendeau, "Comment sortir de l'impasse?" ibid., 15 fév. 1952. He estimated that 2,000 French Canadians were attending Sir George Williams and 40 per cent of the students of Montreal Catholic High, 25 per cent of Newman High, and 20 per cent of D'Arcy McGee were French Canadians.

76 M. Tremblay, "Orientations de la pensée sociale," 202; M. Blain, "Pour une dynamique de notre culture," *Cité libre* 5 (juin-juillet 1952): 23–4; Falardeau, "Conditions et conséquences," 35–7; Henri Pichette et al., "Réflexions de certains aumoniers syndicaux devant notre cours classique," *Ad Usum Sacerdotum* 13 (avril 1958): 78–81.

77 Roger Rolland, "La lettre contre l'esprit: Un témoignage sur l'enseignement secondaire I," *Devoir*, 13 sept. 1952.

78 Rolland, "L'enseignement secondaire II," *Devoir*, 20 sept. 1952; "L'enseignement secondaire III," ibid., 27 sept. 1952. See also A. Tremblay, *Les collèges et les écoles publiques*, 90–1; Laurendeau, "Les conditions d'existence," 386–7.

79 Rolland, "Remarques sur l'éducation et la culture canadienne-française," *Cité libre* 8 (novembre 1953): 40–1.

80 Dansereau, "Communion et communication," 19; Marrou, "Le dilemme de l'éducation contemporaine," 12–15.

81 Lortie, "Le système scolaire," 176; Laurendeau, "Les conditions d'existence," 384–5. He pointed out that despite French Canada's long and unbroken marriage with the traditional humanities little of enduring intellectual or aesthetic value had emerged from French-Canadian society. A strong indigenous literary culture and intellectual tradition had not taken root.

82 FCC, *L'organization et les besoins de l'enseignement classique dans le Québec* (Ottawa 1954), 20, 40–2; A. Tremblay, *Les collèges et les écoles publiques*, 1–4.

83 Pierre Juneau, "Le cinéma canadien; illusions et faux calculs," *Cité libre* 1 (février 1951): 20–1.

84 Rioux, "Remarques sur l'éducation," 42.

85 A. Tremblay, *Les collèges et les écoles publiques*, 11–12, 49–50; Lortie, "Le système scolaire," 173–4, and "The BA Degree in Our French-Speaking Universities," *Culture* 13 (1952): 21–5; Audet, *Histoire de l'enseignement* 2: 270–1.

86 Gérard Pelletier, "Consultation sur les EPS," *Devoir*, 5 nov. 1949; Filion, "Au lieu de se chicaner," ibid., 3 déc. 1949; Lortie, "The BA Degree," 24–5; Adrien Pouliot, "La crise de l'enseignement dans le Québec," *Devoir*, 5 mars 1952.

87 A. Tremblay, "Commentaires," in *Essais sur le Québec contemporain*, 189–91; "Who Goes to University?" 68–71; and "La conjoncture actuelle en éducation," 31.

88 François Zalloni, "L'enseignement secondaire au seuil d'une crise, I–VIII," *Devoir*, 27, 29, 30 déc. 1952, 2, 3, 5, 7, jan. 1953; Laurendeau, "La crise prochaine de l'enseignement secondaire," ibid., 8 jan. 1953; Tremblay, *Les collèges et les écoles publiques*, 75–7. The Tremblay commissioners agreed with this general assessment. *Tremblay Report* 3 bk. 1: 150–4. For the views of the church see Père Gérard Plante, SJ, *La Presse*, 20 nov. 1956 and Père Marie-Joseph d'Anjou, SJ, *Collège et famille* (février 1956), both cited in Moreau, "Les problèmes des laics dans l'enseignement secondaire," *Devoir*, 15 mars 1957.

89 *Rapport du sous-comité de coordination de l'enseignement à ses divers degrés au Comité catholique de l'instruction publique* 37–41. In fact, the introduction of a classical stream in the public sector had come several years earlier when the Arvida, Jonquière, and Shipsaw school boards, influenced and strongly supported by Bishop Georges Mélançon of Chicoutimi, had set up public classical colleges to ensure that working-class students would be given the same opportunity as upper-class children to strive for university careers. The Loi de l'instruction publique was changed to make this development legal but only after much opposition from several conservative bishops and the Duplessis government. Maurice Lebel, "A Survey of the Latest Reforms in the Field of Education in Quebec," *Culture*, 19 (1958): 261–2.

90 Laurendeau, "De nouveau en éducation," *Devoir*, 22 déc. 1953.

91 FCC, *L'organisation et les besoins de l'enseignement classique*, 20–64 (39 quoted);
see also Mgr Réal Thomassin, "Discours à l'ouverture de l'assemblée générale
tenue à Québec les 9 et 10 novembre 1955," *Bulletin* 1 (décembre 1955) : 2–5;
Mgr Pierre Décary, "Evolution du cours classique," ibid., 7 (novembre 1961):
1; and Mgr Pierre Décary, "Is There Any Room Today for Classical Education?" ibid., 3 (juin 1958): 8.

92 A. Tremblay, *Les collèges et les écoles publiques*, chapters 4 and 5 (73 quoted).

93 Laurendeau, "Le cours classique à l'école publique," *Devoir*, 25 avril 1955.
By 1956, when the EPS had evolved into a public secondary system with the
Latin-science curriculum leading to matriculation, the enrolment in this sector
had already outstripped that of the private classical colleges. Audet, *Histoire de
l'enseignement au Québec* 2: 293.

94 A. Tremblay, *Contribution à l'étude des problèmes*, 201n; Galarneau, "Les
collèges classiques," 80.

95 *Tremblay Report* 3, bk. 1: 1977–9. The commissioners had been influenced
strongly by the provincial school boards' desire to expand and modernize the
existing EPS system if given the legal right to do so by the province. See FCS,
Les problèmes des commission scolaires, 38, 150–5, 196; *Mémoire de la Commission
des écoles catholiques de Montréal à la Commission royale d'enquête sur les
problèmes constitutionnels*, 6–7, 12–13, 18.

96 Filion, "Ruée vers le baccalauréat," *Devoir*, 23 mai 1956; "L'éducation, affaire
d'intérêt public," ibid., 15 mars 1957.

97 Trudeau et al., "Des vices mortels aux réformes urgentes ... ," *Devoir*, 15
mars 1958.

98 FTQ, *Mémoire à la Commission Tremblay*, 5–6; CTCC, *Mémoire à la Commission
Tremblay*, 29; FTQ et CTCC, "Memoire sur l'éducation," 210–17; Alliance,
Mémoire à la Commission Tremblay, 21–2.

99 Laurendeau, "Le cours classique et 'le plus grand nombre possible'," *Devoir*,
1 mars 1950; "Sur l'avenir de l'enseignement secondaire," ibid., 27 sept. 1951;
"L'autonomie, ce n'est pas le droit de crever de faim," ibid., 3 déc. 1953;
"Québec a-t-il assez de revenus?" ibid., 21 déc. 1954; "Plus de canons ou plus
de savants?" ibid., 9 avril 1958. Trembley estimated $50 million in 1958. "La
conjoncture actuelle en éducation," 36. Even Filion was strongly recommending free education to the end of the BA. "La peur des fantômes," *Devoir*, 14
jan. 1959.

100 A. Tremblay, *Contribution à l'étude des problèmes*, 187–8. Furthermore, secondary education served provincial as well as local needs and therefore a good
proportion of the costs should be borne by the province. The *Tremblay Report*
agreed (3, bk. 1: 184). Filion, "Il faut un supplement d'effort," *Devoir*, 13
mars 1957; Tremblay, "L'aide nécessaire de l'Etat," ibid., 7 oct. 1957, and
"Le principe de l'égalité des services éducatifs nécessite la centralisation des
revenus," ibid., 8 fév. 1958. He was trying to counter the suggestion put
forward by F. -A. Angers and the Fédération des Commissions scolaires de

Québec that the regional schools administering secondary education could be self-financing.

101 Filion, "Il est temps qu'on définisse le rôle de l'école publique," *Devoir*, 14 déc. 1957.

102 Filion, "C'est la loi de l'amitié qui explique l'étonnante durée du *Devoir*," *Devoir*, 1 fév. 1960.

103 Laurendeau, "Avec plus d'enthousiasme," *Devoir*, 15 juil. 1958. Duplessis had, in fact, confirmed his intransigence by refusing for over a year to see representatives of 18,000 college students, three of whom camped on his doorstep in the legislature for three months. One of them was his daughter. Laurendeau, "M. Duplessis commence à capituler," ibid., 30 août 1958.

104 FCC, *L'organisation et les besoins de l'enseignement classique*, 254–70. Arthur Tremblay rejected this scheme on the grounds that economic parity would result in total state financial support for private institutions. He probably also feared it would retard the development of the public secondary sector. *Contributions à l'étude des problèmes*, 233.

105 *Tremblay Report* 3, bk. 1: 169–70, 178–9, 187–91. Paul-Emile Gingras was infuriated by the *Tremblay Report*'s fear of the state and argued that the colleges could preserve their financial and administrative autonomy much better by dealing directly with the provincial government rather than being wards of the local or regional schools boards. "L'éducation," AN 45 (juin 1956): 889–95.

106 Filion, *Les confidences d'un commissaire d'écoles*; Laurendeau, "Le régime crée pas les nouvelles lois," *Devoir*, 10 mars 1960.

107 V. Décarie, "Fonds publics et enseignement classique," *Cité libre* 27 (mai 1960): 21–4.

108 Laurendeau, "Où va le Canada français? XIII," *Devoir*, 21 mai 1959.

109 Cardinal Villeneuve cited in Jean Désy, "L'université et l'Etat," *Revue de l'Université Laval* 7 (novembre 1952): 205; Abbé Lionel Groulx, "Professionnels et culture classique," *Devoir*, 15 mai 1946.

110 Désy, "L'Université et l'Etat," 207.

111 Filion, "Langue et culture," *Devoir*, 19 jan. 1949.

112 Laurendeau, "Premier but: L'université," *Devoir*, 10 juin 1955; "Où va le Canada français? XIII," ibid., 21 mai 1959.

113 Mgr Alphonse-Marie Parent, CS, "Le rôle des universités canadiennes-français," AN 28 (septembre 1946): 24–5. He was then secretary-general of Laval. See also his "Pour libérer le Québec de l'étranger les universités canadiennes-françaises devront former plus de diplômés," *Devoir*, 15 juin 1956.

114 The Société Saint-Jean-Baptiste de Montréal considered that the "universités canadiennes-françaises ont la responsabilité de travailler directement à l'enrichissement et à l'épanouissement de la culture canadienne-française ... Elles seront à l'avant-garde d'une politique de défense culturelle qui donnera au Canada français les professeurs, les savants, les artistes, les penseurs, et les

écrivains dont il a besoin." *Canada français et union canadienne*, 87, 89.

115 M. Blain, "Pour une dynamique de notre culture," *Cité libre* 5 (juin-juillet 1952): 24–5.

116 Filion, "Faut-il descendre l'Université dans la rue?" *Devoir*, 16 avril 1958; Thérèse Gouin-Décarie, "Le dilemme de l'éducation contemporaine," in *L'éducation*, 22–3; Pelletier, "Baccalauréat et compte en banque," *Devoir*, 3 jan. 1948.

117 J.-Y. Morin, "Le problème social et l'université," *Le Quartier Latin*, 19 March 1953, cited in AGEUM, *Mémoire à la Commission royale d'enquête sur les problèmes constitutionnels* (Montréal 25 février 1954), 4.

118 Laurendeau, "Pourquoi si peu de fils d'ouvrier et de cultivateur à l'Université?" *Devoir*, 7 mai 1953.

119 Pelletier, "Réponse à M. Louis Doux, M.D.," *Devoir*, 6 nov. 1948.

120 Laurendeau, "Où va le Canada français? XIII" *Devoir*, 21 mai 1959.

121 A. Tremblay, *Contribution à l'étude des problèmes*, 303. *Tremblay Report* 3, bk. 1: 191–2.

122 Falardeau, "Où va le Canada français? XII," *Devoir*, 19 mai 1959. See also his "Lettre à mes étudiants," *Cité libre* 23 (mai 1959): 13–14. Falardeau's approach also pervaded the Association des professeurs de Laval's brief to the Tremblay Commission. Perhaps he played a role in its formulation.

123 Dion, "Aspects de la condition du professeur d'université," *Cité libre* 21 (juillet 1958): 26–8. He warned his colleagues of the pitfalls of externally initiated or mission-oriented research. Academics needed to define their own research priorities and objectives.

124 Léger, "La tâche souveraine," AN 45 (avril 1956): 712–15; Faribault, "Où va le Canada français? X," *Devoir*, 15 mai 1959; Brunet, "Où va le Canada français? VIII," ibid., 13 mai 1959; *Tremblay Report* 3, bk. 1: 192; Association des Professeurs de Laval, *Mémoire à la Commission Tremblay*, 18–19.

125 Laurendeau, "Les conditions d'existence," 387–8; "Où le Canada français? XIII," *Devoir*, 21 mai 1959.

126 Maurice Lamontagne, "Le professeur," in *L'éducation*, 48.

127 Cyrias Ouellet, "La liberté académique," *Cité libre* 19 (janvier 1958): 8.

128 J.-P. Lefebvre, "L'éducation populaire au Canada français," *Cité libre* 13 (novembre 1955): 21, 31, 33; Father Gérard Dion made several strong arguments for the need to have continuing education in advanced democratic societies. "Démocratie et education des adults," *Ad Usum Sacerdotum* (octobre 1959), 152–60.

129 *Mémoire de l'université de Montréal à la Commission royale d'enquête sur les problèmes constitutionnels*, 87–90, 120–42.

130 Mgr Alphonse-Marie Parent, "La misère croissante des Universités québécoises," *Devoir*, 16 and 18 jan. 1954; Université Laval, *Mémoire à la Commission Tremblay*, 10–62, 72–4.

131 Cited in Filion, "Que font les catholiques pour leur universités?" *Devoir*,

5 oct. 1957; see also SSJB, *Canada français et union canadienne*, 89-90.

132 Michel Brunet, "The University as a Public Institution in French Canada from Louis XIII to the Electoral Campaign of 1960," *Canadian Public Administration* 3 (December 1960): 344; and his "Nos universités n'ont jamais eu les ressources necessaires à un enseignement supérieur," *Devoir*, 6 fév. 1958.

133 Brunet, "The University as a Public Institution," 349.

134 Pelletier, "Lettre ouverte aux trois étudiants ... ," *Cité libre*, 20 (mai 1958): 4-6; J.-C. Falardeau, "Manquons-nous d'universités? I-III," *Devoir*, 11, 12, 13 avril 1956.

135 Dion, "Aspects de la condition du professeur d'université," 21.

136 Laurendeau, "La banqueroute d'un système," *Devoir*, 17 juin 1953; "La misère croissante des universités," ibid., 7 jan. 1954; Filion, "Le devoir du Québec envers ses universités," ibid., 27 oct. 1956; "Le chantage continuera," ibid., 16 fév. 1957.

137 Filion, "Incompatibilité de nature," *Devoir*, 9 nov. 1957.

138 Filion, "Que font les catholiques pour leurs universités?" *Devoir*, 5 oct. 1957.

139 Laurendeau, "Vivre, et vivre libre," *Devoir*, 9 fév. 1954; Filion, "Les universités continueront à tirer la langue," ibid., 19 jan. 1957; "Pour protéger la liberté académique," ibid., 11 juin 1958. When the Barrette government announced its plans to guarantee the interest on loans taken out by the universities for capital expenditures Laurendeau regretted the government's failure to create an independent commission for higher education "Université: Corps et âme," ibid., 8 mars 1960.

140 Association des Professeurs de Laval, *Mémoire à la Commission Tremblay*, 29-33; Université Laval, *Mémoire à la Commission Tremblay*, 78-83. The Tremblay commissioners' recommendations for higher education were virtually a summary of these two briefs. *Tremblay Report* 3 bk. 1, 195-6.

141 CTCC, *Mémoire à la Commission Tremblay*, 30; FTQ, *Mémoire à la Commission Tremblay*, 5.

CHAPTER NINE

1 Maurice Lamontagne, "Le rôle économique et social du gouvernement," *Relations industrielles* 9 (mars 1954): 135-6.

2 Donald V. Smiley, ed., *The Rowell-Sirois Report, Book 1* (Toronto: McClelland & Stewart 1963); *Dominion-Provincial Conference on Reconstruction: Proposals of the Government of Canada, August 1945*, 1-52.

3 Cf. Robert Bothwell, Ian Drummond, and John English, *Canada since 1945: Power, Politics, and Provincialism* (Toronto: University of Toronto Press 1981), 91-101, 161-4; Leonard Marsh, *Report on Social Security for Canada 1943* (Toronto: University of Toronto Press 1975).

4 Maurice Johnson, "Relations fiscales (1945-1955)," *Thémis* 5 (janvier 1955): 169-70.

5 Ligue d'Action nationale, "Manifeste de la Ligue d'Action nationale sur la conférence fédérale-provinciale," *AN* 27 (avril 1946): 288–300; "Mémoire de la Province de Québec," *Dominion-Provincial Conference (1945): Dominion and Provincial Submissions and Plenary Conference Discussions*, 339–52.

6 Richard Arès, SJ, *Dossier sur le pacte fédératif de 1867: La Confédération: pacte ou loi?*; Laurendeau, "Nous ne souscrirons pas à notre propre déchéance," *Devoir*, 2 déc. 1949.

7 L. Saint-Laurent, "Une défaite libérale mettrait en danger l'autonomie provinciale," *Devoir*, 16 juil. 1948.

8 Laurendeau, "M. Saint-Laurent contre la Confédération," *Devoir* 16 juil. 1948; "Les pouvoirs 'illimités' d'Ottawa," ibid., 23 juil. 1948; 'M. Saint-Laurent suivra-t-il les traces de M. King?" ibid., 1 juin. 1949. See also F.-A. Angers, "Le problème fiscal et la constitution," *AN* 35 (janvier 1950): 13–15, for similar arguments.

9 Paul Sauriol, "Sur une thèse de M. Garson," *Devoir*, 19 nov. 1948; and F.-A. Angers, "Le problème fiscal et la constitution," 16–18.

10 Maurice Lamontagne, *Le fédéralisme canadien: Evolutions et problèmes*; for a synthesis of the book see his "Le rôle économique et social du gouvernement," *Relations industrielles* 9 (mars 1954): 129–43; J.K. Johnson, ed., *The Canadian Directory of Parliament* (Ottawa: Queen's Printer 1968), 317–18. Lamontagne was named assistant deputy minister of northern affairs and national resources in May 1954. He was economic adviser to the Privy Council, 1955–7, and returned as M. Pearson's economic adviser in 1958. After serving as a Liberal member of the House of Commons, 1963–7, Lamontagne was named to the Senate in April 1967.

11 Lamontagne, *Le fédéralisme canadien*, 84–6, 97–9.

12 Ibid., 100.

13 Ibid., 295. Author's emphasis.

14 Ibid., 241–54, 263–70, 257–61.

15 Filion, "Un hold-up sur les provinces," *Devoir*, 11 juin 1949; "Autres pays, mêmes moeurs," ibid., 3 août 1949; "Le Fédéralisme canadien III," ibid., 23 juil. 1954; Sauriol, "Dans un pays sans Québec," ibid., 3 oct. 1953.

16 Filion, "Les déprédateurs d'Ottawa," *Devoir*, 23 sept., 1953. The statistics quoted by Filion are all reconfirmed in Lamontagne, *Le fédéralisme canadien*, 75–83.

17 Laurendeau, "Le vrai crime," *Devoir*, 4 juil. 1953; "La responsabilité de M. Saint-Laurent," ibid., 11 juil. 1953; and "Un autonomiste provinciale à la mode de monsieur St-Laurent," ibid., 25 juil. 1953; "Y a-t-il encore des 'provinces pauvres' au Canada?" ibid., 17 juin 1954; Filion, "Le fédéralisme canadien, I-II," ibid., 21-22 juil. 1954.

18 Paul Sauriol, "Nouvelle offensive fédérale," *Devoir*, 23 avril 1948; "La course au trésor," ibid., 7 juin 1948; "La médecine d'Etat," ibid., 27 août 1948;

Laporte, "La province a bien fait une mauvaise chose," ibid., 10 mai 1951.

19 Laurendeau, "Veut-on détruire l'Etat fédéral?" *Devoir*, 26 sept. 1949; "Que reste-t-il de la Confédération après deux guerres," ibid., 14 nov. 1949; and "Il est temps de se réveiller," ibid., 5 août 1953. In this last editorial Laurendeau warned that Ottawa's technocrats and social planners with the full support of the federal Liberal party were in the process of rewriting the Canadian constitution without being obliged to have recourse to constitutional amendment procedures.

20 Filion, "Une solution de rechange," *Devoir*, 2 oct. 1954.

21 Laurendeau, "Voulez-vous l'annexion?" *Devoir*, 18 mai 1948.

22 Filion, "Le Fédéralisme canadien IV," *Devoir*, 24 juil. 1954. While conceding that Quebec was not always governed by the best men and in the best interest of French Canadians, Filion acknowledged that "j'aime encore mieux être administré par des gens de ma langue et de ma religion, même si je ne les aime pas, que par de gens étrangers à ma langue et à ma religion qui me sont indulgents." See also Laurendeau, "Peut-on nous rendre à Ottawa ce que nous perdons à Québec," ibid., 29 sept. 1949; "Ne lâchons pas la proie pour l'ombre," ibid., 30 sept. 1949.

23 Filion, "Les dépredateurs d'Ottawa," *Devoir*, 23 sept. 1953.

24 Filion, "Pour qui voterons-nous?" *Devoir*, 14 juil. 1948; "Les centralisateurs sont écrasés," ibid., 29 juil. 1948.

25 Pierre Laporte, "M. André Laurendeau passe au crible la politique de l'U. Nationale," *Devoir*, 10 mars 1948; Laurendeau, "Une taxe miraculeuse?" ibid., 21 mars 1950. He pointed to the Ontario government's recent legislation introducing a personal income tax. Premier Frost refused to implement the tax when the federal government refused to collect it for the province.

26 A good insight into Maurice Duplessis' legalistic concept of provincial autonomy can be gleaned from his speeches during federal-provincial conferences. See, for example, *Proceedings of the Conference of Federal and Provincial Governments, December 4-7, 1950*, 25-8; and the second volume of Rumilly, *Maurice Duplessis et son temps*, containing Duplessis' correspondence with King over the appointment of a lieutenant-governor, 26-30, and his views on the issue of family allowances, 62; the search for an amendment procedure, 144-51; and federal grants to universities, 503-5.

27 Laporte, "L'autonomie est en danger, IV," *Devoir*, 16 déc. 1950; "L'autonomie provinciale à la manière d'Honoré Mercier et Maurice Duplessis," ibid., 21 déc. 1950.

28 Rumilly, *Duplessis et son temps* 2: 189-90; interview with F.-A. Angers, 3 June 1972. Latour called upon Angers and several other HEC faculty members, Roger Brossard, Esdras Minville, and Marcel Faribault, to head various committees of the Chambre de Commerce de Montréal.

29 See F.-A. Angers, "Le tour de M. Duplessis," *AE* 12 (juillet 1947): 344-68;

"L'heure de la grande offensive centralisatrice," *AN* 28 (septembre 1946): 9–21; "La situation ce soir ... sur le front fédéral-provincial," *AN* 29 (mars 1947): 178–87.

30 Chambre de Commerce de Montréal, *Mémoire sur les relations fédérales-provinciales en matière d'impôt* vol. 2, *Exposé*, 4–20; The need to undermine socialism was stressed strongly by F.-A. Angers, "La Chambre de Commerce et les relations fédérales-provinciales," *Relations* 10 (juillet 1950): 192–3; clerics like Father Emile Bouvier agreed completely with this strategy. Emile Bouvier, SJ, "Un nouveau fédéralisme s'impose-t-il au Canada?" *Relations* 14 (septembre 1954): 248–51.

31 Filion, "Les hommes d'affaires sont opposés à la centralisation," *Devoir*, 3 mai 1947; "Capitulation sans conditions," ibid., 10 mai 1947.

32 Chambre de Commerce de Montréal, *Mémoire sur le problème financier des universités*, complete text in *Devoir*, 3 oct. 1951. The chamber estimated that Quebec would gain $7 or $8 million in revenue, a sum more than sufficient to serve the needs of the province's universities.

33 Laurendeau, "Encore de l'autonomisme verbal!" *Devoir*, 18 jan. 1952.

34 Rumilly, *Duplessis et son temps* 2: 409. Duplessis attempted to confuse the issue further when he declared that "son gouvernement n'imposera jamais le revenu parce que c'est taxer le travail. Il aime mieux taxer les corporations parce que c'est une taxe sur les profits," *Devoir*, 19 juin 1952.

35 Filion, "L'ennemi public numéro un," *Devoir*, 26 mars 1952; "Une autonomie à zéro pour cent," ibid., 17 mai 1952; Laurendeau, "M. Duplessis a opéré un repli stratégique," ibid., 27 mai 1952.

36 *Commerce-Montréal* editorial cited in full in *Devoir*, 27 mai 1952.

37 Filion, "Maître après Dieu," *Devoir*, 17 juil. 1952.

38 Johnson, "Relations fiscales (1945–1955), 176–8. The agreement was signed on 29 October 1952 after a special session of the Ontario Legislature; Laporte, "L'Ontario, nouveau satellite du gouvernement d'Ottawa," *Devoir*, 3 sept. 1952; Laurendeau, "Un bouche-trou! dit M. Frost," ibid., 4 sept. 1952.

39 Filion, "Si M. Drew veut prendre pied dans Québec," *Devoir*, 6 sept. 1952.

40 Chambre de Commerce de la Province de Québec, *Les relations fédérales-provinciales en matière d'impôts*, 1–2, 13–29, 36–7. See also Rumilly, *Duplessis et son temps* 2: 446.

41 Gérin-Lajoie, "La Commission Tremblay," *Relations* 13 (septembre 1953): 235; Rumilly, *Duplessis et son temps* 2: 446–7. The organizers were two members of the executive of the Chambre de Commerce de Montréal, Gilbert LaTour and Jean-Guy Décarie, a nephew of J.-L. Blanchard, the Union Nationale member for Terrebonne.

42 For Angers' and Bonenfant's testimony see René Durocher and Michèle Jean, "Duplessis et la Commission royale d'enquête sur les problèmes constitutionnels, 1953–1956," *RHAF* 25 (décembre 1971): 341; Gérin-Lajoie confirmed

this interpretation of the events during an interview, 14 Dec. 1972. See also *Devoir*, 27 nov. 1952.

43 Laurendeau and Filion, "Vers une nouvelle phase," *Devoir*, 11 oct. 1952; Laporte "Québec aurait sa commission royale d'enquête," ibid., 27 nov. 1952.

44 Paul Gérin-Lajoie, "La Commission Tremblay," 236; "Quel est l'état de la question," *Devoir*, 29 sept. 1953.

45 Vigeant, "Qu'est-ce que perd la province de Québec a ne pas signer de convention fiscale?" *Devoir*, 16 mars 1953.

46 *Statuts de la Province de Québec*, 2–3 Eliz. 2, c.17 (Québec: Queen's Printer 1954). The terms of the bill set the personal exemptions at $1,500 for an adult, $150 for a child under fourteen, $400 for a child over fourteen, and the rate of taxation was approximately 15 per cent of the federal rates for the same taxable income.

47 Johnson, "Relations fiscales (1945-1955)." The Tremblay commissioners calculated that between 1947 and 1955 the revenue accruing to the province of Quebec would have been $136 million greater had the province signed the tax rental agreements of 1947 and 1952. *Tremblay Report* 1: 211.

48 Rumilly, *Duplessis et son temps* 2: 457, 481, 487.

49 Durocher et Jean, "Duplessis et la Commission d'enquête," 346–8. In November 1953 Duplessis revealed during a press conference that he had tried in November 1951 to get St. Laurent to agree to hand over to the provinces 5 per cent of the federal income tax but the proposal had been flatly rejected. Duplessis rejected St Laurent's counter-suggestion that the province collect its income tax and the taxpayers would be able to deduct up to 5 per cent from their federal taxes. Duplessis to St Laurent, 17 nov. 1951, and St Laurent to Duplessis, 26 nov. 1951; copies of both in Chambre de Commerce de Montréal, *Mémoire à la Commission d'enquête sur les problèmes constitutionnels*, vol. 2, *Les relations fédérales-provinciales* (mimeo, Bibliothèque de la Législature, Québec), Annexe 23, 52–9. André Laurendeau, upon hearing of these November 1951 negotiations, was furious with Duplessis for not having pursued them further by calling for public support for his position. "M. Duplessis et la clause de 5 pour cent," *Devoir*, 17 nov. 1953.

50 Filion, "Québec reprend l'offensive," *Devoir*, 15 jan. 1954; Laurendeau, "Le nouvel impôt sur la revenue," ibid., 12 fév. 1954; "Tous mes biens à mon épouse," ibid., 18 fév. 1954.

51 Chambre de Commerce de Montréal, *Mémoire à la Commission d'enquête . . .*, vol. 2, *Les relations fédérales-provinciales*, 52–5; and Chambre de Commerce de Montréal, "Que l'impôt provincial soit déductible de l'impôt fédéral," *Devoir*, 9 mars 1954.

52 Laurendeau, "Il faut qu'Ottawa rende l'impôt déductible du sien," *Devoir*, 26 fév. 1954; "Au nom de l'unité canadienne," ibid., 25 mars 1954; Filion, "Chef de l'Opposition à vie," ibid., 20 fév. 1954; "Un grand Maillardville, ibid.,

14 avril 1954. See also "Des ententes fiscales 'new look'?" ibid., 17 avril 1954, in which Filion reminds Jean Lesage, a federal cabinet minister, that Duplessis had been partly forced into creating the provincial income tax by nonpolitical associations and groups in the province. It was not an election gimmick of the Union Nationale but constituted the essence of Quebec's concrete proposal to Ottawa.

53 "Rapport moral du président," *Procès-verbal* (Québec 1953), 35–6.

54 *Mémoire annuel de la CTCC au cabinet provincial*, 3 décembre 1952, cited in full in *Le Travail*, 15 déc. 1952.

55 Fernand Dansereau, "Les syndicats appuient le principe de l'impôt provinciale," *Devoir*, 17 jan. 1954. Dansereau later reported that the Conseil central des syndicats nationaux de Shawinigan (CTCC) had called upon its federal MP, J.-A. Richard, to press for full deductibility and suggested strongly that he vote against the budget if the government refused full credit. The union central had a membership of 7,000 and constituted a substantial voting bloc. "Plusieurs syndicats font pression pour la déductibilité," *Devoir*, 24 avril 1954.

56 *Mémoire de la CTCC à la Commission royale d'enquête sur les problèmes constitutionnels, 1954* (mimeo in Bibliothèque de la Législature, Québec), 11; *Mémoire annuel de la CTCC au cabinet fédéral, 10 novembre 1954*, 5.

57 *Mémoire de la Fédération du travail du Québec présenté à ... la Commission royale d'enquête sur les problèmes constitutionnels. Montréal, le 23 juin 1954* (mimeo in Bibliothèque de la Législature, Québec), 10–13, 14–15.

58 *Mémoire de la Fédération des unions industrielles du Québec (CCT) à la Commission royale d'enquête sur les problèmes constitutionnels, 10 mars 1954*, 24–9, 32–7.

59 P.E. Trudeau, "De libro, tributo et quibusdam aliis," in his *Federalism and the French Canadians*, 66–7. The article first apeared in *Cité libre* (octobre 1954). He went on to point out that although Ottawa had altered the terms of the tax rental agreements to suit the needs of the other reluctant provinces, it had steadfastly refused to consider the principle of tax deductibility called for by the government and people of Quebec. As a result, "the federal government and its clever civil servants accommodate themselves only too easily to a system that, at least until 1954, amounted to a manifest defrauding of the Quebec taxpayer," 68–9.

60 *Mémoire de la FUIQ à la Commission d'enquête royale*, 38–41.

61 Ibid., 45.

62 Laurendeau, "La CTCC et les relations fédérales-provinciales," *Devoir*, 17 sept. 1953; Dansereau "Les 3 fédérations syndicals sont d'accord pour reconnaître le droit de la province," ibid., 25 juin 1954.

63 Canada, House of Commons, *Debates*, 1953–4, 4:3730–3. Having considered Quebec's claim for a full 15 per cent credit, Abbott concluded: "Clearly, however, the obvious implication of the principle involved in this proposal is that this parliament should recognize that any province has the right to deter-

mine the amount by which the people of that province may reduce their national tax liability. I consider that any such principle is completely unacceptable" (3732).

64 Dale C. Thomson, *Louis St. Laurent: Canadian*, 377; Laurendeau, "L'opération 'Saxonia'," *Devoir*, 23 sept. 1954.

65 Richard Daignault, "Cri de guerre de M. Saint-Laurent contre le Québec," *Devoir*, 20 sept. 1954; Thomson, *Louis St. Laurent*, 378–80.

66 Laurendeau, "L'opération 'Saxonia'," *Devoir*, 23 sept. 1954. Filion supported this hypothesis when he revealed that the Chambre de Commerce de Montréal and the Board of Trade had arranged a meeting between Duplessis and St Laurent prior to the latter's Saxonia speech on 9 September. The only plausible explanation was that the Keynesian-dominated civil service which controlled policy in Ottawa had succeeded in getting St Laurent to change his mind and adopt an offensive strategy. "Une volte-face inexplicable," ibid., 29 sept. 1954.

67 Vigeant, "Pourquoi nous ne sommes pas séparatistes," *Devoir*, 30 sept. 1954; Filion, "Québec, un Etat Nationale," ibid., 21 sept. 1954; Ligue d'Action nationale, "Discours indigne de M. Saint-Laurent," ibid., 15 oct. 1954.

68 Laurendeau, "M. Saint-Laurent continue d'oublier que Québec est 'différent'," *Devoir*, 24 nov. 1954.

69 Rumilly, *Duplessis et son temps* 2: 506

70 Ibid., 507; Thomson, *Louis St. Laurent*, 380–1.

71 Thomson, ibid., 382–3.

72 Canada, House of Commons, *Debates*, 1955, 1:229–30. St Laurent also released the correspondence he had had on the subject with Duplessis. PAC, *Records of Parliament, 1775–1958*, RG 1H, D2, vol. 626, Duplessis to St Laurent, 11 October 1954, and St Laurent to Duplessis, 14 January 1955. See also Rumilly, *Duplessis et son temps* 2: 511–13, 517–18.

73 Laurendeau, "Trop beau pour être vrai?" *Devoir*, 5 nov. 1954; "Injuste pour tout le monde," ibid., 27 jan. 1955; Sauriol, "Les relations fédérales-provinciales," ibid., 13 oct. 1954; Vigeant, "Blocs-notes," ibid., 29 Nov. 1954; "Ottawa n'offre pas d'entente, mais une concession au Québec," ibid., 18 jan. 1955.

74 Filion, "Une retraite qui est un refus de discuter," *Devoir*, 19 jan. 1955.

75 Trudeau, "Preface à la deuxieme édition," *Mémoire de la FUIQ à la Commission royale d'enquête*, 3–4.

76 Canada, *Proceedings of the Federal-Provincial Conference, 1955*, 14, 16–18; Sauriol, "La conférence fédérale-provinciale," *Devoir*, 5 oct. 1955.

77 Filion, "Il n'y a pas de causes désespérées," *Devoir*, 18 jan. 1956.

78 Filion, "Un accord, non une capitulation," *Devoir*, 29 fév. 1956; "Il y a des mouvements réversibles," ibid., 29 jan. 1958.

79 *Proceedings of the Dominion Provincial Conference, 1957*, 25–6.

80 Filion, "Un accord, non une capitulation," *Devoir*, 29 fév. 1956; "M. Duplessis est satisfait des offres fédérales," ibid., 7 juin 1956; F.-A. Angers, "Rien n'est réglé!" *AN* 45 (mai 1956): 772–84.

81 Canada, House of Commons, *Debates*, 1951, 5: 4278; vote 650, pp. 5, 166.

82 *Report of the Royal Commission on National Development in the Arts, Letters and Sciences*, 355; David Stager, "Federal Government Grants to Canadian Universities," *CHR* 54 (September 1973): 289–91.

83 Stager, "Federal Government Grants," 292. He contends that only Norman Mackenzie favoured such a scheme but fails to point out that Father Lévesque's position was crucial. His negative response would have vetoed the recommendation, but he assured his fellow commissioners that Quebec's universities needed and wanted the grants and the Duplessis government could be persuaded to accept the scheme. Interview with Father Lévesque, 4 Feb. 1974.

84 Stager, "Federal Government Grants," 295–6; Rumilly, *Duplessis et son temps* 2: 403–5.

85 "M. Duplessis tent d'expliquer sa volte-face," *Devoir*, 15 mars 1952. The correspondence outlining the Duplessis–St Laurent negotiations on the issue is located in Chambre de Commerce de Montréal, *Mémoire à la Commission d'enquête . . .*, vol. 2, *Les relations fédérales-provinciales*, Annexe 23, 44–68.

86 Rumilly, *Duplessis et son temps*, 2: 407–10.

87 *Massey Report*, xvii–xviii; see also B.K. Sandwell, "Present Day Influences on Canadian Society," in *Royal Commission Studies: A Selection of Essays Prepared for the Royal Commission on National Development in the Arts, Letters and Sciences*, 1–11. Many of the other studies reflected the same concern with American cultural influences in Canada.

88 "Le père G.-H. Lévesque défend les conclusions du rapport Massey," *Devoir*, 12 nov. 1951; "Le chevauchement des cultures," in Institut canadien des affaires publiques, *Le fédéralisme*, 22–4; Guy Sylvestre, "Le rapport Massey," *Revue Dominicaine* 57 (septembre 1951): 104–12; A. Lamarche, "La vie de l'esprit au Canada," ibid. 57 (juillet-août 1951): 4–10; *Mémoire soumis par l'Université Laval à la Commission royale d'enquête sur les problèmes constitutionnels*, 4 mars 1954 (mimeo in the Bibliothèque de la Législature, Québec), 2–7.

89 Filion, "L'ingérence du fédéral dans l'enseignement supérieur," *Devoir*, 7 juin 1951; Laporte, "Le R.P. Lévesque est-il naif ou optimiste?" *AN* 44 (octobre 1954): 145–6; Angers, "Les solutions du Rapport Massey III–A qui la faute?" *AN* 39 (mai 1952): 267–75.

90 Laurendeau, "La Commission Massey devant 'L'American Way of Life'," *Devoir*, 28 juin 1951; "La Commission Massey est-elle un bureau de réclamations?" ibid., 30 août 1949; "Mon mémoire à la Commission Massey," ibid., 25 nov. 1949; Michel Brunet, "Le Rapport Massey: Réflexions et observations," *L'Action universitaire* 18 (janvier 1952): 39–41; Ligue d'Action nationale, "Mémoire à la Commission royale d'enquête sur les arts, les lettres et les sciences," *AN* 35 (avril 1950): 306–11, 321–2. The author was Father Richard Arès.

91 Filion, "L'ingérence du fédéral dans l'enseignement supérieur," *Devoir*, 7 juin 1951; "Quand des intellectuels se mettent à dérailler," ibid., 14 nov. 1951; Laurendeau, " 'L'éducation académique . . .'," ibid., 17 juil. 1951.

92 Laurendeau, "Ottawa nous refuse ce qu'il a et nous donne ce qu'il n'a pas," *Devoir*, 3 juil. 1951; "Blocs-notes," ibid., 16 nov. 1951. For an even harsher and, to a degree, libellous attack on Father Lévesque see F.-A. Angers, "Deux modèles d'inconscience: Le Premier Saint-Laurent et le Commissaire Lévesque," *AN* 38 (novembre 1951): 205–8. Angers characterized Lévesque as the darling of Anglo-Canadians like Blair Fraser and declared that if the *Massey Report*'s recommendations became reality Lévesque would become known as the French Canadian "qui aura, le premier, ouvert officiellement la porte de notre régime scolaire aux invasions fédérales directes; comme celui qui, sous le couvert de l'aide fédérale aux universités, aura introduit le cheval de Troie ou le cadeau de Grec dans nos murs." Ibid., 208.

93 Laurendeau, "La Commission Massey devant 'L'American Way of Life'," *Devoir*, 28 juin 1951; Filion, "Un tiens vaut mieux que deux tu l'auras," ibid., 19 déc. 1951; Laporte, "Le R.P. Lévesque," 146–52.

94 Revealing his immense feeling for power politics, Filion remarked: "On ne troque pas un droit contre de l'argent. On peut l'échanger contre un autre droit. Si on nous proposait d'échanger l'autonomie culturelle du Québec contre une égalité de fait et de droit à toutes les écoles catholiques et françaises du Canada, nous pourrions discuter. Si on nous disait: Amendons la Constitution; remettons à Ottawa une certaine autorité en matière d'enseignement, mais exigeons que toutes les écoles françaises et catholiques des autres provinces soient traités comme les écoles protestantes du Québec, il y aurait lieu de parlementer." "L'aide fédérale à l'enseignement III–Des naifs ou des traitres?" *Devoir*, 1 avril 1952. See also "Le poisson pourrit par la tête," ibid., 7 juin 1952, in which Filion chastised a section of Quebec's intellectual élite for its total lack of political sense. "La trahison des clercs n'est pas un phénomène particulier a l'élite européenne," he warned.

95 Ligue d'Action nationale, "Mémoire à la Commission Tremblay," 312–16; Michel Brunet, *Canadians et Canadiens*, 26, 29–30, 57–8; Filion, "Nous ne sommes pas des imbéciles," *Devoir*, 7 1953.

96 Louis Saint-Laurent, "Nécessité d'une politique d'éducation," *La Réforme*, 17 oct. 1956; "Address by the Prime Minister," in *Canada's Crisis in Higher Education*, ed., Claude T. Bissell, 249–57; "Québec reste sur ces positions," *Devoir*, 20 oct. 1956; "M. St-Laurent ignore M. Duplessis," ibid., 22 oct. 1956.

97 Mgr Vandry of Laval was on the NCCU executive and Mgr Irénée Lussier of the Université de Montréal spoke out in favour of the new scheme. "Déclarations sur les octrois fédéraux," in Bissell, *Canada's Crisis*, 228–30; Filion, "Le débat est ouvert," *Devoir*, 20 oct. 1956.

98 M. Blain, "Il faut choisir son risque," *Devoir*, 2 nov. 1956; Lambert, "Auto-

nomie provinciale et aide fédérale aux université," ibid., 26 oct. 1956; Dion, "Pouvons-nous? Devon-nous accepter l'offre fédérale d'octroi aux universités?" ibid., 5 nov. 1956; Perrault, "Octrois fédéraux aux universités de la province de Québec," ibid., 9 nov. 1956.

99 Falardeau, "Les octrois fédéraux aux Universités," *Devoir*, 23 oct. 1956.

100 Picard, "L'aide fédérale aux universités est une mesure saine," *Devoir*, 8 nov. 1956.

101 Albert Lévesque, "La 'formule Saint-Laurent': un détournant de fonds," *Devoir*, 23 oct. 1956; Esdras Minville, "Les universités doivent aider la province à reconquérir sa liberté fiscale," ibid., 14 nov. 1956.

102 Brunet, "Le professeur Jean-Charles Falardeau et les besoins universitaires," *Devoir*, 29 oct. 1956. For his critical assessment of the debate see his *La présence anglaise et les Canadiens* 272–4.

103 Trudeau, *Federalism and the French Canadians*, 81–7, 91–2, 95–6.

104 Filion, "Le devoir du Québec envers ses universités," *Devoir*, 27 oct. 1956; "Sommes-nous prêts à accepter l'intervention d'Ottawa?" ibid., 10 nov. 1956; "Demain l'enseignement primaire," ibid., 14 nov. 1956.

105 Filion, "L'aide fédérale aux universités," *Devoir*, 13 oct. 1956.

106 Arès, "Les octrois fédéraux aux universités," *Relations* 16 (décembre 1956): 342.

107 "Québec promet des subsides à l'enseignement," *Devoir*, 15 nov. 1956; Rumilly, *Duplessis et son temps* 2: 590.

108 NCCU, *Proceedings, 1958* (Ottawa n.d.), 115; NCCU, *Proceedings 1959*, (Ottawa n.d.), 139. For the 1958–9 term the grants offered to Quebec's three largest universities were as follows: McGill $1.6 million, Laval $2.1 million, and Montréal $2.8 million.

109 Filion, "La perche est tendue," *Devoir*, 21 juil. 1959; Laurendeau, "Des déceptions, un espoir," ibid., 20 oct. 1959; "Lettre de M. Diefenbaker à M. Sauvé, 9 décembre, 1959," cited in Arthur Tremblay, "Les subventions fédérales aux universités," *Cité libre* 25 (mars 1960): 6–7, 9–10.

110 Filion, "Les conservateurs québécois le dos au mur," *Devoir*, 16 jan. 1960; Laurier L. LaPierre, "The 1960s," in *The Canadians 1867–1967*, ed. J.M.S. Careless and R. Craig Brown, (Toronto, 1968), pt. 1, 353–4. Interview with Senator Arthur Tremblay, 25 Sept. 1981.

111 Laurendeau, "Il faut restaurer le fédéralisme," *Devoir*, 4 mai 1951; "Blocs-notes," ibid., 9 mars 1951.

112 Richard Arès, SJ, *Le fédéralisme: Ses principes de base et sa valeur humaine* (Montréal: Institut social populaire, février 1951, no. 441), 3–7, 21–8. This pamphlet was a collection of four articles originally published in *L'Action nationale* between October 1950 and January 1951. Laurendeau as editor had probably solicited the articles.

113 Ligue d'Action nationale, "Conditions d'un Etat Français dans la Confédération Canadienne: Mémoire à la Commission royale d'enquête sur les relations

fédérales-provinciales," *AN* 43 (mars-avril 1954); 328–30.

114 Ibid., 335, 337–44.

115 Société Saint-Jean-Baptiste de Montréal, *Canada français et union canadienne*, 54–68, 116.

116 Ibid., 125.

117 Ibid., 124; Brunet had first used the term "Statut spécial" in a speech to the AJC in November 1953. *Canadians et Canadiens*, 30. Philippe Ferland, a constitutional expert and law professor at the Université de Montréal, pushed Brunet's analysis one step further and called for the creation of a binational federal state. See his "Il faut refaire la Confédération," *AN* 44 (septembre 1954): 15–52.

118 The commission's members included Judge Thomas Tremblay, a close friend of Duplessis, Esdras Minville, president of the HEC, Paul-Henri Guimont, secretary of the Faculty of Social Sciences at Laval, Honoré Parent, recommended by the Chambre de Commerce de Montréal, John P. Rowat, and Father Richard Arès, associate editor of the ISP and *Relations*. F.-A. Angers was appointed as technical adviser and wrote three special studies for the commission. See Durocher et Jean, "Duplessis et la Commission royale d'enquête," 341–5; Rumilly, *Duplessis et son temps*, 2: 461–2.

119 Laurendeau, "Blocs-notes," *Devoir*, 9 avril 1956; ibid., 7 avril 1956. Those interested in the report had either to consult it in the Bibliothèque de la Législature in Quebec City or obtain a copy from Jean-Charles Bonenfant, the chief librarian, almost as a favour. Little wonder that the first edition of 3,000 copies was hardly depleted in 1960. See Durocher et Jean, "Duplessis et la Commission royale d'enquête," 362.

120 *Tremblay Report* 3, bk. 2: 227–8, 294–5.

121 Ibid., 233–7.

122 Ibid., 264–72, 255–61.

123 Filion, "La clandestine du rapport Tremblay," *Devoir*, 21 avril 1956; and articles by Laurendeau, Sauriol, Filion, "Le rapport Tremblay I–XIX," *Devoir*, 21 avril–19 mai 1956 (quote from article XIX).

124 Filion, "Le rapport Tremblay sera-t-il reflué?" *Devoir*, 27 juil. 1956; Laporte, "La 'résurrection' du Rapport Tremblay," ibid., 24 sept. 1957; "Perdue dans les brumes de la colline parlementaire?" ibid., 27 sept. 1957; F.-A. Angers, P.-E. Gingras, et al., *Compte Rendu*, 22ième Congrès Annuel de la Chambre de Commerce de la Province de Québec, Chicoutimi, 18–22 septembre 1957 (Québec 1957), 1–36.

125 Laurendeau, "Y a-t-il trop de provinces au Canada?" *Devoir*, 26 nov. 1953.

126 Filion, "Le rapport Tremblay, XIX–Le rapport sera-t-il enfoui dans la tombe de M. Duplessis?" *Devoir*, 19 mai 1956; "Faire cavalier seul? Et pourquoi pas?" ibid., 2 mai 1959.

127 Laurendeau, "M. Diefenbaker et les droits provinciaux," *Devoir*, 19 fév. 1958; "Diefenbaker et le Québec," ibid., 1 mars 1958; "M. Diefenbaker et le

dilemme québécois," ibid., 15 mars 1958; and "M. Diefenbaker et le 'melting pot'," ibid., 24 mars 1958; "Ottawa ne bouge guère," ibid., 11 juin 1959.

128 Filion, "Un principe qui se révèle pratique," *Devoir*, 8 juil. 1959.
129 R.P. Arès, "Quel régime Québec doit-il proposer?" *Devoir*, 29 juin 1959; F.-A. Angers, "Propositions concrètes pour la prochaine conférence fédérale-provinciale," ibid., 2 juil. 1959; and Robidas, "Regards sur la constitution canadienne de l'avenir," ibid., 30 juin 1959.

CHAPTER TEN

1 Trudeau, "Réflexions sur la politique au Canada français," *Cité libre* 6 (décembre 1952): 53.
2 Boisvert, Cormier, Blain, "Flèches de tout bois," *Cité libre* 1 (juin 1950): 40–5; Boisvert, "Le Duplessis-soleil," *Cité libre* 3 (mai 1951): 59–60.
3 Jean-Louis Gagnon, "La propagande et le mythe d'Antée," *Cité libre* 6 (décembre 1952): 13; Charles Lussier, "Loi électorale et conscience politique," ibid., 27–8; Filion, "Pour une rédistribution de la carte électorale," *Devoir*, 26 juil. 1952; Laurendeau, "Qui a élu M. Duplessis?" ibid., 27 juin 1956.
4 Kenneth McRoberts and Dale Posgate, *Quebec: Social Change and Political Crisis*, 74.
5 Léger, "De notre démocratie libérale comme expression de la volonté du peuple," *AN* 36 (novembre 1950): 203–12, 186–90.
6 Lussier, "Loi électorale et conscience politique," 31.
7 Filion, "Un moteur solide mais pas de frein," *Devoir*, 18 juil. 1952; "Maître après Dieu," ibid., 17 juil. 1952. Liberals got 48 per cent of the popular vote for 23 seats while the UN held 68 seats with 50 per cent of the vote.
8 Laporte, "Les élections ne se font pas avec des prières XIII, XVI–XVII," *Devoir*, 15, 18–19 oct. 1956. For an analysis of some of the cases studied by the Salvas commissioners see Vincent Lemieux et Raymond Hudon, *Patronage et politique au Québec 1944–1972* (Sillery, Québec 1976), app. 2, 168–73. See also Mario Cardinal, Vincent Lemieux, and Florian Sauvageau, *si l'union nationale m'était contée . . .* (Montréal: Boréal Express 1978), chap. 8, "La caisse électorale," 166–87.
9 Pelletier, "D'ou vient l'argent qui nourri les partis?" *Cité libre* 6 (décembre 1952): 35–41; Filion, "Derrière le rideau de fer," *Devoir*, 13 oct. 1948; Rumilly, *Duplessis et son temps* 2: 101–2, 155–6, 234–5, 473.
10 Laporte, "La machine électorale," *Cité libre* 6 (décembre 1952): 44–6; Pelletier, "D'où vient l'argent qui nourri les partis?" 35–41; Filion, "Le peuple et l'argent se sont prononcés," *Devoir*, 21 juin 1956; Laurendeau, "Echec de la morale politique dans le Québec," ibid., 11 juil. 1956; Laporte, "Les élections ne se font pas avec de prières I–VI," ibid., 1–6 oct. 1956.
11 Pelletier, "D'ou vient l'argent," *Cité libre* 3 (décembre 1952): 35–9; Lauren-

deau, "Qui a élu M. Duplessis?" *Devoir*, 27 juin 1956; Trudeau, "Réflexions sur la politique," 61.

12 Trudeau, "Un manifeste démocratique," *Cité libre* 22 (octobre 1958): 2, 20–1. On the long-standing historical "conspiracy" between the church and the monied classes–English and American–see "Some Obstacles to Democracy in Quebec," in Trudeau, *Federalism and the French Canadians*, 108–9, originally published in *CJEPS* 24 (August 1958).

13 Laurendeau, "Caisses électorales et liberté," *Devoir*, 17 sept. 1956; Trudeau, "Réflexions sur la politique," 61–2; Filion, "Réforme des lois et des moeurs électorales," *Devoir*, 8 août 1956.

14 Laurendeau, "Ce qui était la loi électorale de 1945," *Devoir*, 29 jan. 1953; "Le Conseil législatif votera-t-il cette saleté?" ibid., 30 jan. 1953; "Le Conseil doit écarter . . ." ibid., 4 fév. 1953. The struggle was close. Bill 34 passed by only one vote–8 to 7–in the Legislative Council. See Laurendeau, "Blocs-notes," ibid., 13 fév. 1953.

15 Laurendeau, "Le Bill 34 va subir son premier test," *Devoir*, 3 juin 1953; "Pourquoi l'Union Nationale se bat-elle si fort dans Outremont," ibid., 10 juin 1953; Georges-Emile Lapalme makes the same claim in his *Mémoires* 2: 140–1.

16 Laporte, "Les élections ne se font pas avec des prières," *Devoir*, 12, 13, 23, 24 oct., 6, 13, 14, 22, 23, 24 nov. and 4 dec. 1956.

17 Ibid., 16, 17, 19, 20 nov. 1956. Laporte was an independent nationalist candidate in the Montréal-Laurier riding. His defeat was partially responsible for provoking this highly revealing and, at times, provocative series of articles. The revelations made good copy and sold a lot of newspapers for *Le Devoir*, then on the verge of bankruptcy.

18 Trudeau, "Réflexions sur la politique," 63.

19 Eugène L'Heureux, "La vénalité en politique," *Devoir*, 10 sept. 1956; Laporte, "Les élections ne se font pas avec des prières," ibid., 6 nov. 1956; Laurendeau, "Blocs-notes," ibid., 7 fév. 1953.

20 Laporte, "Une enquête sur le fonctionarisme," *Devoir*, 21, 25, 28 nov., 3, 5, 10, 16, 19 déc. 1947; "Veut-on un gouvernement efficace et progressif?" ibid., 14 oct. 1955; Laurendeau, "Blocs-notes," ibid., 24 mars 1955; "La stabilité et la misère," ibid., 23 mars 1959. Neo-nationalists gained the welcome support of the Chambre de Commerce de Montréal, *Mémoire à la Commission royale d'enquête sur les problèmes constitutionnels*, vol. 6, *Le fonctionnarisme dans la province de Québec* (avril 1955) (mimeo, Bibliothèque de la Législature, Québec), 1–138.

21 Filion, "Du surréalisme fiscal," *Devoir*, 26 fév. 1949; "Régime d'arbitraire," ibid., 18 mars 1950; "Un budget de fraude," ibid., 7 fév. 1953. For a more comprehensive analysis of the Union Nationale's budgetary procedures see Roland Parenteau, "Finances provinciales 1953," *AE* (juillet-septembre 1953); 343–51; and Georges-Emile Lapalme, *Analyse de la situation financière et*

économique de la province de Québec (speech in the Assembly, 7 Feb. 1956, n.p., n.d), 1-63. Lapalme calculated that over a ten-year period, 1945 to 1955, the Duplessis government had spent $363 million over and above the annual budgetary estimates voted by the Assembly (11).

22 Laporte, "Les élections ne se font pas avec des prières," *Devoir*, 17 oct. 1956. See also 20, 22, 25, 26 oct. and 3, 5, 8, 9 nov. 1956.

23 Filion, "Régime d'arbitraire," *Devoir*, 18 mars 1950.

24 Robert Rumilly describes quite unabashedly how this system of discretionary grants worked and how numerous religious and civil leaders expressed their deepest gratitude for the generosity and largesse of Maurice Duplessis and his administration. *Maurice Duplessis et son temps* 2: 212, 327, 345, 357-58, 496, 552, 578-79. For a detailed account of all the grants see Paul Bouchard's election propaganda volume, *La Province de Québec sous l'Union Nationale* (Québec 1956), 1-271.

25 Laurendeau, "Echec de la moralité politique dans le Québec," *Devoir*, 11 juil. 1956; "Une maladie de la démocratie," ibid., 13 juil. 1948.

26 Marcel Rioux, "Requiem pour une clique," *Cité libre* 30 (octobre 1960): 3-4.

27 See chap. 8 above for a detailed discussion of the rationale behind statutory grants.

28 Laurendeau, 'Le diable est-il à gauche?" *Devoir*, 4 fév. 1957.

29 Laurendeau, "Un épilogue," *Devoir*, 28 fév. 1953; Filion, "Il nous faudrait un Bernanos," ibid., 11 août 1956.

30 Filion, "L'anticommunisme électoral redevient à la mode," *Devoir*, 11 juin 1952. Rumilly repeats these inane rumours, *Duplessis et son temps* 2: 216-17.

31 Laurendeau, "Démagogie," *Devoir*, 5 juin 1956; "McCarthyisme: Une arrière saison," ibid., 6 juil. 1956.

32 Gérard Dion et Louis O'Neill, *Deux prêtres dénoncent l'immoralité politique*, 14-15. Originally published as "Lendemains d'élections," *Ad Usum Sacerdotum* 11 (juin-juillet 1956): 198-203, and reprinted in their *Le Chrétien et les élections* (Montréal: Les Editions de l'Homme 1960), 113-23; first reprinted in *Le Devoir*, 7 août and again 14 août 1956. Rumilly was furious at the suggestion that religious personnel, especially the women's orders, had been influenced by anticommunist propaganda. He claimed that the nuns were as enlightened as any respectable Quebec citizen and "Elles n'ont nul besoin de 'mythes' pour les effaroucher, ni d'inquisiteurs pour les torturer." *A propos d'un mémoire "confidentiel,"* 3-12 (12 quoted). It was Filion who revealed the rumour about Lapalme and he blamed the right-wing extremists like Rumilly and Houde for spreading it. "Il nous faudrait un Bernanos," *Devoir*, 11 août 1956.

33 *Deux prêtres*, 8-9. The last reference was to the slogan employed by the Union Nationale in the 1948 and 1952 elections, "Duplessis donne à sa province, les Libéraux donnent aux étrangers."

34 Rumilly, *Duplessis et son temps* 1: 324-9; 2: 215.

35 Pierre Gélinas, "Le parti ouvrier-progressiste," *Cité libre* 6 (décembre 1952):

17–19; Gérard Dion, *Le communisme dans la province de Québec* (Québec 1949), 20–1.

36 Paul Sauriol, "La loi du cadenas," *Devoir*, 1 mars 1948.

37 Jacques Perrault, a law professor at the Université de Montréal and an active supporter of the PSD, made an impassioned plea for the restoration of full civil liberties to all Québécois on a couple of occasions. He was also a member of *Le Devoir*'s board of directors and the newspaper gave the speeches full coverage. See "Les libertés civiles dans le Québec," *Devoir*, 30–31 août 1955; and "Chassons le cauchemar de la peur," ibid., 9 avril 1956.

38 Pelletier, "Les Bills 19 et 20," *AN* 42 (mars-avril 1954): 351–62.

39 Laurendeau, "Il y a deux McCarthy mais un seul Duplessis," *Devoir*, 15 jan. 1954; Filion, "Pour éviter la lutte des classes," ibid., 15 déc. 1953.

40 Laurendeau, "La politique provinciale I–II," *Devoir*, 4, 6 août 1956. The charges against the church were not wholly justified. Cardinal Léger had dealt with the theme of Christians, political action, and democracy at a well-attended meeting in Montreal. See his speech, *Devoir*, 13–14 mai 1955.

41 Laurendeau, "Un réflexe moral," *Devoir*, 13 août 1956.

42 Dion et O'Neill, *Deux prêtres*, 11.

43 Gérard Dion, "La démocratie à l'épreuve," *Devoir*, 23–5 jan. 1957; Père Lévesque, "La civisme, cette grande chose," ibid., 16 sept. 1957; Mgr Pierre Décarie, "L'incivisme: problème actuel," *Bulletin* 4 (mars 1959): 2–6. The Canadian episcopacy also made a declaration favouring improved civic education. See Filion, "L'épiscopat prêche le civisme," *Devoir*, 5 déc. 1956.

44 Pelletier, "Ni contemplateur, ni adulateur . . .," *Cité libre* 28 (juin-juillet 1960): 1–2. Filion defended Abbé Dion's right to speak on the question on the basis of academic freedom. "De la liberté académique," *Devoir*, 17 oct. 1956.

45 Interview with Charles Lussier, 8 Sept. 1976. He confirmed that the *Cité libre* view was influenced heavily by Frank Scott, a McGill Law professor and CCF party activist. See Frank Scott, "Canada et Canada français," *Esprit* (août-septembre 1952): 180–1, 185–6; "L'idée de la liberté dans la politique contemporaine," *La Liberté* (ICAP 1959), 17–19.

46 Lussier, "Loi électorale et conscience politique," 23–4; Trudeau, "Réflexions sur la politique au Canada français," 53–7; "Obstacles à la démocratie," in *Le peuple souverain* (ICAP 1954), 36–40; "La démocratie est-elle viable au Canada français?" *AN* 44 (novembre 1954): 190–200; "Some Obstacles to Democracy," 103–23. For a more extensive study of the question of French Canadians and democracy which follows faithfully the Citélibriste interpretation of Lussier and Trudeau see Pierre Charbonneau's "La Couronne: Essais sur les Canadiens français et la démocratie," in *Les Ecrits du Canada français* 9 (1961): 11–53.

47 "Prières du matin: Elévations matutinales," from a text read over CBF radio station on the morning of the 20 June 1956 provincial election; cited in "Some Obstacles to Democracy in Quebec," 110. For similar pearls of wisdom see André Dagenais, *Dieu et Chrétienté* (Montreal 1955), 108–26.

48 Charles Lussier, "Réhabilitation de l'autorité," *Cité libre* 3 (mai 1951): 21.

49 Trudeau, "Some Obstacles to Democracy," 108–10; "Obstacles à la démocratie," 39–40.

50 Trudeau, "Some Obstacles to Democracy," 104–6.

51 Ibid., 106–7.

52 Trudeau, "Réflexions sur la politique," 53–7; "Obstacles à la démocratie," 36–40; "Some Obstacles to Democracy," 103–7. For a similar view see M. Blain, "Du nationalisme au fascisme," *Devoir*, 5 août 1958.

53 Léon Dion, "L'esprit démocratique chez les Canadiens de langue française," *Cahiers d'éducation des adultes* 2 (novembre 1958): 37.

54 Ibid., 36–9.

55 Ibid., 40–1.

56 Rioux, "La démocratie et la culture canadienne-française," *Cité libre* 28 (juin-juillet 1960): 3–4, 13, and "L'Election vue de l'Anse-à-Barbe," *Cité libre* 3 (décembre 1952): 47–57. Guy Rocher argued that "le Canada français, qui adopte des attitudes du groupe minoritaire, qui a des traits de pays sous-développés, qui est hanté par la survivance, constitue un milieu propice à l'éclosion d'attitudes de type autoritaire tant au plan de la conscience collective qu'au niveau des personalités individuelles," "Liberté et société Canadienne-française," in ICAP, *La Liberté*, 50. Dion confirmed these points in a later analysis of contemporary Quebec by demonstrating the resurgence of a neo-conservative political culture. *Nationalismes et politique au Québec*, 74–83, 131–63.

57 Dion, "L'esprit démocratique," 41–3 (42 quoted).

58 Laurendeau, "L'ère Duplessis," *Devoir*, 23 juin 1956. He wrote, in part, of the French-Canadian people: "Habitué aux travaux durs et prolongé, il s'installe avec émerveillement dans ses loisirs. Ce qu'il ne peut obtenir, il le rêve devant l'écran de la télévision . . . La vraie morale de cette époque aura été un calme et subtil et profond Enrichissez-vous."

59 Laurendeau summarized with approval the points made by Dion, "Blocs-notes," *Devoir*, 4 août 1958.

60 Laporte, "La démocratie et M. Trudeau," *AN* 44 (décembre 1954): 293–96.

61 Laurendeau, "Entre le passé et l'avenir," in *La Liberté*, 30–40 (40 quoted). For a similar expression of views see Fernand Dumont, "La liberté a-t-elle un passé et un avenir au Canada français," in *La Liberté*, 26–33.

62 Filion, "De Constantin à Duplessis," *Devoir*, 18 août 1956.

63 "Some Obstacles to Democracy," 121.

64 Laurendeau, "La théorie du roi nègre, I, II, III," *Devoir*, 4 juil. 5 nov., and 18 nov. 1958. See also Pierre Vigeant "La minorité anglo-québécoise et la moralité publique," ibid., 3 mars 1958.

65 Laurendeau, Théorie du roi nègre, III," *Devoir*, 18 nov. 1958.

66 Filion, "De Constantin à Duplessis," *Devoir*, 18 août 1956; Louis Baudouin, "Rapport général," in *Le peuple souverain*, 52.

67 Pelletier, "Commentaire," in ibid., 14.

68 Trudeau, "Obstacles à la démocratie," 40.

69 *Le Devoir* accuse: Scandale à la corporation du gaz naturel," *Devoir*, 13 and 14 juin 1958; Laurendeau, "Le régime est touché," ibid., 26 juin 1958; Filion, "Nous voulons connaître toute la vérité," ibid., 3 juil. 1958; "Le scandale à Duplessis," ibid., 9 juil. 1958; "La collusion des affaires et de la politique," ibid., 15 août 1958.

70 Interview with Gérard Filion, 4 sept. 1976.

CHAPTER ELEVEN

1 Dion, "L'esprit démocratique chez les Canadiens de langue française," *Cahiers d'éducation des adultes* 2 (novembre 1958): 38.

2 Trudeau, "La démocratie est-elle viable au Canada français?" *AN* 44 (novembre 1954): 198–9; Vadeboncoeur, "Que la 'passion' peut être un guide . . ., *AN* 20 (septembre 1942): 36–42. One political scientist has argued that apoliticism was the common theme of all ideological currents in Quebec in the 1930s. This he explained by the persistence of what he termed, following the Hartzian formula, a "fragment culture" in Quebec which modelled itself on the pre-absolutist monarchies of the ancien régime. See André-J. Bélanger, *L'apolitisme des idéologies québécoise: Le grand tournant de 1934–1936*, 353–68.

3 Laurendeau, "Sur cent pages de Pierre Elliott Trudeau," *Devoir*, 6, 10, 11, oct. 1956; "Blocs-notes," ibid., 7 avril 1959. Léon Dion agrees wholeheartedly with Laurendeau and criticizes those political scientists like Trudeau and Bélanger who perceive conservative nationalism as an apolitical ideology. See his *Nationalismes et politique au Québec*, 35–6.

4 Pierre Laporte, *The True Face of Duplessis*, 119.

5 Robert Boily, "Les hommes politiques du Québec, 1867–1967," in Desrosiers, *Le personnel politique québécois*, 80, 82.

6 Ibid., 77–8, note 47. For a more detailed examination of the characteristics of the political élites in the late 1950s and early 1960s see Robert Boily, "Les élus de 1956 à 1966: principaux caractères sociaux et politiques," in *Quatres élections provinciales au Québec*, ed. Vincent Lemieux, 73–90.

7 Filion, "Le moindre mal," *Devoir*, 8 nov. 1947; "Où conduit le moindre mal," ibid., 20 déc. 1947; Laurendeau, "Pour continuer la lutte," ibid., 9 sept. 1947; "Y a-t-il une crise du nationalisme?" *AN* 41 (janvier 1953): 15–16.

8 Claude Ryan, "Ferons-nous de la politique?" *AN* 37 (juillet 1951): 457–77. Laurendeau saw a strong role for state-controlled electronic media, radio, television, film, in the creation of an urban-oriented popular culture for French Canada. "Les conditions d'existence d'une culture nationale," *AN* 37 (juin 1951): 375–80.

9 Vadeboncoeur, "Une démocratie arrêtée," *Cité libre* 21 (juillet 1958): 27; "Adhésion au PSD," *Devoir*, 6 sept. 1958; "Le Nouveau Parti, une voie car-

rosable pour le socialisme," ibid., 28 nov. 1960; Marcel Rioux, "L'opposition à Québec doit être de la gauche, non de la droite," ibid., 28 nov. 1960. Both expressed confidence that francophone social democrats would feel at home in the new NDP.

10 Trudeau, "L'élection fédérale du 10 août; prodômes et conjectures," *Cité libre* 8 (novembre 1953): 8; "Une lettre sur la politique," *Devoir*, 18 sept. 1954; Thérèse F. Casgrain, *A Woman in a Man's World*, 123–7, 132–6. An active member of the CCF since 1946–national vice-president in 1948 and provincial leader in 1951–she recalls in her memoirs the deep hostility and mistrust encountered by French Canadians, especially those of upper-class origins like herself, who associated themselves with left-wing social and political movements.

11 Angers, "Le parti CCF et la centralisation," *AN* 46 (novembre 1956): 222–31 (231 quoted); "La nouvelle CCF est-elle socialiste?" *AN* 46 (octobre 1956): 105–15.

12 Gérard Dion, "Les catholiques, le socialisme Anglo-Saxon et la CCF," *Ad Usum Sacerdotum* 11 (avril 1956): 138–50. He referred to an article by M.G. Ballantyne, "The Church and the CCF," *The Commonwealth*, 3 March 1944. Thérèse Casgrain recounts the reactions of the traditional political and financial élites to the bishops' declaration. This pressure helps explain the bishops' unwillingness to encourage the publication of the press release making it clear that they meant the CCF. *A Woman in a Man's World*, 120–1.

13 Trudeau et al., "M. Lapalme et le Parti social démocratique," *Devoir*, 1 juin 1956.

14 Laurendeau, "La CCF dans le Québec," *Devoir*, 24 mai 1948.

15 Casgrain, "Lettre au directeur du 'Devoir'," *Devoir*, 9 juil. 1952.

16 Laurendeau, "Blocs-notes," *Devoir*, 31 août 1955; Pierre Laporte, "Le parti CCF est loin du pouvoir dans le Québec," ibid., 4 mai 1955; Filion, "Un coup de barre à droite," ibid., 4 août 1956.

17 Laurendeau, "Le poids de l'histoire," *Devoir*, 6 avril 1959.

18 Laurendeau, "Sans racines," *Devoir*, 5 juil. 1956. The lack of a viable political vehicle to channel the necessary socioeconomic and nationalist reforms prompted J.-M. Léger to suggest that "l'abstention est pleinement justifiée." "Nationalisme et progrès social," *AN* 45 (janvier 1956): 437.

19 Trudeau, "Un manifeste démocratique," *Cité libre* 22 (octobre 1958): 8–9.

20 Pierre Charbonneau, "Défense et illustration de la gauche," *Cité libre* 18 (novembre 1957): 37–9.

21 Dansereau, "Les syndicats ouvriers et l'action politique," *AN* 43 (mai-juin 1954): 491–8; Laurendeau, Les syndicats veulent-ils fonder un nouveau parti?" *Devoir*, 6 juil. 1954; "Les syndicats ouvriers et la politique," ibid., 7 juil. 1955; "Des élections et de l'indifférence," ibid., 3 juil. 1955; Filion, "Pas un parti de classe, mais un parti démocratique," ibid., 14 juil. 1954.

22 Filion, "Aurons-nous des scrupules à battre Maurice Duplessis," *Devoir*, 29 mai 1956; "Nous sommes contre Duplessis," ibid., 16 juin 1956.

23 G.-E. Lapalme, *Mémoires* 2: 23, 68–71, 186–8; Gérard Bergeron, *Du Duplessisme au Johnsonisme 1956–1966*, 25–6. The antilabour Union Nationale continued to retain the support of large numbers of working-class voters, thanks primarily to the persistence of the image, created in the 1930s, of a party of economic protest and a "populist" leader, Duplessis, who carefully cultivated the image of "a man of the people" by using the vernacular, denying that he ever read books, and ridiculing the intellectuals. McRoberts and Posgate, *Quebec: Social Change and Political Crisis*, 79–83.

24 Laurendeau, "Le parti libéral a-t-il un avenir? I–II" *Devoir*, 30 juin and 4 juil. 1956; quote from "Le parti libéral peut-il se renouveler?" *Devoir*, 15 sept. 1956.

25 For Trudeau's negative assessment of the provincial Liberal party see his "Un manifeste démocratique," 5–8. Also Pierre Charbonneau, "Défense et illustration de la gauche," 28.

26 Laurendeau, "La politique provinciale V," *Devoir*, 9 août 1956.

27 Laurendeau, "Le parti libéral a-t-il un avenir? II" *Devoir*, 4 juil. 1956.

28 Laurendeau, "Le diable est-il à gauche?" *Devoir*, 4 fév. 1957; Léger, "Priorité de l'action politique dans le Québec aujourd'hui," *AN* 46 (mars 1957): 483–90; Abbé Louis O'Neill, "Existe-il une gauche au Canada français?" *Devoir*, 20, 21, 23 fév. 1959; Charbonneau, "Défense et illustration de la gauche," 27–35.

29 "Naissance d'un nouveau mouvement politique," *Devoir*, 10 sept. 1956.

30 Bergeron, *Du Duplessisme au Johnsonisme*, 126–7.

31 Le Rassemblement, "Constitution," *Devoir*, 14 sept. 1956.

32 Le Rassemblement, "Déclaration de principes," *Devoir*, 14 sept. 1956.

33 Le Rassemblement, "Décision du congrès spécial," *Devoir*, 1 avril 1957.

34 Casgrain, *A Woman in a Man's World*, 138. The author points out that the Rassemblement grew out of a meeting called by the PSD in April 1956.

35 Bergeron, *Du Duplessisme au Johnsonisme*, 132–3.

36 Interview with Gérard Bergeron, 31 Aug. 1976. Bergeron had met Laurendeau during the summer of 1956 while doing a television program on China. He was impressed with the neonationalist orientation of *Devoir* and when Laurendeau invited him to write a column on Quebec politics he readily accepted. Bergeron was partly responsible for convincing Laurendeau that only a reformed Liberal party and not the half-baked Rassemblement could defeat the Union Nationale.

37 Guy Lamarche, "Le Rassemblement . . . ,"*Devoir*, 2 déc. 1957.

38 Laurendeau, "Blocs-notes," *Devoir*, 3 déc. 1957.

39 Bergeron, *Du Duplessisme au Johnsonisme*, 133–4.

40 Trudeau, "Un manifeste démocratique," 28–9; Guy Lamarche, "La FTQ tentera de réaliser 'l'union démocratique'," *Devoir*, 24 nov. 1958.

41 Michel Roy, "21 personnalités lancent un appel d'urgence aux partis d'opposition; unissons-nous!" *Devoir*, 11 avril 1959; Laporte, "L'union des forces démocratiques est-elle possible pour 1960?" ibid., 30 mars 1959. Laporte

pointed out that the Liberal party had formed, at the direction of delegates attending the fall convention in 1958, a committee composed of Jean Lesage, G.-E. Lapalme, J.-M. Nadeau, André Rousseau, and Alcide Courcy, to study the feasibility of Trudeau's suggestion for the Union des forces démocratiques. It was an astute move because it undermined the charge that the Liberals were not interested in democracy.

42 Trudeau, the Rassemblement's third president, had announced in April 1959 that the Rassemblement's regional groups had been instructed to campaign on behalf of the Union des forces démocratiques and that no dues would be collected for the year 1958-9. Laporte "Le Rassemblement ...," *Devoir*, 22 avril 1959.

43 Cited in Guy Lamarche, "Le Rassemblement," 1 déc. 1958.

44 Trudeau, "Où va le Canada français? III," *Devoir*, 6 mai 1959.

45 Thérèse Casgrain recalls that Trudeau, during his term as president of the Rassemblement, took an extended vacation in Europe. He obviously did not feel that the Union des forces démocratiques was a crucial or urgent matter. *A Woman in a Man's World*, 139.

46 Trudeau, "Un manifeste démocratique," 16-22. Charles Lussier stressed the point that the Citélibristes sincerely believed that a socialist Quebec, because of the persistence of nationalism, would be a totalitarian society. Quebec, it was argued, must experience a liberal era before a social society and political institutions could be established. Interview with Charles Lussier, 8 Sept. 1976.

47 Trudeau, "Un manifeste démocratique," 21.

48 Vadeboncoeur, "Le Club de M. Trudeau," *Devoir*, 9 mai 1959.

49 Filion, "Vers l'unité d'action des forces d'opposition?" *Devoir*, 5 nov. 1958; "Qui veut faire l'ange ...," ibid., 15 avril 1959. Laurendeau, "Pour entreprendre la lutte d'aujourd'hui," ibid., 17 fév. 1959.

50 Bergeron, *Du Duplessisme au Johnsonisme*, 21-7, 33-5 (34 quoted). Bergeron argued that the entrenched Liberal vote was about 40 per cent as compared with 35 per cent for the Union Nationale. Of the remaining 25 per cent, 5 per cent voted for third party or independent candidates, while 20 per cent constituted a floating block. The Union Nationale had managed to hold 15 per cent of that floating block, the rest going to the Liberals. The Liberal party could make gains by enlarging its part of the floating vote or by getting traditionally absentee citizens to vote. In sum, the task was mathematically possible.

51 Ibid., 147-79, 190-2; Lapalme, *Mémoires* 2: 212-18. Interview with Gérard Bergeron, 31 Aug. 1976. He believes his criticism of Lapalme's leadership abilities was used by Gérin-Lajoie and his supporters to push for a leadership campaign. Gérin-Lajoie, of course, hoped to win the leadership if he was given the opportunity.

52 Bergeron, *Du Duplessisme au Johnsonisme*, 180-2, 184-9; idem, *Ne Bougez-Plus!* (Montréal: Editions du Jour 1968), for portraits of Lesage and Gérin-Lajoie,

138–45, 175–82. Lapalme was not chosen as one of the forty politicians sketched by Bergeron!

53 Interview with Father Lévesque, 3 Sept. 1976; Lapalme, *Mémoires* 2: 223–33.

54 Laurendeau, "Une autre 'dernière chance'?" *Devoir*, 8 nov. 1957; Filion, "La chance du parti libéral," ibid., 19 avril 1958; J.-M. Léger, "Le parti libéral du Québec a-t-il un avenir? I," ibid., 29 avril 1958.

55 Laporte, "Lendemains du congrès de Québec I–IV," *Devoir*, 3, 5, 6, 7 juin 1958.

56 Filion, "Triomphateur ou croque-mort?" *Devoir*, 2 juin 1958.

57 Filion, "Comment rétablir l'équilibre des forces démocratiques," *Devoir*, 18 avril 1959; "Le sort du parti libéral," ibid., 13 nov. 1957; "Un avertissement au parti libéral," ibid., 20 août 1958; Laurendeau, "Battre Duplessis," ibid., 28 avril 1958; "Le parti libéral et les 'collaborateurs'," ibid., 26 sept. 1958; Léger, "Le parti libéral du Québec a-t-il un avenir?" ibid., 30 avril 1958; Bergeron, *Du Duplessisme au Johnsonisme*, 35–47. Bergeron was very critical of the liberal and social democrats of *Cité libre* and the unions, as well as the doctrinaire utopians in the PSD, for wasting their time and energy in pursuit of an elusive third party pure of all corruption, traditional politicians, and party organizers. Ibid., 50–3, 132–3, 192–9.

58 Paul-André Comeau, "La transformation du parti libéral québécois," *CJEPS* 31 (August 1965): 358–67.

59 Laurendeau, "Le peuple lui-même," *Devoir*, 28 nov. 1958. Contrary to what he believed some ten years earlier, Laurendeau wrote: "Il n'en reste pas moins artificiel de décrire les masses comme uniquement désireuses de s'angliciser le plus vite possible, en face d'élites nationalistes qui ne feraient que retarder leur mouvements ... Un peuple au contraire se nourrit d'autonomie, et il le sent. Il y aspire, même si d'autres tendances contredisent celle-là. Un être vivant aspire à durer."

60 J.-L. Gagnon, "Que veut, que peut le parti libéral provincial?" *La Réforme*, 18 juil. 1956. See also his "Où va le Canada français? I," *Devoir*, 4 mai 1959; for a similar expression of views see Paul Gérin-Lajoie, "Où va le Canada français? VII," *Devoir*, 12 mai 1959.

61 Bergeron, "Où va le Canada français? IX," *Devoir*, 14 mai 1959.

62 Jean Drapeau, "Pourquoi avoir peur? Nos raisons d'espérer," *Devoir*, 27 oct. 1958; "Peuple esclave et cabinet clandestin," ibid., 13 oct. 1958; "Un 3e parti est nécessaire dans le Québec," ibid., 25 mars 1959; Pierre Desmarais, "La LAC est la seul espoir, même sur le plan provincial," ibid., 29 avril 1959; "Ligue d'Action civique; sections dans 70 comtés," ibid., 18 août 1959. LAC even ran a candidate in a Lac St Jean by-election in August 1959. "Action civique et PSD feront la lutte à l'UN au Lac St Jean," ibid., 22 août 1959.

63 Léger, "Le parti libéral du Québec a-t-il un avenir? IV," *Devoir*, 2 mai 1958; Laporte, "L'Action civique pourrait bien devenir un parti politique en '59," ibid., 9 jan. 1959; Laurendeau, "Pour entreprendre la lutte d'aujourd'hui,"

ibid., 17 fév. 1959; Trudeau, "Le regroupement des forces d'opposition: En reponse à M. Drapeau," ibid., 19 fév. 1959; Jacques Hébert, "Pourquoi j'abandonne la direction de *Vrai*," ibid., 25 avril 1959; Jean Lesage, "Les nouveaux partis ont permis à des 'potentats' de se maintenir au pouvoir," ibid., 1 avril 1959.

64 Laporte, "1759 vu par trois revues à tendances nationalistes," *Devoir*, 1 oct. 1959; Raoul Roy, "L'indépendance du Québec par la voie du socialisme," *Devoir*, 18 juin 1959.

65 Lapalme, *Mémoires* 2: 240–80; interviews with G.-E. Lapalme, 3 Sept. 1976, and Father Lévesque, 3 Sept. 1976. Both tried to justify the need to replace Lesage by arguing that Lesage was very depressed and was drinking heavily. His defeatist attitude, they maintained, would destroy any hope of the Liberals in the next election. Lapalme contended that Paul Sauvé had told him that the UN would do its utmost to defeat Lesage in any riding he chose to run in and that the only potentially safe seat, Québec-Ouest, was not going to be abandoned by the incumbent Liberal J.-P. Galipeau.

66 Laurendeau, "Sauvé déconcerte amis et adversaires," *Devoir*, 13 nov. 1959; "Où les désormais s'arrêtent," ibid., 28 nov. 1959.

67 Laurendeau, "In memoriam Paul Sauvé," *Devoir*, 4 jan. 1960; "Le nouveau premier ministre," ibid., 8 jan. 1960.

68 Lapalme, *Mémoires* 2: 287–8.

69 *1960: Le programme politique du parti libéral du Québec* (Montréal 1960), 3–4. Pamphlet is reprinted in Roy, *Les programmes électoraux du Québec*, 378–88, and in Quinn, *The Union Nationale*, app. C, 225–35.

70 *1960: Le programme politique du parti libéral*, 6–15.

71 Ibid., 15–17.

72 Lesage et al., "Table ronde sur l'Etat provinciale," *Devoir*, 14 juil. 1959; "M. Lesage deplore 'l'illusion' socialiste dans la province," ibid., 5 Dec. 1958. J.-L. Gagnon, "Où va le Canada français? I," ibid., 4 mai 1959. In fact, the Union Nationale party organizers did try to introduce the theme of communism into the campaign (as they had done in 1956) with the publication of a pamphlet *L'anarchie est à nos portes*. It was denounced severely by Laurendeau as well as other journalists in Montreal and Quebec. "Cette anarchie, parait-il, à nos portes?" *Devoir*, 14 juin 1960.

73 Lapalme, *Mémoires* 2: 169–76, 208, 241–42; Laporte, "Le parti revoit son programme," *Devoir*, 2 juin 1958; "Du meilleur et du moins bon dans le programme adopté par les libéraux," ibid., 7 juin 1958; "Québec et les relations fédérales-provinciales," ibid., 26 nov. 1958 (quoted).

74 Jean Lesage, "Lesage réclame une conférence interprovinciale," *Devoir*, 1 juin 1959; "Lesage: Commission d'enquête sur le fiscalité," ibid., 23 mars 1960.

75 Lesage, "Avec Duplessis et Diefenbaker les problèmes constitutionnels ne seront pas réglés bientôt," *Devoir*, 6 juil. 1959. See also Jean Lesage, *Lesage s'engage*, for a similar description of what he termed "Vers une politique de grandeur nationale," 107–14.

76 *1960: Le programme politique du parti libéral du Québec*, 17–19, 20–3.

77 Laurendeau, "L'autonomie provinciale et le programme du parti libéral," *Devoir*, 2 juin 1960; "Le parti libéral et l'autonomie," ibid., 3–4 juin 1960.

78 Laurendeau, "Croyez-vous aux programmes politiques?" *Devoir*, 9 juin 1960.

79 Filion, "Un choix lucide et libre," *Devoir*, 15 juin 1960; "Faut-il que ça change?" ibid., 21 juin 1960.

80 Jean Provencher, *René Lévesque: Portrait d'un québécois*, 131–3; interview with G.-E. Lapalme, 3 Sept. 1976.

81 Interview with Gérard Bergeron, 31 Aug. 1976; Trudeau, "Notes sur l'élection provinciale," *Cité libre* 28 (juin-juillet 1960): 13.

82 Trudeau, "De la notion d'opposition politique," *Cité libre* 27 (mai 1960): 13.

83 Interview with Gérard Bergeron, 31 Aug. 1976; Bergeron, *Ne Bougez-Plus!*, 145–53; Provencher, *Lévesque*, 130–1.

84 Trudeau, "Notes sur l'élection provinciale," 13.

85 Ibid.

86 Jean Hamelin et André Garon, "La vie politique au Québec de 1956 à 1966," in *Quatre élections provinciales au Québec*, ed. Vincent Lemieux (Québec: Les Presses de l'Université Laval 1969), 6–14.

87 Quinn, *The Union Nationale*, 181–6; Roger Mathieu, "Rapport du président général de la CTCC," in *Procès-verbal* (Montréal 1960), 5–25.

88 Laporte, "L'électorat du Québec à décidé: C'est le temps que ça change!" *Devoir*, 23 juin 1960; "L'autopsie de la défaite," ibid., 25, 27, 29, 30 juin 1960.

89 Laurendeau, "Pour demain," *Devoir*, 25 juin 1960; "Cinq mois de régime Lesage," ibid., 2 déc. 1960.

90 Trudeau, "L'élection du 22 juin 1960," *Cité libre* 29 (août-septembre 1960): 3–5 (quoted).

91 Ibid., 7–8. Marcel Rioux, "Socialisme, cléricalisme et nouveau parti," *Cité libre* 33 (janvier 1961): 4–8. Rioux rejected Trudeau's analysis and called for full *Cité libre* support for the newly formed NDP party. This was the beginning of the end for the *équipe* of *Cité libre*. The split would eventually come not over liberal democracy versus social democracy or socialism but rather over the ideology of neo-nationalism. See André Carrier, "L'idéologie politique de la revue *Cité libre*," *CJEPS* 1 (December 1968): 414–28.

Bibliography

PRIMARY SOURCES

Manuscripts

Fondation Lionel Groulx: Fonds André Laurendeau
Public Archives of Canada, Records of Parliament 1775–1958, RG 1H, D2, vol. 626,
  Duplessis–St Laurent correspondence

Interviews

Angers, F.-A.
Bergeron, G.
Dion, L.
Falardeau, J.-C.
Filion, G.

Gérin-Lajoie, P.
Lapalme, G.-F.
Lévesque, G.-H.
Lussier, C.
Tremblay, Arthur

Newspapers and Periodicals

L'Action nationale 1935–60
Cité libre 1950–60
Le Devoir 1947–60

Books and Monographs

Alliance des professeurs catholiques de Montréal. *Mémoire à la Commission royale d'enquête sur les problèmes constitutionnels.* Montréal 1954.
Arès, R. *Dossier sur le pacte fédératif de 1867: La Conféderation: pacte ou loi?* Montréal: Les Editions Bellarmin 1963.
– *Essais de réforme de l'entreprise aux Etats-Unis.* Montréal: Ecole sociale populaire 1950.
Bergeron, G. *Du Duplessisme au Johnsonisme 1956–1966.* Montréal: Parti Pris 1967.
Bissell, C.T., ed., *Canada's Crisis in Higher Education.* Toronto: University of Toronto Press 1957.
Brunet, M. *Canadians et Canadiens.* Montréal: Fides 1954.
– *La présence anglaise et les Canadiens.* Montréal: Beauchemin 1958.
Chambre de Commerce de la Province de Québec. *Les relations fédérales-provinciales en matière d'impôts.* Québec 1952.
Chambre de Commerce du District de Montréal. *Mémoire à la Commission royale d'enquête sur les problèmes constitutionnels.* Vol. 4. *La politique économique du Québec.* Québec 1955.
– *Mémoire sur les relations fédérales-provinciales en matière d'impôt.* Vol. 2. *Exposé.* Montréal 1947.
Commission sacerdotale d'études sociales. *La participation des travailleurs à la vie de l'entreprise.* Compte rendu des Journées sacerdotales d'études sociales de 1947. Montréal: n.p. 1949.
– *L'organisation professionnelle dans le Québec,* Compte rendu des Journées sacerdotales d'études sociales, 1945 et 1946. Montréal: n.p. 1949.
Confédération des travailleurs catholiques du Canada. *Procès-verbal.* Compte rendu des congrès annuels de la CTCC 1945–60.
Cook, R., and M. Behiels, eds. *The Essential Laurendeau.* Toronto: Copp Clark 1976.
Dion, G., et L. O'Neill. *Deux prêtres dénoncement l'immoralité politique dans la*

province de Québec. Montréal: Le comité de moralité publique de la Ligue d'action civique 1956.

Episcopat de la province civile de Québec. *Le problème ouvrier en regard de la doctrine sociale de l'Eglise.* Montréal: Ecole sociale populaire, nos. 433–44, avril-mai 1950.

Falardeau, J.-C., ed. *Essais sur le Québec contemporain.* Québec: Les Presses de l'Université Laval 1953.

Filion, G. *Les confidences d'un commissaire d'écoles.* Montréal: Editions de l'Homme 1960.

Frégault, G. *Canadian Society in the French Regime.* Ottawa: Canadian Historical Association 1954.

Gaudrault, P.-M., OP. *Neutralité, non confessionnalité et Ecole sociale populaire.* Montréal: n.p. 1946.

Gouin, P. *Que devons-nous attendre du Bloc?* Montréal: n.p. 1943.

Hertel, F. *Pour un ordre personnaliste.* Montréal: l'Arbre 1942.

Hughes, E.C. *French Canada in Transition.* Chicago: University of Chicago Press 1963.

Institut canadien des affaires publiques. *La Liberté.* Rapport de la sixième conférence annuelle de l'ICAP, Sainte-Adèle, 1959.

– *L'éducation.* Rapport de la troisième conférence annuelle de l'ICAP, Sainte-Adèle, 1956.

– *Le fédéralisme.* Rapport de la deuxième conférence annuelle de l'ICAP, Sainte-Marguerite, 1955.

– *Le peuple souverain.* Rapport de la première conférence annuelle de l'ICAP, Sainte-Marguerite, 1954.

Labrie, Mgr, CJM *La Côte-Nord et l'industrie sidérugique.* Montréal: Ecole sociale populaire, no. 422, mars 1949.

Lamontagne, M. *Le fédéralisme canadien: Evolutions et problèmes.* Québec: Les Presses de l'Université Laval 1954.

Laporte, Pierre. *The True Face of Duplessis.* Montréal: Harvest House 1960.

Laurendeau, A. *La crise de la conscription: 1942.* Montréal: Les Editions du Jour 1962.

– *Notre nationalisme.* Tracts Jeune-Canada, no. 5. Montréal 1935.

Léger, J.-M. *Notre situation économique: Progrès ou stagnation?* Montréal: Les Editions de l'Action nationale 1956.

Lesage, J. *Lesage s'engage.* Montréal: Editions de l'Homme 1959.

Mémoire de la Commission des écoles catholiques de Montréal à la Commission royale d'enquête sur les problèmes constitutionnels. Montréal 1954.

Mémoire de la Confédération des travailleurs catholiques du Canada à la Commission royale d'enquête sur les problèmes constitutionnels. n.p., n.d.

Mémoire de la Corporation générale des instituteurs et institutrices catholiques de la province de Québec à la Commission royale d'enquète sur les problèmes constitutionnels. n.p., n.d.

Mémoire de la Fédération du travail du Québec à la Commission royale d'enquête sur les problèmes constitutionnels. Montréal 1954.

Mémoire de la Fédération des unions industrielles du Québec (C.C.T.) à la Commission royale d'enquête sur les problèmes constitutionnels, 10 mars 1954. 2nd ed. Montréal n.d.

Mémoire de l'Université de Montréal à la Commission royale d'enquête sur les problèmes constitutionnels. Montréal 1954.

Mémoire du Collège Jean de Brébeuf à la Commission royale d'enquête sur les problèmes constitutionnels. Montréal: Collège Jean de Brébeuf 1954.

Mémoire soumis par l'Université Laval à la Commission royale d'enquête sur les problèmes constitutionnels. Québec 1954.

Miner, H. *St. Denis: A French-Canadian Parish.* Chicago: University of Chicago Press 1939.

Parti Libéral du Québec. *Le Parti Libéral Provincial s'engage.* Montréal: L'Organisation libérale provinciale 1956.

– *1960. Le programme politique du Parti Libéral du Québec.* Montréal 1960.

Rapport du Sous-comité de coordination de l'enseignement à ses divers degrées au Comité catholique du Conseil de l'instruction publique. Québec 1953.

Rioux, A., et al. *Le programme de restauration sociale.* Montréal: Ecole sociale populaire, nos 239–40, décembre 1933–janvier 1934.

Rumilly, R. *A propos d'un mémoire confidentiel.* Montréal: Editions de Notre Temps 1956.

– *L'infiltration gauchiste au Canada français.* Montréal: Editions de l'auteur 1956.

Société Saint-Jean-Baptiste de Montréal. *Canada français et union canadienne.* Montréal: Editions de l'Action nationale 1954.

Tremblay, A. *Les collèges et les écoles publiques: Conflit ou coordination?* Québec: Les Presses de l'Université Laval 1954.

Trudeau, P.E., ed. *La grève de l'amiante.* Montréal: Editions Cité libre 1956.

– *Federalism and the French Canadians.* Toronto: Macmillan of Canada 1968.

Vadeboncoeur, P. *La ligne du risque.* Montréal: Editions HMH 1969.

Articles

Angers, F.-A. "Deux modèles d'inconscience: Le Premier Saint-Laurent et le Commissaire Lévesque." *L'Action nationale* 38 (novembre 1951): 180–210.

– "La nouvelle CCF est-elle socialiste?" *L'Action nationale* 46 (octobre 1956): 105–15.

– "L'avenir économique des Canadiens français." *L'Action nationale* 46 (novembre 1956): 399–409.

– "Le parti CCF et la centralisation." *L'Action nationale* 46 (novembre 1956): 222–31.

– "Le problème fiscal et la constitution." *L'Action nationale* 35 (janvier 1950): 9–34.

- "L'heure de la grande offensive centralisatrice." *L'Action nationale* 28 (septembre 1946): 9–21.
- "Pierre-Elliott Trudeau et 'La grève de l'amiante' I–Réflexions préliminaires." *L'Action nationale* 47 (septembre 1957): 10–22.
- "Pierre Elliott Trudeau et la grève de l'amiante." *L'Action nationale* 48 (septembre-octobre 1958): 45–56.
- "Les raisonnements fallacieux du Rapport Massey: Education et culture." *L'Action nationale* 38 (décembre 1951): 226–52.
- "Les solutions du Rapport Massey I–Un problème mal posé." *L'Action nationale* 39 (mars 1952): 87–120.
- "Les solutions du Rapport Massey II–Quand Ottawa s'en mêle ..." *L'Action nationale* 39 (avril 1952): 214–45.
- "Les solutions du Rapport Massey III–A qui la faute?" *L'Action nationale* 39 (mai 1952): 261–99.
Barbeau, R. "Gauchisme, une forme de nationalisme?" *Tradition et progrès* 1 (mars 1957): 22–36.
Beausoleil, G. "Histoire de la grève à Asbestos." In *La grève de l'amiante*, edited by P.E. Trudeau. Montréal: Editions Cité libre 1956.
- "Histoire des négociations." In *La grève de l'amiante*, edited by P.E. Trudeau. Montréal: Editions Cité libre 1956.
Bilodeau, C. "Education in Quebec." *University of Toronto Quarterly* 27 (April 1958): 398–412.
Blain, J.-G. "La grève de l'amiante." *L'Action nationale* 47 (octobre 1956): 172–8.
- "Inquiétude et tradition." *Esprit* 20 (août-septembre 1952): 241–6.
Blain, M. "Faites vos jeux." *Cité libre* 11 (février 1955): 28–31.
- "Pour une dynamique de notre culture." *Cité libre* 5 (juin-juillet 1952): 20–6.
- "Sur la liberté de l'esprit." *Esprit* 20 (août-septembre 1952): 201–13.
Boisvert, R. "Domiciles de la peur sociale." *Cité libre* 1 (juin 1950): 10–19.
- "La grève et le mouvement ouvrier." In *La grève de l'amiante*, edited by P.E. Trudeau. Montréal: Editions Cité libre 1956.
- "Réflexions sur la justice des hommes." *Cité libre* 11 (février 1955): 12–23.
Brunet, M. "The University as a Public Institution in French Canada from Louis XIII to the Electoral Campaign of 1960." *Canadian Public Administration* 3 (December 1960): 344–9.
- "Toward the Discovery of a New Quebec and the Rebuilding of the Canadian Union." *The Humanities Association of Canada Bulletin* 26 (1965): 29–39.
- "Le Rapport Massey: Réflexions et observations." *L'Action universitaire* 18 (janvier 1952): 39–47.
Chambre de Commerce de Montréal. "Mémoire de la Chambre de Commerce de Montréal à la Commission Massey." *L'Action nationale* 35 (avril 1950): 277–304.
Charbonneau, P. "Défense et illustration de la gauche." *Cité libre* 18 (novembre 1957): 26–46.
- "La Couronne: Essais sur les Canadiens français et la démocratie." *Ecrits du Canada français* 8 (1961): 11–53.

– "Lettre ouverte à Gérard Pelletier sur l'unanimité." *Cité libre* 32 (décembre 1960): 23–35.

Confédération des travailleurs catholiques du Canada et Fédération des travailleurs du Québec. "Les centrales ouvrières du Québec et l'assurance-santé." *Relations industrielles* 13 (1958): 175–208.

– "Mémoire sur l'éducation." *Relations industrielles* 13 (1958): 208–31.

Cormier, G. "Petite méditation sur l'existence canadienne-française." *Cité libre* 1 (juin 1950): 25–36.

– "Pour un humanisme ouvrier; notes sur l'autonomie quotidienne." *L'Action nationale* 30 (novembre 1947): 172–83.

Dansereau, P. "Lettre à un séminariste sur l'aliénation des intellectuels." *Cité libre* 32 (décembre 1960): 14–17.

Décarie, V. "La liberté académique." *Cité libre* 19 (janvier 1958): 3–5.

– "Fonds publics et enseignement Classique." *Cité libre* 27 (mai 1960): 1–24.

Décary, Mgr P. "Allocution du président." *Bulletin de la Fédération des collèges classiques* 3 (octobre 1957): 1–4.

– "Is There Any Room Today for Classical Education?" *Bulletin de la Fédération des collèges classiques* 3 (juin 1958): 8.

Désy, J. "L'université et l'Etat." *La Revue de l'Université Laval* 7 (novembre 1952): 205–19.

Dion, G. "Confessionalité syndicale et régime juridique du travail dans le Québec." *Relations industrielles* 15 (avril 1960): 162–80.

– "Démocratie et éducation des adults." *Ad Usum Sacerdotum* 15 (octobre 1959): 152–60.

– "Invitations à repenser le syndicalisme catholique." *Ad Usum Sacerdotum* 10 (octobre 1954): 1–3.

– "La C.T.C.C. et l'affiliation au CTC." *Ad Usum Sacerdotum* 13 (mars 1958): 52–7.

– "La C.T.C.C. et l'unité ouvrière canadienne." *Relations industrielles* 12 (janvier-avril 1957): 32–53.

– "L'Eglise et le conflit de l'amiante." In *La grève de l'amiante*, edited by P.E. Trudeau. Montréal: Editions Citélibre 1956.

– "L'Eglise et les orientations nouvelles de la C.T.C.C. *Ad Usum Sacerdotum* 12 (novembre 1956): 20–1.

– "Le régionalisme syndicale est-il désuet?" *Ad Usum Sacerdotum* 13 (juin-juillet-août 1958): 124–40.

– "Les Catholiques, le socialisme Anglo-Saxon et la C.C.F." *Ad Usum Sacerdotum* 11 (avril 1956): 138–50.

– "Les groupements syndicaux dans la province de Québec (1955)." *Relations industrielles* 2 (décembre 1955): 1–24.

– "L'université et les relations industrielles." *La Revue de l'Université Laval* 3 (septembre 1948): 56–9.

Dion, L. "Aspects de la condition du professeur d'université dans la société canadienne-française." *Cité libre* 21 (juillet 1958): 8–30.

– "L'esprit démocratique chez les Canadiens de langue française." *Cahiers* (Institut

Canadien d'éducation des adultes) 2 (novembre 1958): 34–43.
- "Le nationalisme pessimiste: Sa source, sa signification, sa validité." *Cité libre* 18 (novembre 1957): 3–18.
Dumont, F. "De quelques obstacles à la prise de conscience chez les Canadiens français." *Cité libre* 19 (janvier 1958): 22–8.
Falardeau, J.-C. "La place des professions libérales dans le Québec." *Revue Dominicaine* 48 (décembre 1942): 274–81.
- "Lettre à mes étudiants." *Cité libre* 23 (mai 1959): 4–14.
- "Perspectives." In *Essais sur le Québec contemporain*, edited by J.-C. Falardeau. Québec: Les Presses de l'Université Laval 1953.
- "The Changing Social Structures." In *Essais sur le Québec contemporain*, edited by J.-C. Falardeau. Québec: Les Presses de l'Université Laval 1953.
Faucher, A., and M. Lamontagne. "History of Industrial Development." In *Essais sur le Québec contemporain*, edited by J.-C. Falardeau. Québec: Les Presses de l'Université Laval 1953.
Filion, G. "Action politique et syndicats." *Relations industrielles* 15 (octobre 1960): 496–9.
Fraser B. "The Fight over Father Lévesque." *Maclean's Magazine*, 1 July 1950, 5, 52–4.
- "The Religious Crisis in Quebec." *Maclean's Magazine*, 10 November 1956, 13–15, 90–1.
- "This is Raymond." *Maclean's Magazine*, 1 January 1944, 9, 30–1.
Gingras, P.-E. "Le rapport Tremblay et l'enseignement." *L'Action nationale* 47 (octobre 1957): 143–60.
- "Le Rapport Tremblay et le financement des collèges classiques." *L'Action nationale* 45 (juin 1956): 889–95.
- "Que deviendront nos collèges classiques?" *L'Action universitaire* 26 (février 1960): 14–18.
Grandpré, de P. "Cette crise de la conscience intellectuelle." *L'Action nationale* 45 (mars 1956): 637–47.
- "Cette 'droite' et cette 'gauche', I." *L'Action nationale* 46 (novembre 1956): 241–7.
- "Le social et le national." *L'Action nationale* 46 (octobre 1956): 126–41.
- "Les Canadiens français et la France." *Chronique sociale de France* 65e année (15 septembre 1957): 481–8.
Harvey, P. "The Economy of Quebec." *University of Toronto Quarterly* 27 (April 1958): 330–40.
Hughes, E.C. "Regards sur le Québec." In *Essais sur le Québec contemporain*, edited by J.-C. Falardeau. Québec: Les Presses de l'Université Laval 1953.
Johnson, M. "Relations fiscales (1867–1945)." *Thémis* 5 (décembre 1954): 71–90.
- "Relations fiscales (1945–1955)," *Thémis* 5 (janvier 1955): 155–85.
Johnstone, K. "Who'll *Le Devoir* battle next?" *Maclean's Magazine*, 14 April 1956, 36–7, 94–6, 98–9.

Jolicoeur, F. "Les problèmes ouvriers du Québec." *Chronique sociale de France* 65e année (15 septembre 1957): 433–42.

Keyfitz, N. "L'exode rural dans la province de Québec, 1951–1961." *Recherches sociographiques* 3 (1962): 303–15.

– "Population Problems." In *Essais sur le Québec contemporain*, edited by J.-C. Falardeau. Québec: Les Presses de l'Université Laval 1953.

– "Some Demographic Aspects of French-English Relations in Canada." In *Canadian Dualism/La dualité canadienne*, edited by M. Wade. Toronto: University of Toronto Press 1960.

Laporte, P. "La démocratie et M. Trudeau." *L'Action nationale* 44 (décembre 1954): 293–6.

– "La machine électorale." *Cité libre* 6 (décembre 1952): 42–6.

– "Le R.P. Lévesque est-il naif ou optimiste?" *L'Action nationale* 44 (octobre 1954): 141–52.

– "Soyons riche, ou nous périrons." *L'Action nationale* 46 (septembre 1956): 26–42.

Laurendeau, A. "Alerte aux Canadiens français!" *L'Action nationale* 16 (novembre 1940): 177–203.

– "Ce peuple chargé de chaines." *L'Action nationale* 17 (mars 1941): 177–89.

– "Conclusions très provisoires." *L'Action nationale* 31 (juin 1948): 413–24.

– "Croisade antifasciste?" *L'Action nationale* 11 (janvier 1938): 41–51.

– "Déclaration au sujet du Bloc populaire." *L'Action nationale* 20 (novembre 1942): 165–74.

– "En guise de préface." *L'Action nationale* 32 (septembre 1948): 3–10.

– "En manière de conclusion." *L'Action nationale* 35 (mai 1950): 388–95.

– "Fécondité de l'argent, mécanisme contre nature," *L'Action nationale* 9 (janvier 1937): 24–43.

– "Humanisme et Patrie." *L'Action nationale* 41 (janvier 1953): 3–5.

– "La conscription et le prétendu 'droit de veto' du Québec." *L'Action nationale* 18 (décembre 1941): 258–65.

– "La politique ne saurait se sauver toute seule." *L'Action nationale* 17 (mai 1941): 351–66.

– "Quatrième état dans la nation." *L'Action nationale* 30 (octobre 1947): 83–92.

– "Les conditions d'existence d'une culture nationale." *L'Action nationale* 37 (juin 1951): 364–90.

– "Les logis de la misère." *L'Action nationale* 30 (septembre 1947): 26–38.

– "L'impossible troisième parti." *L'Action nationale* 17 (avril 1941): 263–74.

– "Nationalisme et separatisme." *L'Action nationale* 44 (mars 1955): 572–80.

– "Nous ne raserons pas la muraille." *L'Action nationale* 19 (janvier 1942): 4–13.

– "Prendre l'offensive." *L'Action nationale* 30 (novembre 1947): 224–31.

– "Y-a-t-il un cas Cité libre?" *L'Action nationale* 37 (mars-avril 1951): 222–34.

– "Y-a-t-il une crise du nationalisme? I." *L'Action nationale* 40 (décembre 1952): 207–25.

– "Y-a-t-il une crise du nationalisme? II." *L'Action nationale* 41 (janvier 1953): 6–28.

Lebel, M. "A Survey of the Latest Reforms in the Field of Education in Quebec." *Culture* 19 (1958): 257–72.

Lefebvre, J.-P. "L'éducation populaire au Canada français." *Cité libre* 13 (novembre 1955): 21–33.

Léger, J.-M. "De notre démocratie libérale comme expression de la volonté du peuple." *L'Action nationale* 36 (novembre 1950): 186–212.

- "Dimensions de la liberté Canada-français." *La Revue socialiste* 3 (hiver 1959–60): 1–6, 61.
- "L'ennemi dans nos murs." *L'Action nationale* 31 (février 1948): 97–109.
- "Etapes de la révolution politique." *L'Action nationale* 37 (janvier 1951): 58–63.
- "Flagrance d'une injustice." *Cité libre* 16 (février 1957): 60–5.
- "La tâche souveraine: Définir une politique du Canada français." *L'Action nationale* 45 (avril 1956): 708–16.
- "Le Canada français à la recherche de son avenir." *Esprit* 20 (septembre 1952): 259–79.
- "Le nationalisme à l'heure de la révolution." *L'Action nationale* 42 (septembre 1953): 7–14.
- "Le temps de l'impatience." *L'Action nationale* 38 (septembre 1951): 60–9.
- "Mesure de notre nationalisme." *L'Action nationale* 39 (juin-juillet 1952): 345–52.
- "Nationalisme et progrès social." *L'Action nationale* 45 (janvier 1956): 433–40.
- "Pour sortir du mensonge." *L'Action nationale* 43 (mars-avril 1954): 372–76.
- "Priorité de l'action politique dans le Québec aujourd'hui." *L'Action nationale* 46 (mars 1957): 483–90.
- "Sus à l'autonomie, ou . . . Quand l'impatience risque de se transformer en trahison." *L'Action nationale* 47 (décembre 1957-janvier 1958): 376–86.
- "Une révolution silencieuse." *L'Action nationale* 39 (mai 1952): 300–8.
- "Une trahison à combattre; une imposture à dénoncer." *L'Action nationale* 45 (juin 1956): 933–40.
- "Urgence d'une doctrine nationale." *L'Action nationale* 32 (décembre 1948): 264–72.

Lemelin, R. "The Silent Struggle at Laval." *Maclean's Magazine*, 1 August 1952, 10, 36–8.

Le Moyne, J. "Jeunesse de l'homme." *Cité libre* 2 (février 1951): 10–14.

- "La liberté académique." *Cité libre* 19 (janvier 1958): 12–15.
- "L'atmosphère religieuse au Canada français." *Cité libre* 12 (mai 1955): 1–14.

Lévesque, G.-H. "Le droit à l'éducation." *Revue Dominicaine* (juillet-août 1958): 1–8.

- L'université et les relations industrielles." *Rapport*. Congrès des relations industrielles, 1946. Québec 1947.

Ligue d'Action nationale. "Mémoire à la Commission royale d'enquête sur les arts, les lettres et les sciences." *L'Action nationale* 35 (avril 1950): 305–31.

- "Conditions d'un état français dans la Confédération canadienne: Mémoire de la Ligue d'Action nationale à la Commission royale d'enquête sur les relations fédérales-provinciales." *L'Action nationale* 43 (mars-avril 1954): 328–50.

- "Manifeste de la Ligue d'Action nationale sur la conférence fédérale-provinciale." *L'Action nationale* 27 (avril 1946): 288–300.

Lortie, L. "Perspectives scientifiques." *L'Action universitaire* 1 (octobre 1947): 43–53.

- "The B.A. Degree in Our French-Speaking Universities." *Culture* 13 (1952): 21–30.

- "Le système scolaire." In *Essais sur le Québec contemporain*, edited by J.-C. Falardeau. Québec: Les Presses de l'Université Laval 1953.

Lussier, C. "La grève dans nos cadres juridiques." In *La grève de l'amiante*, edited by P.E. Trudeau. Montréal: Editions Cité libre 1956.

- "Loi électorale et conscience politique." *Cité libre* 6 (décembre 1952): 23–34.

Marchand, J. "La CSN à quarante ans." *Relations industrielles* 16 (octobre 1961): 471–4.

- "Quelques aspects idéologiques des relations ouvrières-patronales." *Hermès* 3 (octobre 1953): 17–25.

Minville, E. "Conditions de notre avenir." In *Essais sur le Québec contemporain*, edited by J.-C. Falardeau. Québec: Les Presses de l'Université Laval 1953.

- "L'aspect économique du problème canadien-français." *L'Actualité économique* 26 (avril-juin 1950): 48–77.

- "Les conditions de l'autonomie économique des Canadiens français." *L'Action nationale* 33 (mars 1951): 260–85.

O'Neill, L. "Analyse des attitudes de la 'gauche' et de la 'droite' au Canada français." *Ad Usum Sacerdotum* 14 (mai 1959): 98–103.

- "La vraie liberté des laics dans la domaine intellectuelle." *Ad Usum Sacerdotum* 10 (juillet 1955): 186–97.

- "Pourquoi le clergé soutient-il *Le Devoir*?" *Ad Usum Sacerdotum* 10 (février 1955): 76–9.

Ouellet, C. "Les Canadiens français dans les carrières scientifiques." *La Revue de l'Université Laval* 3 (octobre 1948): 133–7.

Parent, Mgr A.-M. "Le role des universités canadiennes-françaises." *L'Action nationale* 28 (septembre 1946): 22–32.

Parenteau, R. "L'émancipation économique des Canadiens français." *L'Action nationale* 49 (juin 1960): 797–810.

- "Quelques raisons de la faiblesse économique de la nation canadienne-française." *L'Action nationale* 45 (décembre 1955): 316–31.

- "Richesse et misère du Canada français." *Chronique Sociale de France* 65e année (15 septembre 1957): 423–31.

Pelletier, G. " '*Cité libre*' confesse ses intentions." *Cité libre* 2 (février 1951): 2–9.

- "Crise d'autorité ou crise de liberté?" *Cité libre* 5 (juin-juillet 1952): 1–10.

- "Dialogue avec un suicidé." *Cité libre* 11 (février 1955): 1–11.

- "D'un prolétariat spirituel." *Esprit* 20 (août-septembre 1952): 190–200.

- "D'où vient l'argent qui nourri les parties?" *Cité libre* 6 (décembre 1952): 35–41.

- "Entretien avec Gérard Pelletier." *Liberté* 7 (mai-juin 1965): 217–53.
- "Feu l'unanimité." *Cité libre* 30 (octobre 1960): 8–11.
- "Histoires de collégiens qui ont aujourd'hui trente ans." *Cité libre* 1 (juin 1950): 5–9.
- "Le syndicalisme canadien-français." In *Canadian Dualism/La dualité canadienne*, edited by Mason Wade. Toronto: University of Toronto Press 1960.
- "Les Bills 19 et 20." *L'Action nationale* 42 (mars-avril 1954): 351–62.
- "Lettre ouverte aux trois étudiants qui 'attendent' à Québec." *Cité libre* 20 (mai 1958): 1–6.
- "Réflexions sur l'état de siège." *Cité libre* 16 (février 1957): 32–40.
- "Refus de confiance au syndicalisme." *Cité libre* 7 (mai 1953): 1–9.
- "Syndicalisme canadien et influence américaine." *Esprit* 22 (1954): 1020–8.

Raymond, M. "What does the Bloc Populaire Stand For?" *Maclean's Magazine*, 1 January 1944, 8–10, 35–6.

Rioux, M. "Idéologie et crise de conscience du Canada français." *Cité libre* 14 (décembre 1955): 1–29.
- "La démocratie et la culture canadienne-française." *Cité libre* 28 (juin-juillet 1960): 3–4, 13.
- "L'élection, vue de l'Anse-à-la-Barbe." *Cité libre* 6 (décembre 1952): 47–52.
- "Remarques sur l'éducation secondaire et la culture canadienne-française." *Cité libre* 8 (novembre 1953): 34–42.
- "Requiem pour une clique." *Cité libre* 30 (octobre 1960), 3–4.

Rolland, R. "Matériaux pour servir à une enquête sur le cléricalisme II." *Cité libre* 7 (mai 1953): 37–43.

Ryan, C. "Ferons-nous de la politique?" *L'Action nationale* 37 (juillet 1951): 451–77.
- "L'Eglise Catholique et l'évolution spirituelle du Canada français." *Chronique sociale de France* 65e année (15 septembre 1957): 443–57.
- "Les classes moyennes au Canada français." *L'Action nationale* 35 (mars 1950): 207–28; 35 (avril 1950): 266–73.
- "Une classe oubliée." *L'Action nationale* 35 (février 1950): 93–110.

Séguin, M. "La Conquête et la vie économique des Canadiens." *L'Action nationale* 28 (décembre 1946): 308–26.

Scott, F. "Canada et Canada français." *Esprit* 20 (août-septembre 1952): 178–89.

Tremblay, A. "Commentaires." In *Essais sur le Québec contemporain*, edited by J.-C. Falardeau. Québec: Les Presses de l'Université Laval 1953.
- "La conjoncture actuelle en éducation." In *L'éducation au Québec face aux problèmes contemporains*. Saint-Hyacinthe: Les Editions Alerte 1958.
- "Les subventions fédérales aux universités: Règlement provisoire: et après?" *Cité libre* 11 (mars 1960): 3–11.
- "Who Goes to University?" In *Canada's Crisis in Higher Education*, edited by C.T. Bissell. Proceedings of the NCCU. Ottawa 1956.

Tremblay, M. "Conflict d'allégeances chez les Canadiens français." *Ad Usum*

Sacerdotum 13 (janvier 1958): 19–25.
- "Orientations de la pensée sociale." In *Essais sur le Québec contemporain*, edited by J.-C. Falardeau. Québec: Les Presses de l'Université Laval 1953.
- "Réflexions sur le nationalisme." *Ecrits du Canada français* 5 (1959): 11–43.
- and A. Faucher. "L'enseignement des sciences sociales au Canada de langue française." In *Les arts, lettres et sciences au Canada 1949-1951*. Ottawa: King's Printer 1951.
Trudeau, P.E. "De la notion d'opposition politique." *Cité libre* 27 (mai 1960): 13–14.
- "La démocratie est-elle viable au Canada français?" *L'Action nationale* 44 (novembre 1954): 190–200.
- "La province de Québec au moment de la grève." In *La grève de l'amiante*. Montréal: Les Editions Cité libre 1956.
- "L'élection du 22 juin 1960." *Cité libre* 29 (août-septembre 1960): 3–8.
- "L'élection fédérale du 10 août: prodomes et conjectures." *Cité libre* 8 (novembre 1953): 1–10.
- "Les octrois fédéraux aux universités." *Cité libre* 16 (février 1957): 9–31.
- "Matériaux pour servir à une enquête sur le cléricalisme." *Cité libre* 7 (mai 1953): 29–37.
- "Notes sur l'élection provinciale." *Cité libre* 28 (juin-juillet 1960): 12–13.
- "Politique fonctionnelle I." *Cité libre* 1 (juin 1950): 20–4.
- "Politique fonctionnelle II." *Cité libre* 2 (février 1951): 24–9.
- "Réflexions sur la politique au Canada français." *Cité libre* 6 (décembre 1952): 53–70.
- "Un manifeste démocratique." *Cité libre* 22 (octobre 1958): 1–31.
Vadeboncoeur, P. "A Break with Tradition?" *Queen's Quarterly* 65 (Spring 1958): 92–103.
- "Critique de notre psychologie de l'action." *Cité libre* 8 (novembre 1953): 11–22.
- "L'irréalisme de notre culture." *Cité libre* 4 (décembre 1951): 20–6.
- "Pour une dynamique de notre culture." *Cité libre* 4 (juin-juillet 1952): 11–29.
- "Que la 'passion' peut être un guide . . ." *L'Action nationale* 20 (septembre 1942): 36–42.
- "Réflexions sur la foi." *Cité libre* 12 (mai 1955): 15–26.
- "Une democratie arrêtée." *Cité libre* 21 (juillet 1958): 31–8.
- "Voilà l'ennemi!" *Cité libre* 19 (janvier 1958): 29–37.

Government Documents

Canada. *Census of Canada* 1941, 1951, 1961, 1971.
- *Dominion-Provincial Conference (1945): Dominion and Provincial Submissions and Plenary Conference Discussions*. Ottawa: King's Printer 1946.
- *Dominion-Provincial Conference on Reconstruction. Proposals of the Government of Canada, August 1945*. Ottawa: King's Printer 1945.

- *House of Commons Debates*, 1951, 1954, 1955.
- *Proceedings of the Conference of Federal and Provincial Governments, December 4–7, 1950*. Ottawa: King's Printer 1951.
- *Proceedings of the Constitutional Conference of Federal and Provincial Governments, January 10–12, 1950*. Ottawa: King's Printer 1950.
- *Proceedings of the Constitutional Conference of Federal and Provincial Governments* (Second Session) *Quebec, September 25–28, 1950*. Ottawa: King's Printer 1950.
- *Proceedings of the Dominion Provincial Conference, 1957*. Ottawa: Queen's Printer 1958.
- *Proceedings of the Federal-Provincial Conference, 1955*. Ottawa: Queen's Printer 1955.
- *Report of the Royal Commission on Bilingualism and Biculturalism. Book* I. *General Introduction: The Official Languages*. Ottawa: Queen's Printer 1967.
- *Report of the Royal Commission on Bilingualism and Biculturalism*. Book III. *The Work World*. Ottawa: Queen's Printer 1969.
- *Report of the Royal Commission on Dominion-Provincial Relations*. Book II. *Recommendations*. Ottawa: King's Printer 1940.
- *Report of the Royal Commission on National Development in the Arts, Letters and Sciences*. Ottawa: King's Printer 1951.
- *Royal Commission Studies: A Selection of Essays Prepared for the Royal Commission on National Development in the Arts, Letters and Sciences*. Ottawa: King's Printer 1951.
Quebec. *Royal Commission of Inquiry on Constitutional Problems. Report*. 5 vols. Quebec: Queen's Printer 1956.

SECONDARY SOURCES

Books and Monographs

Audet, L.-P. *Histoire de l'enseignement au Québec 1840–1971*. 2 vols. Montréal: Holt, Rinehart et Winston 1971.
Bédard, R.-J., ed. *L'essor économique de Québec*. Montréal: Beauchemin 1969.
Bélanger, A.-J. *L'apolitisme des idéologies québécoises: Le grand tournant de 1934 1936*. Québec: Les Presses de l'Université Laval 1974.
- *Ruptures et constantes*. Montréal: Editions Hurtubise HMH 1977.
Black, C. *Duplessis*. Toronto: McClelland and Stewart 1977.
Blanchard, R. *L'Ouest du Canada français: Montréal et sa région*. Montréal: Beauchemin 1953.
Bouchette, E. *L'indépendance économique du Canada français*. 3rd ed. Montréal: Wilson and Lafleur 1913.
Casgrain, T.F. *A Woman in a Man's World*. Toronto: McClelland and Stewart 1972.
Chaloult, R. *Mémoires politiques*. Montréal: Editions du Jour 1969.
Clément, G. *Histoire de l'Action catholique au Canada français*. Montréal: Fides 1972.

Comeau, P.-A. *Le Bloc Populaire 1941–1948.* Montréal: Québec/Amérique 1982.

Comeau, R., ed. *Economie québécoise.* Sillery, Québec: Les Presses de l'Université de Quebec 1969.

Cook, R. *Provincial Autonomy, Minority Rights and the Compact Theory: 1867–1921.* Ottawa: Queen's Printer 1969.

– *The Maple Leaf Forever.* Toronto: Macmillan of Canada 1971.

– ed. *French-Canadian Nationalism.* Toronto: Macmillan 1969.

Cooper, J.I. *Montreal: A Brief History.* Montreal: McGill-Queen's University Press 1969.

Cousineau, Jacques, SJ. *L'Eglise d'ici et le social 1940–1960.* Vol. 1. *La Commission sacerdotale d'études sociales.* Montréal: Bellarmin 1982.

Denis, Roch. *Luttes de classes et question nationale au Québec 1948–1968.* Montréal/Paris: PSI/EDI 1979.

Dion, Léon. *Quebec: The Unfinished Revolution.* Montreal: McGill-Queen's University Press 1976.

– *Le Bill 60 et la société québécoise.* Montréal: Editions HMH 1967.

– *Nationalismes et politique au Québec.* Montréal: Hurtubise HMH 1975.

Dumas, E. *Dans le sommeil de nos os.* Montréal: Leméac 1971.

Dumont, F., et al. *Idéologies au Canada français 1900–1929.* Québec: Les Presses de l'Université Laval 1974.

– et al. *Idéologies au Canada français 1930–1939.* Québec: Les Presses de l'Université Laval 1978.

– et al. *Idéologies au Canada français 1940–1976.* 3 vols. Québec: Les Presses de l'Université Laval 1981.

Elkin, F. *Rebels and Colleagues: Advertising and Social Change in French Canada.* Montreal: McGill-Queen's University Press 1973.

Falardeau, J.-C. *L'essor des sciences sociales au Canada français.* Québec: Ministère des Affaires culturelles 1964.

Gravel, J.-Y., ed. *Le Québec et la guerre.* Montréal: Boréal Express 1974.

Harbron, J.D. *This Is Trudeau.* Toronto: Longmans 1968.

Hamelin, J. *Economie et société en Nouvelle-France.* Québec: Les Presses de l'Université Laval 1960.

Lachance, Micheline. *Le prince de l'Eglise: Le cardinal Léger.* Montréal: Les Editions de l'Homme 1982.

Lapalme, G.-E. *Mémoires.* 2 vols. Ottawa: Les Editions Leméac 1969–70.

Lebel, G. *Horizon 1980: Une étude sur l'évolution de l'économie du Québec de 1946 à 1968 et sur ses perspectives d'avenir.* Québec: Ministère de l'Industrie et du Commerce 1970.

Lemieux, V., and R. Hudon. *Patronage et politique au Québec 1944–72.* Sillery, Québec: Les Editions du Boréal Express 1976.

McRoberts, K., and D. Posgate. *Quebec: Social Change and Political Crisis.* Toronto: McClelland and Stewart 1980.

Minville, E. *Notre milieu*. Montréal: Fides 1947.

– ed. *Montréal économique*. Montréal: Fides 1943.

Ouellet, C. *La vie des sciences au Canada français*. Québec: Ministère des Affaires Culturelles 1964.

Ouellet, F. *Histoire économique et sociale du Québec, 1760-1850*. Montréal: Fides 1966.

Parisé, R. *Georges-Henri Lévesque: Père de la renaissance québécoise*. Montréal: Alain Stanké 1976.

Provencher, J. *René Lévesque: Portrait d'un québécois*. Montréal: La Presse 1973.

Quinn, H.F. *The Union Nationale*. Toronto: University of Toronto Press 1963.

Raynauld, A. *Croissance et structures économiques de la province de Québec*. Québec: Ministère de l'industrie et du commerce 1961.

Rioux, M., and Y. Martin, eds. *French-Canadian Society*. Vol. 1. Toronto: McClelland and Stewart 1964.

Rouillard, J. *Histoire de la CSN (1921-1981)*. Montréal: Boréal Express/CSN 1981.

– *Les syndicats nationaux au Québec de 1900 à 1930*. Québec: Les Presses de l'Université Laval 1979.

Roy, J.-L. *La marche des québécois: Le temps des ruptures (1945-1960)*. Montréal: Les Editions Leméac 1976.

Rumilly, R. *Histoire de la Province de Québec*. Vols. 31-41. Montréal: Fides 1969.

– *Maurice Duplessis et son temps*. 2 vols. Montréal: Fides 1973.

Saint-Germain, M. *Une économie à libérer: Le Québec analysé dans ses structures économiques*. Montréal: Les Presses de l'Université de Montréal 1973.

Séguin, M. *L'idée d'indépendance au Québec: Génèse et historique*. Montréal: Boréal Express 1968.

– *La nation "canadienne" et l'agriculture (1760-1850)*. Montréal: Boréal Express 1970.

Thomson, D.C. *Louis St. Laurent: Canadian*. Toronto: Macmillan 1967.

Tremblay, L.-M. *Le syndicalisme québécois: Idéologies de la C.S.N. et de la F.T.Q. 1940-1970*. Montréal: Les Presses de l'Université de Montréal 1972.

Trofimenkoff, S.M. *The Dream of Nation: A Social and Intellectual History of Quebec*. Toronto: Gage 1983.

Voisine, N., et al. *Histoire de l'Eglise catholique au Québec, 1608-1970*. Montréal: Fides 1970.

Wade, M. *The French Canadians 1760-1967*. 2 vols. Toronto: Macmillan 1968.

–, ed. *Canadian Dualism/La dualité canadienne*. Toronto: University of Toronto Press 1962.

Articles

Barnes, S.H. "The Evolution of Christian Trade Unionism in Quebec." In *Readings in Canadian Labour Economics*, edited by E.A. Kovacs. Toronto: McGraw-Hill 1961.

- "Quebec Catholicism and Social Change." *The Review of Politics* 23 (January 1961): 52–76.

Behiels, M.D. "Le père Georges-Henri Lévesque et l'établissement des sciences sociales à Laval, 1938–1955." *Revue de l'Université d'Ottawa*, 52 (juillet-septembre 1982): 355–76.

- "The Bloc Populaire Canadien and the Origins of French-Canadian Neo-nationalism, 1942–8." *Canadian Historical Review* 63 (December 1982): 487–512.

- "The Bloc Populaire Canadien: The Anatomy of Failure, 1948–58." *Journal of Canadian Studies/Revue d'études canadienne* 18 (Hiver 1983–4 Winter): 45–74.

Blain, J. "Economie et société en Nouvelle-France: L'historiographie des années 1950–1960." *Revue d'histoire de l'Amérique français* 28 (septembre 1974): 163–86.

Boily, R. "Les élus de 1956 à 1966: Principaux caractères sociaux et politiques." In *Quatres élections provinciales au Québec*, edited by Vincent Lemieux. Québec: Les Presses de l'Université Laval 1969.

- "Les hommes politiques de Québec 1867–1967." In *Le personnel politique québécois*, edited by Richard Desrosiers. Montréal: Boréal Express 1972: 55–90.

Brazeau, J. "Les nouvelles classes moyennes." *Recherches sociographiques* 7 (janvier-août 1966): 151–63.

Brunelle, D. "La structure occupationnelle de la main d'oeuvre québécoise 1951–1971." *Sociologie et sociétés* 7 (novembre 1975): 67–88.

Caldwell, A., and B. Czarnacki. "Un rattrapage raté: Le changement social dans le Québec d'après-guerre, 1950–1974: une comparaison Québec/Ontario." *Recherches sociographiques* 18 (1977): 9–58.

Carisse, C. "Fécondité et famille au Canada français." *Revue de l'Institut de sociologie* 1 (1968): 53–65.

Carrier, A. "L'idéologie politique de la revue *Cité libre.*" *Canadian Journal of Political Science* 1 (December 1968): 414–28.

Charest, M. "Le pain du jour: Réginald Boisvert décrit le grisaille d'une petite ville ouvrière." *Le Magazine Maclean*, mars 1964, 20–1, 51–2.

Chartier, R. "Chronologie de l'évolution confessionnelle de la C.T.C.C. (CSN)." *Relations industrielles* 16 (février 1961): 102–12.

Comeau, P.-A. "La transformation du parti libéral québécois." *Canadian Journal of Economics and Political Science* 31 (August 1965): 358–67.

David, H. "La grève et le bon Dieu: La grève de l'amiante au Québec." *Sociologie et sociétés* 1 (novembre 1969): 249–76.

- "L'état des rapports de classes au Québec de 1945 à 1967." *Sociologie et sociétés* 7 (novembre 1975): 33–66.

Dofny, J., and M. Garon-Audy. "Mobilités professionnelles au Québec." *Sociologie et sociétés* 1 (novembre 1969): 277–301.

Durocher, R., et M. Jean. "Duplessis et la Commission royale d'enquête sur les problèmes constitutionnels, 1953–1956." *Revue d'histoire de l'Amérique français* 25 (décembre 1971): 337–63.

Falardeau, J.-C. "Le Québec n'est plus un passé mais un avenir." *Revue de l'Institut de sociologie* 1 (1968): 73–8.

- "L'origine et l'ascension des hommes d'affaires dans la société canadienne-française." *Recherches sociographiques* 6 (janvier-avril 1963): 33–45.
- "Des élites traditionnelles aux élites nouvelles." *Recherches sociographiques* 7 (janvier-août 1966): 131–45.

Faucher, A. "Pouvoir politique et pouvoir économique dans l'évolution du Canada français." *Recherches sociographiques* 7 (janvier-août 1966): 61–86.

Fortin, G. "Le nationalisme canadien français et les classes sociales." *Revue d'histoire de l'Amérique français* 22 (mars 1969): 525–35.

Gagnon, A. "Etude des occupations de la population canadienne-française de la province de Québec." *Contributions à l'étude des sciences de l'homme* 1 (1952): 135–64.

Gagnon, S. "Pour une conscience historique de la révolution québécoise." *Cité libre* 83 (janvier 1966): 4–19.

Garique, P. "Organisation sociale et valeurs culturelles canadiennes-françaises." *Canadian Journal of Economics and Political Science* 28 (May 1962): 189–203.

Guindon, H. "The Social Evolution of Quebec Reconsidered." *Canadian Journal of Economics and Political Science* 26 (Novembre 1960): 533–51.

- "Social Unrest, Social Class and Quebec's Burcaucratic Revolution." *Queen's Quarterly* 71 (Summer 1964): 150–62.

Hamelin, J., J. Letarte, and M. Hamelin. "Les élections provinciales dans le Québec." *Cahiers de géographie de Québec* 4 (octobre 1959-mars 1960): 5–207.

Heintzman, R. "The Political Culture of Quebec, 1840–1960." *Canadian Journal of Political Science* 16 (March 1983): 3–59.

Iglauer, E. "Prime Minister Pierre Trudeau." *New Yorker*, 5 July 1969, 36–42, 44, 46–60.

Isbester, F. "Quebec Labour in Perspective." In *Canadian Labour in Transition*, edited by R.U. Miller and F. Isbester. Scarborough: Prentice-Hall 1971.

Jocas, de Y., and G. Rocher. "Inter-generation Occupational Mobility in the Province of Quebec." *Canadian Journal of Economics and Political Science* 23 (February 1957): 57–68.

Lacoste, N. "Les traits nouveaux de la population du Grand Montréal." *Recherches sociographiques* 6 (septembre-décembre 1965): 265–81.

Lamontagne, M. "Le rôle économique et social de gouvernement." *Relations industrielles* 9 (mars 1954): 129–44.

Langlois, C. "Cultural Reasons for the French-Canadian Lag in Economic Progress." *Culture* 21 (June 1960): 152–70.

Lauzon, A. "Gérard Pelletier: Des ennemis à la douzaine." *Le Magazine Maclean*, 4 novembre 1964, 60–6.

Maheu, P. "Le pouvoir clérical." In *Les québécois*. Montréal: Parti Pris 1971.

Major, A. "Pierre Vadeboncoeur: Un socialiste de condition bourgeoise." *Le Magazine Maclean*, 12 juin 1972, 20–1, 42–3.

Ouellet, F. "Les fondements historiques de l'option séparatiste dans le Québec." *Canadian Historical Review* 43 (Septembre 1962): 185–203.

Parenteau, R. "The Impact of Industrialization in Quebec." In *The Canadian*

Economy: Selected Readings, edited by John J. Deutsch. Toronto: Macmillan 1961.

Rioux, M. "Sur le développement socio-culturel du Canada français." *Contributions à l'étude des sciences de l'homme* 4 (1959): 144–62.

Rocher, G. "Multiplication des élites et changement social au Canada français." *Revue de l'Institut de sociologie* (1968): 79–94.

Rouillard, Jacques. "Mutations de la Confédération des travailleurs catholiques du Canada (1940–1960)." *Revue d'histoire de l'Amérique française* 34 (décembre 1980): 377–405.

Savard, L. "Une idéologie de transition: Du nationalisme à une nouvelle définition du politique." *Recherches sociographiques* 4 (1963): 228–36.

Stager, D. "Federal Government Grants to Canadian Universities." *Canadian Historical Review* 54 (September 1973): 287–97.

Theses

McRoberts, K. "Contrasts in French-Canadian Nationalism." MA thesis, University of Chicago, 1966.

Oliver, Michael K. "The Social and Political Ideas of French Canadian Nationalists 1920–1945." PHD thesis, McGill University, 1956.

Index

Action nationale 6, 15, 20, 24, 28, 29, 32–3, 37, 48, 49, 52,
  56, 58, 86, 88, 94, 195, 234, 266
Agriculture and rural life, decline of 11–13
Alliance des professeurs de Montréal 131, 132, 151, 152,
  153, 171
Alliance Laurentienne 55
Amis du *Devoir* 23, 109
Angers, François-Albert 94–5, 98, 99, 195, 244
Arès, Father Richard 64, 95, 98, 188, 211
Asbestos strike 4, 33, 65–6, 130, 133–4, 136; ideological
  impact of 85–6, 124–9

Barbeau, Raymond 55, 57
Barbeau, Victor 21
Berdiaeff, Nicholas 27
Bergeron, Gérard 265; analysis of Rassemblement 250,
  253–4; analysis of Quebec Liberal party 257–8, 332n36,
  333n50; supports neo-nationalist program 260
Bills 19 and 20 131, 145, 146, 229
Blain, Jean-Guy 86, 95
Blain, Maurice: and future of French Canada 54; founder
  of *Cité libre* 62; career of 67; on Quebec Catholicism and
  cultural alienation 71–2, 73; on Catholics and intellectual
  freedom 80; on nationalism and intellectual rigidity 84,
  89; supports education based on language 156
Bloc Populaire Canadien 24, 36, 39, 44, 111, 125, 141, 242;
  crisis in and demise of 21, 30, 31–2; origins of 29; federal
  and provincial program of 30–1; as advocate of strong
  Quebec state 99, 108, 194
Boisvert, Réginald 69, 138; founder of *Cité libre* 62; career
  of 66–7; on CTCC's radicalization 127–8; CTCC and nationalism 140–1; role in CCF 141
Braun, Father Léopold 75
Brown, Lewis H. 128, 134
Brunet, Michel: critical of traditional nationalism 46–7;